PRODUCING SECURITY

PRODUCING SECURITY

MULTINATIONAL CORPORATIONS,
GLOBALIZATION, AND THE
CHANGING CALCULUS OF CONFLICT

Stephen G. Brooks

PRINCETON UNIVERSITY PRESS   PRINCETON AND OXFORD

Third printing, and first paperback printing, 2007
Paperback ISBN-13: 978-0-691-13031-6
Paperback ISBN-10: 0-691-13031-0

The Library of Congress has cataloged the cloth edition of this book as follows
Brooks, Stephen G., 1971–
Producing security : multinational corporations, globalization, and
the changing calculus of conflict / Stephen G. Brooks.
p.   cm.
Includes bibliographical references and index.
ISBN 0-691-12151-6 (cloth : alk. paper)
1. Security, International.   2. International economic relations.
3. Globalization.   4. Multinational corporations.   I. Title.
JZ5588.B76 2005
337—dc22   2004060154

British Library Cataloging-in-Publication Data is available

This book has been composed in Times Roman

Printed on acid-free paper. ∞

pup.princeton.edu

Printed in the United States of America

3   5   7   9   10   8   6   4

To Deb and Riley

Contents

Figures

Tables

Acknowledgments

OVER THE COURSE of writing this book, I have accumulated many debts. I began this project as a Ph.D. student at Yale, where I had the luxury of having many helpful mentors. Bruce Russett and Alex Wendt provided excellent advice over the entire course of my dissertation. I was very fortunate that Geoff Garrett arrived at Yale during the middle of my graduate study, just as I was plunging into the intricacies of globalization and multinational corporations. Together, these three scholars were a superb dissertation committee: they allowed me the freedom to take on a very wide-ranging project, while also helping me to keep it within manageable bounds. Al Stam, Frances Rosenbluth, and Brad Westerfield all commented on multiple chapters and furthered my dissertation in numerous other ways. Finally, I was especially lucky that Bill Wohlforth came to Yale for two years beginning in my third year of graduate study. He has been a truly exceptional sounding board over many years. Bill now has the distinction of having read more versions of the material in this book than anyone else, as well as having had more conversations with me about its contents.

This project was completed after I became an assistant professor in the Department of Government at Dartmouth College. It is hard to think how I could have a better group of colleagues in international relations than I have at Dartmouth; their comments made this book immensely better. My colleagues Bill Wohlforth and Al Stam have been just as helpful as they were when I was a graduate student. Mike Mastanduno, Ned Lebow, and Dave Kang all provided me with various forms of helpful feedback. My fellow junior international relations colleagues, Daryl Press and Ben Valentino, were invaluable with their encouragement and incisive critiques in countless conversations.

Beyond my mentors at Yale and colleagues at Dartmouth, there are numerous other people who have helped by providing comments on this project. I first wish to thank participants at three American Political Science Association panels and at twenty seminars on this research held at the following universities: Princeton, Stanford, Harvard (three times), University of Chicago, Columbia (twice), UC Berkeley, Georgetown, Brown, Yale (twice), University of Colorado at Boulder, Northwestern, American, University of Pittsburgh, Ohio State, University of Wisconsin, and MIT. Numerous scholars also provided me with written feedback on individual chapters. At the risk of not mentioning some people who provided assistance in this regard, I would like to express my appreciation to Ethan Kapstein, Richard Rosecrance, Robert Gilpin, Vladimir Kontorovich, Matt Slaughter, Joe Grieco, Michael Doyle, Aaron Friedberg, John Mueller, Jonathan Rodden, Ian Hurd, David Lumsdaine, Keith Darden, Barry O'Neill, Dan Reiter, Nigel Thalakada, Keith Crane, Dale Copeland, David

Bach, Tom Bruneau, Riordan Roett, Daniel Markey, Andy Stigler, Susan Rose-Ackerman, Scott Bennett, and Dick Samuels. For their comments and for sharing their wealth of expertise regarding particular literatures in helpful conversations, I would especially like to thank Stephen Kobrin for his help with chapter 2 and Jeff Kopstein and Mark Kramer for their assistance with chapter 6. Finally, Charlie Glaser, David Baldwin, John Hall, Bob Art, and Tom Christensen read the entire manuscript and provided me with useful comments.

I was fortunate to receive generous institutional support over the course of this project. While at Yale, my progress was greatly assisted by fellowships from the National Science Foundation and the Institute for the Study of World Politics as well as a Yale Dissertation Completion Fellowship. Most of my dissertation was written while I was based for two years on a fellowship at Princeton's Woodrow Wilson School. I am especially grateful to Dick Ullman for making sure I had every resource I needed at Princeton. The final draft of the book was written while I was on a fellowship at Harvard's Kennedy School of Government. I want to express thanks to Steve Miller and Steve Walt, in particular, for my enjoyable and productive year at Harvard. At Dartmouth I received numerous financial awards that furthered this project from both the Rockefeller Center for the Social Sciences and the Dickey Center for International Understanding. I am grateful to the various research assistants who helped me: Ben Graham, Emily Mintz, Anne Hunt, Hannah Jacobs, Karen Liot, Spencer Jones, Stratos Pahis, Pooneet Kant, and especially Jeff Arnold. I want to extend a special word of thanks to Chris Wohlforth at the Dickey Center for organizing a symposium on the book that was held at Dartmouth, where I received valuable feedback from participants. I am also indebted to Chuck Myers at Princeton University Press for his interest in my project and guiding the manuscript to completion, and to Richard Isomaki for excellent copyediting.

I wish to express gratitude to my parents for their constant support and encouragement. Finally, my wife, Deborah Jordan Brooks, made all of the challenging phases of this project more manageable in numerous ways. The prospect of having some extra time to spend with her and our daughter Riley provided the strongest possible incentive for me to complete this project.

PRODUCING SECURITY

CHAPTER 1

Introduction

SCHOLARS AND STATESMEN have debated the influence of international commerce on war and peace for thousands of years. Around A.D. 100, Plutarch maintained that international commerce brought about "cooperation and friendship" and that the cessation of commercial exchange would cause the life of man to be "savage and destitute."[1] This line of reasoning became particularly prominent in the eighteenth and nineteenth centuries with the writings of philosophers such as Adam Smith, Jeremy Bentham, Immanuel Kant, Thomas Paine, Jean-Jacques Rousseau, Montesquieu, and John Stuart Mill.[2] These men were united in their belief that enhanced international commerce made war among states more costly and, thus, that "the natural effect of commerce is to lead to peace,"[3] as Montesquieu maintained in 1748. Many of them also believed that commerce was a dynamic force having a progressively stronger stabilizing effect over time. In the eyes of Kant, "the spirit of commerce, which is incompatible with war, sooner or later gains the upper hand in every state."[4]

This sanguine view of commerce as having a strong, positive effect on interstate relations has not been universally embraced. Indeed, many have argued the opposite is true. Perhaps the most prominent early pessimistic statement in this regard was advanced by Alexander Hamilton. Writing in 1787, he devotes most of Federalist 6 to critiquing the notion that the "spirit of commerce has a tendency to soften the manners of men and to extinguish those inflammable humors which have so often kindled into wars." After running through a series of historical examples, Hamilton ultimately concludes that numerous wars were "founded upon commercial motives" and that "spirit of commerce in many instances administered new incentives" for conflict.[5] Another prominent early pessimist is Frederick List, who argued during the middle of the nineteenth century that reducing participation in international commerce is, in the absence of a universal republic, the surest route to enhancing a state's security.[6] At the dawn of the twentieth century, John Hobson famously maintained that the business activities of firms led to imperialism; a few years later,

---

[1] Irwin 1996, 11.
[2] See the discussion in Silberner 1946; and Doyle 1997, chap. 7.
[3] Montesquieu 1989, 338.
[4] Kant 1957, 32.
[5] Hamilton 1961, 56, 57.
[6] See Silberner 1946, chaps. 8 and 9.

Lenin then took one step further, emphasizing that not just imperialism but eventually war among capitalist states would be the inevitable result of capitalism.[7]

The belief that international commerce can strongly shape security relations is reflected not just in the writings of scholars over the centuries, but in policy discussions and governmental decisions. Over the years, the optimistic perspective on commerce and security has most strongly and directly shaped policy. David Lloyd George, Cordell Hull, Woodrow Wilson, Richard Cobden, William Gladstone, and Bill Clinton are prominent examples of politicians who have advanced policies premised on the notion that international commerce can promote peace.[8] As we move into the twenty-first century, this view continues to significantly influence important aspects of policy. In the United States, the decision to push for China's entry into the World Trade Organization is the most prominent recent example. In his 28 January 2000 State of Union Address, President Bill Clinton exhorted: "Congress should support the agreement we negotiated to bring China into the WTO, by passing Permanent Normal Trade Relations with China as soon as possible . . . [because] it will plainly advance the cause of peace in Asia." While the foreign policy approaches of the Clinton and George W. Bush administrations differ greatly on many issues, a key common theme is the notion that promoting economic globalization throughout the world can foster a stable security environment.[9]

Despite the prominence of the view among scholars and policymakers that international commerce significantly influences security relations, up until the 1990s essentially no empirical analysis of this issue existed.[10] In the final phase of the Cold War, prominent scholars such as Richard Rosecrance and Kenneth Waltz continued the centuries-old debate on the effects of commerce on peace, but this discussion was confined to the level of theory.[11] The rapidly growing scope of international economic integration, termed "globalization," has over the past decade led international relations scholars to renew their attention to how shifts in the international economy affect states' security behavior. Unlike almost all previous scholarship on this general subject, the most recent wave of investigations was empirically focused.[12] The general finding emerging from this literature—that trade linkages between states reduce the likelihood of conflict—is important in its own right and, more generally, indicates that the

---

[7] Hobson 1902; and Lenin 1917.

[8] See Way 1998, chap. 1.

[9] On this point, see Rose 2003.

[10] On this point, see, for example, Levy 1989, 261–62.

[11] Rosecrance (1986) argues that commerce promotes stability, whereas Waltz (1979, esp. 138) advances the opposite position.

[12] For useful reviews of this recent literature, see McMillan 1997; Barbieri and Schneider 1999; and Mansfield and Pollins 2001.

centuries-old contention that the business activities of firms can significantly shape security affairs is, in fact, valid.[13]

BRINGING IN THE GLOBALIZATION OF PRODUCTION

Given the great importance of economic globalization in the international environment, it is crucial to carefully evaluate its influence on security. The recent literature examining how the international economy influences security has produced important new insights, but it suffers from a major limitation: it neglects the most significant feature of today's global economy. Over the centuries, scholars have generally treated the questions "Does international commerce influence security?" and "Do trade flows influence security?" as synonymous. Not surprisingly, virtually all studies in this recent wave of scholarship examine the security repercussions of international trade flows.[14] In the past, such an overarching focus on the security implications of trade made sense. It no longer does. Until recently, trade was "the primary means of organizing international economic transactions."[15] Today, however, trade is a second-order phenomenon: where and how multinational corporations (MNCs) organize their production activities is now the key integrating force in global commerce.[16]

MNC international production strategies have changed in a variety of fundamental ways over the past three decades. These new strategies are characterized by an increased cross-border dispersion of production. For this reason, analysts commonly use the short-hand term *globalization of production* as a descriptor of these recent changes in MNC production—a practice I will also adopt here.[17] As will be shown in chapter 2, MNCs are geographically dispersing production activities both internally and externally—that is, within the firm itself as well as through the development of more extensive interfirm linkages across borders. More specifically, MNCs have greatly enhanced the intrafirm international division of the production process through a new role for foreign

---

[13] This is not to say that there is uniform agreement concerning how trade linkages influence security behavior. The prevailing view is that higher levels of trade interdependence lower the likelihood of conflict (on this point, see, for example, the discussion in Mansfield and Pollins 2001). Some scholars, however, continue to express reservations about the validity of this finding (see, for example, Green, Kim, and Yoon 2001; Barbieri 2002; and Bennett and Stam 2003, esp. 95–98).

[14] A partial list of these studies includes Oneal and Russett 1997, 1999; Russett and Oneal 2000; Oneal et al. 1996; Hegre 2000; Kim 1998; Copeland 1996; Barbieri 1996; Barbieri and Levy 1999; and Polachek 1992. For a full set of citations, see the bibliographies in Barbieri and Schneider 1999; McMillan 1997; and Mansfield and Pollins 2001.

[15] Kobrin 1995, 26.

[16] A multinational corporation is a firm that owns, coordinates, or controls value-adding activities in more than one country.

[17] See, for example, Dunning 1992, 128–32. The "geographic dispersion of MNC production" is a more accurate, but also more cumbersome, short-hand descriptor that I will also sometimes use.

affiliates; at the same time, they have pursued deeper relationships with foreign suppliers and cooperative partners located abroad through international subcontracting and international interfirm alliances.

Although analysts use the language of globalization in describing these shifts, the geographic dispersion of MNC production activities is not truly global in scope. These shifts in MNC production have had powerful effects on some states, but have largely bypassed many others. Specifically, it is among the economically most advanced states that the geographic dispersion of MNC production has been most prominent; the rise of international interfirm alliances, for example, is a trend largely restricted to North America, Western Europe, and Japan. It is also important to recognize that the geographic dispersion of MNC production is not occurring equally across all industries. As will be shown in chapter 2, internationalization strategies have become prominent only in certain sectors.

The unprecedented nature of the globalization of production is a key feature distinguishing it from international trade. Many analysts argue that what we call economic globalization resembles the international economy during the "golden age" of capitalism from 1870 to 1914. However, this similarity is strong only if we treat economic globalization as an aggregate; when we break economic globalization into its constituent parts, we reach a very different answer. The globalization of production clearly represents an ongoing qualitative change in the international economy; trying to advance the same claim about the other two economic globalization trends—of international trade and international financial markets, respectively—is more problematic. In the end, the geographic dispersion of MNC production is the most historically novel aspect of contemporary economic globalization.

Despite the substantive significance and historical novelty of the globalization of production, there has so far been no systematic empirical analysis of its implications for security relations among states. The last detailed empirical examination of how international production by MNCs can influence security affairs was written in 1935.[18] A number of prominent analysts have recently noted that changes in MNC production strategies may have significant repercussions for security affairs, but this is not a primary focus of their analysis, and they do not empirically evaluate the notions they advance.[19] Because systematic data on the geographic dispersion of MNC production does not exist, there is a dearth of quantitative studies of international conflict that use measures of this global production shift.[20] A significant literature did develop in the middle and late 1980s that analyzed the United States' increased reliance upon

[18] See Staley 1935.

[19] See, for example, Kapstein 1992; Rosecrance 1999; and Friedman 1999.

[20] For useful discussions of the limitations of data on the international production activities of MNCs, see OECD 2002, 159; UNCTAD 1993a, 164; World Bank 1997a, 52; and Dunning 1992, 6–10, 22, 28–29. The best data we have on the globalization of production concerns foreign direct

foreign suppliers for parts and components of military weapons systems.[21] However, this literature, as well as the studies following in its wake, focuses almost exclusively on the consequences of the globalization of production for U.S. defense policy or the structure of the U.S. economy rather than upon the repercussions for international security more generally. This literature also centers upon increases in international subcontracting, which is only one element of the geographic dispersion of MNC production.

Empirical analyses of the security repercussions of trade flows can no longer eclipse examinations of how the globalization of production affects security relations. This book is the first systematic study of how this unprecedented change in the global economy influences international security. Since the geographic dispersion of MNC production is a novel and dramatic shift in the international environment, it is critical to know how it changes the prospects for peace. This analysis shows that the globalization of production has led to major changes in the global security environment that collectively improve the security climate in some regions while decreasing it in others.

THE GLOBALIZATION OF PRODUCTION LEADS TO CHANGES IN CAPABILITIES, INCENTIVES, AND ACTORS

Within the literature that examines how the international economy can influence security, scholars outline a wide variety of arguments. In practice, these disparate arguments can be boiled down to three general mechanisms: the global economy can influence security by changing capabilities, incentives, and

---

investment (FDI); however, FDI data captures the geographic dispersion of MNC production only partially and, moreover, covers only some countries. Through 2003, there are only two published analyses I am aware of that seek to employ a systematic measure relating to the globalization of production, each of which is plagued by severe data limitations. In the first study, Gartzke, Li and Boehmer (2001) seek as part of their analysis to broaden the notion of economic interdependence beyond an exclusive focus on trade flows between countries to also include FDI linkages. Because systematic dyadic data for FDI does not exist, there is no way of comprehensively measuring the theoretical construct they are interested in: FDI interdependence between pairs of states. Their study uses the total amount of inward and outward FDI as a proportion of a country's GDP, which is of no help in determining the extent of FDI interdependence between each pair of states (that is, the level of FDI from country A in country B and vice versa). In the end, therefore, the dyadic test this study uses is inappropriate and its analysis can therefore tell us little. A second analysis by Rosecrance and Thompson (2003) actually does contain a measure of FDI interdependence. As they note, however, the scope of their analysis of FDI interdependence was greatly circumscribed by data limitations: "Unfortunately, few nations except the United States collect data on FDI flows with particular countries. Thus . . . we had to limit ourselves to looking at data on U.S. FDI and conflict with other countries over the period 1950–1992" (389). The problem is that the United States is a very special case in the international system: it is the largest source of FDI and is also simultaneously the most powerful state—economically, politically, and militarily.

[21] Much of this literature is discussed in Moran 1990.

the nature of the actors. This book shows that the globalization of production has reshaped the global security environment via each of these three general mechanisms.

Regarding capabilities, the key puzzle is whether the globalization of production has fundamentally changed the parameters of weapons production. As Richard Bitzinger notes, throughout history, "most countries traditionally have preferred to be self-sufficient in arms production."[22] The reasons are straightforward: "going it alone" in defense production makes it possible to guard against vulnerability to supply interruptions and to ensure that strategic competitors do not have easy access to the same vital military technologies. States continue to have a preference for relying on their own resources for weapons production; the key question is how capable they are of pursuing this strategy. Analysts agree that going it alone has become harder in defense production in recent years.[23] Until now, however, we have lacked an understanding of exactly how much more difficult it has become. The analysis in this book reveals that the scales have decisively shifted against a strategy of autarkic defense production: no state, including the great powers, can now effectively remain on the cutting edge in military technology if it does not pursue significant internationalization in the production of weaponry.

Concerning incentives, the key unanswered question is whether the geographic dispersion of MNC production has changed the economic benefits of conquest. Economic gain has historically been a significant motivating force for conflict, and wars of conquest unfortunately still occur, as is demonstrated by Iraq's 1991 invasion of Kuwait and the occupation of western Congo by Uganda, Burundi, and Rwanda from 1998 to 2002. Irrespective of the motivation for war, the prospects for stability—that is, peacefulness—will decrease if aggressors are able to extract significant economic resources from newly occupied territory. The current benchmark study of the economic benefits of conquest concludes that conquerors are still in a position to effectively extract economic resources from vanquished wealthy countries.[24] In order to determine whether this is truly the case, we need to investigate how recent economic transformations within the most advanced countries affect the economic benefits of conquest. Until now, this key issue has been neglected in the literature. This analysis reveals that while conquerors are still in a position to effectively extract economic resources from a subset of wealthy countries, they can no longer do so from most. Specifically, I find that the globalization of production has greatly reduced the economic benefits of military conquest among the most advanced countries.

With respect to shifts in the nature of the actors, the primary puzzle is whether the geographic dispersion of MNC production can reshape security by

---

[22] Bitzinger 1994, 172.

[23] See, for example, Moran 1990; Bitzinger 1994; and Vernon and Kapstein 1991.

[24] See Liberman 1996.

influencing the prospects for regional economic integration. Because regional integration can alter the interests of the group's respective members, scholars conclude that such institutions can play a significant role in the development of stable, peaceful security relationships.[25] Although this line of argument is compelling, a key question remains: under what conditions will states with security tensions be able to consolidate integration in the first place? All the theory we have indicates that it is the consolidation of deep regional economic integration, and not simply the formation of an agreement, that has significant positive security repercussions. And yet, scholars who study international cooperation generally agree that states with security tensions will be least likely to engage in deep economic cooperation.[26] We need to examine whether the globalization of production can exert sufficient pressure to induce even those states with a history of security rivalry to consolidate regional integration. The analysis here shows that it can. I find that this global production shift can, under certain conditions, enhance the prospects for peace by contributing to the consolidation of deep regional economic integration among long-standing security rivals.

The globalization of production has significant ramifications for security affairs by virtue of the fact that it has altered the parameters of weapons development, the economic benefits of conquest, and the prospects for regional economic integration among security rivals. These three mechanisms are the focus of this book both because of their significance in the literature and because they can be directly examined empirically. However, these mechanisms are not the only means by which the geographic dispersion of MNC production can potentially influence security; in total, there are five other mechanisms, all of which I analyze in this book. Two of these additional mechanisms are briefly discussed in chapter 3, while the remaining three are examined in detail in chapter 8. As will be seen, these five other mechanisms are all prospective in nature: they have the potential to influence security relations in the future, but do not appear to have yet played a role. The bottom line is that the globalization of production has already reshaped the international security environment in dramatic ways and may have an even greater influence in the years ahead.

THE GLOBALIZATION OF PRODUCTION ACTS AS A SIGNIFICANT FORCE FOR GREAT POWER STABILITY

The influence of the globalization of production on security is clearest and also most consequential with respect to great power relations. A massive amount of

[25] See, for example, Wendt 1994; Deutsch et al, 1957; Nye 1971; and Russett and Oneal 2000, chap. 5.

[26] See, for example, Grieco, Powell, and Snidal 1993.

literature within international relations is devoted to examining the most dangerous potential outcome in the system: a great power that attempts to fundamentally upset the territorial status quo and is successful in doing so because the gains of military conquest are cumulative. The possibility of this outcome has cast a long shadow over researchers working within every different approach and method in the field.[27] This focus is not surprising. Although great power war is not an everyday occurrence, it is one that holds great peril: in World War II, over 50 million were killed, and the possibility that the nature of the system could be transformed by the Axis powers was far from remote. Moreover, the mere threat of great power revisionism is grave and consequential: the U.S. effort to contain the Soviet threat to the system during the Cold War was incredibly expensive in economic terms (for decades America committed between 5 and 14 percent of its GDP to defense spending), and U.S presidents repeatedly engaged in brinkmanship that ran the risk of escalation to global thermonuclear destruction.

Many different factors influence the prospects for great power stability.[28] What is crucial is to identify which factors are important and whether they are likely to have a positive or negative influence. The findings of this book collectively indicate that the globalization of production now acts as a force for stability among the great powers. Put most precisely, the conclusion of this study is that the increased geographic dispersion of MNC production will, ceteris paribus, increase the stability of great power relations.

Of course, some say that the rise of what we now call economic globalization is partly due to the "long peace" that emerged among the great powers after 1945.[29] This is true. There are many different sources of this long peace, which, in turn, provided a favorable environment for the onset and acceleration of economic globalization. This book is not about the causes of the long peace, nor the genesis of economic globalization. Instead, the motivation for this study is to understand the repercussions of the globalization of production for security relations throughout the world in recent years and in the years to come. With the fading of Cold War security structures, a number of prominent analysts now see an increased threat of security competition among great powers.[30] This is where the geographic dispersion of MNC production enters in. As this study will show, now that the globalization of production is here, it works independently to reinforce stability among the great powers in a positive feedback loop via a specific set of mechanisms.

This analysis, in short, greatly strengthens the argument that international commerce now acts as a force for peace among the great powers. This book's

[27] Mearsheimer 2001; Rosecrance 1999; and Stam and Smith 2001 are recent examples.

[28] The most significant recent empirical analysis emphasizing this point is Bennett and Stam 2003.

[29] For this argument, see, for example, Buzan 1984. On the long peace, see Gaddis 1987.

[30] See Mearsheimer 2001; Kupchan 2002; Waltz 2000; and Huntington 1993.

conclusion—that the production activities of MNCs contributes to stability in a way that is different from and stronger than trade—undercuts those who advance pessimistic projections about the great powers in the years ahead. Significantly, these analysts all maintain that international commerce now provides no reason for optimism about the future. The most forceful proponent of this gloomy perspective, John Mearsheimer, certainly does recognize that economic globalization is a significant force in world politics that has the potential to dramatically influence security affairs, but ultimately concludes that it does not reduce the force of his pessimistic predictions. Mearsheimer asserts there is essentially no difference between the nature and extent of international commerce in today's global economy and that of the pre-1914 era; he then reasons that if extensive international commerce did not prevent World War I, "a highly interdependent world economy does not make great-power war more or less likely" and that we ultimately have no reason to think that the current wave of economic globalization will act as a significant constraint on the severity of conflict among the great powers in the years ahead.[31]

Mearsheimer's treatment of economic globalization suffers from the standard problem in the security field at large: an overly narrow and static conceptualization of international commerce. Trade linkages before World War I were very extensive, to be sure. But trade comprises only one part of what international commerce now consists of, a minority portion at that. Before World War I, there was nothing like the geographic dispersion of MNC production that exists today. Given that the globalization of production is historically novel and is now the pivotal driver of international commerce, analyses such as Mearsheimer's that dismiss the current security repercussions of economic globalization of parallels with pre–World War I trade make no sense. Indeed, they are biased.

It turns out that once we factor in the globalization of production, Mearsheimer's pessimistic argument concerning the future of great power security relations loses steam. In his analysis, whether substantial power gains can be accrued through military conquest has a fundamental influence on the prospects for great power conflict.[32] Much of the basis for Mearsheimer's overall pessimism is a reflection of this in combination with his assessment that great power conquerors can, in fact, still effectively extract the economic wealth of those societies they vanquish on the battlefield and forcibly occupy.[33] As recently as World War II, it appears that great powers were in a position to conquer other great powers and effectively extract economic benefits from

[31] See Mearsheimer 2001, 371. This is the same line of argument advanced in Waltz 2000; and Kupchan 2002, esp. 103. Huntington goes one step further, arguing that commerce is now destabilizing among the great powers; see Huntington 1993, 25–27.

[32] Of the four strategies Mearsheimer identifies for states to enhance their power, it is conquest that plays by far the most significant role in his account and in the historical record; see Mearsheimer 2001, esp. 147–55.

[33] Mearsheimer 2001, esp. 148–50.

occupation.[34] This is no longer the case: a key finding of this book is that the globalization of production has greatly lowered the economic benefits of conquest in the most economically advanced states, and hence among all of the current and future great powers. This alone significantly undercuts Mearsheimer's pessimistic portrait of great power security relations in the years ahead.

The reasons why Mearsheimer places great stress on the economic benefits of conquest as an influence on great power stability are, of course, particular to his specific analysis. However, we need not agree with his particular theory of world politics to appreciate why the reduction in the economic benefits of conquest among the most advanced countries caused by the globalization of production significantly enhances stability among the great powers. Numerous other scholars employing approaches very different from Mearsheimer's similarly emphasize the economic benefits of conquest as a key influence on great power stability.[35] Irrespective of why a state seizes territory beyond its borders, the prospects for stability are greatly reduced when a great power can use one military conquest as a springboard for the next. During World War II, for example, the Nazis achieved great initial success and were hard to defeat in large part because they were able to effectively extract economic resources from the territory they occupied; these resources provided capacity that the Nazis could use to protect captured territory and acquire more. Had the Nazis been unable to effectively extract economic resources from vanquished territory, then their strategic vulnerability would have increased as they extended themselves militarily. This example makes it evident why a reduction in the economic benefits of conquest among the most advanced countries would enhance stability among the great powers.

Through its influence on the economic benefits of conquest, the geographic dispersion of MNC production acts as a force for continued peacefulness among the great powers. Although significant, this is not the only reason why this global production shift promotes great power stability. This study's finding that great powers can no longer effectively go it alone in defense-related production points in the same direction. While the consequences of a change in the benefits of conquest for great power stability has received extensive scholarly treatment, the potential significance of a shift in the ability of states to pursue an autarkic defense production strategy has not yet been examined. There is good reason for this, since until very recently great powers retained the ability to be self-sufficient in defense production.

To put it simply for now, this book's finding that an autarkic defense production strategy has been fundamentally undermined augurs well for peaceful security relations among the great powers for two basic reasons.[36] First,

---

[34] See Liberman 1996, chap. 3.

[35] Three of the strongest recent statements in this regard are Van Evera 1999, chap. 5; Stam and Smith 2001; and Rosecrance 1999, esp. 17, 81.

[36] A more detailed version of this argument is presented in chapter 7.

consider what would happen if a great power were to go it alone in defense production in the current environment. Any state that pursues this course will not have leading-edge military equipment and will thus be in a weaker position to pursue revisionist aims. Modern history makes clear the significance of this development: the three main revisionist great powers from the past 75 years (imperial Japan and Nazi Germany in World War II, and the Soviet Union during the Cold War) were largely closed off from the international economy at the time they challenged the status quo.

Second, the finding that states can no longer effectively produce leading-edge military technologies on their own means that any great power that makes a fundamental challenge to the territorial status quo will be easier to subdue; this is the case irrespective of which defense production strategy is pursued. The great powers that have made fundamental challenges to the status quo over the past century all acted largely on their own and provoked a counterbalancing coalition that imposed a supply cutoff upon them. The problem is that these supply cutoffs were far from effective in reducing the ability of the revisionist great power to develop and produce competitive military weaponry.[37] The world of today is much less threatening in this regard: the globalization of production greatly magnifies the degree to which a supply cutoff like those imposed in World War II would degrade the military capacity of a revisionist great power that acts alone.

The marked reduction in the benefits of conquest among the most advanced countries and the change in the parameters of weapons development caused by the globalization of production are both stabilizing for security relations among the great powers on their own. Of key importance, however, is that these changes overlap and reinforce each other: as chapter 7 shows, these two shifts in combination make less acute the most dangerous threat in the system. Significantly, this is true regardless of what motivates great powers. No matter whether the ultimate goal is power, security, prestige, or wealth, the geographic dispersion of MNC production has structurally shifted the scales against any great power that tries to overturn the fundamental nature of the system through force. Given that the globalization of production is a major, historically novel shift in the international environment, we are fortunate that it has a stabilizing influence on great power relations.

IS THE GLOBALIZATION OF PRODUCTION LEADING TO UNIVERSAL PEACE?

The view that economic shifts can influence the political world is one of the most enduring notions within political science and the social sciences more

---

[37] For a useful overview, see Mearsheimer 2001, 90–96.

generally. Although sometimes viewed as being exclusively associated with Marxist theory, it is an intellectual project of incredible diversity. Unfortunately, many analysts go so far as to advance economic determinist arguments.[38] A prominent example of this tendency with respect to international security is John Stuart Mill's argument in 1848: "It is commerce which is rapidly rendering war obsolete, by strengthening and multiplying the personal interests which are in natural opposition to it. . . . [Commerce is] the principal guarantee of the peace of the world."[39]

Mill's optimistic forecast that international commerce was rendering war obsolete, like many similar predictions that followed in its wake, proved to be greatly in error.[40] His understanding was not simply wrong at the time; it necessarily will always be wrong.[41] The simple reason is that international commerce is only one of the variables that influences the likelihood of war. This study is motivated by the need to better understand whether international commerce now has a positive or negative influence on security relations; in pursuing this goal, I recognize that it does not serve as a master variable.

Although the globalization of production does not provide any guarantee of peace among the great powers, it does act as a force for stability among them. This raises a key question: does this global production shift have beneficial repercussions for security throughout the world or only in certain regions? For many, the term *globalization* connotes a system or process that encompasses all countries and industries. As stressed above, the globalization of production is not, in fact, 'global' but instead remains bounded in important respects: it is an ongoing process, not an end point.[42] It is, consequently, vital to examine the nature of this production change in its current form rather than to speculate about some hypothetical future international economy that is perfectly globalized.[43] Once we do so, it becomes clear that there is no reason to expect that the geographic dispersion of MNC production will have a uniform effect on security relations throughout the world.

The unfortunate conclusion of this book is that while the geographic dispersion of MNC production is stabilizing among the great powers, it will not promote peace elsewhere in the world. Indeed, the analysis in the concluding section of the book shows that this global production shift is likely to have a net negative influence on security relations among developing countries. As will be

---

[38] Here, economic determinism is taken to mean that "the tendencies, forces, and outcomes of economic processes exert an independent, determining influence on other aspects of social development, such as political organization and cultural beliefs" (Bimber 1994, 91).

[39] Mill 1920, 582.

[40] The most famous of these forecasts was advanced by Norman Angell; Angell 1910.

[41] See the discussion in Keohane and Nye 1998, 81.

[42] On this point, see Dicken 1998, 5.

[43] Some globalization proponents are more extreme in this respect; see, for example, Reich 1991; and Ohmae 1995.

seen, this is partly because developing countries have not yet participated in the globalization of production to nearly the same extent that the great powers have. Far from acting as a general force for improved security relations, as some prominent analysts aver is the case, the positive influence of the global-ization of production, I conclude, will be geographically circumscribed for the foreseeable future.[44]

PLAN OF THE BOOK

The remainder of this book is divided into seven chapters. Chapter 2 is devoted to outlining several key features of the globalization of production. In the final portion of this chapter, I argue that this global production shift is the most novel aspect of contemporary economic globalization.

Chapter 3 outlines the theoretical foundations for the book. The chapter be-gins by providing a detailed portrait of the three key puzzles that need to be ad-dressed and the specific mechanisms by which the globalization of production can influence security that I will evaluate empirically. I reveal how these three mechanisms correspond with the main theoretical approaches to the influence of the global economy on international security. The second portion of chapter 3 outlines the deductive basis for the three theories that will be analyzed in the empirical analysis. These theories concern, respectively, how the globalization of production influences (1) the ability of states to effectively rely on their own resources in defense production; (2) the prospects for regional economic inte-gration among security rivals; and (3) the economic benefits of conquest.

Chapters 4–6 evaluate the three theories developed in chapter 3. Chapter 4 shows that even those states with the largest and most advanced economies in the system—the great powers—now must strongly pursue globalization of defense-related production if they wish to remain on the leading edge in military technology. This is made clear through an examination of the least likely case: the United States, which has long been the country in the best position to pursue an autarkic defense production strategy due to its economic size and domestic technological capacity. Beginning in the mid-1970s, the United States moved away from its long-standing approach of minimizing its reliance on international sources for key aspects of defense production. I demonstrate that the United States strongly shifted away from its default autarkic approach in the mid-1970s because the gains of globalization in weapons production—reduced cost and, es-pecially, enhanced quality—were dramatic. I also find that the globalization in defense-related production was an important factor in the United States deci-sively pulling ahead of the Soviet Union in military technology during the 1980s.

---

[44] The most prominent statement that the globalization of production will act as a general force for improved security relations is Friedman 1999, esp. 257.

Chapter 5 demonstrates that the geographic dispersion of MNC production can enhance the prospects for peace by contributing to the consolidation of deep regional economic integration among long-standing rivals, but only under certain conditions. Because of the nature of these conditions, the key test case is Mercosur (the Southern Cone Common Market), an integration agreement formed in 1991 by Argentina, Brazil, Paraguay, and Uruguay. I show that incentives created by the globalization of production helped propel Mercosur policymakers to take great strides toward the consolidation of regional integration during the group's early years. I also find that this early consolidation of Mercosur helped make it possible for Argentina and Brazil to decisively move beyond their 150-year-long history of security rivalry and consolidate a stable and peaceful security relationship.

Chapter 6 reveals that the geographic dispersion of MNC production has led to shifts in the structures of the most advanced states that prevent a conqueror from effectively extracting economic gains from occupation. The chapter examines the only recent example of military conquest of any economically advanced societies in which extraction was attempted: the Soviet empire in Eastern Europe. Two key findings emerge. Through an investigation of Hungary from the early 1970s through the early 1990s, I show that a vanquished advanced country will be greatly constrained in its ability to participate in the globalization of production following conquest. By analyzing Soviet policy toward Eastern Europe from the early 1960s through the 1980s, I also demonstrate that a conqueror of an advanced society will be prone to use mechanisms of imperial control that greatly hinder innovation in the "knowledge-based" sectors that have become the key focus of those countries whose firms have participated most strongly in the globalization of production.

The specific empirical findings detailed in chapters 4–6 are significant and help to resolve a number of important puzzles in the security literature. Given the salience and historically unprecedented nature of the globalization of production, we need to know what general effects it has on international security. Addressing this issue is the purpose of the concluding section of the book. Chapter 7 draws together my empirical findings into a series of bottom-line implications for international security. I delineate why the geographic dispersion of MNC production now acts as a force for stability among great powers but, at the same time, has a net negative effect on security relations in the developing world. I also explain why this global production shift currently has a mixed effect on security relations between the great powers and developing countries.

Chapter 8 then looks toward the future security environment. I outline and critically assess a series of additional mechanisms by which this global production shift can potentially influence interstate relations in the years ahead. I conclude that none of these additional mechanisms is likely to alter the initial assessment derived in chapter 7 concerning the general security repercussions of the globalization of production. In the end, therefore, the final conclusion of this book is that the geographic dispersion of MNC production has a differential effect on security relations: positive among the great powers; mixed between the great powers and developing countries; and negative among developing countries. This is true not just now, but is likely to remain so for many years to come. The final portion of this chapter argues that future research on the globalization of production's security repercussions should focus on nonstate actors, particularly terrorists. I then discuss the four main ways this global production shift may influence the threat from terrorism in upcoming years.

CHAPTER 2

Understanding the Globalization of Production

THE GLOBALIZATION of production is a historically unprecedented change in the international economy. Because of the novelty of this global production shift, many of its key elements are insufficiently understood by international relations scholars, especially analysts who focus on security issues. The principal goal of this chapter, therefore, is to outline several key features of this dramatic ongoing change in the global economy.

This chapter is divided into five sections. The first section provides a general portrait of the rapidly growing significance of multinational corporations (MNCs) in the global economy. The second, third, and fourth sections, respectively, review three global production changes of particular importance. The final section critically discusses the common view that contemporary economic globalization is "nothing new." Although this claim has some merit with respect to both international trade and international financial markets, this is not the case with respect to the globalization of production.

THE ENHANCED SIGNIFICANCE OF MULTINATIONAL CORPORATIONS IN THE GLOBAL ECONOMY

MNCs have long existed, but it is only very recently that they have become "the primary movers and shapers of the global economy."[1] Up until a short while ago, trade had always been the most important integrating force in global commerce. Trade flows are still very important; today, however, international production by the massive number of MNCs (65,000 with 850,000 affiliates) is now much more significant as a driver of commerce.[2] Although data on the globalization of production is limited, the paramount status of MNC production is revealed in a number of different statistics.

We do have a fair amount of data on foreign direct investment (FDI) flows, which increased much more rapidly than global trade flows during the 1980s and 1990s.[3] In turn, as figure 2.1 reveals, the total accumulated stock of global FDI increased rapidly as a share of global output during this period.

[1] Dicken 1998, 177.

[2] UNCTAD 2002a, xv.

[3] Held et al. 1999, 242. FDI is a category of international investment. The defining feature of FDI is that it is international investment undertaken with the goal of exercising control over an

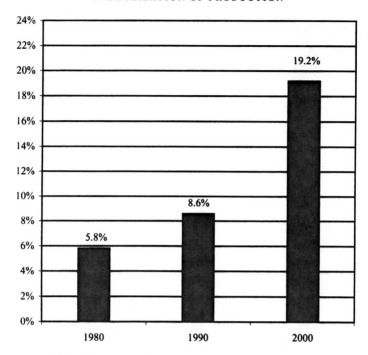

Figure 2.1 FDI Outward Stock as a Share of Global GDP
Source: UNCTAD FDI/TNC Database.

However, FDI flows can change dramatically from year to year, and, at any rate, FDI only reflects the globalization of production to a partial degree. The geographic dispersion of MNC production is better reflected by the sales and gross product of MNC foreign affiliates; each of these measures is estimated to have grown much more rapidly than trade and world output in recent decades, as figure 2.2 shows. At present, the value of the sales of MNC foreign affiliates is more than twice that of world exports.[4]

If we look beyond growth rates, all estimates reveal that the globalization of production now significantly outstrips trade as an organizing feature of the international economy. There are many indicators, but several stand out. For

---

enterprise; this is what differentiates FDI from international portfolio investment. As the OECD outlines: "Foreign direct investment reflects the objective of obtaining a lasting interest by a resident entity in one economy ("direct investor") in an entity resident in an economy other than that of the investor ("direct investment enterprise"). The lasting interest implies the existence of a long-term relationship between the direct investor and the enterprise and a significant degree of influence on the management of the enterprise" (OECD 1996, 7–8).

[4] Kobrin 2003, 15.

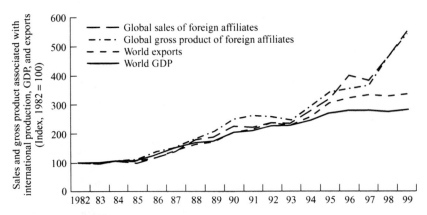

Figure 2.2 The Growth of Sales and Gross Product Associated with MNC International
Production, GDP and Exports, 1982–1999 (Index, 1982 = 100)
Source: UNCTAD 2000a, 6.

one thing, much trade today is simply a by-product of the geographic dispersion of MNC production. Most notable in this respect is intrafirm trade: "While
estimates are hard to come by, it appears that between 30 and 50 percent of
world 'trade' is actually composed of intra-firm transfers between units of
multinational firms; for example, a recent study of U.S. trade patterns found that
38% of transactions were intra-firm."[5] Also significant in this regard is international subcontracting: in 1990, offshore subcontracting by U.S. manufacturing
firms accounted for almost 12 percent of total U.S. nonenergy purchases.[6]

In terms of annual value, international production by MNCs is now much
more significant than trade. As one analysis concludes: "The size and scope
of international production are amplified further by the activities of MNCs
in forms other than FDI, such as subcontracting, licensing and franchising,
through which markets for goods, services, and factors of production can be
reached and international production organized. Global sales in international
markets associated with this more broadly defined international production
amounted to an estimated $7 trillion in 1992, compared to some $3 trillion in
arm's-length trade" (see figure 2.3).[7]

If we look at the United States in particular, which has the most reliable
and systematic data on MNCs, then the same basic portrait emerges. When it
comes to serving foreign markets, for example, trade is now much less important than production by the foreign affiliates of U.S. MNCs, as figure 2.4

[5] Kobrin 2003, 15; see also the discussion in Jones 1996, 56; and Dicken 1998, 43.
[6] World Bank 1997a, 45.
[7] UNCTAD 1995, xx.

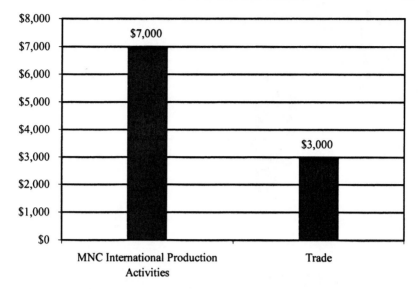

Figure 2.3 Estimated Value of MNC International Production Activities Compared to Arm's-Length Trade in 1992 (in U.S.$billions)
Source: UNCTAD 1995, xx.

reveals. In the end, it is clear that trade now has secondary status in the international economy. The only issue under contention is the magnitude of the disparity vis-à-vis MNC production.

It is necessary to descend from this level of abstraction if we are to gain a better grasp of how the structure of global production has changed in recent years. I am not interested in explaining where the globalization of production came from, and so will not dwell on its complex origins. Moreover, no attempt will be made to fully discuss the massive literature on the production strategies of MNCs.[8] Instead, the aim of the next three sections is to provide a brief overview of three specific global production changes that are particularly important to understand: (1) the increased geographic dispersion of MNC production activities; (2) the increased geographic dispersion of technological development by MNCs; and (3) the increased opportunity cost of being closed off from MNCs. The first two involve the changing behavior of *firms*; the third concerns the changing behavior of *states*. While these three changes are examined separately below, it is important to recognize that in practice these three transformations are not distinct but instead overlap and reinforce each other.

[8] For a general analysis of MNCs, see Dunning 1992. Some of the key theoretical contributions on the existence, growth, and strategies of MNCs include Hymer 1976; Buckley and Casson 1976; Vernon 1966; Caves 1971; and Dunning 1977.

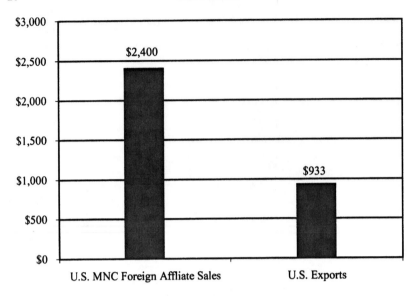

Figure 2.4 U.S. Exports Compared to Sales of U.S. MNC Foreign Affiliates in 1998
(in U.S.$billions)
Source: Quinlan and Chander 2001, 88.

GLOBAL PRODUCTION CHANGE NUMBER 1:
THE INCREASED GEOGRAPHIC DISPERSION
OF MNC PRODUCTION ACTIVITIES

This section outlines the two most significant shifts that have increased the geographic dispersion of MNC production activities over the past three decades: the rise of international subcontracting and the shift away from stand-alone foreign affiliates.

The Rise of International Subcontracting

For a variety of reasons, many firms have recently chosen to specialize more than they did previously. In particular, many large firms have moved away from contributing at all phases of the value-added chain and instead specialize in those aspects of the value-added chain that use resources and capabilities in which the firm has a perceived competitive advantage—what is termed a "core competency" strategy.[9] This core competency trend is reflected in the increasing trend toward subcontracting (or outsourcing), a production strategy in which "the firm offering the subcontract requests another independent enterprise to undertake the production or carry out the processing of a material, component, part or subassembly for it."[10]

Of course, firms have always engaged in subcontracting. But for cultural, political, geographic, and other reasons, firms generally have a preference to use suppliers within their own country before turning to those located elsewhere. As a result, almost all subcontracting until recently occurred *within* countries. This has greatly changed: "One of most significant developments of the past thirty years has been the extension of subcontracting across national boundaries: the emergence of *international subcontracting* as an important global activity. The revolution in transport and communications technology, together with developments in the production process itself, have created the potential for firms to establish subcontracting networks over vast geographical distances."[11] In the extreme, some firms now rely on subcontracting for virtually their entire production: Nike, for example, subcontracts all of its shoe manufacturing activities to dozens of different locations, most of which are located in South and Southeast Asia.[12]

One indicator of the rapid growth of international subcontracting is a recent World Bank survey of 628 North American and 240 European industrial groups or firms, which found that "offshore outsourcing rose about 30 percent between 1987 and 1995 in response to growing cost competition and the restructuring of business."[13] A better indicator of the growing significance of international subcontracting is the escalating degree of offshore purchasing by U.S. manufacturing firms, which until a few decades ago secured almost all of their parts and components from either (1) their own foreign affiliates or (2) the vast range of other companies that were based in the United States. As figure 2.5 shows, international subcontracting by U.S. manufacturing firms exploded in value beginning in the early 1970s. Of course, overall U.S. imports also increased significantly over this period. As figure 2.6 shows, however, international subcontracting by U.S. manufacturing firms more than doubled as a percentage of nonenergy purchases during the 1972–87 period.

A New Role for Foreign Affiliates

While international subcontracting has the obvious effect of dispersing production across borders, these activities are not located within the global firm's

---

[9] See, for example, Jones 1996, 142.
[10] Holmes 1986, 84.
[11] Dicken 1998, 233.
[12] Dicken 1998, 235–36.
[13] World Bank 1997a, 43–44.

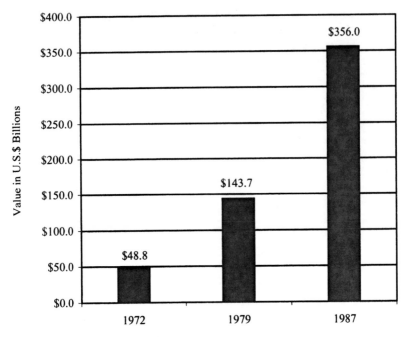

Figure 2.5 Value of International Outsourcing by U.S. Manufacturing Firms
(selected years)
Source: World Bank 1997a, 45.

direct managerial control: international subcontracting does not involve resource transfers from affiliate to parent or vice versa, but rather involves sourcing from third parties. In recent years, many MNCs have also moved toward
developing much greater integration of their productive activities across wide
geographic expanses *within* the firm itself. This is a marked shift from the pre-
dominant pattern prior to the 1970s, where the foreign affiliates of MNCs were
a miniature replication of their parent organizations in the home country.[14] International production linkages within the firm were quite weak in this period:
with the notable exceptions of transfers of technology and capital from the parent firm, affiliates prior to the 1970s invariably were "stand-alone" affiliates—
that is, they were largely independent of the parent firm in the host country.
Stand-alone affiliates essentially replicate the entire value-added chain of the
parent firm within a different market.

While stand-alone affiliates are of course still common, FDI has increasingly become a means for MNCs to access particular factors of production
as part of a strategy for organizing production globally in the most efficient

[14] Dunning 1992, 127.

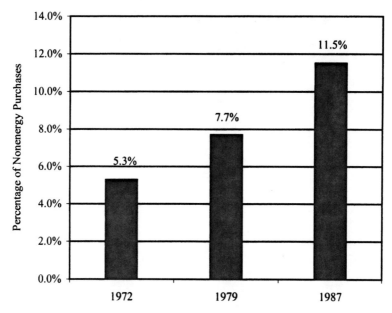

Figure 2.6 International Outsourcing by U.S. Manufacturing Firms as a Percentage
of Nonenergy Purchases (selected years)
Source: World Bank 1997a, 45.

manner possible. For those phases of the value chain that global firms continue
to specialize in, many MNCs have sought to reap various locational advantages
by locating each part of the value chain in the area that is most advantageous
from a production standpoint.[15] As one analysis concludes: "Firms increasingly
seek locations where they can combine their own mobile assets most efficiently
with the immobile resources they need to produce goods and services for the
markets they want to serve. As a consequence, firms split up the production
process into various specific activities (such as finance, R&D, accounting,
training, parts production, distribution), or segments of these activities, with
each of them carried out by affiliates in locations best suited to the particular
activity. This process creates an international intra-firm division of labor and a
growing integration of international production networks."[16] Global production
links within the firm pursuing this new affiliate strategy are obviously very
extensive. In the extreme, "any affiliate operating anywhere may perform,

[15] See, for example, UNCTAD 1993a; Vernon 1992; Krugman 1995; Dunning 1992, 1994;
Jones 1996, 143; and UNCTAD 1998, 111–12. The value chain, or value-added chain, refers to
"the various stages of economic activity that make up a production sequence of a specific product
or service from start to finish" (Dunning 1992, 189). Other authors in this literature prefer the term
production chain (Dicken 1998).

[16] UNCTAD 1998, 111–12.

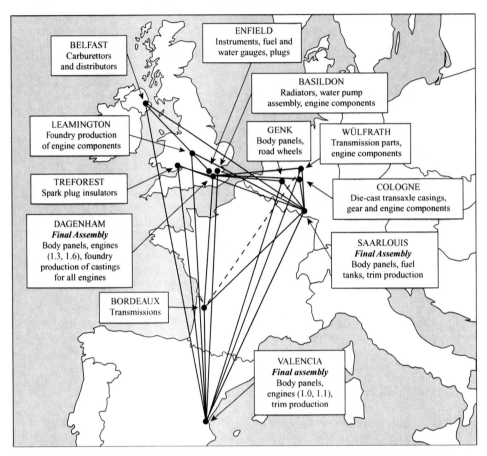

Figure 2.7 The Ford Fiesta Production Network in Western Europe
Source: Dicken 1992, 300.

either by itself or with other affiliates or the parent firm, functions for the firm as a whole."[17]

Even within a particular region, it is possible for an MNC to geographically disperse its production activities to a very significant degree in order to take advantage of locational advantages of particular countries. This is made clear in figure 2.7, which shows the geographic dispersion of production of the Ford Fiesta throughout Europe as of the early 1990s. The figure only shows production dispersion within Ford itself, which accounts for around 45 percent of the value of a Fiesta; the remaining production for this automobile is performed via an subcontracting network that consists of hundreds of outside suppliers.[18]

[17] UNCTAD 1993a, 121.
[18] Dicken 1992, 300.

Lack of data unfortunately makes it impossible to parse the precise extent of the intrafirm international division of the production process.[19] Looking at U.S. data is the best route available: "the most detailed data on multinational activities are widely recognized to be those on U.S. multinational enterprises maintained by the U.S. Bureau of Economic Analysis. On many specialized questions, therefore, analysis in this area is often restricted to consideration of U.S. multinationals alone."[20] One indicator of the growing significance of the geographic dispersion of MNC production activities is that "the share of exports in sales of U.S. majority-owned affiliates has more than doubled, from less than 20 percent in 1966 to more than 40 percent in 1993."[21] Similarly, the employment level in foreign affiliates as a percentage of total employment for U.S. manufacturing MNCs increased from 21 percent in 1966 to 36 percent in 1997.[22] Because of the upgraded production role for U.S. foreign affiliates, many of them have become very significant global players in their own right: "As U.S. multinational corporations increasingly disperse different stages of production among different countries, their affiliates have also become world-class exporters of intermediate goods and components. In 1998, the exports of U.S. affiliates totaled $623 billion."[23]

Overall, foreign affiliates "now account for one-tenth of world GDP," and employment by foreign affiliates is currently estimated to account for about 54 million people, as compared with around 24 million in 1990.[24] Perhaps the most striking indicator of the increased significance of foreign affiliates is that many of them now have their *own* network of affiliates. As table 2.1 shows, many U.S. manufacturing MNCs now have a tiered structure of affiliates: "the first tier consists of affiliates owned by the ultimate parent, the second tier by affiliates owned by first-tier affiliates, and so on."[25]

The most widely cited general indicator of the enhanced intrafirm international division of the production process is the emergence of intrafirm trade as an important feature of the global economy over the past few decades. Intrafirm trade has, of course, always existed, but "apart from the long-established intrafirm trade in natural-resource products . . . intrafirm trade in intermediate products and services is primarily a phenomenon of the past few decades."[26] As noted previously, intrafirm trade now accounts for somewhere between 30 and 50 percent of world trade,[27] as compared to around 20 percent

[19] See, for example, OECD 2002, 159; UNCTAD 1993a, 165; World Bank 1997a, 52; and Dunning 1992, 6–10, 22, 28–29.
[20] World Bank 1997a, 52.
[21] World Bank 1997a, 41.
[22] Rangan 2001, 7.
[23] Quinlan and Chander 2001, 90.
[24] UNCTAD 2002a, xv.
[25] UNCTAD 1993a, 141.
[26] UNCTAD 1994, 143.
[27] Kobrin 2003, 15.

TABLE 2.1
Multitiered Ownership Structures of U.S. MNCs, 1991

Number of Tiers of Affiliates		Percentage of MNCs
1		32
2		22
3		28
4		12
5		6
Average	2.4	Total	100

Note: The data are based on a survey of 318 of the largest U.S. manufacturing MNCs with at least 5 percent of their total assets or sales abroad and at least $50 million in sales. Of that universe, a total of 51 MNCs responded in full. Those MNCs showed no bias when compared to the universe of 318 MNCs.
    Source: UNCTAD 1993a, 141.

in the early 1970s.[28] It is also telling that the composition of intrafirm trade appears to increasingly be shifting toward intermediate goods.[29]

Are MNC Production Activities Globalized?

It is clear that in recent years many MNCs have increasingly sought to "slice up the value chain," as Paul Krugman aptly puts it: they have simultaneously moved toward a higher reliance on international subcontracting (that is, enhanced interfirm production linkages across borders) and a greater intrafirm international division of the production process (that is, enhanced intrafirm linkages across borders).[30] Underlying the increasing prominence of these production dispersion strategies is a simple goal on the part of MNCs: the location of each element of the production process in the geographic region offering the greatest locational advantages. Perhaps the best indicator of the growing significance of the strategy of slicing up the value chain is the rapid rise in the ratio of imported to domestic sources of intermediate inputs: between the early 1970s and the mid-1980s, this ratio rose by 40 percent in Japan, 47 percent in Canada, 81 percent in France, 86 percent in the United States, and 131 percent in the United Kingdom.[31]

---

[28] Jones 1996, 56.

[29] UNCTAD 1994, xxi.

[30] Krugman 1995.

[31] Calculated from data in Levy 1993, 31. Levy also presents data for one other country, Germany, for which no statistics are available for the early 1970s. Levy does show, however, that ratio of imported to domestic sources of intermediate inputs in Germany increased by 38 percent between the mid-1970s and the mid-1980s.

Why have so many MNCs moved toward slicing up the value chain in the last few decades? The simplest answer is because they now can. MNCs have always had incentives to pursue geographic dispersion in production, but long faced barriers to doing so. These hurdles have now been greatly reduced; two factors are of key significance in this regard. As will be described in detail below, in response to the great increase in the opportunity cost of being isolated from MNCs, the past three decades have witnessed a push by states to create a more favorable investment climate for global firms. The second factor—the one highlighted most prominently in the literature—is that this shift toward greater geographic dispersion by many MNCs has been facilitated by recent technological shifts.[32] In particular, recent technological changes have led to a marked reduction in the geographic constraints that formerly existed on the dispersion of MNC production activities: the dramatic "shrinkage of space"[33] in recent decades has made it much easier to coordinate across firm boundaries and over wide regions.[34] Regarding transportation, for example, the introduction of containerization and the development of superfreighters caused sea freight unit costs to decline in real terms by almost 70 percent from the early 1980s to 1996.[35] Regarding communications, the "cost of a telephone call from London to New York has decreased since 1930 by a factor of 1500."[36] Figure 2.8 shows the dramatic reduction in telephone costs over the past few decades.

Significantly, improvements in communications have not only reduced costs, they have also undergone a *qualitative* change: the switch to fiber optics, increased coverage by satellite networks, the rise of the Internet, and other technological changes have increased the ease of disseminating financial data, contracts, and technical specifications throughout the world.[37] Of key significance is that these communications improvements have been complemented by dramatic advances in computers, which have become far less expensive in recent decades. According to one analysis, the "price of computing power has dropped in real terms by 99 per cent since 1970."[38]

As pioneer MNCs have dispersed their production geographically in order to reap locational efficiencies, they have created incentives for other firms to follow suit: "In today's globalizing world economy, the increasing competitive pressures faced by firms of all sizes impel more and more of them to establish an international portfolio of locational assets to remain competitive."[39] In this

---

[32] See, for example, Lipsey 1997, esp. 79; Kobrin 1997, 2003; Brooks and Guile 1987; Malone and Rockhart 1993; Dicken 1998, 145–76; Mytelka 1991; Casson 2000, 87; and Dunning 1995.

[33] Two good summaries are Dicken 1998, 151–61; and World Bank 1997a, 36–37.

[34] See, for example, Brooks and Guile 1987; Malone and Rockhart 1993; Casson 2000; and Dunning 1992, 605–6.

[35] World Bank 1997a, 37.

[36] OECD 2001, 12.

[37] See, for example, Brunn and Leinbach 1991; and Malone and Rockhart 1993.

[38] OECD 2001, 12.

[39] UNCTAD 1999, 4. See also the discussion in UNCTAD 1993a, 147, 154–55; and UNCTAD 1998, 111–12.

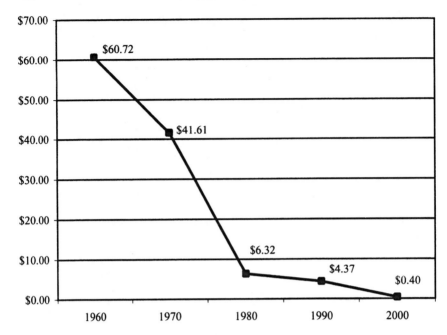

Figure 2.8 Cost of a Three-Minute Telephone Call From New York to London, 1960–2000
(in 2000 U.S.$)
Source: Masson 2001, 6.

way, increased global competitiveness and the globalization of production
have become linked in a feedback cycle. Because MNCs that pursue geographic dispersion reap locational advantages, pressure increases on their competitors to pursue globalization. In short, the internationalization of production
increases competitive pressures to internationalize production.

While the strategy of slicing up the value chain is growing rapidly in significance, MNC production is *not dispersed equally across all industries*. The geographic dispersion of MNC production activities appears to be most prominent
in those sectors of manufacturing characterized by "high levels of research and
development and significant firm-level economies of scale," such as machinery, electronic components, and computers.[40] That MNC production activities
in these sectors of manufacturing have been most geographically dispersed is
best reflected in U.S. data on MNCs. The latest data reveals that exports from
U.S. foreign affiliates as a share of total affiliate sales is now highest in the
following sectors: computer and office equipment (66 percent), industrial machinery and equipment (61 percent), electronic and other electrical equipment

[40] World Bank 1997a, 42; see also Hanson, Mataloni, and Slaughter 2001, 12.

TABLE 2.2
U.S. Trade in Products with the Highest Degree of Intrafirm Trade (percent)

	Share of Total Imports or Exports	Intrafirm Trade
Imports		
Transportation equipment	17.7	75.6
Computer and electronic products	20.8	66.3
Chemicals	6.4	59.3
Machinery, except electrical	6.6	50.3
Electrical equipment, appliances, and components	3.3	50.0
Exports		
Transportation equipment	15.6	41.2
Plastics and rubber products	2.2	40.7
Chemicals	9.9	39.3
Computer and electronic products	20.7	36.9
Electrical equipment, appliances and components	3.3	35.1

Source: OECD 2002, 166.

(57 percent), and transportation equipment (52 percent).[41] In other words, it is in these sectors—in which U.S. foreign affiliates now export the majority of goods that they sell—that the shift away from stand-alone affiliates has been most dramatic.

Data on intrafirm trade within U.S. MNCs reveals the same basic set of manufacturing industries as exhibiting the greatest extent of globalization. As of the early 1990s, the industries with the highest level of intrafirm exports relative to total exports were (1) machinery, (2) electronic components, (3) transportation, and (4) office and computing machines.[42] The latest data indicates the same basic pattern. Table 2.2 shows the industries in which U.S. MNC production is geographically dispersed to the greatest extent.

Why are these the industries in which U.S. MNC production activities have become most geographically dispersed? There are two primary reasons. First, these are industries that "involve production stages—design, component, production, final assembly—that are physically separable. Firms need not perform these tasks in the same location, and so can locate different stages in different countries." The second reason is that these are industries in which the "production stages exhibit different factor intensities," giving firms in these

[41] Hanson, Mataloni, and Slaughter 2001, 41.

[42] See Hanson, Mataloni, and Slaughter 2001, 41.

sectors strong incentives to slice up the value chain in order to exploit differences in factor costs across countries.[43]

In those sectors where MNC production activities have become most geographically dispersed, many analysts stress that a new general form of production has emerged: the "network" form of production.[44] Within a network, the headquarters of an MNC essentially serves as a "central nervous system" that manages large flows of resources within the firm (from parent to affiliate and vice versa, and between affiliates) in combination with extensive linkages with external firms. As Dunning puts it, "The large international firm . . . is increasingly assuming the role of an orchestrator of production and transactions within a system of cross-border internal and external relationships, which may, or may not, involve equity involvement but are intended to serve its global interests."[45]

It is important to recognize, however, that the geographic dispersion that occurs within production networks is not necessarily global in nature. In large part due to the influence of regional economic integration agreements, many production networks have a strong regional focus.[46] Figure 2.7 shows that an example is Ford's production network in Western Europe for the Fiesta. Since much geographic dispersion occurs within, rather than across, regions, the term *globalized* is a misnomer even for many industries that are now characterized by a network form of production.

GLOBAL PRODUCTION CHANGE NUMBER 2: THE GEOGRAPHIC DISPERSION OF TECHNOLOGICAL DEVELOPMENT BY MNCS

Creating a product or a good is a complicated process. One way to conceive of this process is to bifurcate it into a front-end, preproduction stage and a back-end, production stage. The previous section delineated the enhanced geographic dispersion of MNC activities in the production stage—that is, the various steps taken to actually produce the good or product. This section outlines the growing geographic dispersion in the front-end stage, focusing specifically on how MNCs develop new technologies used in the production process.

In recent years, technological development *within* MNCs has become increasingly dispersed geographically.[47] "Under competitive pressures, R&D is increasingly undertaken abroad. For example, expenditure on R&D undertaken by foreign affiliates has been growing disproportionately faster than the size of

---

[43] Hanson, Mataloni, and Slaughter 2001, 20.

[44] On production networks, see, for example, Kobrin 1997, 153–55; and Dunning 1988, 344–46.

[45] Dunning 1992, 602.

[46] Gilpin 2001, 292–93.

[47] For useful discussions, see Cantwell 1995, 1998; Florida 1997; UNCTAD 1999, 200–202; Cheng and Bolon 1993; and Blanc and Sierra 1999.

their operations: between 1985 and 1995, it grew by a factor of 3.4, while sales increased by 2.5 and employment by 1.7. One study has found that, between 1991 and 1995, 11 per cent of United States registered patents of the world's largest firms were generated by research undertaken in countries outside the home country of the parent company."[48] Significantly, one recent analysis concludes that "four-fifths of technology flows are internalized within MNCs."[49]

The growing level of technological linkages within MNCs is important. However, when it comes to the enhanced geographic dispersion of technological development by MNCs, what is most significant is not what has recently happened *within* firms, but *between* them. This is because there was a dramatic increase in the number and importance of interfirm alliances beginning in the 1970s. Exactly what interfirm alliances are, and how and why they have grown so rapidly in recent years, is discussed below.

Interfirm Alliances

Interfirm alliances are different from mergers, since interfirm collaboration occurs only in a portion of business activities and can be very limited in time span. The impermanence of interfirm alliances is, in fact, one of the primary features that make them attractive to firms, since many of the benefits of collaboration associated with mergers can be achieved without incurring the complicated issues associated with changes in long-term ownership.

An example that makes these characteristics clear is the interfirm alliance that IBM, Siemens, and Toshiba formed in 1992 to develop a new semiconductor chip. The three firms shared the U.S.$1 billion development costs for the chip and had several hundred engineers drawn from all three firms working together to develop it in one of IBM's facilities in East Fishkill, New York under a Toshiba manager. After three years, the chip was successfully developed, and the three firms then dissolved the alliance and went their separate ways in producing the chip.[50]

The rise of interfirm alliances is very recent. Starting essentially from a base of zero in the early 1970s, interfirm alliances have grown remarkably in recent years, as figure 2.9 indicates. While comprehensive data on interfirm alliances does not exist, "virtually every attempt at data-gathering reveals their dramatic growth."[51] According to one estimate, "high technology strategic alliances' compound annual growth rate in the 1980s was 31 per cent."[52] In turn, a recent

[48] UNCTAD 1999, 154.

[49] Dunning 2000, 14.

[50] See *Business Week*, 27 July 1992, 59; UNCTAD 1993a, 143; and *Wall Street Journal*, 14 July 1992, B1.

[51] Kobrin 1997, 150; For an excellent recent analysis, see Hagedoorn 2002.

[52] As cited in Kobrin 1995, 22.

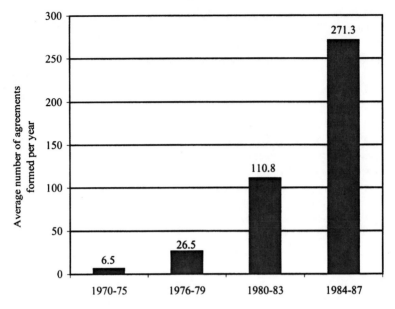

Figure 2.9 Interfirm Alliances in Information Technology and Biotechnology
Source: Mytelka 1991, 11.

OECD analysis finds that the number of interfirm alliances formed "in the 1990s is significantly higher than those observed in the 1980s," with a total of sixty-two thousand partnerships created between 1990 and 1999.[53] Many MNCs now have several *hundred* interfirm alliances.[54] By the late 1980s Philips, for example, had "over 800 strategic alliances, one or the other of which involve most of the leading electronics and telecommunications companies in the world."[55]

Why have interfirm alliances become so prevalent in recent decades? Scholars highlight technological change as the principal driving force behind this trend.[56] The relative significance of technology as a source of international competitiveness has accelerated due to speedier rates of product obsolescence[57] and the increased global competitive pressures faced by firms.[58] In recent years, the cost, difficulty, complexity, and scale of technological development

[53] Kang and Sakai 2000, 7.

[54] Dunning 1995.

[55] Dunning 1988, 342.

[56] On the motivations for interfirm alliances, see, for example, Mytelka 1991; Dunning 1995; Hagedoorn 1993; OECD 1992; Kobrin 1995, 1997; and Terpstra and Simonin 1993.

[57] See Dicken 1998, 162; Kobrin 1995, 22; and Mytelka 1991, 19 and the sources cited therein.

[58] See, for example, Dunning 1995; and UNCTAD 1995.

has also greatly increased in many sectors.[59] This is best reflected in the rapid escalation of research and development (R&D) costs. One study finds that "between 1975 and 1995, expenditure on all kinds of research and development in the OECD economies rose three times the rate of output in manufacturing industry."[60] Within the United States, R&D spending as a percentage of sales doubled in the 16 years between 1976 and 1992,[61] while absolute spending by U.S. MNCs on manufacturing technology R&D increased by 43 percent (in constant 1987 dollars) from 1981 to 1991.[62]

In this technological environment, interfirm alliances are useful for a variety of reasons. For one thing, the shortening of product life cycles has made interfirm alliances attractive as a means of increasing the efficiency and speed of production. In turn, the nature of many current commercial technologies now "requires them to be combined with other technologies, produced by a different group of firms. Thus the latest generation of large commercial aircraft requires the combined skills of metallurgy, aeronautical engineering and aeroelectronics . . . New telecommunication devices embrace the latest advances in carbon materials, fibre optics, computer technology and electrical engineering."[63] Finally, the increased cost, risk, scope, and complexity of technological development has caused many MNCs to enter into alliances with other firms to minimize the risk and cost of engaging in R&D and augment the potential for innovation. As Chesnais points out, in an environment of "rapid and radical technological change, the new forms of agreements offer firms a way of ensuring, in a wide variety of situations, a high degree of flexibility in their operations. When technology is moving rapidly, the flexible and risk-sharing (or indeed risk-displacing) features of interfirm agreements offer firms a wide range of opportunities for acquiring key scientific and technical assets from outside their own walls . . . inter-firm agreements can likewise provide firms with a possibility of pooling limited resources in the face of rising R&D costs."[64] In explaining why it was necessary for Toshiba to initiate the aforementioned interfirm alliance with Siemens and IBM to develop a new semiconductor chip, Tsuyoshi Kawanishi (Toshiba's senior executive vice president) noted that the costs of staying on top of technological developments "are close to surpassing the point that any single company can manage."[65]

In keeping with these technological trends, a recent survey of four thousand strategic alliances found that dealing with the changed parameters of

---

[59] See, for example, Kobrin 1997, 149–50; and Mytelka 1991, 16–21 and the sources cited therein.

[60] See Dunning 2000, 9.

[61] As reported in Kobrin 1997, 150.

[62] UNCTAD 1995, 149.

[63] Dunning 1988, 334.

[64] Chesnais 1991, x.

[65] *Washington Post*, 14 July 1992, D1.

TABLE 2.3

Interfirm Alliances by Sector in the 1980s

Sector	Alliances	
	Number	*Percent*
Information technology based	1,660	39.7
Microelectronics	383	
Telecommunications	366	
Software	344	
Industrial automation	278	
Computers	198	
Other	91	
Biotechnology	847	20.3
New materials technology	430	10.3
Chemicals	410	9.8
Aviation/defense	228	5.5
Automotive	205	4.9
Heavy electric/power	141	3.4
Instruments/medical technology	95	2.3
Consumer electronics	58	1.4
Food and beverages	42	1.0
Other	66	1.6
Total	4,182	100.0

Source: Dicken 1998, 229.

technological development was the most important motivating factor for engaging in interfirm collaboration.[66] Indeed, interfirm alliances are sometimes referred to in the literature simply as "inter-firm technology cooperation agreements."[67]

While interfirm alliances have occurred in a wide range of industries in recent years, they have been overwhelmingly concentrated in sectors with rapidly changing technologies and high entry costs.[68] This concentration is reflected in table 2.3, which presents the results of an analysis of the sectoral distribution of interfirm alliances formed during the 1980s.

It is noteworthy that the majority of these interfirm alliances in technology-intensive sectors are between competitors.[69] That so many competitors are entering into interfirm alliances is a further indication of the rapid evolution of technological change in recent years: even though MNCs are now spending

[66] Hagedoorn 1993. See also OECD 1992; Kobrin 1995, 1997; and Terpstra and Simonin 1993.

[67] See, for example, Mytelka 1991, 1.

[68] See, for example, Dicken 1998, 229; Hagedoorn and Schakenradd 1990; OECD 1992; Jones 1996, 144; and Kobrin 1997.

[69] One survey of 839 interfirm alliances formed between 1975 and 1986 found that 71 percent of them were between two companies in the same market; see Dicken 1998, 228.

more on R&D than ever before, they less and less often have the capacity to manage technological development on their own. As Kobrin emphasizes, "the range of technologies that must be brought to bear on product and/or process development is increasingly beyond the core competencies of even the largest and most global firms. Technologies have become so complex and change so rapidly that even industry leaders cannot master them internally."[70]

The significance of this newfound willingness—indeed, eagerness—on the part of MNCs to engage in technological cooperation with competitors should not be underestimated. "Collaboration in research and development reverses a fairly long tradition of directly appropriating knowledge through in-house research and development that dates back to the development of science-based industries in nineteenth century Europe and North America."[71] Firms have traditionally preferred to internalize technological development for two key reasons: (1) internalization offers the potential to reduce transaction costs; and (2) the possession of unique technological assets has traditionally been the principal source of rents for firms in many industries.[72] To many analysts, the dramatic turnaround in the willingness of so many MNCs to share control of their technological assets with their competitors represents a profound, ongoing change in the strategic behavior of firms. In this respect, John Dunning argues persuasively that the increased significance of interfirm alliances is representative of a sea change in organizational form away from hierarchical capitalism—which emphasized competition between firms—toward what he calls "alliance capitalism"—which involves simultaneous competition and cooperation between firms.[73] This shift is propelled by the fact that interfirm alliances increase company profits and performance.[74]

It is important to recognize that an MNC can engage in a large number of *simultaneous* alliance agreements with another firm. In the area of information technology, for example, AT&T and Sun Microsystems had more than seven separate alliance agreements with each other in 1990.[75] This large number of simultaneous alliances reflects the fact that interfirm alliances occur only in a portion of business activities and do not typically involve a direct equity relationship between firms. Hence, they can be formed in particular areas on an as-needed basis and retained only as long as useful, perhaps no more than a few months if only a very specific area requires collaboration. When a partnership between two firms is successful, the process often feeds on itself: alliances in one area spill over into cooperation in others. For example, after the success of the alliance between IBM, Siemens, and Toshiba in the development of one

[70] Kobrin 1995, 23.
[71] Mytelka 1991, 9.
[72] See, for example, Hymer 1976; and Buckley and Casson 1988.
[73] Dunning 1994, 1995.
[74] See the discussion in Kang and Sakai 2000, 5, 37.
[75] See Hagedoorn and Schakenraad 1990, 170.

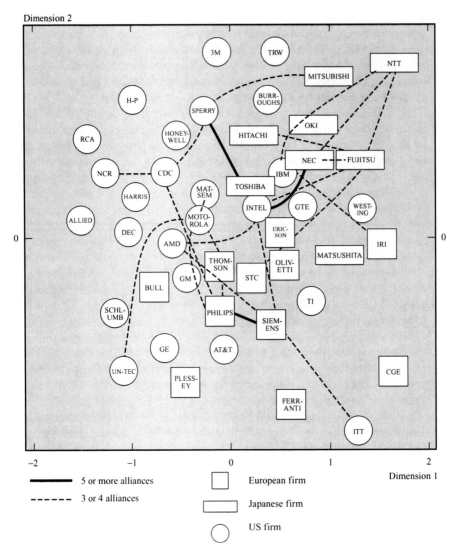

Figure 2.10a Interfirm Alliances in Information Technology, 1980–1984
Source: Hagedoorn and Schakenraad 1992, 169–70.

semiconductor chip, the three firms set up a separate interfirm alliance to develop a different advanced chip.

Some MNCs engage in interfirm alliances with just one other MNC. However, many firms form alliances with a number of firms simultaneously. For example, in 1990 AT&T had multiple agreements with, among others, Toshiba,

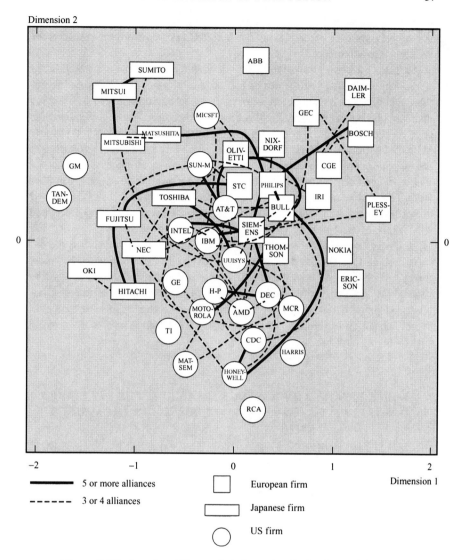

Figure 2.10b Interfirm Alliances in Information Technology, 1985–1989
Source: Hagedoorn and Schakenraad 1992, 169–70.

Intel, Sun Microsystems, Hewlett-Packard, Bull, and Olivet. The net result is
that many high-technology industries are now characterized by a complex web
of interfirm alliances involving a large number of companies. Figure 2.10
shows this network in the information technology sector, and how it rapidly developed during the 1980s. It should be noted that Figure 2.10 does not show all

interfirm alliances in this sector; it is limited to "those agreements made by firms in which the transfer of technology through R&D or other innovative efforts are central to the agreement."[76]

Recent advances in communications technology have made it possible for specifications, plans, and data to be shared in real time, permitting collaborative technological development across vast geographic distances to a degree that would have been impractical a few decades ago. While comprehensive data on interfirm alliances does not exist, most of these agreements do appear to be international—that is, between MNCs with headquarters in two different countries. According to one recent analysis of interfirm alliances formed in the 1990s, 68 percent of the partnerships were international in scope.[77] Another study found that in the information technology sector, U.S. MNCs formed almost twice as many interfirm alliances with Japanese and West European MNCs during the 1980s as they did with other U.S. firms.[78]

That being said, it is not the case that interfirm alliances encompass the entire globe. In fact, the overwhelming majority (more than 90 percent by many estimates) now exist within the triad of Western Europe, the United States, and Japan.[79] In large part, this specific geographic concentration of interfirm alliances reflects the fact that they are primarily concentrated in industries with rapidly changing technologies and high entry costs, which tend to be based in the triad.

GLOBAL PRODUCTION CHANGE NUMBER 3: THE INCREASED OPPORTUNITY COST OF BEING CLOSED OFF FROM MNCS

The two global production changes discussed above concern the behavior of MNCs. The third and final change highlighted here concerns the behavior of states—namely, their general response to the recent increase in the opportunity cost of being closed off from MNCs. In response to these changed incentives, there has been a marked global trend since the late 1970s toward increased openness to MNCs. The reduction in barriers to inward FDI is of particular salience. Recent changes in state policies that influence international interfirm alliances are less relevant to our discussion, since states have traditionally been less able to restrict, and also less interested in, interfirm alliances (owing in large part to the very recent genesis of this trend and also to the fact that interfirm alliances, unlike FDI, occur only in a portion of business activities and are often limited in their time span).

[76] Hagedoorn and Schakenraad 1991, 163.
[77] Kang and Sakai 2000.
[78] Hagedoorn and Schakenraad 1990, 177.
[79] See, for example, Kobrin 1997, 150.

Among economists, there is considerable debate over whether unfettered global capital flows are beneficial.[80] Concerning FDI, the dozens of cross-national studies that have appeared in recent years have not produced a comparable debate concerning whether it has a negative or positive effect on growth. Instead, the debate in this literature now centers on the magnitude and scope of the FDI growth effect.[81] Although FDI has always been an important way for countries to gain access to technology and investment capital, the combination of the increased difficulty and importance of technological development and the enhanced competitiveness of global markets has caused the opportunity cost of being closed off from FDI to increase substantially in recent years.[82]

Regarding technological development, MNCs can be important not simply as sources of new production methods and technology that might otherwise be difficult to obtain, but also because they provide training to their employees that can foster technological innovation within the host country.[83] MNCs may also enhance indigenous technological innovation by engaging in technical support and establishing other linkages with local supplier firms.[84] In addition, the presence of MNCs may result in indirect spillover effects that lead to improved technological capacity within a host country.[85]

While FDI has always been a key source of technology, in recent years the increased risk, cost, complexity, and importance of technological development has for three overlapping reasons magnified the importance of attracting MNCs. First, MNCs have become critical sources of technology: MNCs now account for an estimated three-quarters of the world's civilian R&D expenditures.[86] Second, firms without the latest technology now face greater difficulties in becoming internationally competitive, due to factors such as the shift to technology-intensive production in many industries and the increased ability of firms to serve markets throughout the world.[87] Third, the ability to access technology from MNCs through licensing and other nonequity arrangements is

[80] For an excellent overview of the debate, see Garrett 2000, esp. 963–65.

[81] Some cross-national studies find that FDI benefits all countries, but has an even larger positive effect on growth when accompanied by economic stability, open markets, and human capital (see, for example, Bengoa and Sanchez-Robles 2003; and Lipsey 2000). Other studies find that FDI plays an important role in contributing to economic growth, but that it is crucial for a country's local financial markets to attain a certain level of development for these positive effects to be realized (see, for example, Hermes and Lensink 2003; and Alfaro et al. forthcoming). Finally, some studies find that FDI is positive for many countries while being neutral for those that lack the conditions to benefit from technological spillovers (see, for example, Oliva and Rivera-Batiz 2002; Ram and Zhang 2002; and Choe 2003).

[82] See, for example, World Bank 1997a, 44–47; UNCTAD 1992, 111–90; and Garrett 2000, 965–67.

[83] See, for example, Chen 1983; Gerschenberg 1987; and UNCTAD 2001, 144–48.

[84] See, for example, Schive 1990; Ismail 1999; and UNCTAD 2001, 142–43.

[85] See, for example, UNCTAD 1995, 139 and the sources cited therein.

[86] UNCTAD 1995, 149.

[87] Dunning 1992.

TABLE 2.4
National FDI Regulatory Changes, 1991–2000

Item	1991	1992	1993	1994	1995	1996	1997	1998	1999	2000
Number of countries introducing changes in investment regimes	35	43	57	49	64	65	76	60	63	69
Number of regulatory changes of which	82	79	102	110	112	114	151	145	140	150
More favorable to FDI[a]	80	79	101	108	106	98	135	136	131	147
Less favorable to FDI[b]	2	–	1	2	6	16	16	9	9	3

Source: UNCTAD 2001, 6.

[a] Including liberalizing changes or changes aimed at strengthening market functioning, as well as increased incentives.

[b] Including changes aimed at increasing control as well as reducing incentives.

no longer as effective as in the past, for a variety of reasons. Most importantly, the increased pace of technological development, and the concomitant shortening of product life cycles, means that technology is likely to be obsolete by the time firms are willing to license it. This is because MNCs normally transfer their most recent technological advances only to affiliates and alliance partners; generally, only older technologies are licensed.[88]

As a result, the importance of attracting FDI as a means of gaining access to technology has been greatly increased in the last several decades. At the same time, the changed parameters of technological development and intensified competition within global markets place an increased premium on capital accumulation as a source of international competitiveness. And for many states, FDI has become a vital source of capital. This is especially the case for developing countries. Since the early 1990s, most external resource flows to developing countries have been private: official (government to government) flows have averaged around $50 billion per year in recent years, while private flows have been around $250 billion per year. In turn, the majority of private resource flows to developing countries in recent years have come in the form of FDI. In short, FDI is now the most important source of external resource flows to developing countries.[89]

It is thus clear that attracting MNCs in order to secure access to technology and capital has become more important in recent years. In response to the enhanced opportunity cost of closure to MNCs, states have rushed to change policy so as to reduce barriers to inward FDI and make themselves more attractive to MNCs. This is reflected in table 2.4, which shows that out

[88] UNCTAD 1992, 141.
[89] UNCTAD, 2000a, 22.

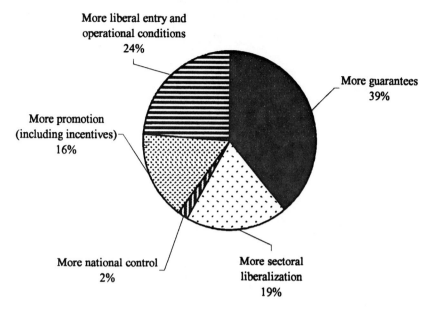

Figure 2.11 Types of Changes in FDI Laws and Regulations, 2000
Source: Dicken 2003, 137.

of the 1,074 regulatory changes made by states in their FDI policies during the 1991–2000 period, 95 percent created a more favorable investment climate for FDI.

These FDI policy changes come in a variety of forms. Figure 2.11 shows the breakdown of the regulatory policy changes toward inward FDI that were enacted during 2000.

One other important change that reduces barriers to investment is specific to developing countries: the disappearance of expropriation of MNC assets as a policy tool beginning in the early 1980s. There were only six expropriation acts during the 1982–86 period and no cases whatsoever during the 1987–92 period.[90] Figure 2.12 shows the historical significance of this decline.

Finally, beyond the wide variety of policy changes that have been enacted in recent years to lower barriers on MNCs, direct and indirect forms of payments by states to attract FDI have also greatly increased in recent years: "One of the most striking developments of the last two or three decades has been the enormous intensification in competitive bidding between states. . . . A recent study by UNCTAD found that only four countries out of 103 did not offer some kind

[90] Minor 1994, 180. In light of the dramatic trend that Minor reports, it is not surprising that his is the last available study that tracks expropriations.

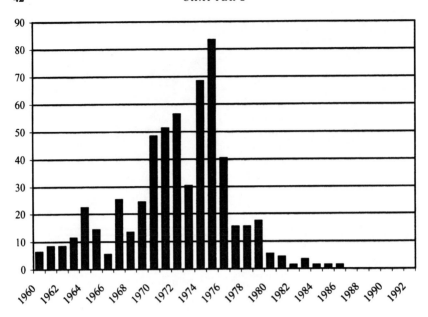

Figure 2.12 Total Number of Expropriation Acts by Year
Source: Minor 1994, 180.

of fiscal incentive to inward investors during the early 1990s while financial incentives were offered in 59 out of 83 countries surveyed."[91]

The sheer number of countries now seeking to lure MNCs—and the incentives and policies they offer—is unprecedented. Never before have MNCs had so many favorable options in location. This openness to MNCs strengthens and accelerates the first two global production changes noted above. Giving MNCs an even wider range of favorable investment sites from which to choose enhances production dispersion strategies, which, in turn, indirectly promotes the development of a wider range of international interfirm alliances. In this respect, the three global production changes outlined in this chapter are not distinct, but are rather elements of an integrated, reinforcing global production system.

We have not had anything like the geographic dispersion of MNC production before, and hence cannot use history as a guide to what might happen in the future. Obviously, the trend toward an improved investment climate for MNCs could slow. But any significant, general reversal is extremely unlikely. Unlike global capital flows, FDI is not subject to rapid, destabilizing shifts: because they are liquid, international financial investments can be withdrawn at

[91] Dicken 1998, 271.

the first sign of trouble, whereas FDI is much harder to move, and is therefore more durable. This is a key reason why the debate over the benefits of financial market liberalization does not carry over to FDI.[92] Most states throughout history have had to be convinced or coerced to reduce barriers to trade; in comparison, states have eagerly created a better climate for MNCs in recent decades. Significantly, no international FDI regime has so far been needed: unlike the increased levels of openness to international trade that occurred after World War II, this dramatic recent opening to MNCs has not depended on "any successful outcome of negotiations designed to enhance economic efficiency through multilateral cooperation."[93] Ultimately, the main reason why we should not expect a significant reversal of the trend toward greater openness to MNCs is that technology lies at its root.[94] Barring some unexpected, dramatic shift that makes technology less expensive, less risky, less important, or less desirable, states will be prone to seek greater access to MNCs; general openness to MNCs is therefore likely to remain a permanent feature of the global economy.

Analysts generally agree that the globalization of production is stable now that it has emerged. Since MNCs have already extensively dispersed production, they present a powerful political force that will fight any restrictions on their continued ability to do so.[95] Turning back the clock to the old, geographically concentrated form of production would also be extremely costly for national economies. As the most detailed treatment of this issue concludes:

> Technological change . . . has resulted in new, deep forms of networked integration which would be very costly to reverse in terms of the difficulty of unraveling them and the efficiency loss of doing so. . . . The closure of the international economy in the 1930s was accomplished relatively easily through high tariff walls and limits on investment. In many instances domestic or "home-spun" goods could be substituted for imports. While the costs were considerable in terms of deepening and prolonging the Great Depression, they were still marginal and incremental. At this point, unraveling the very complex networks of international production would be considerably more difficult and costly. Closing national borders would require recreating complex, internationalized systems of production domestically. It is far from clear that individual firms, or even national economies, have that capability. . . . Technological change has altered significantly the costs of alternative models of organization of the world economy to the point where our range of choice is limited.[96]

[92] For a particularly helpful comparison of the debate over finance and FDI, see Garrett 2000.
[93] Kobrin 1995, 24; see also, for example, Garrett 2000, 945.
[94] See, for example, the discussions in World Bank 1997a, 44–49; UNCTAD 1992, 102, 141; Kobrin 1995, 24, 29; and Garrett 2000, 965–67.
[95] Milner 1988 and 1989.
[96] Kobrin 2003, 7, 11, 17.

In short, although it is possible that the globalization of production could come to a crashing end, any significant reversal seems very unlikely. We will know only in the future how resilient the globalization of production is, but since it now exists, we need to know how it influences security.

IS THE GLOBALIZATION OF PRODUCTION HISTORICALLY UNPRECEDENTED?

Perhaps the most striking aspect of the globalization of production is how recent this shift is. Subcontracting has always existed, but *international* subcontracting arrived in force for the first time only around three decades ago. Cooperation between firms across borders is of course nothing new, but the scope of the international interfirm alliances that rose to prominence in the 1970s—and their importance in the global strategies of MNCs, especially high-technology firms—is simply unprecedented in the international economy. And while large MNCs have long had holdings that spanned the globe, only in the past few decades have we seen the "emergence of the truly global enterprise . . . [in which] the motive for foreign production is not so much to gain the economic rent that marketable advantages can earn, as to capture the economics of integration and diversification arising from such production."[97]

Some analysts suggest that we already have globalized production, asserting that geography no longer matters and that MNCs can establish dispersed global production networks at little cost.[98] This is wrong. That production is rapidly becoming more geographically dispersed is clear, but we are far from having truly globalized production. Production appears to have been globalized to the greatest extent in high-technology sectors and those sectors of manufacturing characterized by high levels of R&D and significant economies of scale. Many areas of production have not yet become globalized to a significant degree, and many others never will be.

That being said, the nature of global production—especially in high-technology sectors and many manufacturing sectors—is being transformed into a something *qualitatively* different than before, even compared to three decades ago. In this respect, the globalization of production stands apart from the other two globalization trends (of trade and international financial markets), which have important antecedents in the 1870–1914 period—the so-called golden age of capitalism. With respect to international financial markets, the *speed* of global capital flows is unprecedented, but the level and significance of capital market integration may only have just recently reached their peak

[97] Dunning 1992, 129.
[98] A prominent example is Ohmae 1995.

during the golden age of capitalism.[99] Noteworthy is that trade flows were much higher prior to World War I than through most of the twentieth century.[100] And while international trade flows are now higher than their peak before World War I, the increased level of trade in today's international economy does not represent a *structural* change in the international economy—it is a quantitative increase rather than a qualitative change.[101] In comparison with the golden age of capitalism, arguably the two most important qualitative changes in recent years in international trade—the increased significance of intrafirm trade and international subcontracting—are a by-product of the globalization of production.

Some analysts have suggested that MNC production is little more geographically dispersed today than before 1914, pointing out that the world FDI stock as a share of world output is estimated at 9 percent in 1913, essentially the same as in 1990.[102] This conclusion is highly misleading for a number of reasons. First, the current FDI level is more than twice the 1913 estimate: in 2000, FDI as a share of global output reached 19 percent.[103] Moreover, a great proportion of internationalized production now involves (1) extrafirm production linkages (most notably, international subcontracting), (2) nonequity linkages between global firms (most notably, interfirm alliances) and (3) intra-MNC service flows. These connections do not show up in calculations of the total FDI stock. In comparison, nonequity firm cooperation, international subcontracting, and intra-MNC service flows were negligible prior to World War I— in large part because of the poor quality of communications and information technology.[104] World FDI stock as a share of world output is therefore a biased means of comparing the current extent of internationalized production to the golden age of capitalism.

Even if world FDI stock as a share of world output were an appropriate means of comparing these two historical eras, one still could not conclude that the globalization of production is "nothing new." This is because the vast majority of FDI prior to World War I did not involve the globalization of production as we use the

---

[99] The best discussion of this issue is Obstfeld and Taylor 1998.

[100] See McKeown 1991.

[101] Measured in constant prices, the export-to-GDP ratio in Western Europe is almost twice as high as in 1913 (Maddison 1995, 38). However, Glyn argues that constant price comparisons are grossly misleading because "export prices rise systematically more slowly than do prices for output as a whole" and that "to correct for these differential price changes, we should focus on export shares at *current* prices" (1997, 6; emphasis in original). Glyn finds that, measured in current prices, "the 1994 share of exports in GDP did not much exceed 1913 levels" (6). See also the discussion in Held et al. 1999, 169.

[102] See Bairoch and Kozul-Wright 1996, 10.

[103] UNCTAD FDI/TNC database.

[104] Dunning 1992; see also Malone and Rockhart 1993. As one analysis notes, "In 1860, sending two words across the Atlantic cost the equivalent of $40 in today's terms" (OECD 2001, 11–12).

term today. In the pre-1914 era, "at least three-quarters of world FDI was concerned with the exploitation of natural resources."[105] The great importance of natural resource extraction as a motivating force for FDI is reflected in the fact that 76 percent of the world FDI stock was based *outside* North America and western Europe in 1914, with a scant 8 percent being based in Western Europe itself.[106] Current figures reflect the shift in motivations for FDI. By 1993, natural resources accounted for only 11 percent of FDI, and the vast majority of FDI is now based in the developed world—43 percent of the world total in western Europe and 27 percent in North America.[107]

The above discussion bears directly on the common claim in the literature that economic globalization is not especially novel. Katzenstein, Keohane, and Krasner, for example, assert that "this era of increasing transboundary activity [that] is variously called 'internationalization' or 'globalization' . . . is not an unprecedented development."[108] On what do they base their claim? They point out, correctly, that "international financial markets were highly integrated at the end of the nineteenth century—perhaps even more so than they have been since, at least until very recently. Trade flows were also much higher at this time than for most of the twentieth century."[109] The key shortcoming of their analysis is omission of recent global *production* changes. In the end, it would be very hard to argue that the geographic dispersion of MNC production does not represent a qualitative change in the international economy. However, Katzenstein, Krasner, and Keohane are correct that the same claim about the other two globalization trends—of international trade and international financial markets—is more problematic.

It is thus true that what we now call "economic globalization" has important antecedents in the high levels of economic integration that existed from 1870 to 1914. But when we break economic globalization into its three constituent parts, we reach a different, more nuanced answer. This is not to say that recent changes in trade and international capital markets are "nothing new," nor that they will have not important effects on states' security behavior. But if we are to take seriously John Gaddis's call for scholars in international relations to think more carefully about how security behaviors can change *over time*, then there are strong reasons for us to pay close attention to the globalization of production.[110]

[105] Jones 1996, 32.
[106] Jones 1996, 31.
[107] Jones 1996, 54, 55.
[108] Katzenstein, Keohane, and Krasner 1998, 684.
[109] Katzenstein, Keohane, and Krasner 1998, 684.
[110] See Gaddis 1992–93, 38; and Gaddis 1997, 79–80.

CHAPTER 3

Theoretical Foundations

IN THIS CHAPTER, I provide the theoretical foundations for the book. The first section delineates the three key puzzles that require analysis and the specific mechanisms I focus on. I show how these mechanisms correspond with the main theoretical approaches to the influence of the global economy on security. The remainder of the chapter outlines the deductive basis for the three theories examined in the empirical analysis. The second, third, and fourth sections specify the expected influence of the globalization of production on the economic benefits of conquest, the dynamics of regional economic integration among developing countries, and the trade-off between autarky and openness in defense-related production.

INCENTIVES, ACTORS, AND CAPABILITIES

As noted previously, the global economy can influence security by changing (1) incentives, (2) the nature of the actors, and (3) capabilities. With respect to each of these three general categories, I delineate below the primary mechanisms the literature points to by which the globalization of production can influence security, and identify the key unanswered questions that require analysis.

The Globalization of Production and Changes in Incentives

Liberal theories emphasize that changes in the global economy shift the cost/benefit ratio for war and that changed incentives, in turn, influence the likelihood of conflict.[1] With respect to the globalization of production, the only prominent argument in this regard is advanced by Richard Rosecrance, who maintains that recent production shifts by multinational corporations have caused the structure of the most advanced countries to change in a way that reduces greatly the economic benefits of seizing territory, thereby lowering the likelihood of war.

Rosecrance underscores that new MNC production strategies have facilitated the transformation of the most advanced states toward knowledge-based

---

[1] See, for example, Rosecrance 1986; and Oneal and Russett 1997.

economies.[2] The dramatic shrinkage of space over the past several decades has allowed MNCs in the most advanced countries to increasingly specialize in sectors of production that used skilled labor in their home country operations.[3] Nike represents an extreme example: its management and R&D is based in Oregon, while all of its production, which is based on non-skill-intensive activities, is located outside the United States. According to Rosecrance, the key reason why states with knowledge-based economies are less profitable to conquer concerns the mobility of the economic surplus. For most of human history, land was the fundamental factor of production in all societies. Under these circumstances, the conquest of territory coincided with increased control over the economic assets that provide the bedrock of political power.[4] Rosecrance highlights that land is fixed and can be captured, but people, and the information they possess, are mobile. For this reason, he argues in societies where production is largely a reflection of human capabilities, much of the economic surplus available to the conqueror can no longer be definitively seized.[5]

If the people in a conquered knowledge-based society have the opportunity and willingness to flee from a conqueror, then the economic benefits of capturing territory are reduced to a significant degree. However, a large proportion of a conquered country's citizens may not be able to escape a potential conqueror. It is true that citizens with the highest skills are often those who are most mobile. At the same time, even those with access to international transportation may not have a chance to flee a conqueror who strikes swiftly and who is ruthless in closing down borders. As a result, the mobility of people will not necessarily reduce the economic benefits of conquering a knowledge-based economy to a meaningful degree; the extent of the reduction will ultimately depend upon how a conqueror acts after subjugation.

We need to consider one other argument about why the shift to knowledge-based economies in the most advanced countries reduces the economic benefits of conquest. Stephen Van Evera argues: "Today's high technology post-industrial economies depend increasingly on free access to technical and social information. This access requires a free domestic press, and access to foreign publications, foreign travel, personal computers, and photocopiers. But the police measures needed to subdue society require that these technologies and

[2] Rosecrance 1999, xii. U.S. data gives some indication of the significance of this change: "whereas in the 1950s, 80 per cent of the value added in US manufacturing industry represented primary or processed foodstuffs, materials or mineral products, and 20 per cent knowledge, by 1995, these proportions had changed to 30 and 70 per cent respectively" (Dunning 2000, 8).

[3] In this respect, a recent analysis by Feenstra and Hanson concludes that "the fragmentation of production into discrete activities which are then allocated across countries" has contributed to a shift in "employment towards skilled workers within industries. . . . Our main finding is that outsourcing can account for 31–51 percent of the increase in the relative demand for skilled labor that occurred in U.S. manufacturing industries during the 1980s" (1996, 1, i).

[4] See the discussions in Rosecrance 1986; Kaysen 1990; and Gilpin 1981.

[5] See Rosecrance 1996, 48, 58; and Rosecrance 1999, esp. 30–31.

practices be forbidden, because they also carry subversive ideas. Thus critical elements of the economic fabric now must be ripped out to maintain control over conquered polities. . . . This is a marked change from the smokestack-economy era, when societies could be conquered and policed with far less collateral economic harm."[6]

This line of argument has been strongly criticized by Peter Liberman, who asserts that recent technological advances do not simply increase the willingness for popular resistance but also simultaneously increase the conqueror's capacity for coercion: "the subversive potential of information technologies must be weighed against their contribution to state surveillance. Bar codes, miniature microphones, video cameras, and computerized data banks—if not photocopiers—all have more Orwellian than libertarian applications."[7] Neither Van Evera nor Liberman provides any basis for evaluating whether the technologies in knowledge-based societies give an organizational edge to the conqueror or those in the populace who engage in resistance; it is possible that the factors they identify essentially cancel each other out.

Unlike the examinations of economic benefits of conquest by Van Evera and Rosecrance, Liberman's analysis of the issue is empirically based. His book—which is based on a detailed historical analysis of five occupations of industrial societies in the twentieth century (Belgium and Luxembourg 1914–18, Ruhr-Rhineland, 1923–24, the Japanese empire 1910–45, the Nazi occupation of western Europe 1940–44, and the Soviet empire in Eastern Europe, 1945–89)—is the benchmark study of the economic benefits of conquest. Liberman's ultimate conclusion is that ruthless conquerors, such as the Nazis in World War II, can suppress popular resistance and can thereby effectively extract economic resources from a vanquished advanced country. Indeed, he argues, economic modernization actually enhances the profitability of conquest.[8]

Is Liberman correct? Most analysts would agree that countries with high GDP per capita whose economies are tied to extractable resources (e.g., Kuwait) still offer high cumulative gains to a conqueror.[9] On the basis of Liberman's book, however, we cannot conclude that a conqueror will be able to effectively extract gains from the most economically advanced societies. His assertion in this regard is, at best, premature. The reason is that the analyses by Van Evera and Rosecrance do not provide a comprehensive understanding of how recent changes in the economies of the most advanced countries can influence the economic benefits of conquest. Much more detailed theoretical and empirical analysis along these lines is now needed.

In this regard, it is crucial to further examine how globalization influences the economic benefits of conquest. The first empirical puzzle that this book

---

[6] Van Evera 1990–91, 14–15.
[7] Liberman 1996, 28.
[8] Liberman 1996, 28, 26.
[9] See, for example, Rosecrance 1999, xiv–xv, 4, 169, 200.

will explore, therefore, is whether the globalization of production has changed the economic structures of the most advanced states in ways that prevent a conqueror, even a ruthless one, from effectively extracting economic gains from the occupation of vanquished territory.

The Globalization of Production and Changes in Actors

Although Marxism, transnationalism, and constructivism differ markedly, they share a general understanding of how the global economy can influence security. All three emphasize that changes in the global economy can lead to shifts in the nature of the actors, and can thereby result in a new security environment. However, the specific dynamics toward which each of these three theories points diverge dramatically.

Transnationalists often only indirectly addressed security issues, but this literature's general argument that transnational actors—in particular MNCs—were rising to prominence and replacing states as the key actors in world politics had important implications for security affairs.[10] The transnationalist literature suffered from withering criticism and largely disappeared from view after the 1970s.[11] A principal reason is that the state never faded away, as this literature predicted. In the realm of security policy, it is clear that the preferences of MNCs are hardly the most important factors that policymakers consider when making decisions. Moreover, to the extent that MNCs do have an ability to influence security policy, they have cross-cutting interests. The U.S.-led invasion of Iraq in 2003 is a case in point: some U.S. defense and oil firms may benefit because they will obtain larger contracts, but many other U.S. firms were hurt by the higher oil prices and economic uncertainty associated with the conflict as well as by the damaged relations between the United States and Western European countries. In short, MNCs do not have a dominant role in security policy, and they do not have monolithic interests.

While unlikely, it is of course conceivable that MNCs could replace states as the key actors in security affairs at some point. Current trends suggest, however, that they will not do so for at least the next several decades. Looking through the recent literature, one might doubt this is the case: speaking for many, Susan Strange maintains that "the impersonal forces of world markets . . . are now more powerful than the states to whom ultimate political authority over society and economy is supposed to belong."[12] This conclusion is wrong; the only way to reach it is if one conflates two separate questions: (1) who are the "main" actors

---

[10] Some transnationalists did make explicit arguments about security: Morse, for example, argued that the rise to prominence of MNCs would lead to foreign policies within the most advanced countries that "are primarily non-conflictual" (1970, 377, 387).

[11] See, for example, Krasner 1978.

[12] Strange 1996, 4; cf. Gilpin 2001, 297–300.

in world politics? and (2) are nonstate actors in the global economy—including MNCs—having an increasingly important influence on world politics? An important premise of this book is that the answer to the second question is yes. That being said, the answer to the first question is clearly states, especially with respect to security affairs. It is now crucial to better understand how the changing production activities of MNCs are influencing the security behavior of states.

What about Marxist theory? The basic Marxist perspective is that a state's international behavior is derivative of class structure.[13] A Marxist would argue that the globalization of production will lead to changes in class structure and thereby influence security. But Marxist theories have never worked well with respect to security affairs, and it is hard to see why the geographic dispersion of MNC production will improve their applicability.[14]

What about the more specific argument derived from world systems theory that the economic prospects of countries currently furthest behind are being most harmed as economic globalization accelerates?[15] Were it true, this pattern could lead to changes in the structure of such countries that might have significant repercussions for security affairs.[16] As emphasized in chapter 2, while debate continues among economists over whether unfettered global capital flows are beneficial for developing countries, no comparable controversy exists with respect to the production side of globalization.[17] It is exactly because FDI is beneficial that there has been such a rush to attract MNCs within developing countries in recent decades.

A key tenet of constructivist theory is that changes in the international environment can lead to shifts in the interests of states, thereby leading to a new security environment.[18] With respect to the global economy, the best-developed constructivist statement in this regard concerns regional economic integration. Extending the work of integration theorists such as Ernst Haas and Karl Deutsch, Alexander Wendt argues persuasively that the pursuit of regional economic integration has the potential to lead to new patterns of interaction that cause the group's members to develop a more collective understanding of their interests, leading to a positive transformation in the nature of their security relationships.[19] The significance of this line of argument is made plain by the fact that regionalism has emerged as a major feature of the international economy: during the 1990–98 period, a total of 82 regional trade agreements (RTAs) entered into force, as compared to 14 agreements between 1980 and 89.[20] As of 2000,

[13] For a useful overview of the Marxist understanding of international relations, see Doyle 1997, 315–88.

[14] See, for example, Waltz 1979, 20–36; and Rose 2003.

[15] Wallerstein 1996.

[16] Relevant here is the discussion in Kennedy 1993.

[17] See the review of the literature in Garrett 2000.

[18] For a comprehensive overview of constructivist theory, see Wendt 1999.

[19] Wendt 1994.

[20] World Bank 1999, 54.

Mongolia, China, and Japan were the only countries that were not members of at least one RTA.[21]

The theoretical argument that regional economic integration helps promote peaceful security relationships is certainly very compelling. It is critical to recognize that it is the actual experience of consolidating deep integration—and not merely forming a group—that leads to the processes scholars highlight as beneficial for improved security ties.[22] This leads to a key question: under what conditions will states with security tensions be able to consolidate successful regional economic integration agreements? This question is especially puzzling given that scholars agree that countries with mutual security tensions are the *least likely* to engage in deep economic cooperation because of fears about how the gains of cooperation will be distributed.[23] This is hardly an idle question, given that the most successful regional economic integration scheme in the twentieth century—the European Economic Community/European Union—was consolidated in the presence of a common external security threat. Moreover, mutual security tensions are a nonissue among the members of what are probably the two next most successful regional economic integration schemes—the European Free Trade Association (EFTA) and the North American Free Trade Agreement (NAFTA). In contrast, numerous regional economic integration schemes have fallen apart due to security tensions among their respective members. This has especially been the case in the developing world.[24]

The general notion that states with security tensions can engage in regional economic cooperation when faced with a common external threat may be on target, but it is currently too narrowly focused on shared *security* threats. A key unanswered question is whether the globalization of production has led to a new common external threat facing states—isolation from FDI—that not only creates pressure for states to consolidate regional integration, but may even be strong enough to facilitate deep economic cooperation among states that have long-standing security tensions.

As chapter 2 showed, the opportunity cost of being isolated from MNCs has greatly increased in recent years, along with the competition to attract FDI. Many have argued that this escalating competition is, in fact, a key factor propelling the recent growth of regionalism. Robert Gilpin, for example, maintains that "one important motive for regional arrangements is to enable groupings of states to attract investment by MNCs. This last factor helps explain the rapidity

---

[21] World Trade Organization 2001, 37. Macau and Hong Kong were also not members of an RTA in 2000.

[22] In addition to Wendt 1994, see also, for example, the analysis in Deutsch et al, 1957; Haas 1964; and Nye 1971.

[23] See Baldwin 1993, especially the chapters by Powell, Grieco, and Keohane. See also Grieco, Powell, and Snidal 1993.

[24] For a discussion of this point, see Brooks 1994.

with which regional arrangements have been spreading around the globe."[25] This notion that competition for FDI promotes regionalism has not yet been empirically evaluated, however.[26] This is not to say MNCs' influence on regional integration has been ignored. In analyses of the European Union (EU) and NAFTA, great attention has been paid to the role of MNCs *internal* to these integration groupings that lobby governments within the region in favor of enhanced integration.[27] What scholars have so far failed to adequately examine is the influence of MNCs from *outside* the region on the integration process.

If we were to ask, "Where can contemporary regional integration potentially have the greatest overall influence on intraregional security behavior?" scholars would undoubtedly point to the developing world—the so-called zone of turmoil.[28] For regional economic integration agreements involving developing countries, it is only MNCs from *outside* the region that are likely to contribute to the integration process; the reason is that relatively few significant MNCs are based in these countries.[29] In recent years, economists have outlined compelling theoretical arguments for why pursuing regional integration can help developing countries compete for new FDI from outside the region.[30] These theoretical models provide a useful starting point, but they are inadequate because they neglect politics: they specify why integration offers potential economic advantages in terms of attracting increased FDI, but do not delineate when policymakers are more likely to pay the significant political costs associated with consolidating regional integration to compete for MNCs. Neglecting these political costs is a major problem, given that "building institutions in world politics is a frustrating and difficult business. Common interests are often hard to discover or to maintain."[31] Prior to the 1990s,

[25] Gilpin 2000, 109. Numerous political scientists and economists have made assertions similar to that advanced by Gilpin; see, for example, Ethier 1998a, 1156–58 and 1998b, 1242; Fernandez and Portes 1998, 202; Blomstrom and Kokko 1997, 1; Mattli 1999a, 155; Hurrell 1995, 172; Heinrich and Konan 2000, 2; and Narula 2001, 1–2.

[26] None of the analyses in the previous note provides direct supporting evidence or cites any other studies that do so.

[27] See, for example, Milner 1997; Chase 1998; Frieden 1996; Green Cowles 1995; Fioretos 1997; Sandholtz and Zysman 1989, 116–18; Hufbauer and Schott 1992, 71–75; Bornschier 2000, 28–32; Haggard 1995, 90–91; and Mattli 1999a, 49–50 and 1999b, 16–17. This internal emphasis makes the most sense for the EU and NAFTA. Scholars point out that MNCs based in these regions, particularly those with extensive intraregional investments, gain efficiency benefits from enhanced integration, including greater economies of scale in production (see, for example, Milner 1997), stronger protection of relation-specific investments (Yarbrough and Yarbrough 1992, 94–103) and, in the case of the EU, reduced costs associated with exchange rate fluctuations (see, for example, Frieden 1996).

[28] See Singer and Wildavsky 1993; and Goldgeier and McFaul 1992.

[29] On this point, see UNCTAD 2000a, 71–74, 81–83.

[30] See especially Ethier 1998a and 1998b; Fernandez and Portes 1998; and Blomstrom and Kokko 1997.

[31] Keohane 1984, 246.

significantly, none of the RTAs undertaken in the developing world achieved long-term success.[32]

The poor record of the first wave of regional economic integration in the developing world is, in many respects, not surprising. As compared to the developed world, numerous built-in constraints—most notably, the fact that developing countries typically do not have complementary economies—make regional economic integration among developing countries much less viable and, consequently, much less likely to be successfully consolidated.[33] The presence of these constraints has important implications for security in the developing world: policymakers in the region clearly look with envy at the legacy of greatly improved security relations in Western Europe—especially the dramatic decline in the long-term rivalry between Germany and France—that coincided with the achievement of deep levels of regional economic integration.[34] Benazir Bhutto, for example, stressed in 1999 that a regional economic integration agreement between India and Pakistan would be an ideal means to improve security relations between these two countries.[35] In light of the built-in constraints on regional economic integration that pulled down the first wave of efforts in the developing world, the frequent declaration by developing country policymakers that pursuing integration can be beneficial for security relations may strike most analysts as unrealistic.

The second empirical puzzle this book addresses is thus whether isolation from FDI is a new kind of common external threat that generates pressure toward the consolidation of RTAs in the developing world. If so, and if this external pressure is strong enough to lead to extensive economic cooperation even among states with a long-standing history of security rivalry, then regional integration can potentially enhance the prospects for peace in the developing world.

The Globalization of Production and Changes in Capabilities

Realist scholars emphasize that the global economy can lead to shifts in state capabilities, and thereby to changes in security. With respect to MNCs, the key argument in this regard is advanced by Robert Gilpin. In his 1975 book *U.S. Power and the Multinational Corporation,* Gilpin stresses that MNCs can lead

---

[32] Writing in 1985, Okolo succinctly concludes that "while regional integration efforts have been successful in more advanced countries, no scheme in the Third World has yet achieved concrete success" (1985, 121). See also de la Torre and Kelly 1992, 32–33.

[33] For a review of the various factors militating against the success of the first wave of regional economic integration efforts in the developing world, see Brooks 1994.

[34] For arguments that European regional integration had a positive impact on West European security affairs, see, for example, Monnet 1978; and Gerbet 1983.

[35] *New York Times,* 8 June 1999, A27.

to the dispersion of advanced technologies from the leading powers, thereby allowing rising powers to catch up more quickly.[36] In his view, the high level of FDI outflow from the United States in combination with a low FDI inflow would contribute to American relative decline and hence hasten a power transition. In the current environment, the key application of this general line of argument would obviously be to the United States and China, since the latter is the only country that can potentially match the size of the former in the foreseeable future.

Few would dispute that FDI from U.S. MNCs allows China to gain access to American technology and thereby grow more quickly. That being said, the "outward FDI by the leading power causing a power transition" dynamic that Gilpin highlights will not be a very important force in world politics for at least several decades. There are two main reasons for this. First, the United States is now so far ahead in all of the components of power vis-à-vis China that a power transition cannot occur in the foreseeable future.[37] Second, while China does benefit greatly from FDI inflows from U.S. MNCs, if one were to ask which country most benefits from the globalization of production, most analysts would likely choose the United States. On the FDI front, much has changed in the three decades since Gilpin's book: the United States has long been the most popular destination for FDI, having attracted nearly one-fourth of world FDI inflows during the 1990s.[38] In 1975, the U.S. FDI ratio was 4.5:1—that is, "its outward investment was four-and-a-half times greater than its inward investment." In recent years, in comparison, the U.S. FDI ratio has hovered right around "a perfect balance in terms of outward and inward" FDI.[39] By 2000, foreign firms (excluding banks) located in the United States employed a total of 6.4 million American workers.[40] If we look beyond FDI, U.S. MNCs have been leaders in employing new global production strategies designed to reap locational efficiencies; Chinese firms, in comparison, have almost no experience in this area.[41] U.S. MNCs have also been at the forefront in establishing cooperative partnerships with foreign firms in order to enhance innovation in advanced technologies; in contrast, developing country firms, including China's, remain largely isolated from this production strategy (probably more than 90 percent of interfirm alliances occur among the triad of the United States, Japan, and western Europe). Based on current trends, if and when China does match the power of the US—a potential development that is far in the future—it is thus unlikely that MNCs' production activities will have played a large role in producing this outcome. Contrary to the situation when

[36] Gilpin 1975.

[37] See the discussion in Brooks and Wohlforth 2002a.

[38] UNCTAD FDI/TNC database.

[39] Dicken 2003, 59.

[40] *Wall Street Journal*, 4 April 2003, A1.

[41] Reflective of this is that China's outward FDI stock as a percentage of GDP remains tiny; in 2000, it stood at just 2 percent (UNCTAD FDI/TNC database).

Gilpin's book was written, the leading power and the main rising power are simultaneously large beneficiaries of global production shifts directed by MNCs.

Although the globalization of production is thus unlikely to significantly contribute to an overall power transition in the foreseeable future, it nevertheless holds important potential implications for how states develop and produce weaponry—and thus may lead to important shifts with respect to military capabilities. Specifically, the geographic dispersion of MNC production may influence the choice that states make between autarky and openness in defense-related production.[42] Realists and other scholars have long emphasized that states face strong incentives toward relying on their own capabilities for defense production.[43] The disadvantages of openness in defense production are clear: "If pools of advanced technology are located beyond a state's borders, it means that countries may not be able to access the technologies in a timely fashion, and that potential adversaries will be fishing in the same technological pond."[44] Not surprisingly, therefore, the lure of an autarkic defense production strategy has been strong over the centuries and remains so to this day: one would be hard-pressed to find any current policymaker who prefers to rely on international sources for key aspects of defense production.

In recent years, however, the parameters of the choice between openness and autarky have shifted. A number of analysts have argued that the pendulum has swung against an autarkic strategy in defense production.[45] But how far? Arguably the strongest claim in the literature is advanced by Vernon and Kapstein, who assert that "most countries are likely to accept heavy reliance on foreign technologies and foreign components as an inescapable condition for maintaining their defense establishments."[46] At first blush, this statement seems very bold. It is not: the word "most" denudes it of any force. Most countries are small in economic size: as of 2000, 94 percent of countries had GDPs below U.S.$500 billion.[47] Such small states cannot be on the leading edge in military technology today without participating in the globalization of production. But this is beside the point: the inability of small states to compete in military technology while pursuing an autarkic strategy is overdetermined. Because of the long-standing importance of economies of scale in both production and R&D in the military sector, only the largest states could be at the cutting-edge in military technology while following an autarkic strategy, even *before* the globalization of production. It is, therefore, banal to say that most states must participate

---

[42] To be clear, I use the term *autarky* here simply as a shorthand for a state that strives for self-sufficiency.

[43] See, for example, Carr 1946, 120–24; Waltz 1979, esp. 104–7; and Snyder 1991, 24–25.

[44] Kapstein 1992, 191.

[45] Prominent examples include Moran 1990; Kapstein 1992; Bitzinger 1994; and Vernon and Kapstein 1991.

[46] Vernon and Kapstein 1991, 19.

[47] Calculated using GDP data at market exchange rates. Data available at http://www.worldbank.org/data/databytopic/GDP.

in the globalization of production if they are to have any hope of being on the cutting-edge of military technology.

This brings us to the third and final empirical puzzle this book addresses: has the opportunity cost of isolation in defense-related production now become so high that strong participation in the globalization of production is a necessary prerequisite for staying at the forefront in military technology even for the states with the largest and most advanced economies, the great powers? Put another way, have the costs of going it alone in military technology now become so steep that all states now face a structural imperative to give up the benefits of autarkic defense production? While a number of analyses have touched on this question, no strong, empirically grounded answer has so far been forthcoming. We know that gains are accrued by moving away from autarky, but we are still in the dark as to whether internationalization of defense-related production is now a necessity for any great power that wishes to be on the leading edge in military technology.

THEORY NUMBER 1: THE GLOBALIZATION OF PRODUCTION AND THE ECONOMIC BENEFITS OF CONQUEST

With respect to changes in incentives, the key unanswered question is whether the globalization of production has shifted the structures of the most advanced states in ways that would prevent a conqueror from effectively extracting economic gains from the vanquished country. In this section, I outline how this global production shift is likely to influence the economic benefits of conquest within the most advanced countries.[48]

Credibility of Commitment, MNCs, and the Economic Benefits of Conquest

As stressed in chapter 2, the opportunity cost of being closed off from MNCs has increased markedly in recent years. This point has significant repercussions for the benefits of conquest: there are strong reasons to expect the flow of inward FDI to decline markedly in an advanced country after it is vanquished by an extractive conqueror and also that it will become much more difficult for firms in the conquered territory to establish and sustain international interfirm alliances.

Highly relevant on this issue is the formal theoretical literature that examines the influence of credible limits on the exercise of state power, which finds the level of investment within an economy is influenced by the credibility of commitment of the governing authority not to confiscate a society's wealth or extract excessive rents.[49] As Douglass North and Barry Weingast stress, "the

---

[48] Some of the discussion in this section draws on Brooks 1999.

[49] See, for example, North and Weingast 1989; Olson 1993; North 1993; Shepsle 1991; Furubotn and Richter 1993, 2; and Weingast 1993.

more likely it is that the sovereign will alter property rights for his or her own benefit, the lower the expected returns from investment and the lower in turn the incentive to invest. For economic growth to occur the sovereign or government must not merely establish a set of rights, but must make a credible commitment to them."[50] How can leaders increase their credibility of commitment? The only real way is "by being constrained to obey a set of rules that do not permit leeway for violating commitments."[51]

The general conclusion in this literature is that democracies with strong institutions have the highest credibility of commitment, since leaders in such systems face both institutional and electoral constraints on their ability and willingness to confiscate wealth or extract excessive rents. Another key conclusion concerns the influence of time horizons: "Credible commitment can only be realized over a very long time period of time. . . . Time is crucial for the constituents since uncertainty about the ruler's behavior can only be mitigated by the ruler establishing a reputation and by learning on the part of constituents."[52]

How do extractive conquerors fare regarding credibility of commitment to leave wealth alone? Mancur Olson argues out that the general form of government with the lowest credibility regarding confiscation of wealth is an external invader that engages in economic extraction, which he aptly terms a "roving bandit."[53] He notes that even if an invader wishes to extract only a minimal level of economic wealth from the vanquished country, there are two reasons why they cannot credibly commit to refrain from more comprehensive extraction: they normally have short time horizons, and they have no institutional or electoral constraints on their power within the vanquished country.

Of course, if there is little governing authority and a consequent lack of property rights in the area prior to conquest, then even an extractive conqueror might be a relative improvement.[54] In all of the advanced economies of today, however, strong governing authority does exist; as a result, credibility of commitment regarding wealth confiscation will always be relatively lower in an advanced country after occupation by an extractive conqueror. In addition to the reasons highlighted by Olson, conquerors are, to a greater degree than other rulers, likely to change the economic rules of the game in erratic ways in response to threats to the security of their rule. All leaders face a dilemma between promoting economic efficiency, on one hand, and ensuring security of rule, on the other.[55] For many reasons, this dilemma will be particularly acute

---

[50] North and Weingast 1989, 803.

[51] North and Weingast 1989, 804.

[52] North 1993, 15.

[53] Olson 1993, 568. Shepsle similarly notes that invasion is a key factor that reduces the incentives to invest (1991, 245).

[54] See, for example, Staley 1935.

[55] See North 1993, 14.

for an extractive conqueror, and sharp, unanticipated shifts in economic policy are likely as threats, to a conqueror's rule eventuate.

An important point to recognize is that even if the "correct" policies were initiated that might attract MNCs to a conquered territory, such policies would not be credible over the long term, for the reasons noted above. An extractive conqueror will not be able to assure foreign investors that it will abide by these policies and will not seize assets of MNCs, extract excessive rents from them, or generally shift policies in ways that reduce the cost-effectiveness of their investments.[56] This matters greatly: "Unless there is appropriate and credible protection against a major change in economic policy, economic reform may fail because the gains of economic agents are inadequately protected. . . . Inadequate attention to securing the political foundations of reform can create a form of equilibrium trap in which economic reform fails despite the apparently 'correct' economic policies."[57] On top of this, the conqueror's tenure as governing authority in the vanquished territory will be unclear because it faces the continual prospect of expulsion by forces outside or inside the country. Long-term investments will be particularly constrained by uncertainty about how long the rules of the game established by the conqueror will last.

The preceding discussion is particularly significant for FDI, since it is a form of investment that is especially sensitive to the long-term credibility of commitment of a host government. There is a variety of overlapping reasons why this is the case.[58] First, the foreign investor has no direct recourse if the host government decides to shift policy in a less advantageous direction. In turn, many of these investments entail high fixed costs that are recoverable only if the MNC is allowed to use the facilities in which it has invested over an extended period of time. Finally, the exit options of MNCs are much more limited than those of other "liquid" financial investments by foreign investors, such as stocks, bonds, and currencies: "FDI, while mobile ex ante, is relatively illiquid ex post."[59] In combination, these three factors make MNCs highly sensitive to an extractive conqueror's low credibility of commitment.

It is not just access to FDI that is likely to be greatly reduced following conquest. For those firms within the conquered advanced economy that are highly dependent upon maintaining interfirm alliances with firms in other countries, their continued ability to create and maintain these cooperative agreements, and hence their productivity, is also likely to be imperiled due to the extractive

[56] In addition to outright expropriation itself, MNCs "face considerable political risks in terms of expropriation of revenue streams. Governments can renegotiate tax rates, depreciation schedules, tariff rates, and a host of other policies that directly affect multinational corporations. Other indirect factors, such as the imposing of capital controls, devaluations, or other macroeconomic decisions not targeted specifically at multinational firms, but affecting the profitability of the investment, are also important" (Jensen 2003, 594).

[57] Weingast 1993, 288.

[58] The discussion in the remainder of this paragraph owes much to Frieden 1994.

[59] Jensen 2003, 594.

conqueror's low credibility of commitment. In an interfirm alliance, the relationship between firms "frequently involves sensitive information, which might cause damage if used opportunistically by the firms involved, and therefore requires a high level of trust between the parties."[60] MNCs will be unlikely to undertake an interfirm alliance with a firm in an occupied country because the conqueror will be unable to provide assurances that it will not someday use the knowledge or technology generated from the alliance in an opportunistic fashion. Given the conqueror's low credibility of commitment, firms in the conquered advanced country will simply not be in a position to reassure current and potential alliance partners in other countries that they will not someday be exploited. MNCs can often choose from many different potential alliance partners; to the extent that this is the case, MNCs are unlikely to form or continue a cooperative partnership with a particular firm in a conquered territory given the nature of the risks involved.

Beyond the credibility-of-commitment dynamic, many MNCs are likely to shy away from the conquered country for one additional basic reason: collateral damages. Given that a conqueror is likely to face both internal and external threats to its rule, MNCs face the prospect that their foreign affiliate's facilities, or one of the firms in the vanquished country that the MNCs depend upon, will be damaged or destroyed during a military engagement. The looming and unpredictable nature of this threat is likely to cause many MNCs to be averse to set up long-term production arrangements that rely on facilities in the conquered country and, more specifically, to refrain from technological upgrading of any affiliates they have based there.

In sum, there are strong reasons to expect that military conquest will greatly reduce the inflow of FDI into an advanced country that is occupied as well as make it much harder for firms in the vanquished country to establish and maintain international interfirm alliances. Given this, we should expect the economic benefits of occupying territory to decline as the opportunity cost of isolation from MNCs intensifies, as has clearly been the case in recent years. Benefits are likely to be especially constrained over the long term, as reduced access to FDI and interfirm alliances within the conquered country are likely to have strong cumulative effects.

Geographic Dispersion by MNCs and the Economic Benefits of Conquest

As noted in chapter 2, the production activities of MNCs have become increasingly dispersed geographically in recent decades. Many MNCs have sought to reap locational efficiencies by relying to a greater degree on international

---

[60] Sölvell and Birkinshaw 2000, 86.

subcontracting or by slicing up the value-added chain and dispersing different aspects of production within the firm itself to those countries that are most advantageous. Because the vast majority of MNCs are based in the most economically advanced countries, it is these societies in which production has become most geographically dispersed.[61]

How does this influence the economic benefits of conquest within the most advanced countries? The increased geographic dispersion of MNC production activities means that conquering an advanced country may only result in possession of a portion of the value-added chain, perhaps a very small portion. Until recently, if a conqueror invaded a country with, for example, an automotive sector, then the conqueror would be able to take possession and resume production of virtually the entire range of inputs necessary to produce the car. Now, however, the car's engine might be produced in one country, the body panels in a second country, the suspension in a third, the transmission in a fourth, and so on. As a result, to take control of the car's entire value-added chain would require conquering many countries. This obviously becomes extremely difficult, thereby reducing the overall payoff of conquest. Moreover, it means that a conqueror would not be in a position to shift a significant portion of the vanquished country's industrial capacity back to the conqueror's homeland, as the Soviets did when they removed entire factories from East Germany immediately after Word War II.[62]

It is important to recall that the geographic dispersion of MNC production activities has not occurred equally across all industries. As noted in chapter 2, this shift appears to be most prominent in those sectors of manufacturing characterized by high levels of research and development and significant economies of scale, such as machinery, computers, electronic components, and transportation.[63] This has significant implications for the benefits of conquest, since it is these and other similar manufacturing sectors that would be especially valuable to a hypothetical conqueror because they are, to use Van Evera's apt terminology, highly "cumulative resources": possessing them would magnify the power of the conqueror and increase its capacity to protect, control, or acquire other resources.[64]

Critics might respond to the above argument in three ways. First, is it necessary to capture the whole value-added chain? If, for example, a conqueror takes over a country with a car transmission factory, won't that transmission factory have great value on its own? There are a number of reasons to think it will not. As Jeff Frieden underscores: "A local affiliate is an integral part of a corporate network, and if separated from this network it loses most of its value. The assets of the local affiliate are specific to their use within a broader international

[61] UNCTAD 1995, 10.
[62] See Liberman 1996, 126–27.
[63] World Bank 1997a, 42.
[64] See the discussion in Van Evera 1999, chap. 5.

enterprise, generally for technological, managerial, or marketing reasons. Most of the value of an overseas Ford affiliate, for example, is inseparable from the affiliate's connection with Ford. . . . This may be because the affiliate makes parts (or requires inputs) which are used (or supplied) only by the parent company, or because the affiliate depends on the reputation and managerial expertise of the international firm. . . . Once the assets are separated from the integrated corporation, they lose much of their value."[65]

Ultimately, the most plausible conclusion is that the transmission factory, though still valuable, will be proportionately less valuable than if the conqueror were able to take over the full value-added chain of car production. In order to fully exploit the factory, the conqueror will need to secure supplies of the remaining aspects of the value-added chain through one of three mechanisms: by establishing a new production plant to produce them, by retooling an existing production plant to produce them, or by purchasing supplies on the open market. While it may be possible to secure the remaining aspects of the value-added chain through these strategies, all of them involve significant costs. These costs did not exist, or, at least, were much lower, when production was much more geographically centralized, and where most or all of the value-added chain could be captured through the invasion of a single country.

Second, is it necessary for the conqueror to replicate the entire value-added chain to produce the end product? Can't the conqueror simply sell the portion of the value-added chain that it has captured on the open market, thereby reaping a substantial profit? While the component would not be worth as much on its own as it would be as part of a finished product, it would still be worth something. Exactly how much will partly depend upon the importance of the captured component in the value-added chain. If the conqueror captures a stage of the value-added chain that is important, then the conqueror may have significant leverage regarding price with the global firms needing the component, and vice versa. To the extent that the conqueror does have leverage regarding price, its duration will depend upon how easily global firms can switch to another supplier; the easier it is to switch, the shorter the time frame during which the conqueror will be able to sell the component for a significant profit. Significantly, one of the hallmarks of economic globalization is that the pool of potential suppliers has greatly increased. Moreover, many MNCs now take active steps to geographically diversify their affiliates and sources of supply from third parties in order to reduce various forms of risk, including "the risk of over-reliance on a single source whose operations may be disrupted" due to events such as strikes, accidents, or breakdowns.[66] For these and other reasons, it will often be very easy for MNCs to switch to alternative suppliers; in general, therefore, a conqueror's leverage is likely to be low.

---

[65] Frieden 1994, 571. For a similar assessment, see Lipson 1985, 29.

[66] Dicken 1998, 218. For a discussion of some of the other reasons why MNCs geographically diversify in order to guard against various forms of risk, see Rugman 1979, 1980; and Lessard 1982.

Even if a conqueror does not try to sell the component for an inflated price, the conqueror's ability to continue production of the component and sell it to the MNC requiring it is likely to be temporally restricted to a significant degree. In our hypothetical example, the MNC that owns or relies upon the transmission factory located in the vanquished territory may be willing to purchase components from the conqueror in the short term but is unlikely to rely upon this source over the longer term. The key reason is the conqueror's low credibility of commitment in the vanquished advanced country: the MNC will be averse to relying on the transmission factory because the conqueror will be unable to provide assurances that it will not unexpectedly change policies in ways that reduce the cost-effectiveness or accessibility of this particular supplier. There are in addition three other reasons why the MNC will be disinclined to depend on the transmission factory over the long term: (1) the transmission factory within the conquered territory might be destroyed or damaged during a military reprisal; (2) transportation networks are normally greatly disrupted by warfare, which often makes moving goods in and out of a conflict area difficult and expensive; and (3) the conquest of territory during the second half of the twentieth century has typically been followed by substantial economic sanctions that restrict the ability of the aggressor state to participate in international markets. To guard against supply disruptions or cost increases following conquest, the MNC is likely to strive to reduce its reliance on the transmission factory within the conquered territory. This becomes especially likely given the large number of substitutable production sites and alternative suppliers that are now typically available. Moreover, if the transmission factory is an affiliate, the MNC is unlikely to continue to invest in technological improvements to the factory given the high risks involved. Given the rapid rate of technological change, this means that the transmission affiliate is likely to quickly become outdated, and hence not valuable: "To seize [it] is to seize only physical assets that will soon be outmoded."[67]

Third, critics might posit that the increased geographic dispersion of MNC production will not appreciably lower the economic benefits of conquest since most MNC headquarters are located in advanced countries to which all profits from abroad will eventually return. Capturing profits is one thing; capturing productive assets that have the capacity to strengthen the conqueror's military power in the short term is something altogether more valuable. Profits are also based upon the ability to continue producing finished products. To the extent that the geographic dispersion of production makes it relatively more difficult and costly for MNCs based in the conquered territory to complete the process for reasons just outlined, profits following conquest will be reduced. Moreover, not all MNC profits will, in fact, return to the home country following conquest. The number and significance of regional headquarters of MNCs has

---

[67] Lipson 1985, 29.

greatly increased in recent years.[68] Some of these regional headquarters have been created to coordinate a particular product line of an MNC; some are designed to coordinate all of the MNC's affiliates in a particular region; and others are responsible for a particular function of the MNC's entire worldwide production.[69] Because of the conqueror's low credibility of commitment regarding the confiscation of wealth and, in turn, because liquid capital is now so easy to transfer electronically, the increasing prominence of regional headquarters means that some MNC profits—perhaps a large proportion—will not flow to the home country headquarters following conquest, but will instead be directed toward regional headquarters. Even in the absence of regional headquarters, it is likely that a significant portion of MNC assets will be directed toward safer havens in response to conquest. Iraq's recent occupation of Kuwait is instructive in this respect. As Rosecrance points out, "Saddam Hussein ransacked the computers in downtown Kuwait City in August 1990, only to find that the cash in the bank accounts had already been electronically transferred."[70]

All of the discussion so far in this section has considered the influence of the geographic dispersion of MNC production activities on the benefits of conquest. Recall from chapter 2 that the geographic dispersion of MNC technological development also increased in recent years in large part because of the rising importance of interfirm alliances.[71] Recall also that interfirm alliances have been primarily concentrated in sectors with rapidly changing technologies and high entry costs, such as aerospace, computers, new materials, and microelectronics. Significantly, these and other such high-technology sectors are highly cumulative resources, since they provide much of the foundation for military power in the modern era.

Much of the basic logic outlined above concerning why the geographic dispersion of production lowers the benefits of conquest also applies to the geographic dispersion of technological development. Until recently, a conqueror would likely be able to capture in entirety a particular technology or a research project that existed within a country. Now, in contrast, a hypothetical conqueror of a state whose firms have many international interfirm alliances might capture only a portion of a certain technology or research project—which would be less valuable for the reasons sketched above regarding why capturing only a part of the value-added chain is less advantageous. Again, this dynamic is restricted to the most economically advanced countries, since the overwhelming majority, probably more than 90 percent, of interfirm alliances now exist within Western Europe, the United States, and Japan.

---

[68] See, for example, Dicken 1998, 208–11; and UNCTAD 1996, 135–41.

[69] UNCTAD 1996, 135.

[70] Rosecrance 1996, 48.

[71] As emphasized in chapter 2, the rise of interfirm alliances is not the only factor propelling the geographic dispersion of technological development. Technological development *within* MNCs themselves has also become increasingly geographically dispersed in recent years.

Knowledge-Based Economies and the Economic Benefits of Conquest

As noted previously, the globalization of production has facilitated the switch to knowledge-based economies in the most advanced countries. Although the specific arguments advanced by Rosecrance and Van Evera to show why this shift to knowledge-based economies in the most advanced states leads to a reduction in the economic benefits of conquest are subject to compelling counterarguments, one additional issue needs to be considered: how the mechanisms of control used by a conqueror are likely to influence the economic dynamism of these societies. Of particular importance is an analysis of how conquest influences the level of innovation within a vanquished knowledge-based country.

Innovation is much more significant in knowledge-based economies than in agricultural-based or industrial-based economies.[72] What implications does this have for the benefits of conquest? Two points need to be considered. The first concerns the financing of innovations. Innovations are by definition risky. If the requisite financial backing is not forthcoming, then an innovation may never come to fruition even if its benefits are recognized. In this respect, the importance of risk capital is much greater in knowledge-based societies. Significantly, the pool of risk capital within the vanquished territory available to bring innovative ideas to the marketplace is likely to be significantly diminished following conquest. The cost of borrowing on international capital markets will be higher: "Interest rates rise in war. . . . Belligerents present a higher than normal probability of default. Lenders make borrowers pay for this higher risk by charging a higher interest rate."[73] Of course, capital from the conqueror's economy can be used to finance innovations within the conquered country. But doing so entails significant opportunity costs: there will be less capital available within the conqueror's economy itself. A relatively greater amount of capital will have to be drained from the conqueror to maintain productivity within a conquered knowledge-based economy, precisely because innovation is relatively more important than within agricultural or industrial economies.

The second point that needs to be considered is more substantively important and also more difficult to explain. To begin with, it is necessary to recognize that the centralization of economic authority reduces innovation. This basic point has been stressed repeatedly in numerous literatures. One of the key ways that corporations have sought to increase rates of innovation in recent years is by weakening hierarchical structures within the firm; that is, by decreasing the extent to which workers are monitored and directed by superiors.

---

[72] This is reflected in a number of recent trends within knowledge-based economies, including the increased risk, cost, and complexity of research and development and much faster rates of product obsolescence; see, for example, Dunning 1995; and Kobrin 1997.

[73] Gholz and Press 2001, 12; see also 13, 30–31.

These decisions are consistent with studies that show that centralized, hierarchical structures within firms tend to impede rates of innovation.[74] These findings on firms, in turn, mirror those in organizations more generally: "Centralization has usually been found to be negatively associated with innovativeness; that is, the more power concentrated in an organization, the less innovative that organization tends to be."[75] Finally, there is widespread agreement that these general findings regarding firms and organizations can be extended to states themselves. Many studies find that states pursuing economic centralization—that is, states where the central governing authority strongly monitors and directs firms and other economic actors—have lower rates of innovation than states with less economic oversight.[76]

The rise of knowledge-based economies increases the significance of the inverse relationship between innovation and economic centralization.[77] A key question, then, is whether a conqueror will undertake economic centralization within a vanquished knowledge-based country. For several reasons, we should expect it to do so.

In the first place, economic centralization gives the conqueror a greater ability to shape production in the vanquished territory to ensure that useful materials and goods are being produced. The goals of firms and of the conqueror will not necessarily overlap. Conquerors may, for example, wish to switch production in the vanquished territory over to war material. Commercial firms, in contrast, may be averse to giving up their market share and becoming cogs in the conqueror's war machine. This basic conflict of interest was evident during the early stages of World War II, when German firms and the Nazi regime had very different views of how best to exploit the conquest of France, Austria, Czechoslovakia, and Poland. Many German firms wished to capitalize on the commercial opportunities in the newly occupied territories. Nazi officials, in contrast, felt that economic activity in the territories "should serve not the profit motive. . . . but the common good"; that is, the production of material should be geared to Germany's strategic needs.[78] In the end, the commercial firms lost

---

[74] See, for example, Russell and Russell 1992; and Cohn 1981.

[75] Rogers 1983, 359–60.

[76] These economic literatures are examined in Winiecki 1986 and 1988. See also Hanson and Pavitt 1987; and Evangelista 1988, 29–33. It should be noted that as a descriptor of a state's economic structure, the term *centralization* is also used by many scholars as a general means of distinguishing the degree of power held by the central government as compared to state governments in federal systems. This particular understanding of centralization is not employed in the discussion that follows.

[77] This effect is the foundation for Robert Bates' argument: "When firms that used high proportions of plant and machinery relative to human skill formed the basis of economies, then centrally directed systems tended to work; mid-century, the Soviet Union competed successfully with capitalist nations as measured by rates of economic growth. But as the economies of nations have moved towards forms of production that require a high level of human capital, these forms have proved increasingly inefficient" (Bates 1991, 27). See also Winiecki 1986, 326–27.

[78] Overy 1986, 305.

out: Hermann Göring ordered in 1940 that "the endeavor of German industry to take over enterprises in the recently occupied territory must be rejected in the sharpest possible manner. Travel of industrialists into the occupied territory must not be permitted for the present."[79] The vast majority of firms in the vanquished territories were ultimately placed under the political control of the Nazis, under Göring's direction. As he explained, the territories under German occupation "formed a homogenous area with manifold, mutual obligations which makes necessary a coordinated supervision from Berlin. . . . In order to exploit the territories . . . in the best way to achieve the Fuhrer's goals, the property . . . must be safeguarded and administered in a co-ordinated way."[80]

Perhaps the main force pushing conquerors to undertake economic centralization, however, is that it provides a convenient means of dealing with a general dilemma that Douglass North identifies: "The ruler continually faces a tradeoff between the higher income he can obtain by relaxing restrictions on constituents (thereby increasing their productivity and both their and his income) and the increasing threat to his security that the relaxed restrictions entail because his subjects have both more freedom of action and resources to overthrow him."[81] All rulers face this trade-off, but it is most pronounced in conquered societies. Economic centralization enables the conqueror to shape production within the conquered territory so as to maintain stability in three primary ways. First, the conqueror has more control over the nature and extent of production of military hardware. Second, and relatedly, the conqueror can more easily ensure that economic resources are not used to support resistance. Finally, economic centralization allows the conqueror to restructure production in the vanquished country to make it dependent, improving the conqueror's leverage and bolstering imperial authority. Centralization, in short, is valuable because it restricts freedom of action in a vanquished society and limits resources available for rebellion.

The preceding incentives for promoting economic centralization apply to all nonagricultural societies. What about knowledge-based economies specifically? Is there a greater need for economic centralization following the conquest of a knowledge-based economy? There are strong reasons to suspect that this is the case. Before a conqueror can secure economic gains from the occupation of conquered territory, it must establish territorial control sufficient to attempt extraction of economic resources; the key finding from Liberman's study of conquest is that this degree of territorial control is possible in advanced societies only if a conqueror is extraordinarily ruthless in suppressing nationalist resistance.[82] Numerous reasons, some of which are stressed below, indicate that resistance cannot be ruthlessly suppressed unless the conqueror pursues

[79] Overy 1986, 308.
[80] Göring as cited in Overy 1986, 305, 322.
[81] North 1993, 14; see also the related discussion in Hall 1996, 55–57.
[82] Liberman 1996.

economic centralization in an advanced country. Liberman himself acknowledges the potential significance of this underlying dynamic.[83]

In short, the rise of knowledge-based societies shifts the basic trade-off North identifies—between increasing income and reducing threats to security by minimizing the resources and freedom for rebellion—to the disadvantage of the conqueror. In a vanquished society with an economy based on physical labor, natural resources, or basic manufacturing, a conqueror can monitor the output and activities of workers with relative ease. In such a society, a conqueror can more safely err on the side of enhancing income. In a knowledge-based society, in contrast, output and workers are much more difficult to monitor, for the simple reason that it is very hard to evaluate what is inside people's heads. Not only do workers in a knowledge-based society have more freedom of action to oppose a conqueror, they also have a greater range of resources that can challenge the conqueror's authority that can be used quickly, perhaps even anonymously, by a small number of individuals. Using computers to conduct information warfare is the most obvious example.

For these reasons, the conqueror of a knowledge-based society will face a relatively greater need to focus on limiting the freedom of workers and firms and the resources available for resistance. There are many means of doing so, but economic centralization is probably the most secure. This is the best means to precisely control individuals' access to resources that could be used to challenge the conqueror. In turn, findings on principal-agent relationships strongly suggest that a conqueror's need for direct monitoring in order to curb freedom of action will be highest in knowledge-based societies. Within principal-agent relationships, "hidden action" by the agent—that is, when it is difficult for the principal to observe whether the actions of the agent are in the principal's best interests—increases the need for monitoring.[84] The problem of hidden action will obviously be far greater in knowledge-based societies than in industrial, agricultural, or resource-based economies.

In nonadvanced economies, it might be feasible for a conqueror to establish a relatively stable set of prohibited or approved activities for firms and workers that could be easily administered within a decentralized structure; this would not be possible in a knowledge-based society. There the central authority will need strong oversight of economic activity and constantly updated guidelines concerning which activities by firms and workers will be permitted and which proscribed. The simple reason is that the tasks workers and firms perform, and the resources they have access to, evolve quickly in a knowledge-based economy; in setting up guidelines, the conqueror of such a society is always chasing a moving target.

A basic insight from studies of collective action suggests a further reason

[83] See, Liberman 1996, 143, where he notes, "perhaps tyrannical rule over modern industrial societies can function only with centralized economic control."

[84] See Kiewiet and McCubbins 1991, 25–26.

why a conqueror will be more likely to pursue economic centralization within a vanquished knowledge-based economy. Urban workers are more geographically concentrated, and hence can more easily than rural workers overcome problems of collective action to organize against the ruler.[85] As a result, economic policies that give urban workers enhanced autonomy will be a greater threat to a conqueror than economic policies that give rural or agricultural workers more autonomy. Because knowledge-based economies are always accompanied by significant urbanization,[86] the need for economic centralization to restrain freedom of action and access to resources is likely to be higher in these societies than in other kinds of economies.

Shirking will also be a much more significant problem facing a conqueror of a knowledge-based economy. In resource-based, agricultural, and basic industrial economies, it is relatively easy to gauge the amount and quality of effort by laborers. This is because the physical tasks performed are basic and routinized and output is measurable and tangible. In knowledge-based societies, by contrast, a supervisor may have great difficulty determining whether a worker is shirking or, for example, incubating a solution to a complex problem. This is another reason why we expect the need for careful monitoring by a conqueror to be relatively higher in a knowledge-based society. And while monitoring knowledge-based workers to ensure they are not shirking is not an impossible task, it will necessarily create additional pressure toward economic centralization. Again, the key reason is that the nature of work responsibilities in knowledge-based societies evolves greatly over time. As a result, a central authority must constantly make decisions about how long workers and firms should devote to particular tasks, or when the line has been crossed that indicates footdragging.

For the preceding reasons, conquerors will face increased incentives to pursue centralization within knowledge-based economies. This does not mean, however, that conquerors will feel pressure to impose command-style economies, for economic centralization does not require central planning. This is because conquerors have means of exerting centralized control short of direct management of all economic output. The authority exercised by the Nazi regime over firms in the territory it occupied in the early years of World War II reflects the range of economic centralization strategies available to conquerors.[87] Although most firms were placed under direct Nazi political control, not all were. Some foreign firms in the occupied countries were managed by German MNCs under trusteeships, in which all output was the property of the Nazi regime, which exercised various forms of control over production, including over prices and sales. In addition, some German MNCs were allowed to take over foreign firms in the conquered countries without operating under trusteeships. However,

---

[85] On this point, see Bates 1981.

[86] For a discussion of this point, see Sassen 1998.

[87] The information in this paragraph is drawn from Overy 1986.

even without such trusteeships, these MNCs ultimately "were subject to a set of regulations and controls over investment policy, product policy, and labour dictated by the state economic apparatus."[88] These three mechanisms—direct state control, trusteeship, and oversight—vary in the extent of direct economic management exercised by the central authority. Through a mix of these three mechanisms, the Nazis maintained tight control over the output in the occupied territories.

The bottom line is that nationalism and the globalization of production now mix in such a way that the ability of a conqueror to extract economic resources from a vanquished advanced society is likely to be much lower than in previous eras. To extract economic resources, a conqueror will need to ruthlessly suppress nationalist resistance.[89] And in order to constrain challenges to their rule, conquerors will be prone to pursue economic centralization, especially in knowledge-based societies whose emergence in recent years has been facilitated by the globalization of production. Yet economic centralization reduces innovation, which is the lifeblood of knowledge-based societies. To the conqueror's detriment, this constriction will increase over the long term due to the cumulative adverse effects of centralization on innovation within a conquered knowledge-based economy.

Specific Hypotheses

The preceding theoretical analysis identifies a series of reasons why the globalization of production is expected to reduce the economic benefits of conquest in the most advanced countries. Three specific hypotheses emerge from this discussion:

1. A vanquished advanced country is unlikely to attract significant FDI following conquest, and its firms are unlikely to be able to form or sustain extensive international interfirm alliances.

2. In the most advanced states, the ability of a conqueror to extract economic resources is likely to be much lower than in the past because production and technological development are now less concentrated geographically.

3. Conquerors are likely to pursue economic centralization, especially in a vanquished knowledge-based economy.

If the second hypothesis is valid, then a conqueror will be in a weaker position to seize the resources of a vanquished advanced society and employ them to

---

[88] Overy 1986, 299.
[89] See Liberman 1996.

protect or acquire other resources. If the first and last hypotheses are valid, then the conquest of an advanced state will lead to a great reduction in economic dynamism, significantly constraining the long-term gains of the conqueror.

THEORY NUMBER 2: THE GLOBALIZATION OF PRODUCTION AND REGIONAL ECONOMIC INTEGRATION IN THE DEVELOPING WORLD

With respect to changes in the nature of the actors, the key unanswered question is whether isolation from FDI is a new kind of common external threat that generates a strong pressure for the consolidation of regional trade agreements (RTAs) in the developing world; if so, then extensive economic cooperation may occur even among states with a long-standing history of security rivalry. This section begins by briefly reviewing theoretical analyses developed by economists explaining why the pursuit of regional integration is now an attractive option for developing countries wishing to compete for increased FDI. The second part of this section then extends the basic logic of these theoretical models.

Why Competition for FDI Makes Regional Integration More Attractive for Developing Countries

In several recent theoretical analyses, Wilfrid Ethier stresses that competition for FDI is now likely to play a significant role in the decision of developing countries to pursue regional economic integration.[90] He notes that competition for FDI is now intense and argues that, under these conditions, even a small national advantage may help attract FDI.[91] This is because "direct investment is lumpy: you have to put a factory in one place" and with many "similar countries competing, small advantages can prove decisive."[92] In today's global economy, he maintains, membership in an RTA may be just such a slight advantage, allowing an economically small country or one that has recently engaged in reforms "to distinguish itself from its rivals" and attract FDI.[93] In outlining this theoretical argument, Ethier concentrates on the particular case in which a developing country pursues regional integration with an industrial country, as in Mexico's integration agreement with the United States. However, Ethier's general theoretical argument, concerning why competition for FDI is now likely to

[90] See Ethier 1998a, 1998b.
[91] Ethier 1998b, 1242.
[92] Ethier 1998b, 1156.
[93] Ethier 1998a, 1157.

spur interest in regional integration, also applies to RTAs comprising only developing countries.

Economists identify two principal advantages to membership in an RTA for developing countries that want to attract FDI. The first is increased market size: "Regional integration should enhance the attractiveness of investing in the region as a whole by creating a larger common market."[94] Large regional markets open opportunities for MNCs to exploit economies of scale and engage in production specialization within the region.[95] Numerous empirical studies have found that market size is, in fact, a key determinant of FDI.[96] For developing countries in particular, a comprehensive recent analysis finds that market size is the most important determinant of FDI inflows.[97]

Beyond increased market size, Raquel Fernandez and Jonathan Portes have recently outlined the deductive basis for a number of "nontraditional" gains from regional integration, some of which directly address how developing countries can use integration as a strategy to attract increased FDI.[98] Of particular relevance is their argument that regional integration makes it possible for developing countries to signal MNCs in two different ways and thereby attract higher levels of FDI. Because of the relative newness of economic reform efforts undertaken by many developing countries, there is often significant information asymmetry between governments and investors. Given this information asymmetry, Portes and Fernandez argue that a developing country may wish to use regional integration to signal its true liberal intentions. They maintain that regional integration can act as a signal to MNCs that the parties to the agreement are, in fact, liberal. Their basic logic is straightforward: because exposing firms to greater competition from regional competitors entails political costs and requires liberal policies, it provides the government with an effective signaling mechanism, since only a government with liberal intentions would pursue this course.[99] In addition, they contend that regional integration may be a useful signal in a second respect: to "signal not the policies of individual governments but their future relationships. . . . Investors may only be prepared to invest in one or both countries if both signal their future good relationship by signing" an RTA that provides assurances that trade barriers between the agreement's members will not be reimposed at some point in the future.[100]

---

[94] Blomstrom and Kokko 1997, 9.

[95] See, for example, Blomstrom and Kokko 1997, 9; Lunn 1980, 95; Narula 2001, 5; Buckley, Clegg, and Forsans 1998; and Dunning 1980.

[96] See, for example, Lunn 1980; Ajami and Ricks 1981; Beer and Cory 1996; UNCTAD 1998, 135–40; Tsai 1994; and the series of studies noted in Dunning 1992, 170.

[97] UNCTAD 1998, 138–39.

[98] Fernandez and Portes 1998.

[99] Fernandez and Portes 1998, 208.

[100] Fernandez and Portes 1998, 209.

Bringing Politics In

This general logic outlined by economists is compelling, but it needs to be extended. These various models leave out politics, and hence do not tell us much about when regional integration is likely to be consolidated. While an RTA may be a useful tool for developing countries in attracting FDI, successfully consolidating integration is politically difficult because it involves exposing domestic industries to increased international competition. Moreover, scholars agree that security rivals are the least likely to engage in deep regional economic cooperation because of fears as to how the gains will be distributed.[101] Both of these political constraints on regional integration are likely to be especially strong in the developing world. It is partly because the political costs associated with integration are so significant that none of the dozens of RTAs in the developing world before 1990 succeeded.[102]

Under what conditions are policymakers in developing countries more likely to bear the political costs associated with consolidating regional integration in order to attract increased FDI? Among those developing countries that initiate an RTA, we would expect their willingness to bear the political costs associated with consolidating regional integration efforts to be greater if both of the following conditions are met: (1) the ability of the group's members to meet their potential for attracting FDI without pursuing integration is low; and (2) the economic size of the RTA they join is large, and the group is able to achieve significant economic size with relatively few members.

The basis for the first condition is clear enough. If a state does not place a high value on attracting FDI, or is able to meet or come close to its potential for securing FDI without pursuing regional integration, then we would expect it to be less willing to pay the political costs associated with consolidating an RTA to secure increased FDI than states that value FDI but fall short attracting it on their own. An explanation of the basis for the second condition, which is more complicated, follows.

The integration group's size is directly relevant to the first FDI motivation delineated by economists (using regional integration to enhance market size). Two findings from the literature on the determinants of FDI are of key importance in this respect. First, a group must reach a certain minimum economic size before the market-related factors that attract MNCs become operative: "A small market prohibits firms from exploiting scale economies and limits the degree to which factors of production can be specialized. Eventually, if the market keeps growing, economies of scale can be exploited and large scale production can begin. There exists a 'threshold' that must be crossed before a firm will

---

[101] See, for an example of the consensus in the literature on this point, Grieco, Powell, and Snidal 1993.

[102] On this point, see, for example, Okolo 1985, 121; and de la Torre and Kelly 1992, 32–33.

invest in the area for the first time."[103] Significantly, the height of this threshold has rapidly increased over the past several decades due to the dramatic rise in the scale and complexity of technology.[104] The literature also indicates that once this threshold is crossed, the amount of FDI will, ceteris paribus, be a function of the region's market size. A series of empirical studies finds that "once a market attains a size that permits local production to become cost-effective. . . . at and after that point, the level of FDI in that market is . . . closely related to market size."[105]

The economic size of the RTA is also relevant for the second FDI motivation outlined above (using regional integration as a signaling mechanism). This is most obvious with respect to the second dynamic that Fernandez and Portes identify, whereby states use an RTA to signal MNCs that the states will maintain open trading relationships and that a regional market will endure. Fernandez and Portes are correct in arguing that MNCs may sometimes invest only when there is a high level of certainty about the nature of the trading relationships within a region.[106] But this dynamic will likely be of much greater import when the RTA is economically large due to the same "threshold" size point just mentioned. If investing in a region or country only makes sense when the MNC can use a production site as a base for exporting to other countries in the region or can set up regional production strategies, then uncertainty about whether trade barriers in the region may be imposed will influence the MNCs' decision to invest. However, strong concerns of this kind are likely to be present only with respect to large RTAs. In smaller RTAs for which none or few MNCs are in a position to reap significant profits by serving a regional market from a single production plant or profitably set up regional production strategies, investment decisions are not likely to be influenced strongly by concerns about future trade barriers in a region. For this reason, we would not expect policymakers in small RTAs to have a significant willingness to pay the political costs associated with consolidating integration in order to benefit from the second signaling dynamic identified by Portes and Fernandez.

The economic size of the agreement is also relevant to the first signaling dynamic that Fernandez and Portes identify (in which states utilize regional integration to signal MNCs that they are, in fact, liberal). In the literature that examines signaling, analysts tend to assume active and close monitoring. Yet this need not always be the case; actors may sometimes wish to signal their true type to other actors who are not actively monitoring their behavior. For example, decision makers in states that have recently undertaken economic liberalization may want MNCs that had written them off as undesirable investment sites to once again pay attention to their country or region. If a state wishes to

---

[103] Lunn 1980, 95. On this threshold point, see also Dunning 1992, 170; and World Bank 2000, 37.

[104] The best discussion of this point with respect to regional integration is Kobrin 1995.

[105] See Dunning 1992, 170 and the studies cited therein.

[106] Fernandez and Portes 1998, 209.

use regional integration to signal MNCs in this manner, the agreement needs to be substantial enough that MNCs will actually be aware of the group's progress and thus receive the signal. As sizable as many MNCs are, they have limits in their ability to gather information about suitable investment sites.[107] If an RTA is large, MNCs are more likely to invest resources to monitor the group's progress. In turn, the larger the RTA, the more likely the media or others will undertake analyses of it that MNCs can profitably use. In contrast, if an RTA is small in economic size, then MNCs and other analysts will tend to overlook it and, hence, using regional integration to signal to MNCs is likely to be relatively ineffective. As a result, policymakers are unlikely to bear significant costs in order to pursue a signaling strategy.

Economically large RTAs thus have several key benefits in terms of attracting enhanced FDI.[108] That being said, augmenting the number of countries that are party to an international agreement will reduce the ease of engaging in cooperation by making it more difficult to bargain, resolve disputes, detect opportunism, and enforce agreements.[109] The manner in which an RTA achieves significant economic size is thus another factor influencing the likelihood that policymakers will bear the political costs associated with consolidating regional integration to attract additional FDI. Very succinctly, the fewer countries that must be party to an RTA in order for it to be significant in economic size, the better. More specifically, we would expect the chances of successful consolidation of the RTA—and hence the willingness to invest in the agreement in order to attract FDI—to decrease as more countries are needed for the RTA to achieve significant economic size.

Specific Hypothesis

One conclusion of the preceding discussion is that the incentives for developing countries to initiate regional integration agreements to attract MNCs have increased in recent years. Forming a group, is relatively easy; however, if the group makes no progress, it is also inconsequential. Over the past several decades, developing countries have indeed shown great affinity at forming RTAs; it is the consolidation of these groups that has proven elusive. The key conclusion of the preceding theoretical discussion is that among those developing

---

[107] On this point, see, for example, UNCTAD 2000b, 112.

[108] To be clear, nothing here is meant to imply that economic size is a necessary requirement for attracting FDI; the experience of small countries like Singapore clearly indicates this is not the case. Regional integration influences some, but not all, of the factors that affect the decision by MNCs to undertake FDI. The key point is that all of the mechanisms identified by scholars through which regional integration can potentially lead to greater FDI are likely to be present only for economically large RTAs.

[109] See Yarbrough and Yarbrough 1992, 69, 74–75; Nye 1971, 105–6; Oye 1986, 19–20; and Ethier 1998a, 1153.

countries that initiate RTAs, competition for FDI is likely to act as a significant force for the consolidation of integration only under certain conditions. The specific hypothesis that emerges from the theoretical analysis is the following:

> Regional integration among developing countries is more likely to be consolidated when the RTA is economically large but has few member states, and when the group's members have difficulty attracting FDI on their own, ceteris paribus.

If the two conditions specified here are strongly met, then the pressure to consolidate regional integration may be sufficiently great to promote extensive economic cooperation even among states with a long-standing history of security rivalry.

THEORY NUMBER 3: THE GLOBALIZATION OF PRODUCTION AND THE TRADE-OFF BETWEEN AUTARKY AND OPENNESS IN DEFENSE PRODUCTION

The final means by which the globalization of production can influence security is by changing capabilities. The key unanswered question in this regard is whether the scales have shifted so far against an autarkic strategy that significant internationalization in defense-related production is now a necessity for any great power that wishes to be on the leading edge in military technology. Unlike the first two mechanisms discussed previously, no detailed theoretical analysis is necessary for this final mechanism since the deductive basis for the hypothesis to be examined has already been established by scholars.

A key theme in the literature on globalization is that the need to internationalize production in order to remain on the cutting-edge in the leading commercial sectors has increased dramatically in recent decades. Stephen Kobrin provides the clearest statement: "In industries such as telecommunications, pharmaceuticals, semiconductors, and aerospace . . . states are now faced with a discrete decision rather than a marginal tradeoff: participate in the world economy or forgo technological development. . . . The choice is to compete transnationally or forgo the next generation of microprocessors, pharmaceuticals or telecommunications technology entirely."[110]

While Kobrin's statement is perhaps overstated, no scholar would likely disagree with his underlying contention: in today's global economy, states that are isolated from MNCs and in which firms are constrained from pursuing internationalization strategies face huge handicaps in remaining competitive in the leading commercial sectors. Numerous analysts advance arguments that accord with Kobrin's contention.[111] In particular, scholars underscore that (1) if a

[110] Kobrin 1997, 156.
[111] Prominent examples in the international political economy and economics literatures respectively are Frieden and Rogowski 1996 and Bayoumi, Coe, and Helpman 1999.

state is isolated from FDI, it will have reduced access to the latest technologies and production methods; and (2) if a state's firms are unable to participate in the globalization of production, they will not be able to reap the key advantages associated with internationalization strategies—in particular, multiplying opportunities for innovation via interfirm alliances and reaping locational advantages by slicing up the value chain. Of course, these are long-standing handicaps associated with international economic isolation. But analysts uniformly agree that these handicaps increased greatly over the past several decades.[112]

The question is not whether the opportunity cost of closure has increased to the point that states feel great pressure to open up to MNCs. We know this is the case; it is exactly for this reason, as shown in chapter 2, for states' dramatic rush to openness to MNCs in recent years. The question is also not whether the need to pursue globalization has become so significant that production in the leading commercial sectors—especially high technology and those sectors of manufacturing characterized by high levels of R&D and significant economies of scale—will be marked by a significant and rapidly growing level of internationalization. Chapter 2 shows that this is indeed the case. The only remaining question is whether the opportunity cost of closure to the globalization of production has increased so dramatically that significant internationalization is now a necessity even for the states with the largest and most advanced economies, the great powers, if they wish to remain competitive in military technology. In defense production above all other areas states face strong incentives to not pursue openness and in which they historically have been most willing to take costly steps in order to pursue a strategy of autarkic production.

To explain the rapid increase in the internationalization of production by MNCs in the leading commercial sectors, analysts highlight two factors: (1) coping with a simultaneous increase in the importance of technological development and the escalating cost, difficulty, complexity, and scale of developing new technologies; and (2) accessing the best possible location for production. As in the commercial realm, the importance and difficulty of technological development in production of weaponry has greatly increased in recent decades. It is obvious that the reliance of modern weapons on advanced technology has skyrocketed in recent decades. U.S. fighter jets provide a telling example: "Computers and software accounted for less than 2 percent of development costs for the F-4 Phantom, the mainstay of the U.S. fighter inventory during the 1960s and early 1970s. The corresponding percentage for the F-15 was over 26 percent, and that for the F-18 was greater than 40 percent."[113] It is also common knowledge that the cost and difficulty of developing the new advanced technologies that are employed in modern weaponry has spiraled upwards in recent decades. "During the 1950s, the up-front R&D costs associated with weapons

[112] See the overall assessment of the literature on this point in Garrett 2000, especially 965–67.
[113] CIA 1987a, 3.

acquisition comprised only 5 percent of the cost of the system; by the 1980s, this had risen to 50 percent."[114] Just during the 1985–99 period, the development costs for semiconductors increased tenfold.[115]

What is less well known is how incredibly complex modern weapons systems have become in number of parts and components. There is general recognition that a massive weapons system such as the B-2 bomber requires thousands of parts and components in its production. But weapons systems far smaller in scale and cost are also highly complex. A 1992 Commerce Department study, which to date is the only "comprehensive analysis of sourcing by weapons system at lower tier subcontractor levels,"[116] undertook an exhaustive examination of the supply chain for three weapons systems—the HARM missile, the Mark-48 ADCAP torpedo, and the Verdin communication system—that were chosen as "representative" weapons used by the U.S. Navy.[117] A stunning finding emerged: for just these three weapon systems, a total of "15,000 companies were identified at the subcontractor level, with 11,638 companies still serving as active suppliers to the prime contractors for the three weapons systems" (6,818 for the HARM missile, 1,483 for the Verdin, and 3,336 for the Mark-48 torpedo).[118]

It is thus clear that the production of modern weaponry has the same basic characteristics as the commercial high-technology and advanced manufacturing sectors: as compared to a few decades ago, technology is both more important and difficult to develop, while the number of parts or components, and hence needed suppliers, is now much greater. The logical expectation, therefore, is that the same conclusion scholars have reached with respect to commercial sectors—that strong participation in the globalization of production is now a necessity for all states, even the economically largest and most advanced ones, to remain internationally competitive—now applies with equal force to the production of weaponry.

Specific Hypothesis

The key conclusion from the preceding discussion is straightforward: the scales have decisively shifted against going it alone in military technology. This is true not just for small states, but for the great powers as well—who, by virtue of their economic size, are in the best position to pursue a strategy of autarkic defense production. This leads to the following specific hypothesis:

If a state does not pursue significant internationalization in defense-related production, it will be unable to remain on the cutting edge in military technology.

[114] Kapstein 1991–92, 668.
[115] Kobrin 1995, 22; emphasis added.
[116] Commerce 1992, 8. For a similar assessment, see Blackwell 1992, 197.
[117] Commerce 1992, i.
[118] Commerce 1992, 6, 10, 14, 16.

THE STAKES OF THE ANALYSIS

The hypotheses advanced in this chapter suggest that the globalization of production: (1) greatly reduces the ability of a conqueror to reap economic gains by conquering an advanced state; (2) under certain conditions is likely to push developing countries—including those with long-standing security rivals—to consolidate regional economic integration in order to attract MNCs; (3) makes it impossible for all states, including the great powers, to remain competitive in military technology if they go it alone in defense-related production.

The next section of the book is devoted to empirically evaluating the specific hypotheses delineated in this chapter. Chapter 4 analyzes whether the geographic dispersion of MNC production has altered the trade-off between autarky and openness in defense-related production. Chapter 5 examines whether competition for FDI has shifted the dynamics of regional integration among developing countries. Finally, chapter 6 evaluates whether the globalization of production alters the economic benefits of conquest in the most advanced countries.

CHAPTER 4

The Globalization of Production and Military Technological Competitiveness

MILITARY TECHNOLOGY has always played a pivotal role in security affairs. With the onset of the industrial revolution, the importance of technology greatly increased: "Where once war was waged by men employing machines, more and more war was seen as a contest between machines that are served, maintained and managed by men."[1] By the dawn of World War II, the development of military technology had achieved such scale and importance that governments began to devote vast resources to enhance their long-term military technological competitiveness.[2] Over the centuries, "most countries have preferred to be self-sufficient in arms production."[3] The dynamics of international security would be reshaped in important ways if states can no longer effectively "go it alone" in the production of weaponry.

Few would deny that an autarkic defense production strategy has been fundamentally undermined for economically small states. But is the same also now true for the great powers? The theoretical analysis in chapter 3 suggests that it is. The United States is by far the least likely case for the specific hypothesis that emerged from this discussion: if a state does not pursue significant internationalization in defense-related production, it will be unable to remain on the cutting edge in military technology. The reasons why are straightforward. First, the United States has long been the country in the best position to attain economies of scale in defense production because of its immense economic size.[4] Second, for decades the United States has been the world's leading technological power in general, and with respect to military technology in particular. In the last several decades, the Soviet Union was the only country that came close to the U.S. ability to pursue a strategy of autarkic defense production.

For four overlapping reasons, the most appropriate test for the hypothesis is to examine the experience of the United States during the last two decades of the Cold War. First, before 1970, there was relatively little in the way of the globalization of production from which U.S. firms could be isolated. Second, at present, technological development is more complicated, and the geographic

[1] Van Crevald 1989, 225.

[2] On this point, see Herrera 1995; and Pearton 1982.

[3] Bitzinger 1994, 172.

[4] For a useful overview of the importance of achieving economies of scale in defense production, see Buzan and Herring 1998, 35.

dispersion of MNC production is more advanced, than was the case during the 1970s and 1980s; for this reason, the opportunity cost of going it alone in defense production in those decades was not as high as it is today. Focusing on this earlier period is thus a tougher test of the hypothesis advanced here. Third, the United States was engaged at this time in a military competition with the highest possible stakes, and defense planners had a strong preference for domestic defense production, other thing being equal. Fourth and finally, during the Cold War, U.S. policymakers and the U.S. public were willing to pay a high premium for defense: "When the Soviet Union was rattling its saber . . . the Pentagon did not seem too bothered that weapons programmes usually overran their budgets."[5]

In short, the United States had greater opportunity and willingness to pursue autarkic defense production during the 1970s and 1980s than today. Given this fact, if the United States shifted during this period away from its long-standing course of not strongly relying on international sources for key aspects of defense production, it would not do so for capricious reasons. Rather, the United States would be expected to strongly move toward openness only if the gains of internationalization—in terms of reduced cost and, especially, enhanced quality—were substantial. The first and second sections below are consequently devoted to respectively examining whether U.S. defense production did, in fact, become significantly more globalized during this period and, in turn, whether there were strong gains to be accrued by taking this route that were recognized by U.S. defense policymakers. As shown below, this is indeed the case. The third section examines the effect of the enhanced level of internationalization of U.S. defense production during this period. The question at issue is whether this shift was a contributing factor to the United States decisively pulling ahead of the Soviet Union in military technology during the 1980s. It is demonstrated that isolation from the globalization of production had an independent, negative effect on Soviet ability to remain competitive with the United States in key dual-use industries and defense-related technologies during the 1980s. In the end, the various streams of evidence analyzed in this chapter reveal that the geographic dispersion of MNC production has fundamentally shifted the scales, such that even the great powers cannot effectively pursue autarkic defense production.

THE GLOBALIZATION OF U.S. DEFENSE PRODUCTION

Before the mid-1970s, the United States achieved "a remarkable degree of autarky" in its defense production.[6] After this time U.S. defense production came to be marked by a significant degree of internationalization. That the United

---

[5] *Economist*, 14 June 1997, Survey, 4.
[6] Kapstein 1992, 180.

States was essentially autarkic in defense production during the initial decades of the Cold War might seem surprising, in light of the country's liberal ideology regarding international economic matters. However, U.S. national security policymakers had had a preference for autarkic defense production ever since the days of Alexander Hamilton.[7] And during much of the Cold War, the United States was very effective while pursuing autarky because of the country's economic size and technological dynamism. After the mid-1970s, the technological context changed.

Licensed Production, Coproduction Programs, and Codevelopment Programs

The three forms of internationalization of U.S. defense production that are most apparent and easiest to measure are (1) licensed production, (2) coproduction programs, and (3) codevelopment programs. Each of these strategies became much more prominent after the mid-1970s, for the United States in particular and for worldwide defense production. In the aggregate, the total number of licensed production and coproduction/codevelopment programs in 1986–90 was almost 200 percent greater than in 1961–65 and more than 50 percent greater than in 1971–75.[8] Although internationalization strategies rose greatly in importance during the final phase of the Cold War, this does not, in fact, provide strong evidence in favor of the notion that pursuing globalization in defense-related production offered large potential economic gains for the United States at this time. Why this is the case is detailed below.

Licensed production "entails the transnational sale or transfer of the rights to manufacture a weapon system that was originally developed in the supplier's country."[9] For the United States, licensing is "almost entirely a 'one-way street' for technology flows."[10] As a result, this internationalization strategy did not offer any substantial gains for U.S. defense production during the Cold War, at least with respect to enhancing the quality of U.S. weaponry.

Coproduction concerns the joint manufacture of either an entire weapons system or particular components that were originally produced in one country. A paradigmatic example is the F-16 fighter "in which four West European countries (Belgium, Denmark, the Netherlands, and Norway), in addition to assembling the plane for their own forces, also produced components and subsystems that went into F-16s designated for the US Air Force."[11] However, coproduction typically occurs for political, not economic, reasons. Rather

---

[7] See the discussion in Baldwin 1985, 92–93.
[8] Calculated from data in Bitzinger 1994, 176.
[9] Bitzinger 1994, 175–76.
[10] Bitzinger 1994, 176.
[11] Bitzinger 1994, 177.

than being driven by firms for quality and cost reasons, portions of the production process are spread across various countries at the behest of governments in order to increase domestic employment, promote alliance cohesion, reduce trade imbalances, or promote other noneconomic goals. As a result, coproduction "usually results in higher per unit costs."[12] Coproduction thus clearly did not lead to significant economic gains for the United States during Cold War.

In codevelopment programs, companies from different countries work together to develop and produce weapon systems. Codevelopment is distinguished from coproduction because the former consists of international collaboration throughout the entire value-added chain. Moreover, it is typical that "the major collaborative impetus comes from industry rather than government."[13] Codevelopment thus does offer the potential for significant gains "by reducing duplicative R&D and achieving economies of scale through longer production runs."[14] U.S. defense firms did participate in some codevelopment programs with other international firms during the 1970s and 1980s, such as the AV-8B Harrier II fighter jet that was jointly developed by McDonnell Douglas, British Aerospace, and Rolls-Royce. Prior to 1990, however, codevelopment efforts were much more extensive among European firms on prominent projects such as the Jaguar fighter jet, the Tornado fighter jet, the Alpha jet, and the NH-90 helicopter.[15] Moreover, although U.S. firms did accrue advantages from codevelopment projects, the bulk of technology transfer in these cooperative ventures still tended to be from U.S. firms to foreign firms rather than vice versa.[16] During the Cold War, U.S. defense firms thus derived only limited economic gains from this method of internationalization.

In the literature on the globalization of defense production, the preceding three internationalization strategies have received the lion's share of attention.[17] The likely reason is that these internationalization efforts are very visible: they clearly involve defense production, and they are normally undertaken by military prime contractors. Moreover, they also often entail substantial political bargaining between governments. During the final phase of the Cold War, however, the globalization of U.S. defense production achieved its greatest salience, and was most substantively important, at the subcontractor level in dual-use industries. Evidence to this effect is presented below.

[12] OTA 1990, 44.

[13] OTA 1990, 44.

[14] OTA 1990, 44.

[15] See, for example, Kapstein 1991–92; and OTA 1990, 13.

[16] U.S.-Japanese codevelopment programs in fighter aircraft are a prominent example in this regard. Japanese firms prized codevelopment over licensing or coproduction precisely because the former strategy offered much greater access to engineers in U.S. companies and their wealth of production experience in defense-related production; on this point, see Samuels 1994, esp. 240–41, 244, 275–77.

[17] See, for example, Bitzinger 1994 and the literature analyzed therein.

The Overlap between Dual-Use Industries
and the Globalization of Production

In the mid-1970s, the division between the development of military technology and civilian-commercial technology—which had been pronounced throughout much of the twentieth century—became much more porous.[18] As the number and significance of dual-use technologies rapidly expanded after the mid-1970s, development of military technology and development of civilian technology no longer moved on separate tracks. Increasingly, advancement in the latter depended upon improvements in the former, as figure 4.1 indicates.[19] These various commercially driven technological shifts led to fundamental changes in the nature of weapons development.

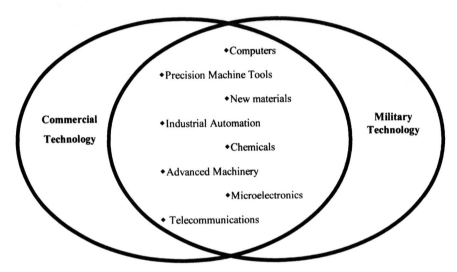

Figure 4.1 The Significance of Dual-Use Technologies

It is useful to recall the particular industries in which production was becoming most geographically dispersed. As was discussed in chapter 2, inter-firm alliances during the 1970s and 1980s were most concentrated in those sectors with rapidly changing technologies and high entry costs—such as microelectronics, new materials, aerospace, computers, telecommunications, and chemicals—while MNC geographic dispersion strategies were most

---

[18] See Herrera 1995.

[19] For example, "three-quarters of the computing power in the state-of-the art Aegis cruiser depends on commercial equipment" (Samuels 1994, 27). For discussions of the rising significance of dual-use technologies, see, for example, Cohen 1996, 42–43, 51; OTA 1990, 53; OTA 1989, 33–35; Samuels 1994, 27–30; Cha 2000, 396; Feigenbaum 1999, 98; Kapstein 1992, 7; Alic et al. 1992; Moran 1990; and Friedberg 2000b.

significant in those sectors of manufacturing with high levels of R&D and significant economies of scale—such as machinery, computers, and electronic components. Reading through these sectors, one encounters a "who's who" of dual-use technologies.

As the significance of dual-use technologies increased and, in turn, productivity in these sectors became increasingly tied to the degree to which firms pursued strategies of internationalization, what was the result? Very simply, this dynamic was the most important driving force behind the globalization of U.S. defense-related production during the 1970s and 1980s. Beginning in the mid-1970s, there was an explosion in significance of both interfirm alliances and international sourcing in key dual-use sectors.

Growing Interfirm Alliances
in Defense-Related Production

Interfirm alliances became much more prominent within the aerospace and defense sector during the 1980s, with a total of 228 interfirm alliances formed in this sector during this period.[20] However, in dual-use industries the significance of interfirm alliances became especially dramatic during the 1980s. Three key dual-use sectors—information technology, new materials technology, and chemicals—together accounted for 60 percent of all interfirm alliances formed during the 1980s.[21]

The information technology sector had great importance for the kind of advanced U.S. weapons systems coming online during this period; hence, even if this sector had been the only one in which interfirm alliances existed, it still would have had great substantive significance for American defense production. In fact, the information technology sector alone accounted for 40 percent of interfirm alliances in the 1980s.[22] Figure 4.2 shows the dramatic jump in the number of interfirm alliances in this sector during the 1980s.

As noted previously, technological development is the key driving force behind the rapid increase in interfirm alliances that began in the late 1970s: collaborating with other firms makes it possible for MNCs to minimize the risk and cost of developing new technologies while simultaneously enhancing the potential for innovation. Interfirm alliances thus gave U.S. MNCs important advantages in the aerospace and defense sector and, especially, in dual-use industries.

However, a key question remains: did U.S. MNCs gain from *international* interfirm alliances with MNCs based elsewhere? Given the historical strength of U.S. MNCs in advanced technologies, one might expect that a large number

[20] Dicken 1998, 229.

[21] Dicken 1998, 229. On the importance of these three dual-use sectors for defense production, see DoD 1990.

[22] Dicken 1998, 229.

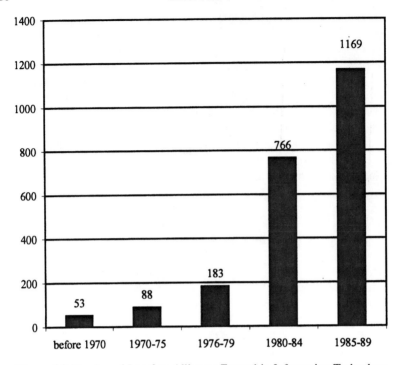

Figure 4.2 Number of Interfirm Alliances Formed in Information Technology
from the Early 1950s to 1989

of interfirm alliances in these sectors would simply be between U.S.-based
firms. This is indeed the case. Detailed analysis of interfirm alliances in the information technology sector reveals that 24 percent of these agreements in the
1980s included only U.S. firms.[23] However, international collaboration by U.S.
MNCs in this sector was of relatively much greater significance: 22 percent of
interfirm alliances in information technology formed during the 1980s were
between U.S. and West European MNCs, while 17 percent were between U.S.
and Japanese MNCs.[24]

General Assessments of International Sourcing in Defense-Related Production

U.S. firms thus strongly shifted toward partnering with other global firms in the
development of dual-use technologies via interfirm alliances during the final
phase of the Cold War. At the same time, many U.S. firms involved in defense

[23] Hagedoorn and Schakenraad 1990, 177.
[24] Hagedoorn and Schakenraad 1990, 177.

production were also moving toward greater internationalization at the lower tiers of weapons production through increased reliance on foreign affiliates and international subcontracting. This evolution is revealed by studies undertaken during the 1980s by the U.S. government and think tanks that sought to gauge the level of "foreign sourcing" in the production of U.S. weapons systems. In almost all of these analyses, foreign sourcing was defined by the location of production facilities rather than according to the firm's nationality. As a result, these analyses lump together two different internationalization strategies pursued by U.S.-based MNCs: (1) enhanced international subcontracting to firms based outside the United States and (2) increased reliance on the foreign affiliates of U.S.-based MNCs. The general findings from the major analyses of foreign sourcing in defense production are reviewed briefly in what follows.

Beginning in the mid-1980s, the Department of Defense undertook or sponsored an extensive number of studies that examined the degree of foreign sourcing. One survey that analyzed the findings from 10 DoD studies of this issue conducted in the mid-1980s sums them up as follows:

> Significant foreign dependencies exist in major weapons systems. The phenomenon is widespread and probably exists in most defense systems. This conclusion is the consensus of a number of studies which, directly or indirectly, addressed the question of foreign source dependencies as they relate to national defense and the production of military hardware. The dependencies spread across a wide range of production inputs. They include a few instances of total systems purchased offshore, such as chemical protective suits purchased from England. They progress down the production chain to include major sub-systems such as heads-up displays, electronic assemblies, and electronic components including semiconductors and ceramic packages.[25]

A later DoD analysis conducted in 1988 similarly concluded, "Foreign sourcing of key parts, components, and complete products is an extensive and growing business practice in both commercial and defense manufacturing."[26]

The findings from these DoD studies were echoed in analyses conducted by the Office of Technology Assessment (OTA) in the late 1980s and early 1990s. A 1990 OTA report noted: "Much weapons technology . . . is developed by large multinational companies with manufacturing facilities around the world. . . . Many US weapons systems depend, partly by design and partly by chance, on Japanese and European technology, parts, and components. Interdependence in the defense industries is a fact of life."[27] A 1991 OTA report concluded: "Almost all US weapons systems contain component parts from foreign sources, predominantly incorporating 'dual-use' technologies with both military and civilian applications, such as microelectronic chips, composite materials,

[25] Vawter 1986, 4. The 10 studies surveyed are listed on p. 8.
[26] DoD 1988, 192, 155, 157.
[27] OTA 1990, 10–11.

and flat-panel displays."[28] Similarly, a 1988 OTA report found that internationalization of defense production "is most pronounced in those industries—e.g. semiconductors, machine tools, structural materials, and optics—that are vital lower tier suppliers for defense projects, but do most of their business in the commercial marketplace."[29]

A 1991 General Accounting Office (GAO) analysis reached a similar finding: "Foreign sources of supply, manufacturing, and technology abound in both the commercial and defense sectors."[30] This report examined a selected set of items from the M1 Abrams tank. The analysis found that foreign subcontracting occurred for each of these items, which included: (1) a portion of the seal connecting the engine and the air intake system; (2) the ammunition storage racks; (3) an extrusion used in the louvers of the tank's ballistic doors; (4) the optical glass in the gunner's primary sight; and (5) the tank's ballistic computer. The Canadian company that built the ballistic computer was also found to rely on foreign subcontracting for a number of core technologies and components.[31]

A 1989 analysis by the Center for Strategic and International Studies examined statistics on import penetration of key industrial sectors that the DoD heavily depends upon as a means of gauging the extent of foreign sourcing specifically in the defense sector. This approach had the principal advantage of having comprehensive statistics available and the key shortcoming of not providing a direct measure of foreign sourcing specifically in the defense sector. In this study, import penetration in the defense industrial base "was observed to have grown between 1980 and 1986 in 104 of 122 critical defense sectors for which data are available." It also found that "in 1980, and again in 1986, 52 critical defense sectors had import concentration greater than US manufacturing as a whole."[32] This examination discovered that the "greatest import penetration is in the components and subassemblies tier, with nearly 19 percent of domestic consumption coming from foreign sources in 1986."[33]

Among the major analyses of foreign sourcing conducted during this period, the principal outlier to the preceding characterization of internationalization of U.S. defense production is a National Defense University study of precision guided munitions (PGMs) undertaken in 1987. This analysis concluded that sourcing outside of Canada and the United States accounted for only 2 percent of the total value of procurements for PGMs.[34] What accounts for the discrepancy between this report's conclusion and that of other analyses? One possibility is

[28] OTA 1991, 69.
[29] OTA 1988, 15.
[30] GAO 1991, 2.
[31] GAO 1991, 18–21.
[32] CSIS 1989, 38.
[33] CSIS 1989, 37.
[34] Libicki, Nunn, and Taylor 1987, 109.

that PGMs have a different set of production requirements from other kinds of weapons systems. A more likely possibility is that this PGM study was specifically focused on the top level of production, centering on prime contractors.[35] As the next section reveals, the globalization of production in U.S. weapons systems occurred to the greatest extent in dual-use industries in the lower tiers of production. Analyses that do not examine lower-tier suppliers, such as the PGM study, are therefore likely to underestimate the extent of internationalization in U.S. weapons systems production.

Analysis of International Subcontracting in U.S. Weapons Production

Although useful, the various studies reviewed above do not provide specific figures concerning the extent of foreign sourcing at the subcontractor level of weapons production—that is, foreign sourcing at the level below prime contractors. This lack of information is more than just a minor problem: during the late 1980s, the DoD estimated that "materials and components purchased by prime contractors from lower-tier industries represent 50 to 85 percent of our total expenditures."[36]

There is a simple reason why the studies just examined did not have concrete figures concerning the precise extent of foreign subcontracting: keeping track of the scores of firms that are subcontracted for each weapon system is a daunting exercise given the great complexity of most modern systems. As one industry group noted recently, it is virtually impossible for firms involved in defense production "to create, much less certify, an authoritative list of countries of origin of the hundreds or sometimes thousands of discrete components in a particular computer or telecommunications switch or radar control unit."[37] The complexity and difficulty of this task notwithstanding, the DoD was regularly criticized by Congress and the GAO in the middle and late 1980s for not gathering such information.[38] In 1988, the Commerce Department responded to this gap by undertaking "the first known comprehensive analysis of sourcing by weapons system at lower tier subcontractor levels, both domestic and foreign."[39]

As was briefly described in chapter 3, this landmark Commerce study examined three weapons systems—the HARM missile, the Mark-48 ADCAP torpedo, and the Verdin communication system—that were chosen as "representative" weapons used by the U.S. Navy.[40] If one defines the revolution in

---

[35] Libicki, Nunn, and Taylor 1987, 45.
[36] DOD 1988, 156.
[37] Information Technologies Association of America 2003, 3–4.
[38] See, for example, GAO 1989; and DOD 1988.
[39] Commerce 1992, 8. For a similar assessment, see Blackwell 1992, 197.
[40] Commerce 1992, i.

military affairs (RMA) as a process by which "the application of information technology is bringing about a change in the practice of warfare,"[41] then the three weapons surveyed represent a continuum between traditional systems and RMA systems, since they vary in their reliance upon information technology. Of the three systems, the most traditional is the Mark-48, a torpedo with a six-hundred-pound warhead that is used on both attack and strategic submarines.[42] The system most reliant on information technology is the "electronics-intensive" Verdin, "a shore-to-ship transmit/receive communications system designed to provide reliable, secure, single and multi-channel communications in the very low/low frequency range with US submarines."[43] It is deployed on strategic missile submarines, ships, and the E-6A aircraft (an airborne command, control, and communications platform).[44] Finally, somewhere between these two systems is the HARM missile, "a high-speed antiradiation surface missile that is designed to suppress and destroy enemy radar defense systems." It is deployed on a range of U.S. fighter jets.[45] It should be noted that the Commerce study examined only the HARM missile itself (rocket motor, warhead, etc.). It did not examine the launch computer and associated software for the HARM system—which receives data about the target, processes it, determines target priority, and so on—which are separate from the missile and installed directly on the airframe.

Beyond providing a detailed portrait of the extent of foreign sourcing at the subcontractor level, two very important general findings emerged from this Commerce study. The first general finding, concerning the incredible complexity and scope of the production chain for modern weaponry, was already highlighted in chapter 3. It is worth repeating again here. For just these three weapon systems, a total of "15,000 companies were identified at the subcontractor level, with 11,638 companies still serving as active suppliers to the prime contractors."[46]

The second general finding concerned dual-use industries. The Commerce study revealed that the farther one moved down the supplier chain, the more prevalent such industries became. Specifically, the analysis found that "the percentage of total shipments for defense applications decreased by tier—with 28 percent of second tier shipments but only 7.5 percent of third tier shipments destined for defense applications."[47] For reasons already stressed, this means that looking at defense prime contractors alone will lead analysts to underestimate the extent of internationalization in weapons systems production. In turn,

---

[41] For this definition, see Orme 1997, 145; see also the references cited therein.
[42] Commerce 1992, 12.
[43] Commerce 1992, iii.
[44] Commerce 1992, 14.
[45] Commerce 1992, 9.
[46] Commerce 1992, 6.
[47] Commerce 1992, ii.

this pattern indicates why monitoring the extent of globalization of weapons systems is such a daunting exercise, since keeping track of lower-tier suppliers is difficult.

The study's primary focus was to identify foreign-sourced items, which were defined as "materials, parts, components, or subassemblies manufactured, assembled, or otherwise processed outside of the United States."[48] As in most other studies of this issue, "foreign subcontracting" is thus a general category that lumps together (1) international outsourcing to third-party firms and (2) items obtained from a foreign affiliate of a U.S.-based MNC. In the aggregate for the three weapon systems, the Commerce study revealed that foreign subcontracting accounted for 13 percent of all procurement at the subcontractor level in 1988 (10 percent of second-tier procurements and 14 percent of third-tier procurements).[49]

Given the significance of information technology in most RMA systems and the fact that information technology is one of the sectors in which production became most internationalized in the 1980s, one might expect that the extent of globalization of production of the three weapons systems would reflect where they fell on the traditional-RMA continuum. This is indeed the case. The Commerce study found that the Mark-48 torpedo was the least globalized of the three systems, with around 5 percent of procurements going to foreign subcontractors at both the second tier and third tier. The next most globalized weapons system was the HARM missile, with foreign firms accounting for 5 percent of second-tier subcontracting and 18 percent of third-tier subcontractors. Finally, the "electronics-intensive" Verdin was the most globalized of the three, with 40 percent of second-tier procurements going to foreign subcontractors.[50]

From the Commerce study one can gain a sense of the extent and nature of foreign subcontracting for weapons systems. In total, the Verdin system drew on 163 foreign subcontractors from 26 different countries: Australia, Austria, Brazil, Canada, Denmark, Finland, France, Germany, Hong Kong,

---

[48] Commerce 1992, 4.

[49] Commerce 1992, 50, 32.

[50] Commerce 1992, iii. Figures for third-tier foreign subcontracting for the Verdin are unclear. The study reports that "*Identified* third-tier foreign sources for the Verdin declined to 16 percent of total purchases" (Commerce 1992, iii; emphasis added). However, the report outlines several reasons why this is very likely a significant underestimate. In the Commerce study, the "trail" of foreign subcontracting stopped with the first identified foreign firm in the production chain: "While information on foreign sources was gathered at each tier, these foreign firms were not surveyed because Department of Commerce mandatory information collection authority does not extend beyond United States borders" (Commerce 1992, 16). As a result, the report notes that "the large number of foreign second tier Verdin suppliers [52 in total] could not be surveyed in order to identify their third tier suppliers" (16, iii). Many of these foreign firms probably subcontracted to other foreign firms, since, as the Commerce study points out, "foreign suppliers . . . likely had a greater tendency to make use of non-U.S. lower-tier suppliers" (ii). In the end, therefore, it impossible to know the extent of third-tier foreign subcontracting for the Verdin.

India, Ireland, Italy, Japan, Malaysia, Mexico, Philippines, Singapore, South
Africa, South Korea, Sweden, Switzerland, Taiwan, Thailand, United Kingdom, Zaire, and Zimbabwe.[51] A very wide range of components and technologies were secured via foreign subcontracting from these 26 countries. While
too expansive to fully list here, these include ceramic packaging and ceramic
piece parts from Japan; capacitors, resistor ceramic cores, cathode foil, and resistor caps from Germany; silicon wafers from Denmark; electronic components from Hong Kong; transistors from South Korea; ceramic bases and lids
from Singapore; woven fiberglass, burn-in services, and diodes from Taiwan;
castings from Canada; machine components from Switzerland; and linear actuators and various electronics from the United Kingdom.[52]

THE SCOPE OF U.S. GAINS FROM THE
GLOBALIZATION OF WEAPONS PRODUCTION

The previous section revealed that during the final phase of the Cold War, U.S.
defense production shifted to become significantly internationalized. The high-
stakes competition with the Soviet Union continued, as did the strong preference of U.S. defense policymakers for domestic defense production, other
things being equal; as a result, we would expect this shift to occur only if there
were significant gains to be accrued from internationalization. The first portion
of this section provides a portrait of the scope of the gains the United States
was able to reap by moving away from its long-standing autarkic course in
defense production. The second portion examines whether U.S. defense policymakers did, in fact, recognize the economic gains associated with moving
toward internationalization and promoted globalization of defense-related
production based on this assessment.

The Scope of Gains

For a series of overlapping reasons, we would expect U.S. firms involved in defense production to avoid significant internationalization during the 1970s and
1980s: (1) various government policies designed to favor domestic production,[53] (2) direct political pressure against internationalization by Congress,[54]
(3) continued strong DoD preference for domestic sources, other things being
equal,[55] and (4) the fact that U.S.-based defense companies had, for decades,

---

[51] See Commerce 1992, 16, 53–63.
[52] See Commerce 1992, 53–63.
[53] See, for example, DoD 1989; OTA 1990, 10, 28–30; and Graham and Krugman 1991, 115.
[54] See, for example, DoD 1989, 17.
[55] See, for example, OTA 1990, 29.

been able to avoid heavy reliance on foreign sourcing and many preferred not to have to move in that direction.[56] Given these various incentives, the fact that U.S. defense production became internationalized to a significant degree suggests that globalization offered substantial advantages for U.S. defense firms.

In this respect, it is not surprising that studies reveal that numerous U.S. defense contractors did strongly support policies that gave them freedom to pursue internationalization. A 1990 OTA study, for example, reports that "the large aerospace and electronic defense companies, among others, favor policies that promote international collaboration, because it gives them the flexibility to team, subcontract, and form alliances with suppliers and partners around the world."[57] This same analysis cites one top defense executive as noting: "The best thing the government could do for our international business would be to get out of the way."[58] In a more recent study, the Aerospace Industries Association underscores that restrictions on the ability of U.S. defense contractors to pursue internationalization would mean that "the Defense Department would have to pay more for its products and wouldn't have access to the most advanced electronics and information technologies. . . . Defense transformation and the acquisition of new technologies could be drastically slowed or curtailed. . . . An inefficient technology base serving defense only may have to be constituted at great expense in funding and time. The long-term result would be less equipment and technology in the hands of the war fighters."[59]

Critics might respond that while there were gains from enhanced globalization of defense-related production in the final phase of the Cold War, they may have been relatively minor. Looking at the results of the Commerce study, they might agree that the extensive level of foreign sourcing in the Verdin indicates the presence of substantial gains from pursuing internationalization for this system, but would likely note that the other two weapons systems examined had a much lower level of foreign sourcing. This objection points to a substantial weakness of the Commerce study: while the specific items obtained through foreign subcontracting are identified, there is no systematic way to gauge their collective importance other than to look at the aggregate amount of procurement dollars devoted to foreign subcontracting or the total number of foreign subcontractors as a proportion of all subcontractors. These are obviously very crude measures. From a military competitiveness standpoint, what exactly

---

[56] As Norman Augustine, the chairmen of Lockheed Martin, noted, "We don't always see eye to eye with our allies, so it's difficult to be over-dependent on them" (*Economist*, 17 June 1997, Survey, 4). At this time, some U.S. defense contractors had explicit rules against strongly relying on foreign sourcing. McDonnell Douglas, for example, had in 1991 a " '50 percent' rule which requires that 50 percent of the structural components, such as wings or fuselage pieces, be domestically sourced" (GAO 1991, 17). See also the discussion in OTA 1990, 33.

[57] OTA 1990, 11.

[58] OTA 1990, 27.

[59] Aerospace Industries Association 2003, 1, 2–3.

does it mean, for example, that foreign subcontracting accounted for 5 percent of the HARM missile's second-tier procurement dollars and 18 percent of third-tier procurement dollars, or that foreign subcontractors accounted for 712 out of the 6,818 identified subcontractors? On the one hand, foreign subcontracting for the HARM missile does not account for anywhere near the majority of the total procurement dollars or number of contributing companies. On the other hand, the substantive importance of the components, technologies, and materials obtained through foreign subcontracting might be much greater than these general numbers imply. In more concrete terms, how important is it that foreign subcontracting could be used to secure items such as ceramic packaging, ceramic piece parts, semiconductors, resistor cores, silicon ingots, magnetic cores, and UV lenses from Japan; wiring boards and various electronics from Canada; linear actuators, rocket motor cases, gear motors, and various electronics from the United Kingdom; silicon wafers from Denmark and Italy; resistor end caps from France; machine parts, carbide bearings, and semiconductors from Switzerland; CMOS wafers and electrolytic capacitors from Taiwan; polpropylene film from France; needle roller bearing and silicon carbide shapes from Sweden; and castings, capacitors, ceramic substrates, cathode foil, resistors, X-ray technology, and polycarbonate base capacitor film from Germany? What would the direct and indirect costs have been in the hypothetical scenario in which U.S. domestic sourcing had been pursued—whether due to protectionist restrictions or some other constraint—for these and all other foreign-sourced items used in the production of the HARM missile?

When gauging the potential cost of the United States going it alone in defense production, it is important to remember that weapons platforms declined in significance during the final phase of the Cold War. As Eliot Cohen underscores: "The platform has become much less important, while the quality of what it carries—sensors, munitions, and electronics of all kinds—has become critical. A modernized 30-year-old aircraft armed with the latest long-range air-to-air missile, cued by an airborne warning plane, can defeat a craft a third its age but not equipped or guided."[60] Why does this matter for assessing the U.S. gains to be accrued by pursuing globalization? During the final phase of the Cold War, it does not appear that production was internationalized to a significant degree with respect to U.S. weapons platforms. All the evidence does indicate, however, that U.S. defense production became globalized to a significant degree with respect to the sensors, electronics, new materials, information technology, and other "add-ons" produced by lower-tier subcontractors and grafted onto weapons platforms. The important point is that even though the production of U.S. weapons platforms was not globalized significantly during the 1980s, this does not mean U.S. gains from pursuing internationalization were not substantial, for the simple reason that it is the lower tiers of production

[60] Cohen 1996, 45.

that "develop much of the innovative and leading-edge technologies" in modern weaponry.[61]

The M1 tank is instructive on this score. The M1 was designed and developed in the 1970s and underwent substantial technological upgrading during the 1980s. As noted previously, the 1991 GAO study that examined the extent of foreign sourcing in the upgraded version of the M1 tank examined only a few elements of its production. However, even just the finding that foreign subcontracting existed for its optical sight and ballistic computer is very significant. As was demonstrated in the 1991 Gulf War, these technologies gave the M1 a decisive advantage over the most advanced Iraqi tanks.[62] With its advanced computer-guided firing mechanism, the M1's 120 mm cannon (which, it should be noted, was itself designed by the Rheinmetall Corporation of Germany) was able to destroy Iraqi tanks from 4 km away and to regularly score first-round hits of Iraqi tanks from three kilometers.[63] The Iraqi T-72 simply did not have the commensurate capacity. The M1's advanced sights also gave it a marked advantage in detection over the T-72: the M1 could detect T-72s from four times the distance that the latter could detect the former.[64] As a result of these two technological advantages, M1 tanks could "detect and destroy Iraqi vehicles from *outside* the Iraqis' maximum range."[65] The decisive battlefield significance of these foreign-sourced items in the M1 is hardly atypical. As one analysis concludes: "Foreign purchases . . . often involve the very parts that make weapons perform. For example, FMC Corp.'s Bradley fighting vehicle depends on a sophisticated sensor system from the Netherlands to inform soldiers of potential threats and targets. Without this part tucked into the turret of the armored vehicle, the Bradley would be comparatively helpless on the battlefield."[66]

Of course, even if foreign-sourced items have a crucial influence on the battlefield effectiveness of weapons, a critic might argue that it was not necessary for the United States to find foreign sources for these components. Fortunately, the Commerce study sheds light on this issue: it undertook a detailed survey (the first—and to this author's knowledge, the last—of its kind) that assessed the motivations of U.S. firms for engaging in foreign subcontracting in defense production. The most important reason for relying on foreign subcontracting (cited by 53 percent of the respondents in the Commerce survey) is that no known U.S. supplier existed. Foreign subcontracting when there is no U.S. supplier is not surprising. More puzzling is why foreign subcontracting occurred when a potential U.S. source existed. In the Commerce survey, by far the most frequently cited reason (mentioned by more than 33 percent of

[61] OTA 1990, 28.

[62] See the discussion in Bonsignore 1992; Press 1997, 2001, 37; and Held and Sunoski 1993, 6.

[63] Press 2001, 37; and Held and Sunoski 1993, 6.

[64] Press 2001, 37; see also Bonsignore 1992; and Press 1997, 139.

[65] Press 1997, 139.

[66] *Wall Street Journal*, 24 March 1988.

respondents) for choosing a foreign-based supplier over a domestic supplier was, "Foreign source produces a higher quality item."[67] The next most cited motivation for making this choice (cited by 23 percent of respondents) was, "Foreign source offers item at a lower price."[68]

The Commerce survey thus clearly shows that U.S. firms did not undertake foreign sourcing in defense production during the 1980s for capricious reasons, but rather to meet concrete needs. This result indicates that the costs and difficulty of moving toward domestic sourcing for all of the items necessary for weapons systems such as the HARM missile would be very significant. The difficulty of moving away from foreign subcontracting becomes even more apparent when we consider weapons systems collectively. For production of the HARM missile alone, 712 foreign-based suppliers would have to be replaced (in addition to an unknown number of foreign-based suppliers for the launch computer and associated software). Taking this approach simultaneously for all U.S. weapons systems would have involved thousands of foreign suppliers.

The Commerce study demonstrates that modern weapon systems have such complex production chains that the degree of foreign sourcing cannot be determined without a detailed analysis of all tiers of suppliers. Duplicating the effort of the Commerce study for U.S. defense production in its entirety would be nearly impossible.[69] Even the Commerce study could not determine the full extent of foreign sourcing, since it was unable to track when foreign subcontractors themselves engaged in international subcontracting. At any rate, no additional analyses along the lines of the Commerce study were undertaken for defense production during the 1980s. For this reason, it is impossible to know in what areas U.S.-based firms actually did rely on foreign sourcing for defense-related production during this period; we therefore cannot reach any kind of precise assessment of exactly how much the United States gained in the aggregate by moving toward openness in defense production. The best indicator in this regard is an analysis conducted by the DoD in 1990—the Critical Technologies Plan (CTP)—which revealed a wide range of technologies for which foreign sourcing offered significant potential gains for U.S. weapons production.

The CTP examined the 20 technologies considered most critical to the "qualitative superiority of United States weapons systems."[70] These technologies were divided into three levels of priority, although the report stresses that "since these 20 critical technologies are already those selected as 'most essential' . . . the further prioritization should not be overemphasized."[71] The

---

[67] Commerce 1992, 64–65.

[68] Commerce 1992, 64. Reasons 3 through 7 as cited by firms are as follows: (3) "Foreign source used to supplement domestic sources"; (4) "Item is imported as part of a global marketing strategy"; (5) "Foreign sources provide quicker delivery"; (6) "Other sourcing reasons"; and (7) "Item is imported as a result of an 'offset agreement.'"

[69] See the discussion in OTA 1990, 35.

[70] DoD 1990, ES-1

[71] DoD 1990, ES-2.

first category—"most pervasive technologies"—consists of those considered most critical.[72] Eight general technologies were included: composite materials; computational fluid dynamics; data fusion; passive sensors; photonics; semiconductor materials and microelectronic circuits; signal processing; and software producibility. A second category—"enabling technologies"—consists of technologies that "offer the most immediate advances in weapons systems capabilities." It included general technologies: air-breathing propulsion; machine intelligence and robotics; parallel computer architectures; sensitive radars; signature control; simulation and modeling; and weapon system environment. The remaining five technologies fell in a third category—"principally emerging technologies"—which is irrelevant for the analysis in this chapter since it is comprised of those technologies that, as of 1990, had only future applications.[73] This third category of technologies will therefore not be addressed in the discussion that follows.

Within each of the twenty technological categories, the CTP looked at a series of more specific technologies and for each assessed "the capability of others to contribute to the technology." The capability of foreign contribution was evaluated using the following four-point scale: (4) other countries are significantly ahead in some niches of technology; (3) other countries are capable of making major contributions; (2) other countries are capable of making some contributions; and (1) other countries are unlikely to have any immediate contribution. It is unlikely that those technologies receiving a score of 1 or 2 would involve extensive foreign sourcing; at any rate, using foreign sources would not provide significant gains for the United States. In contrast, technologies receiving a score of 3 or 4 were likely to involve significant foreign sourcing and to also offer large potential gains.

Table 4.1 shows the technologies the CTP rated 3 or 4. Each specific technology is listed below a broader technological category (the first six general technological categories are from the "most pervasive" category, the remainder from the "enabling" category). The country or alliance having superiority or being capable of making major contributions is noted in parentheses. Table 4.1 is the best snapshot available of the key defense-related technologies in which globalization offered significant potential advantages for U.S.-based firms during the 1980s.

In reading through table 4.1, one should note that the CTP undercounts the number of technologies in which globalization offered significant potential gains for U.S. defense production, since the report evaluates technological competitiveness on a country-by-country basis rather than at the level of firms. Yet in many defense-related sectors, it is likely that U.S.-based firms attained strong technological capacity in part by participating in interfirm alliances with MNCs based in other countries or by establishing or upgrading foreign affiliates abroad.

[72] DoD 1990, ES-2.
[73] DoD 1990, 7.

TABLE 4.1

1990 DoD Assessment of Key Defense-Related Technologies in Which
Globalization Offered Significant Advantages

Photonics
  1. Increased volume production of high-power laser diode rays (Japan)
  2. Greater than 2 Gibit LAN (Local Area Network) (NATO and Japan)
  3. Ultra low-loss (less than 0.001 db/km) fibers (Japan)
  4. Research in photonics, bistable devices, other specific components (Japan and
     NATO)
  5. Increased volume production of high-power laser diode rays
     (NATO)
  6. Development of optical interconnects, including fiber optic backplanes
     (Japan)

Passive sensors
  1. Material processing and fabrication of large-scale detector arrays
     (NATO and Japan)
  2. Fiber Optic Sensor System (Japan)

Semiconductor materials and microelectronic circuits
  1. VLSI/VHSIC <0.3 micron features size (Japan)
  2. Implementation of Bi-CMOS and GaAs MMIC circuits (Japan)
  3. Bulk or epitaxial growth of compound semiconductor materials
     (Japan and NATO)
  4. Radiation hardening (Japan)

Data fusion
  1. Enhanced man/machine interface, rapid assimilation and processing of large data
     sets (Japan and NATO)
  2. Real-time OS for secure distributed processing (NATO)
  3. Intelligent data extraction from text; pattern recognition (including application
     of neural nets) (Japan)

Signal processing
  1. Application of massively parallel processors and neural networks to
     signal processing (Japan)

Software producibility
  1. Enhanced software development environments (Japan and NATO)
  2. Algorithms, languages, and tools for advanced parallel architectures
     (Japan)

Machine intelligence and robotics
  1. Application of advanced structural materials to robots (having high dynamic
     loads or required to operate in hostile environments) (Japan)
  2. Integration of smart sensors and improved actuators (Japan)
  3. Development of specialized techniques for AI applications of advanced
     processing architectures (NATO and Japan)
  4. Practical telecontrol of military vehicles (NATO)

TABLE 4.1 (*Continued*)

5. Application of advanced structural materials to robots (having high dynamic loads or required to operate in hostile environments) (NATO and Japan)
6. Integration of smart sensors and improved actuators (NATO)

Simulation and modeling
1. Effective application of advanced computing architectures to real-time and faster-than-real-time simulation of complex situations/environments (Japan)
2. Development of numerical algorithms for modeling of nonlinear processes on advanced computing architectures (NATO and Japan)
3. Development and empirical validation of physical models of materials (including material reaction to extreme conditions) (Japan)

Weapon system environment
1. Effective integration of remote sensing data (NATO)
2. Accurate predictions of localized weather conditions (NATO)
3. Undersea acoustic research, especially that correlated with bathymetry data (NATO)

Air-Breathing propulsion
1. Development and design integration of lightweight/high-temperature/ high-strength materials (NATO and Japan)
2. Reduction of observables in high temperature air-breathing propulsion systems (NATO and Japan)

Parallel computer architectures
1. Improved packaging (including interconnect and thermal management) and massively parallel hardware (Japan)
2. Development of software and development tools to exploit massive parallelism (NATO and Japan)

Sensitive radars
1. Beam steering, application or coherent laser diodes, laser radar (Japan)
2. Active element arrays conformal antennas (Japan)

Signature control
1. Structural RAM components and ferrites/polymer composites (Japan)
2. Helicopter acoustic signature reduction (NATO)

Composite materials
1. Development of composite materials capable of retaining structural properties at high temperature (NATO and Japan)
2. Application of structural composites to reduce observables (NATO and Israel)
3. Development of improved NDE techniques for advanced composites (NATO and Japan)
4. Improved characterization of composite material response to weapon effects (NATO)
5. Improved modeling and prediction of life cycle failure (NATO and Japan)

Source: DoD 1990.

Recognition of the Gains of Internationalization
by U.S. Defense Policymakers

In light of the evidence presented here, we would expect to find a strong recognition within the DoD that restricting internationalization would increase the cost and reduce the quality of U.S. weapons. This is indeed the case. As one prominent DoD analysis conducted in 1988 concluded: "As a nation and as a continent, we no longer are totally self-sufficient in all essential material or industries required to maintain a strong national defense. . . . The United States could not build fortress America, even if this were a desirable objective. Nor could the Department of Defense reverse worldwide economic trends, such as the internationalization of manufacturing."[74]

In an interview, then secretary of defense Dick Cheney similarly stressed that buying exclusively from U.S.-based companies "would be nice if it were possible," but noted that using domestic sources only would mean "spending money on things that I could get cheaper elsewhere, and it raises the specter of having to rely upon less than first-rate technologies." It would be impractical for a defense firm to "only buy from American suppliers," Cheney remarked, "if by going to the international market they can acquire capability or quality or price that they can't get here at home."[75]

The clearest indication, however, of recognition within DoD that an autarkic U.S. defense-production strategy held significant disadvantages are the studies during the 1980s that examined the consequences of congressional restrictions on the ability of U.S. defense firms to use foreign sourcing. The rapid increase in foreign sourcing within U.S. defense production in the 1980s hurt uncompetitive U.S.-based defense suppliers, who called upon Congress to enact "Buy American" restrictions. Congress responded by sharply increasing the number of Buy American restrictions: 18 restrictions were added during the 1980s to the 8 that were in place prior to 1980.[76] This rapid increase was the catalyst for DoD studies on the consequences of relying on domestic sourcing for defense production.

Two initial DoD studies conducted in 1986 both concluded that congressional efforts to mandate the exclusive use domestic sources would have unfavorable

---

[74] DoD 1988, 192, 155.

[75] As quoted in *Aerospace Daily*, 23 January 1992. This basic assessment is also reflected in the numerous statements from DoD officials that stressed the advantages of greater collaboration on defense-related production within NATO; see, for example, Carlucci 1988, who notes (9) that taking this route would "improve U.S. and allied defense capabilities and operation effectiveness by access to, and use of, and protection of the best technology to meet military requirements." See also Moodie and Fischmann 1990 for a useful overview of various DoD reports issued during the 1980s that make this point.

[76] See DoD 1989, 15–22.

effects on the quality and cost of weapons systems and would not be in the interests of the DoD.[77] In 1989, the DoD completed a comprehensive analysis of Buy American restrictions and issued a sharply critical assessment.[78] This report found that negative effects of the restrictions included "procurement and delivery delays when domestic products are not available," "cost increases for DoD procurements," and "impediments to technological cooperation with US allies and to the flow of modern technology to the United States."[79] On the subject of technology, the report noted further: "To remain competitive, US industry must have access to technology developed by our allies. . . . Other nations have made significant accomplishments in high technology that would greatly benefit US industrial competitiveness and weapons capabilities."[80] In the end, the report's main recommendation was "that most congressionally mandated Buy American restrictions be abolished" and, in turn, that "Congress should avoid future use of Buy American restrictions in procurement."[81]

It is thus clear that U.S. defense policymakers recognized the strong gains associated with globalization in weapons production. Of course, recognizing this benefit is one thing; taking actions based on it is something altogether different. Other things being equal, U.S. defense policymakers strongly preferred to be self-sufficient in defense production; their doing nothing appreciable to block the rapidly growing internationalization of U.S. defense-related production during this period is therefore telling.

The DoD did not simply refrain from blocking the globalization of U.S. defense-related production; it also took direct actions to facilitate it. This is most apparent with respect to the Buy American restrictions just discussed. As the 1989 report makes clear, the DoD was concerned about efforts to restrain international sourcing, and it put pressure on Congress to refrain from creating Buy American restrictions.[82] Moreover, the DoD took active steps to circumvent those restrictions already in place. In response to DoD concerns, Congress allowed numerous exceptions to Buy American restrictions and granted the secretary of defense the authority to issue waivers. During the 1980s, the DoD rigorously exploited these loopholes. In an analysis of Buy American restrictions affecting the F/A-18 aircraft and the M1 Abrams tank, the GAO found that "they are of limited impact because of the many exceptions allowed.[83] James Blackwell similarly concludes that the DoD successfully avoided Buy American restrictions by securing "waivers and exceptions for a variety of

[77] See Vawter 1986, 16–17 and 22–24 for an analysis of these two 1986 DoD studies.
[78] DoD 1989.
[79] DoD 1989, 35.
[80] DoD 1989, 11.
[81] DoD 1989, 12
[82] See, for example, the discussion in Haglund and Busch 1990, 248; and *Wall Street Journal*, 24 March 1988.
[83] GAO 1991, 6.

reasons, including price, quality, and availability."[84] In fact, the DoD's circumvention of these restrictions during the 1980s was so comprehensive that one industry association brought suit in 1988 against the DoD to try to force it to comply with the Buy American Act.[85]

THE GLOBALIZATION OF PRODUCTION AND ENHANCED U.S. MILITARY TECHNOLOGICAL COMPETITIVENESS

This final section is devoted to examining the effect of the increased level of internationalization of U.S. defense production. Ideally, we would be able to compare U.S. military technological competitiveness during this period with another state that (1) remained wedded to autarkic defense production; (2) strove to remain on the cutting edge in military technology; (3) was of the same economic size; and (4) had identical domestic technological capacity. The only state that comes close to meeting these conditions is the Soviet Union. It is clear that the Soviet Union strongly meets the first two conditions. Concerning the third condition, the Soviet Union was only around 60 percent the size of the U.S. economy in 1970.[86] In defense-related production, however, the Soviet Union more than made up for its smaller economic size by draining the civilian economy and devoting massive resources to weapons development.[87] Taking this route, the Soviet Union actually exceeded the United States in some important areas of defense production capacity, most notably military R&D. The CIA estimates that the Soviet Union's total spending on military R&D was twice the U.S. level in 1980.[88] In the end, therefore, the Soviet Union and the United States were not dissimilar in terms of size of defense-related production.

It was in the fourth condition, domestic technological capacity, that the two countries differed most dramatically: the economic structure of the United States gave it a leg up in technological innovation over the Soviet Union. For the economy as a whole, the two countries were night and day with respect to innovation.[89] With respect to innovation in defense production, however, the difference between the two countries was not nearly so great, at least until the early 1980s.[90] Their respective approaches to production were also more similar

[84] Blackwell 1992, 197.

[85] OTA 1990, 84; see also Blackwell 1992, 197.

[86] See Brooks and Wohlforth 2000–2001, 21.

[87] See, for example, Gaddy 1997.

[88] CIA 1983, 1. A later CIA analysis found that the Soviets devoted about 4 percent of GNP to military R&D in the late 1980s and that the comparable figure for the US at this time was 0.7 percent of GNP (CIA 1991, 2).

[89] See, for example, Deudney and Ikenberry 1991.

[90] See, for example, Holloway 1982; Burghart 1992, 37; Smith 1983, 73; and Campbell 1972, 606. See also Evangelista's comprehensive survey of weapons innovation in the Soviet Union and United States, which finds that domestic structure gave each side advantages and the net result was

with respect to defense than for any other sector. On the U.S. side, it is in defense production that the country was arguably most economically centralized: decisions about what to produce, who would produce, and how they would produce were made by the federal government to a greater degree than probably any other sector.[91] As for the Soviets, the defense sector was substantially insulated from the problems that typically plagued their command economic structure:

> In the defense sector of the USSR, the main barriers to innovation in the Soviet economy—insufficient resource, taut plan targets, and problems of interdepartmental coordination—are substantially minimized. . . . Not only do Soviet defense industries receive first priority in the procurement of personnel and materials, but supply arrangements are more dependable, thus eliminating a major source of uncertainty that impedes innovation. Taut production targets, which in the civilian sector create a reluctance to introduce new processes or products, do not hamper defense industries. . . . Soviet defense industries have been granted considerably more organizational flexibility than other sectors of the economy. In the high-technology fields of aviation and missile production, design bureaus are attached directly to experimental plants that produce prototypes, thus bridging the research/production chasm that plagues other industries. . . . Defense quality inspectors have the right to reject substandard goods, reinforcing the incentive to innovate and upgrade products.[92]

While the innovation gap between the Soviet Union and the United States was smaller in weapons production than in the economy as a whole, a gap nevertheless existed. For this reason, the Soviet Union would have had trouble keeping up with the United States in military technology even if it had abandoned autarkic defense production when the United States did and had participated in the globalization of production. Of course, the Soviet Union's command economic structure was a constant handicap throughout the Cold War. Of key interest, therefore, is the directional change during the 1980s: did Soviet isolation from the globalization of production make it *even more difficult* to remain competitive in military technology during this period?

Soviet Isolation from the Globalization of Production

During the 1970s and 1980s, U.S. defense firms and Soviet weapons producers took opposite paths in the globalization of production. While U.S. MNCs were

---

essentially a draw: while the "openness and decentralization of U.S. society encourage technological innovations in weaponry," the Soviet Union was ultimately able "to concentrate its resources and respond to U.S. initiatives in ways that ultimately redound to the disadvantage of both countries" (Evangelista 1988, 267).

[91] See, for example, Kapstein 1992, 26.

[92] Smith 1983, 73.

greatly expanding cooperative links with other international firms, Soviet enterprises remained isolated from international interfirm alliances.[93] U.S. MNCs were at the forefront in dispersing production throughout the globe to reap locational advantages; in comparison, the operations and supply networks of Soviet producers were almost completely confined to the Eastern bloc.[94] Soviet enterprises lacked the technological capacity or managerial experience to engage in international interfirm alliances or to geographically disperse production.[95] The Soviet enterprises' incapacity to engage in internationalization was, in turn, partly caused by a more general form of isolation from the globalization of production: lack of FDI.[96] During the 1980s, the Soviets remained isolated from FDI, while the United States grew rapidly as a host country: "the magnitude of direct investment in the United States doubled from 1980 to 1985, and again from 1985 to 1990."[97] One reflection of the surge of FDI into the United States during this period is that the foreign affiliate share of U.S. domestic manufacturing rose from 3.9 percent in 1980 to 14.8 percent in 1992.[98]

Lack of FDI meant that the Soviets had reduced access to the latest technologies and production methods from around the world and were instead largely dependent upon autonomous improvements. Of course, this was a longstanding handicap. However, this disadvantage increased in relative importance as the cost, complexity, and pace of technological development spiraled upwards and as the military competition with the United States shifted to weapons systems that depended upon rapid advances in microelectronics and other dual-use sectors.

Much the same story can be told about Soviet enterprises' lack of access to international interfirm alliances. While U.S. firms involved in defense-related production were multiplying their opportunities for technological innovation and reducing the risks and difficulty of R&D through interfirm alliances that spanned the entire globe, the Soviets could only draw upon the producers within the Eastern bloc. Thus, while U.S. MNCs were able to adapt to the microelectronics revolution and rapid general change in the parameters of technological development by increased global collaboration, Soviet enterprises did not have this strategy available.

The consequences of the inability of Soviet enterprises to geographically disperse production are not as clear-cut. The increasing tendency of U.S. firms

[93] Jones 1996, 144.

[94] Jones 1996, 46.

[95] Dunning 1993a, 74. A variety of studies have found that managerial and technological competence is a key prerequisite to engaging in global operations and FDI; see, for example, Pearce 1993.

[96] A range of analyses have found that a significant presence of MNCs within a country has strong learning and demonstration effects on domestic firms, showing them how to pursue internationalization; see, for example, Aitken, Hansen, and Harrson 1997.

[97] Feenstra 1999, 332.

[98] Held et al. 1999, 251.

involved in defense-related production to engage in international outsourcing and other geographic dispersion strategies during the 1980s was seen by many American defense analysts as a central concern.[99] To many contemporary observers, increased reliance upon foreign sources of supply generated only negative effects because of the loss of autonomy. Lost in these arguments about reduced autonomy is the fact that the gains the United States derived from globalizing defense production were a source of *relative* advantage over the Soviets. The Soviets could only wish for the "autonomy problems" the United States had. Instead of drawing upon the best global suppliers, as U.S. firms could, Soviet enterprises were forced to perform almost all of their technological development and production within the Eastern bloc. Only the United States had the luxury of worrying about a possible *long-term* loss of autonomy because it was so incredibly efficient; moreover, the legitimacy of these American fears of lost autonomy was always questionable, since there was no chance that Japan, West Germany and other key suppliers would switch sides in the Cold War. On the other front, the Soviets, as will be stressed below, were struggling to deploy the necessary weapons onto the field of engagement in the *short term*. It is important to bear in mind that short-term military readiness was of crucial importance to the Soviets, since all of their conventional war-fighting plans depended upon a quick initial victory over NATO forces. Once geographically dispersing production became a linchpin of many Western MNCs' strategies, the Soviets' lack of ability to do so became a significant handicap.

In sum, as the importance of dual-use industries and technologies grew in weapons production and as the productivity of U.S.-based firms in these sectors became increasingly tied to internationalization, one would expect a magnification of the difficulty the Soviets had in keeping up with the United States in military technology. Remaining economically isolated in the wake of ongoing changes in the structure of global production, did the Soviet Union have greater difficulty competing with the United States in military technology? This question is explored below.

The Growing Gap in Military Technology

There is widespread agreement that the Soviet Union's technological lag grew significantly during the 1980s.[100] Soon after assuming power, Gorbachev sternly "criticized his predecessors for failing to keep abreast of the faster-paced West in the scientific and technological revolution."[101] In a 1987 speech,

---

[99] For a discussion of the concerns created in the United States in the 1980s, see Moran 1990.

[100] I thank Bill Wohlforth for numerous helpful conversations about these issues as part of our research collaboration and for directing me to a number of these sources; see the related discussion in Brooks and Wohlforth 2000–2001, 25–26.

[101] Schmickle 1992, 30.

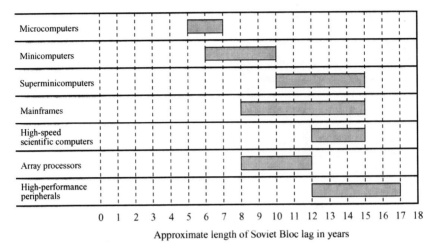

Figure 4.3 Lags in Soviet Computer Technology Relative to the West, 1989
Source: CIA 1989, 2.

he noted more pointedly, "In our country, scientific and technical progress is slowing down."[102] Comparisons on the basis of technological competitiveness— as opposed to older indicators that focused on raw industrial output, such as steel production—reveal that the Soviets were rapidly falling behind the United States and the West.[103] Soviet trade statistics tell a similar story. While the Soviets had been somewhat successful in exporting machinery and equipment to Western Europe in the 1970s, by the late 1980s only 2 percent of Soviet exports to the West were "of machinery and equipment and only 0.23 percent in high-tech goods."[104] At the same time, increasing amounts of Soviet imports (40 percent in 1986) were of machinery, and much of that consisted of technologically advanced machine tools that the Soviets could not produce themselves.[105]

A recently declassified CIA analysis reveals that the gap in Soviet computer technology vis-à-vis the West increased sharply beginning in the late 1970s. In mini/superminicomputers, the Western lead over the Soviets, which was around five years in the early and mid-1970s, increased to around seven years in the late 1970s and early 1980s, and grew further to around ten years by the middle and late 1980s.[106] Figure 4.3 shows the CIA's 1989 estimate of the extent of the Soviet lag relative to the West in various aspects of computer technology.

[102] As cited in Schroeder 1989, 47; see also the discussion in Bennett 1999, 270–72.

[103] See Wohlforth 1993, 242–43. For contemporary analyses by Western scholars of the increasing technological lag, see, for example, Cooper 1991; Judy and Clough 1989; Hanson and Pavitt 1987; and Winiecki 1988.

[104] Shmelev and Popov 1989, 226.

[105] Evangelista 1996, 171.

[106] See CIA 1989, 8.

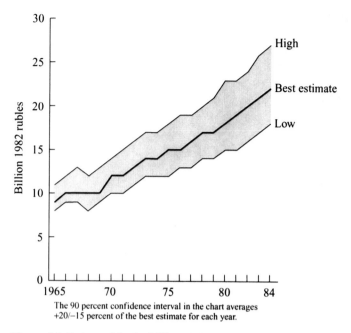

Figure 4.4 Estimated Soviet Military R&D Expenditures, 1965–1984
Source: Firth, and Noren 1998, 220.

What about military technology in particular? While hard data on military R&D inputs and outputs and overall efficiency are not available,[107] numerous analyses find that Soviet military technology became much less competitive in the 1980s.[108] As one leading analyst of Soviet technology sums up: "In the past the Soviet Union managed to match all Western revolutions in military technology: tanks and aviation in the prewar period, nuclear weapons in the 1940s, missiles in the 1950s, and the numerous improvements of the 1960s and 1970s. . . . In the 1980s the Soviet Union suffered a setback in an area in which it had previously been spectacularly successful: military competition with the West. . . . The boastful official cliché of 'a new correlation of forces in the world' gave way to the alarmist 'threat of becoming a second-rate power.' "[109]

Of particular significance is that the Soviets witnessed a steady decline in the productivity of their military R&D expenditures and, as a consequence, were compelled to shift more and more R&D expenditures from the civilian to the defense sector.[110] As figure 4.4 shows, Soviet military R&D expenditures

[107] See Kontorovich 1990, 264.

[108] See, for example, Gaddy 1997; Nichols 1993; Odom 1990; Herspring 1989; Friedberg 2000b; Ellman and Kontorovich 1998; Kontorovich 1990; and Cohen 1996.

[109] Kontorovich 1990, 255.

[110] Kontorovich 1990, 1992. These trends were clearly recognized by the CIA at the time; see, for example, CIA 1985b.

rose dramatically during the 1970–85 period—far faster than the rate of growth in the Soviet economy as a whole.[111]

In explaining why the Soviets were spending progressively more on military R&D but falling behind in weapons technology, many analysts highlight the increasing shift in the West to a new generation of conventional weapons based on dual-use technologies.

> It was becoming clear to Soviet military leaders that they were facing a third wave of new military technologies. The developments in micro-electronics, the semi-conductor revolution and its impact on computers, distributed processing, and digital communications were affecting many aspects of military equipment and weaponry . . . During his tenure as chief of the General Staff, Marshal Ogar-kov . . . was explicit in calling their impact yet another revolution in military af-fairs,[112] rivaling the change generated by nuclear weapons. Although doctrine and military planning moved quite far in adjusting to the potential of "advanced conventional munitions" as they are called, the large bureaucratic Soviet-military industrial-complex was proving unable to hold up its end. . . . Soviet military in-dustry has lost the competition to exploit technology for qualitatively superior weapons. . . . [The] new revolution in military affairs was demanding forces and weapons that the Soviet scientific-technological and industrial bases could not provide.[113]

U.S. intelligence analysts discerned that the Soviets were having increased difficulty remaining competitive in military technology in the 1980s because of the microelectronics revolution and other technological shifts.[114] "By the mid-1980s, US intelligence analysts were reporting that much of the overall Soviet disadvantage in advanced military technologies could be traced to failings in a handful of 'underlying technologies,' in particular, computers . . . microelec-tronics production techniques . . . and precision instrumentation to monitor ex-periments and control production."[115] The most detailed assessment of this kind is a recently declassified 1990 analysis by the CIA, which identified the "foundation technologies [that] are the key bottlenecks inhibiting Soviet progress in military-related production."[116] These are shown in table 4.2.

What is most striking about the list of sectors in table 4.2 is how much it overlaps the "most globalized" sectors identified in chapter 2. The key point is that a large proportion of the core defense-related technologies in which the

[111] For a review of the various estimates of Soviet economic growth during the 1970–85 period, see Brooks and Wohlforth 2000–2001, 14–21.

[112] The first so-called revolution in military affairs occurred in response to "the new techniques of aviation, motorization, and chemicals weapons that emerged in World War I. The advent of nuclear weapons brought about a second revolution" (Odom 1990, 55).

[113] Odom 1990, 52–53, 63–64.

[114] See, for example, CIA 1989, iii; 1987, 13.

[115] Friedberg 2000b, 296–97. A good overall treatment is CIA 1990.

[116] CIA 1990, 3.

TABLE 4.2
CIA Assessment of the Key Technological Bottlenecks Inhibiting Soviet
Progress in Military-Related Production, 1990

Microelectronics production equipments
  Automatic test equipment
    Logic circuit testers
    Memory circuit testers
  Material deposition equipment
    Plasma-enhanced chemical vapor deposition
    Metal-organic chemical vapor deposition
    Molecular beam epitaxy
    Chemical beam epitaxy
    Electron cyclotron resonance deposition
    Magnetically enhanced sputtering
  Computer-aided design equipment
  Lithography equipment
    Stepping mask aligners
    Electron beam lithography
    Ion beam lithography
    X-ray lithography
  Single-crystal compound semiconductor growth equipment
    High-pressure Czochralski
    Liquid encapsulated Czochralski
  Etching equipment
    Reactive ion etchers
    Reactive ion beam etchers
    Electron cyclotron resonance etchers
    Magnetically enhanced etchers
  Defect detection equipment
  Ion implantation equipment

Computers and peripherals
  High-performance computers
  Design technology and workstations
  Disk drives
  Manufacturing technology

Advanced manufacturing
  Computer numerically controlled machine tools
    High-precision machine tools
    Computer numerical controllers
  Precision turning machines
  High-accuracy measuring equipment
  Flexible manufacturing systems
  Robotics

(Continued)

TABLE 4.2 (*Continued*)

Telecommunications
    Fiber optics
    Repeaters
    Digital switches
    High data rate microwave

Advanced materials
    Fiber and filamentary materials
    Composite structures manufacturing
        Filament-winding equipment
        Tape-laying equipment
        Interlacing equipment
    Hot isostatic presses

Source: CIA 1990, 2.

Soviet Union fell furthest behind during the final phase of the Cold War are exactly those in which production became most geographically dispersed during the 1980s.

Within the Soviet Union itself, there was widespread recognition in the 1980s that the microelectronics revolution and other shifts in key dual-use sectors had created a new and difficult challenge for the Soviet defense industry. This is not to say there was a general perception that the entire current generation of conventional military technology (as of the mid-1980s) had become woefully uncompetitive with that of the West. This is not the case.[117] What a great number of Soviet policymakers and analysts, including many in the Soviet military, were anxious about was the *increasing difficulty* of keeping up with the United States.

While the Soviets were upbeat about their technological competitiveness in conventional weapons in the 1970s, there was growing pessimism by the 1980s.[118] The Soviet military foresaw "a steepening of the curve of technological progress that was both unprecedented and dangerous," and "military writers then began an all-out campaign of alarmism on the issue of conventional technologies in the early 1980s."[119] In the early 1980s, "the Soviets found their reading of the military future profoundly disheartening" because they realized that "their country, incapable of manufacturing a satisfactory personal computer, could not possibly keep up in an arms race driven by the information technologies."[120] On this score, General M. A. Gareev (former deputy chief of the General Staff who was in charge of military-scientific work in the General

---

[117] On this point, see, for example, Evangelista 1999.
[118] See, for example, Nichols 1993, 95–96.
[119] Nichols 1993, 115, 116.
[120] Cohen 1996, 39.

Staff in the late 1980s) noted pointedly: "Our inferiority in this area was manifest in our reconnaissance technologies, navigation equipment, target identification systems, electronic countermeasures, computers—all the equipment which uses electronics."[121] Many, including Marshal Ogarkov and others within the Soviet military, were particularly concerned about what would happen when the United States deployed its next generation high-tech conventional weapons, being developed in the 1980s, which truly took advantage of the microelectronics revolution.[122] As Col. Gen. Mikhail Moiseev noted, the United States was moving toward equipping "their armed forces with the kinds of weapons systems for which the search for countermeasures will demand many times more time and resources from the Soviet Union."[123]

The most recent evidence concerning Soviet hard-liners is also instructive. Even though they face strong incentives to argue that the Soviet Union was capable of continuing the military rivalry with the United States, most now hold that Moscow could not sustain the Cold War status quo.[124] An important example is Marshal Dmitry Yazov, who was defense minister under Gorbachev and also a leading figure in the August 1991 coup. When asked in a recent interview whether the Soviet Union had to get out of the Cold War, Yazov responded: "Absolutely. . . . We had to seek a dénouement. . . . We had to find an alternative to the arms race. . . . We had to continually negotiate, and reduce, reduce, reduce—especially the most expensive weaponry."[125]

Of principal concern to Soviet civilian policymakers during the 1980s was the opportunity cost of finding stop-gap remedies to match U.S. high-tech weapons.[126] The Soviet Union had previously been able to sustain competitiveness in military technology by draining the commercial economy in service of the military sector.[127] As a result, much of the country's resources in R&D and technological development were already being channeled into the military. The possibility that further increases would be necessary to remain technologically competitive in the arms race was a truly ominous prospect.[128] As Odom reports, "a surprisingly broad consensus existed among most of the Soviet elite that the Soviet economy was in serious trouble and that the burden of military expenditures was much to blame."[129] For this reason, many shared Gorbachev's

---

[121] Gareev as cited in Ellman and Kontorovich 1998, 63.

[122] See, for example, Nichols 1993, esp. 115–20; Odom 1990, 63; Fitzgerald 1987, 9–10; Heymann 1990, 97–98; Herspring 1990; and Kass and Boli 1990, 392.

[123] Moiseev as cited in Nichols 1993, 213.

[124] See the discussion in Brooks and Wohlforth 2000–2001, 42–29; and Brooks and Wohlforth 2002b, 104–10.

[125] This quote is drawn from Brooks and Wohlforth 2001, 46.

[126] See, for example, Gorbachev 1996, 215.

[127] Gaddy 1997, 56. See also Bleaney 1988, 73–74.

[128] See, for example, Gaddy 1997; Gorbachev 1996, 215, 564; Aslund 1989; Hewett 1988; Ellman and Kontorovich 1992; Lundestad 2000, 5–6; and Doc. No. 59 in National Security Archive 1998.

[129] Odom 1998, 115.

assessment concerning "the need to drastically reduce our defense budget—an indispensable condition for improving the economy."[130]

The Cost of Soviet Isolation from the Globalization of Production

If the Soviets' lack of ability to internationalize defense-related production and isolation from MNCs were having a negative influence on their ability to remain competitive in military technology during the 1980s, what would we expect to discover in the historical record? We would expect to find evidence of: (1) an awareness within the Soviet Union that the nature of global production was shifting and an acknowledgment by analysts and policymakers that isolation from Western firms and ongoing production changes in the global economy must be reversed to prevent the Soviet Union from becoming a second-rate technological power; (2) augmented efforts by policymakers to undertake politically and ideologically costly actions to augment access to Western MNCs as part of an effort to reverse the country's decline in key dual-use sectors such as computers; (3) strong support for increased openness to Western firms even among conservative, military-industrial officials who were resistant to economic reform at the domestic level and who were ideologically insulated from the appeals of pro-Western intellectuals; and (4) a recognition that stealing or importing from the West had become far less effective than FDI as a means of gaining access to advanced technology. These four observable implications are successively reviewed below.

HEIGHTENED SOVIET AWARENESS OF THE COSTS OF ISOLATION

By the late 1970s and early 1980s, many Soviet analysts recognized that international economic linkages were increasing and changing qualitatively, that MNCs were becoming more significant in the global economy, and that MNCs were taking actions leading to the "internationalization" of production.[131] Many Soviet analysts attributed these changes not to an ephemeral set of circumstances but instead to ongoing technological advances: in the words of Pavel Khvoinik, the "transition of the internationalization of production to a new, higher level" was due to "the objective need of productive forces for a further deepening of the specialization of cooperation of production in conditions of the scientific-technical revolution."[132] There was also a recognition that the internationalization of production was occurring specifically in the military realm. As one Soviet analyst noted in 1985, the "sharply intensifying

---

[130] Gorbachev 1996, 564.

[131] On the lengthy and involved Soviet debate on the changing nature of the international economy, see Hough 1986, 94–97.

[132] As cited in Hough 1986, 95.

internationalization" in the West was leading to a "rise in the number of joint international arms production programmes, agreements on specialization, cooperation and exchange of the results of scientific, technological and design work in the military field."[133]

Many policymakers recognized this general shift in the global economy as well. Gorbachev, for example, noted in his speech to the Twenty-seventh Party Congress in February 1986 that the reach of global firms had "gained strength rapidly. . . . By the early 1980s, the transnational corporations accounted for more than one-third of industrial production, more than one half of foreign trade, and nearly 80 per cent of the patents for new machinery and technology in the capitalist world."[134]

While few ventured as far as Russian economist Grigorii Khanin, who argued that "International integration is the chief strength of the Western economy," there was increased recognition in the 1980s among Soviet analysts that the ability of Western MNCs to exploit international linkages had become an important relative advantage over the Soviets, and one of ever increasing saliency.[135] In turn, many in the Soviet Union realized that the country needed to participate in the international division of labor (in nonsocialist parlance, to expand Soviet access to global firms and the international economy) to prevent an erosion of the Soviet Union's technological capacity.[136] Even a conservative such as Valery Boldin, a hard-liner who joined the August 1991 anti-Gorbachev coup, recognized that the Soviets were falling behind technologically in the 1980s, in significant part due to "our lack of world experience, our country's lack of access to world markets. . . . We stewed in our own juices for the simple reason that most of our electronics went to defense purposes, and defense was a completely closed sector."[137]

The appreciation that Soviet economic isolation from global firms was increasingly costly did not immediately translate into frequent dramatic public announcements by policymakers. This is to be expected, though. For one thing, Soviet leaders "were typically secretive about foreign economic policy."[138] More importantly, ideological and political constraints continued against discussing the closed nature of the Soviet economy as a major obstacle facing the country. Initially, the changing views of Soviet analysts were manifested in the dramatically altered parameters of the debate about the developing world. Specifically, in the early 1980s many Soviet analysts began to strongly challenge the

[133] Buzuev 1985.

[134] Gorbachev 1987, 3:192.

[135] Grigorii Khanin as cited in Hanson 1991, 119.

[136] As Evangelista puts it, there was an increased awareness that "the USSR was isolating itself from the global 'scientific-technological revolution,' and would fall behind if it did not integrate itself" (1996, 172). See also, for example, the discussions in Hough 1988a, 1988b; Hewett 1988; Hewett and Gaddy 1992; and Geron 1990.

[137] This quote is drawn from Brooks and Wohlforth 2000–2001, 38.

[138] Hewett and Gaddy 1992, 62.

decades-old dogma that FDI in the developing world was necessarily exploita-tive. Ivan Ivanov, for example, argued in 1983: "The young states . . . all the more often receive access to the technical-financial potential of the transnational cor-porations while preserving national sovereignty over natural resources and their economies."[139]

As the 1980s progressed, economic analysts, liberal and conservative alike, openly challenged the long-accepted orthodoxy of Soviet autarky itself. Un-doubtedly, this sea change among analysts toward criticizing autarkic policies as weakening technological development strongly reflected the changing views of Soviet policymakers at this time. Recall that Soviet analysts did not write in a vacuum: their analyses were closely monitored, and those who outlined posi-tions contrary to the prevailing views of high officialdom ran the risk of cen-sorship or damage to their prospects for promotion. "From a policy point of view, the important thing was not that such statements passed censorship, but that they won such wide support among specialists. They were seldom challenged directly. . . . The scholars who made these strong statements . . . were fairly high members of a policy-oriented world, and were looking to their future careers. It is hard to believe that the community would have swung so far to one side in criticizing current Soviet policy if it had not had a sense that its views were shared by the successor generation of high officialdom."[140]

NEW POLICY DIRECTIONS

Recognizing the increased costs of Soviet economic isolation was easy; politi-cally costly decisions to rectify the situation were entirely different. As noted above, powerful ideological, political, and bureaucratic constraints confronted any policymaker who ventured to reverse the Soviets' long-standing autarkic poli-cies, particularly those regarding FDI. Thus, upon entering office, Gorbachev's preference was to try to redress the growing technological gap with the United States through "transfusions" of ideas and innovations from within the USSR and the Soviet bloc.[141] Gorbachev pinned his hopes, in large part, on a policy of *ac-celeration*, including: increased emphasis on quality control; technocratic stream-lining; a greater focus on investment in existing factories rather than construction of new ones; and, in particular, trying to get the commercial sector to learn from the supposed efficiency of the military sector.[142]

At the same time, the Soviets attempted on a reduced scale to duplicate the observed internationalization of production occurring within the global econ-omy by moving toward greater production integration within the Eastern bloc itself. As Rogowski notes: "Astonishing as it may seem, Eastern Europe's

---

[139] As cited in Hough 1988a, 58.

[140] Hough 1988a, 59.

[141] *Time*, 9 September 1985, 25.

[142] Gaddy 1997, 47–61; and Aslund 1989, 26–30.

Soviet mentors were so persuaded of the merits of their own home policy of autarky that they heartily seconded each of their new satellite regimes' pursuit of self-sufficiency, initially eschewing even specialization within the Socialist bloc. This led inevitably to grossly inefficient duplication of industrial capacities."[143] Increased recognition of these inefficiencies and the possibility that eliminating them would enhance the Soviets' technological competitiveness without the political and ideological costs of opening up to the global economy offered a tempting option to Soviet policymakers.[144] Specifically, this opportunity led the Gorbachev team, as Prime Minister Nikolai Ryzkhov stated in 1986, to push COMECON "away from largely trading links toward interaction in production, toward a high degree of specialization and coproduction."[145]

By 1987, it became apparent to Gorbachev and others that his initial policy package for redressing the Soviets' technological lag with the United States was doomed to failure. The policy of acceleration was going nowhere. In particular, Gorbachev recognized that the attempt to apply the productivity "secret" of the military sector to the commercial sector was a dead end. This was because "the 'secret' was that the military sector cannibalized the economy . . . To ask the military industry to apply its methods to serve civilian industry was not simply politically impossible but also illogical."[146]

At the same time, it also became clear that efforts to duplicate on a reduced scale the international production linkages in the West by expanding specialization and production linkages within COMECON would bear little fruit.[147] Increased specialization within COMECON was fine in principle, but it was evident that none of the countries in the Eastern bloc had the capacity to match the West technologically using indigenous sources. This is most made apparent by examining East Germany, which had long been the most economically competitive member of the Eastern bloc.[148] Even in East Germany, major reforms and policy initiatives in the 1980s intended to match the productivity and technological capacity of the West in areas such as computers and microelectronics were utterly disastrous.[149]

Thus, it soon became clear that the Soviets would not be able to shore up their declining technological competitiveness using Gorbachev's initial "internal" policy package. It was in this context that, in 1987, Gorbachev began to

[143] Rogowski 1993, 1.

[144] See Adomeit 1998, 224.

[145] Speech by Nikolai Ryzkhov to COMECON in December 1986, as cited in Palmieri 1992, 170. See also Adomeit 1998, 224–27.

[146] Gaddy 1997, 56.

[147] See Geron 1990, 43; and Adomeit 1998, 227.

[148] In 1988, when Soviet exports totaled U.S.$108 billion by official reckoning, the GDR (with about one-fifteenth the population) exported just under U.S.$48 billion; Maier 1997, 66–67.

[149] See, for example, Maier 1997; and Rogowski 1993. For further discussion of this point, see chapter 6, esp. p. 164.

discuss *publicly* the mounting costs of Soviet international economic isolation.[150] And it was only at this point that the politically difficult decisions were taken to increase openness. For the Soviets, the most notable and consequential step in this regard was the decision in 1987 to legalize FDI within the Soviet Union for the first time since the 1920s.[151] By some accounts, the opening to FDI was "the boldest step of perestroika, [since it] amounted to no less than a complete reversal of a strong ideologically motivated aversion to Western capital."[152] To be sure, initial Soviet moves regarding joint ventures were quite modest (foreign participation in joint ventures were limited to 49 percent), and efforts were made to camouflage the nature, extent, and existence of these reforms.[153] But, as time progressed and as the nature of the Soviets' technological lag became even more apparent, efforts to attract FDI expanded. While majority Soviet equity in joint ventures had initially been the "*sine qua non* of the Soviet leadership," in December 1988 majority *foreign* ownership (theoretically up to 99 percent) of joint ventures was permitted in an effort to greatly increase the attractiveness of the Soviet Union as an investment site for MNCs.[154]

"From the Soviet standpoint, while foreign ownership of a controlling interest was an ideological and psychological anathema, the benefits to be gained outweighed what was given up. . . . It was envisioned by many in the Soviet hierarchy that these [joint] ventures would play a major part in assuring the success of the Gorbachev reforms."[155] Although the Soviet leadership advanced many reasons for pursuing joint ventures, "the main ones were to acquire technology and management know-how."[156] And with respect to joint ventures, it was in the computer sector that the Soviets were interested first and foremost in establishing strong links with Western firms.[157]

Of course, a number of analysts argue that Gorbachev became increasingly disposed toward economic openness neither in response to the failings of his initial batch of "internal" reforms, nor because of objective indicators that the Soviets' isolation from Western firms was making it more difficult to remain technologically competitive in key dual-use sectors. Specifically, they depict a Gorbachev who was far more "consumerist" in his motivations for international economic reform—that is, with a primary interest in improving consumer welfare and not in reversing the technological lag with the United States.

The notion that Gorbachev was driven primarily by consumerist motivations is belied by his actions (rhetoric aside, he made no effort to increase outlays for

---

[150] Hough 1988b, 199.
[151] See, for example, Hewett and Gaddy 1992, chap. 2; Cutler 1992, 171; and Burghart 1992, 107.
[152] Samonis 1995, 6.
[153] See Hough 1988a, 56–57.
[154] Geron 1990, 47; and Palmieri 1992, 172.
[155] Burghart 1992, 85, 107.
[156] Hewett and Gaddy 1992, 77; see also Burghart 1992, 76, 82–83.
[157] The best source here is Burghart 1992.

consumer welfare in this period) and his statements (three months before assuming power in 1985, for example, Gorbachev stressed that "only an intensive economy which is developed on the most modern scientific-technical basis can . . . safeguard the strength of the country's position in the international arena and allow it deservedly to enter the twenty-first century a great and prospering power").[158] Whatever Gorbachev's underlying motivations, distinguishing a "consumerist-welfare" motive from a "reversing the technological lag with the United States" motive is extremely difficult. For one thing, "in a world in which power rests increasingly on economic and industrial capabilities, one cannot readily distinguish between wealth (resources, treasure and industry) and power as national goals."[159] Distinguishing these motives becomes even more difficult given the central significance of dual-use industries at this time. As stressed above, the geographic dispersion of MNC production occurred to the greatest extent in the 1980s in dual-use industries such as microelectronics, new materials, machinery, and computers. The Soviets' lack of access to the international economy in sectors such as these was thus simultaneously harmful to the civilian economy *and* the country's military technological competitiveness with the United States. Ending their isolation thus essentially offered a "two-for-one" deal for the Soviets.

SOVIET HARD-LINERS RECOGNIZE THE INCREASED COSTS OF CLOSURE

If being closed off from Western firms had an independent, negative influence on Soviet military technological competitiveness, then we would expect to find strong support for increased international economic openness even among those officials with strong defense-industrial credentials who were disinclined toward economic reform at the domestic level and, in turn, who were ideologically insulated from the appeals of pro-Western intellectuals.[160] Indeed, we find a number of Party officials with impeccable defense-industrial credentials who played key roles in pushing for increased international economic openness—most significantly, Prime Minister Ryzhkov and Lev Zaikov, the chairman of the Military-Industrial Commission. What these two men shared, beyond a strong commitment to Soviet power, was concrete experience running large defense plants, and thus first-hand knowledge of the real capacities and needs of the military-industrial sector. Both understood the need for technological upgrading in order to maintain Soviet relative power—it was essential, in Zaikov's words, to have "the production of machines, instruments and equipment . . . correspond

---

[158] Gorbachev as quoted in Hough 1988b, 11.

[159] Gilpin 1975, 37.

[160] I thank Bill Wohlforth for numerous helpful conversations about these issues as part of our research collaboration; see the related discussion in Brooks and Wohlforth 2000–2001, 38–39.

to the world level."[161] Both were opposed to significant domestic economic reforms (Zaikov to a greater extent than Ryzhkov). Both were insulated from appeals from pro-Western intellectuals. And while Ryzkhov was not especially supportive of military interests, Zaikov was.

And yet both Zaikov and Ryzkhov strongly favored opening up the Soviet economy in general and to Western MNCs, in particular. Ryzkhov was particularly forceful in his calls for joint ventures. Key for him was gaining access to advanced Western technologies.[162] Significantly, there are many reasons to suspect that "both Ryzhkov and Zaikov based their enthusiasm for reform of the foreign trade system on their experiences of military machine-building."[163]

Ryzhkov and Zaikov not only spoke of the need for increased international economic openness, but also undertook important steps in implementing policies. Indeed, by some accounts, Ryzhkov and Zaikov were more decisive early on in this respect than Gorbachev.[164] In the end, the actions of these men make it impossible to believe that the Soviets moved away from autarky simply because of a general interest in consumer welfare or because of the influence of pro-Western intellectuals.

We will never know exactly to what extent most Soviet hard-liners actually *wanted* increased international economic openness: there was little point in hard-liners publicly taking the lead on this issue when there were plenty of other policymakers who were already doing so. Because Zaikov was an incessant supporter of the military, Aslund suggests that "we may surmise military support" for Zaikov's economic policy program.[165] But this is hardly strong evidence on this score.

Ultimately, the more important question is not whether Soviet hard-liners played a key role in the *initiation* of the shift toward openness, but rather whether they were going to expend any political capital to try to *prevent* this dramatic change in policy from occurring. As one contemporary analyst noted, "the failure of economic autarky to produce high-technology, high-quality growth leaves them [hard-liners] without a convincing policy argument."[166] At the same time, Gorbachev and other reformers in favor of change could "plausibly say that reform was indispensable. They could say that Russia would not remain a great power unless the Soviet Union raised its technology to world levels, and they could say an opening to the West was necessary for that end."[167] The connection between isolation and the technological lag thus helps explain why hard-liners

[161] Zaikov as cited in Aslund 1989, 46.
[162] Aslund 1989, 40.
[163] Aslund 1989, 46–47.
[164] Aslund 1989, 61.
[165] Aslund 1989, 47.
[166] Hough 1988b, 218.
[167] Hough 1988a, 25.

did not put up a credible fight against a policy of increased international economic openness.[168]

RECOGNITION THAT STEALING AND IMPORTING TECHNOLOGY IS INFERIOR TO FDI

Of course, a key question is why gaining access to Western firms was viewed by traditionalists such as Ryzhkov and Zaikov as essential to redress the Soviet Union's growing lack of competitiveness in key defense-related technologies. After all, the Soviets had alternative strategies to obtain Western technology available to them, most obviously importing or stealing foreign technologies. Especially during the 1970s, the Soviets sought to enhance their technological competitiveness through outright purchases of Western technology. It is also clear that the Soviets had long engaged in an intensive strategy of stealing key Western technologies, including many important military technologies and commercial technologies with direct military applications.[169] This Soviet effort, which was extensive throughout the Cold War, was enhanced in scope in the early 1980s.[170] A recently declassified CIA analysis conducted in 1987 concludes: "Since 1975 the Soviets have imported 2,500 pieces of major manufacturing equipment related to the microelectronics industry, most of it illegally."[171]

By the 1980s, however, gaining access to technology via FDI emerged as the preferred alternative. Simply stealing technology from the West was seen by many as having reduced utility at this time.[172] There was also widespread recognition within the Soviet Union by the mid-1980s that "Brezhnev's policy of importing foreign technology was basically a failure."[173] As one analyst concludes: "The Soviet record of assimilating technology that has not been accompanied by the human element has been chequered at best; at worst, the failure to have some kind of human involvement with either hardware or information transfers has resulted in the total inability to incorporate that technology, making such transfers of little or no value in spite of the cost and effort involved in the physical transfer process."[174] Significantly, "even turnkey operations, which shared

---

[168] In turn, the link between isolation and the technological lag made it more difficult for hardliners to put up opposition to military retrenchment, which was a necessary precursor to increased international economic openness due to the West's restrictive "economic containment" policies (see the discussion of this point in Brooks and Wohlforth 2000–2001, 40–42). On the West's "economic containment" policies, see Mastanduno 1992; and Shambaugh 1996.

[169] See, for example, Burghart 1992, 40; and CIA 1985b.

[170] See CIA 1987b, 24; 1985, 2.

[171] CIA 1987b, 17.

[172] See the discussion in CIA 1987a, 4; 1989a, 3; Cooper 1991, 48; Friedberg 2000b, 318; and Odom 1990, 63.

[173] Hough 1988b, 83. On this point, see also Winiecki 1986, 330; Schmickle 1992, 30; Hough 1988a, 89; Hewett and Gaddy 1992, 29; CIA 1982, 6; and Cooper 1991.

[174] Burghart 1992, 151.

some of the same benefits of Joint Ventures, had been found to suffer once the installation was in place, for without the ability to modify and develop the original facility, these plants soon became stagnant and outmoded."[175]

Soviet policymakers also realized that their reduced ability to steal or purchase technology from abroad was harming their technological competitiveness in the military realm. "The large bureaucratic Soviet military-industrial complex was proving unable to hold up its end. . . . The sense of crisis was compounded by the realization that in dealing with the new challenge, the Soviet economy would be less able than previously to exploit what economists have called 'the advantages of backwardness,' i.e. the possibility of borrowing technology from advanced industrial states and thereby avoiding the costs of development."[176] By the mid-1980s, the key conclusion for Soviet policy was straightforward: the lack of "extensive cooperative relations with Western firms . . . and R&D communities" had become a key liability in the Soviet quest to develop "the weapons of the future."[177]

Why did many Soviet decision makers conclude that buying or stealing technology was no longer as useful as in the past and that FDI was preferable? There are four basic reasons. First, if the Soviets purchased or stole technology rather than obtaining it through FDI, they were closed off from technical support, training, and other forms of direct consultation—all of which became increasingly important as the cost, risk, and complexity of technological development spiraled upwards.[178] As Carol Clark notes in her survey of the decline of Soviet and Eastern European technological competitiveness: "Effective imitation of new technology, technology that may be firm-specific or include knowledge and processes that are not easily copied at arm's length, require a sustained learning-by-doing process to acquire the needed technical know-how. Long term, close ties between supplier and recipient, as in the case of foreign direct investment, can facilitate the learning process and can thereby greatly enhance the effectiveness of technology transfers."[179] By the 1980s, many advanced technologies required highly skilled workers with specialized training and experience.[180] Because of the Soviets' lack

---

[175] Burghart 1992, 83.

[176] Odom 1990, 63. See also CIA 1987c, 1.

[177] Odom 1985, 11.

[178] See, for example, Chen 1983; Gerschenberg 1987; and Schive 1990.

[179] Clark 1993, 185; see also Turner 1988, 515; and Schroeder 1989, 41 who notes: "When foreign technology was purchased, the firm not infrequently found that the new machine did not fit well into the old plant, that employees had to be trained how to use it, and that needed auxiliary materials were not available domestically."

[180] See, for example, Kenney and Florida 1993; UNCTAD 1992, 102; and Dunning 1994. With respect to Soviet weapons development, Odom noted in 1985 that all of the "weapons of the future . . . which Soviet military analysts see as changing the nature of war, rely on a variety of innovations in the use of new technologies. Most of these innovations are being made in the West, and moving them into serial production is not easy, even for Western firms. Although espionage may give the USSR access to the new technologies, only extensive cooperation with Western firms that have applied them in mass production will allow the USSR to achieve a respectable indigenous production capacity" (11).

of access to direct training in using these new technologies, "higher than usual construction cost overruns [were] associated with the installation of the more sophisticated equipment" from foreign suppliers that the Soviets were able to obtain.[181] For the Soviets, a key attraction of joint ventures at this time is that they "offered the opportunity for long-term contacts with Western scientists, managers, and workers. . . . The end result, it was hoped, would be transfer of knowledge relating to production capability."[182]

Second, "the domestic economic system had resisted technology imports, which often seemed to fall into an economic black hole, protecting the economy from any outward rippling, stimulating effect."[183] One of the key reasons FDI is valuable is that MNCs often develop significant linkages with local supplier firms,[184] thereby promoting spillover effects in related industries and enhancing technological innovation in the economy as a whole.[185]

Third, as the pace of technological development accelerated, simply buying technology would not do much to help the Soviets remain competitive with the United States in key technologies, for the simple reason that MNCs generally only license older technologies.[186] The Soviets found that passive technology transfers "have the major weakness that, as a rule, they do not provide access to the latest technology at the research frontier of development. The technology acquired has usually passed through the processes of development and commercialization, so that the Soviet Union finds itself in a permanent follow-up situation involving a built-in time lag. As a rule, passive modes of technology transfer do not permit the elimination of technological gaps."[187] Similarly, a recently declassified 1987 CIA analysis finds that "the Soviets have not been satisfied with their use of Western equipment and technology" because it is often "outdated by the time production begins."[188]

Fourth and finally, the enhanced complexity and pace of technological change caused "reverse engineering" to become an increasingly ineffective route for redressing the Soviets' gap in defense-related technologies.[189] One challenge in this respect concerned the acquisition of technologies. As the complexity of Western military technology increased, the number of companies involved in the

[181] Winiecki 1986, 330. See also CIA 1987b, which concludes (20) that "Soviet industry as a whole was making poor use of foreign manufacturing technology."

[182] Burghart 1992, 83, 152. On this point, see also CIA 1989b, 31.

[183] Schmickle 1992, 30.

[184] See, for example, Ismail 1999; and UNCTAD 2001, 142–43.

[185] See, for example, UNCTAD 1995, 139.

[186] MNCs normally transfer their most recent technological advances only to affiliates and alliance partners; licensing is generally done only of relatively older technologies (see UNCTAD 1992, 141).

[187] Cooper 1991, 48.

[188] CIA 1987c, 2.

[189] On Soviet recognition of the greatly enhanced difficulty of reverse engineering during the 1980s, see, for example, CIA 1989a, 3; 1987a, 4.

production of any given weapon also increased. To illegally acquire technologies and then engage in reverse engineering, the Soviets needed to steal from an increasing number of Western companies, significantly increasing the cost and difficulty of industrial espionage. A second challenge concerned the enhanced difficulty of reverse engineering itself. "Reverse engineering . . . works only for simple products. In cases where the products and processes are complex or the technologies involved unfamiliar and even unknown, successes are few. And, even if the process can be successfully duplicated and the product reproduced, the time involved often makes the product and the technology obsolete before it can be duplicated on a broader and useful scale."[190]

Computers are a telling example on this score. "Unfortunately for the Soviets, computers and the increasingly miniaturized components of which they were constructed proved extremely difficult to 'reverse engineer' and copy. According to one account it took Soviet engineers longer to copy the IBM 360 computer than 'IBM took to develop it in the first place.'[191] Because of the difficulty of reverse engineering in information technology, the CIA concluded in 1987 that "the Soviets traditional answer to the their shortcomings—a crash program to acquire and copy—is of limited value."[192] As minister V. Kolesnikov bluntly concluded in 1987, "simply copying a Western computer, circuit for circuit . . . is no longer feasible."[193]

Summary Assessment

The strands of evidence surveyed in this section indicate that the Soviets' economic isolation from ongoing global production changes helps to explain why the country fell so far behind the United States in key dual-use and defense-related technologies during the final phase of the Cold War. The analysis also indicates that the globalization of production's negative influence on Soviet military technological competitiveness would have escalated ever further if the Cold War had continued beyond the 1980s and the Soviets had remained economically isolated.

Before we can have full confidence in these conclusions, we must consider the alternative explanations for the Soviet Union's reduced ability to remain competitive with the United States in key defense-related technologies in the 1980s. Some might argue that the Soviets were rapidly falling behind in military technology at this time precisely because the Reagan administration deliberately sought to increase the technological sophistication of U.S. weapons. The problem with this explanation is that, as Aaron Friedberg demonstrates,

---

[190] Burghart 1992, 152.
[191] Friedberg 2000b, n. 58.
[192] CIA 1987a, 13.
[193] As reported in CIA 1989b, 3.

the United States had been employing this "technological sophistication" strategy for 25 years before the Reagan administration came to power.[194] Why did this long-standing U.S. strategy suddenly have such a strong effect in the 1980s? This analysis suggests that "playing the technology card" became a particularly effective strategy for the United States only when the cost, complexity, and difficulty of technological development became especially high and, in turn, when the West had achieved a relative advantage in technological innovation that the Soviets could not match with a "hunkering down" strategy (that is, allocating increased resources away from consumers and toward military technology development). Of key importance is that U.S. firms involved in defense-related production quickly adapted to the changed parameters of technological development by increasing internationalization while the Soviet defense establishment did not. However, this relative advantage achieved salience in the 1980s due to factors beyond the immediate control of American policymakers. It is not that the Reagan administration's policies were unimportant; clearly they were. However, acknowledging this fact does not give us much leverage on the specific question at hand: it is very hard to explain why a long-standing, U.S. "technological sophistication" strategy that had been in place since at least the mid-1950s suddenly made it very difficult for the Soviets to keep up in military technology in the 1980s using their traditional hunkering-down strategy.

When asking why it was specifically in the 1980s the Soviet Union began to lag seriously in military technology, the most obvious alternative explanation is inefficiencies associated with the country's domestic economic structure. If we were to highlight only one factor to explain the overall difficulty the Soviets had in keeping up in military technology throughout the Cold War, the inefficiency of their command economy would clearly be the one. However, as an explanation for why the gap began to sharply widen specifically in the 1980s, it is hardly sufficient. The Soviet command economic structure was a constant throughout the Cold War, and it is not easy to explain rapid changes in a dependent variable—in this case, military technological competitiveness—with a constant. That being said, while the Soviets' command structure was a constant, technology was not: many analysts stress that command economies can do fairly well with simple technologies, but do much more poorly with complex ones.[195] This argument is a compelling one. Yet even those scholars who advance this line of argument most forcefully recognize the salience of the growing costs of Soviet closure to the global economy and see it as an independent factor behind its declining technological competitiveness. Winiecki, for example, recognizes that isolation from Western MNCs "accelerated the onset of the 'time of troubles' in Soviet-type economies."[196]

---

[194] Friedberg 2000b. On this point, see also Evangelista 1988.

[195] The best sources here are Winiecki 1986 and 1988.

[196] Winiecki 1986, 326.

When factoring in the significance of the Soviets' command economy, there are two other points we need to consider. First, right up until the end of the Cold War, the United States was hardly an archetype of a decentralized, capitalist economic system when it came to defense production at the prime contractor level. At this level, the U.S. government made many of the crucial choices on American weapons parameters. Moreover, many of these production decisions were not made primarily on the basis of economic efficiency; congressional pork barrel politics was the most significant drain in this regard. At the prime contractor level, the Soviets had long been able to compete very effectively, in large part because of their ability to concentrate huge amounts of money and technological personnel on military-specific production tasks. The United States only began to pull substantially ahead of the Soviets in weapons development during the 1980s, just at the time that dual-use technologies became especially significant at the lower tiers of weapons production. Significantly, this is the precise area in which U.S. defense production was least micromanaged by Washington and in which it became most globalized. From the U.S. standpoint, it may turn out to have been fortunate that gathering data on the extent of globalization in American defense production is so difficult because the production chains of modern weapons are so extraordinarily complex. Had it been possible to accurately determine which specific foreign companies and affiliates were contributing to individual U.S. weapons systems at the lower tiers of production, it is possible that Congress would have used this information to constrain the internationalization of American weapons production in response to domestic political pressures as well as to the "autonomy concerns" so prevalent during the 1980s with respect to Japan and other countries. As it was, the globalization of U.S. weapons production advanced rapidly largely below the radar screen, and hence was spared widespread interference from Washington.

A second point to consider is that we cannot simply take the efficiency of the U.S. domestic economy as exogenously given; as Peter Gourevitch reminds us, we need to keep in mind how international economic exposure influenced the structure of the U.S. economy during the final phase of the Cold War.[197] If U.S. MNCs had been unable to increasingly rely on international outsourcing and on their foreign affiliates for key aspects of the production process, and unable to form cooperative ventures with foreign firms to develop new technologies, then the U.S. domestic economy would have been structured such that it was less able to push the technological envelope in the areas that it specialized in. Because of the globalization of production, many U.S. MNCs were increasingly able to concentrate their home country operations on those aspects of technological innovation that they were best at.[198] Of course, it is not simply the geographic dispersion of MNC production that

---

[197] Gourevitch 1978.

[198] For an excellent analysis of this point, see Rosecrance 1999.

contributed to this development—international trade is obviously also of vital importance. Yet over the final phase of the Cold War, the former was more important. As stressed in chapter 2, during this period trade was a second-order phenomenon in the international economy compared to where and how MNCs organized their production activities, especially in key dual-use sectors.

Ultimately, the preceding analysis does not indicate that the Soviets' international economic isolation had a stronger negative effect on their technological competitiveness than did their command economy. One might be tempted to conclude from the Soviet leadership's "staged" approach to addressing the country's technological lag in the 1980s (first, through internal reforms and, once these failed, through opening up to global firms) that international economic openness offered greater potential gains than did internal economic reforms. This conclusion is a mistake, however. The simple reason is that the internal acceleration reforms pursued at this time never tackled the Soviet Union's command economy in a profound manner. The failure of this policy to reverse the Soviets' growing lag cannot be attributed to a lack of potential gains for internal reforms.

The conclusion we can draw from the preceding examination is that Soviets' isolation from the globalization of production had an independent, negative effect on their competitiveness in key dual-use industries and defense-related technologies during the final phase of the Cold War. Before the 1980s, the Soviets were already running uphill in the arms race because of their inefficient command economy. The rapid acceleration of the globalization of production, and Soviet isolation from it, made the incline steeper and would have done so to a progressively greater extent had the Cold War continued.

CONCLUSION

States have always had strong incentives to rely on their own resources for weapons production. The degree to which an autarkic strategy has been undermined in recent years has not been specified up to this point. The existing literature clearly indicates that small states cannot be competitive in military technology if they do not strongly participate in the globalization of production. But this conclusion is essentially irrelevant, since these smaller states were not in a position to be on the cutting edge in military technology while following an autarkic strategy even before the onset of the globalization of production; only the great powers have had this option in recent decades owing to the importance of economies of scale in defense-related production.

Out of all states, the United States is the least likely case for the argument that autarkic defense production has been decisively undermined. If the United States can no longer effectively pursue autarky, then no other state has any hope of doing so. The analysis here shows that the United States strongly pursued globalization in defense-related production during the 1970s and 1980s and that this shift was undertaken because defense policymakers and defense firms recognized the significant gains to be accrued by internationalizing production. U.S. military technological competitiveness was, in fact, enhanced by a strategy of openness during the final phase of the Cold War; isolation from the geographic dispersion of MNC production had an independent, negative effect on Soviet ability to remain competitive with the United States in key dual-use industries and defense-related production during the 1980s.

This examination thus shows that autarkic defense production has been fundamentally undermined. This is true not just for some states, but for all of them. It was already true in the 1980s, and has only solidified as the geographic dispersion of MNC production in areas related to weaponry increases.

What does this conclusion mean for the United States specifically? It does not mean that U.S. weapons systems now have, or are likely to have in the future, high levels of internationalization at all tiers of production. At the defense prime contractor level, where much weapons production is still military-specific, U.S. defense companies are still the key drivers of weapons production for a variety of political and economic reasons, and will probably remain so. It is at the lower tiers of defense production, where dual-use items are key, that U.S. weaponry is now heavily internationalized. It is important to keep in mind that the United States had a greater opportunity and willingness to pursue an autarkic strategy during the final phase of the Cold War than it does today. The exact extent to which U.S. defense production is now globalized is unclear, but there is every reason to think that it is much more significant now than during the 1980s. Michael Wynne, the undersecretary of defense for acquisition, recently estimated that "about 40 percent of machine tools used on U.S. weapons systems come from foreign suppliers."[199]

This analysis does not mean that the United States would now be unable to replicate domestically all of the technologies, parts, and components used in defense-related production that it now receives from international sources. If the United States was willing to devote Soviet-like levels of expenditure to defense, there is no telling what it could do on its own. But such spending is not going to happen. Even at the outer limit of foreseeable U.S. defense budgets, autarkic weapons production would be infeasible. It is useful to recall what it would have taken in the late 1980s for the United States to replace the international contributions for a single munition, the HARM missile. Pure domestic sourcing would have required replacing 712 foreign subcontractors that contributed to production of the missile at the lower tiers, as well as an unknown number of foreign companies that contributed to the launch computer and associated software. In addition, all sourcing from the foreign affiliates of U.S. MNCs would have required curtailment, as would all collaboration between U.S. companies

---

[199] *Washington Post*, 28 June 2003, E1.

and foreign-based firms and researchers on the technologies used in the HARM missile.

If the United States were to try to go it alone in weapons production, direct budgetary outlays to create or improve the needed domestic industries and technologies would be massive, but the opportunity cost would also be great. This is partly because the United States has a limited number of domestically based technological personnel available to draw upon at any point in time.[200] Also significant is that the Pentagon buys only a small percentage of the market in dual-use items that the United States relies upon in defense-related production.[201] A switch to domestic production of these items for the Pentagon would result in much shorter production runs than are associated with the current, dual-use firms producing for the global market; as a result, the benefits of economies of scale, as well as various learning effects associated with intensive production, would be lost by going the autarkic route. For these and other reasons, a go-it-alone strategy would be inefficient and would come at the expense of future improvements in those areas that U.S.-based talent and resources now specialize in.

Put another way, we cannot take the current U.S. technological and economic base as a given and ask: "How much extra would it cost to replicate what comes from abroad?" A go-it-alone effort in weapons production would be costly in direct terms and also indirectly, since it would degrade the current strengths of the U.S. economy as technological talent and resources were drained to work on duplicating foreign-sourced items. And this is a best-case scenario; at worst, after huge outlays and slowed technological progress in those areas that are the current focus of U.S. firms and personnel, the United States could very well turn out to be unable to develop domestically all that is required to produce weapons systems. Among other challenges that might be insurmountable, the U.S. government would need to consistently make the right choices in terms of which dual-use technologies to invest in for future Pentagon use; no longer would the United States have the luxury, as it does now, of waiting to choose the best of many different dual-use technologies that emerge from a global competition among firms from dozens of countries.

The immense difficulty of moving away from globalization in defense-related production is reflected in recent DoD actions. In May 2003, Congressman Duncan Hunter, chairman of the House Armed Services Committee, spearheaded an effort to strengthen Buy American regulations concerning military procurement.[202] Defense Secretary Donald Rumsfeld—who a month earlier had requested that Congress grant him greater leeway to bypass existing Buy American requirements—responded by threatening that President Bush

---

[200] On this point, see, for example, the discussion in *Aviation Week*, 24 October 1966, 33.

[201] See, for example, Pages 1996, 10; and Alic et al. 1992, 260.

[202] For a useful overview, see Towell 2003.

would veto the 2004 defense authorization bill if the proposal championed by Hunter were included.[203] In an 8 July 2003 letter to Hunter, Rumsfeld underscored that his proposal "would deny to U.S. forces critical technologies and capabilities available only, or most economically, from non-U.S. sources."[204] Undersecretary Michael Wynne also warned that the proposed strengthening of Buy American restrictions would "have a devastating effect on our ability to provide war fighting equipment on any kind of economic basis." He estimated that adopting just one of the restrictions under consideration—that major weapons purchased by the DoD be manufactured with U.S.-made machine tools—would raise U.S. weapons prices by 20 to 40 percent.[205]

DoD's strong reaction to the congressional effort—in combination with vigorous lobbying from numerous defense industry groups, including the National Defense Industrial Association, the Aerospace Industries Association, and the Information Technologies Association of America—makes unlikely any significant strengthening of Buy American restrictions in the foreseeable future.[206] Anyone in Congress who wants U.S. weapons systems to be as capable as possible would be wise not to challenge the DoD's strong preference. In keeping with the analysis presented in this chapter, defense analyst Loren Thompson recently concluded: "If these foolish [Buy American] provisions manage to survive conference in the Senate, the Bush administration can forget about transforming the military into anything other than a technological backwater. . . . The Soviet Union had a 'Buy Russian' policy that closed its economy to most of the world, and everybody knows how that worked out."[207]

---

[203] *Defense Daily International*, 11 July 2003. It should be noted that the secretary of defense currently has great freedom to bypass Buy American restrictions; Rumsfeld's request was for the system of exemptions to be made even more liberal. Under existing rules, Buy American regulations can, for example, be waived if a product is not manufactured in the United States in sufficient quantity or quality, or if the regulations are deemed to be "inconsistent with the public interest," or if a domestic contractor causes "unreasonable" costs or delays.

[204] Rumsfeld 2003.

[205] *Washington Post*, 28 June 2003, E1. As an example of how Hunter's proposal could reduce access to key technologies not available from U.S. sources, Suzanne Patrick, deputy under secretary of defense for industrial policy, pointed to the tilt fan rotor technology used in the Marine variant of the F-35, which is produced by Rolls-Royce of Britain. In a hearing before the House Armed Services Committee, Patrick underscored: "We would not be able to field the Marine Corps variant of the Joint Strike Fighter if we have to rely solely on U.S. content. . . . It's innovative new technology. It is not technology that has been available in the United States" (see Patrick 2003).

[206] See Information Technologies Association of America 2003; Aerospace Industries Association 2003; and Snyder 2003, 13.

[207] As quoted in the *Wall Street Journal*, 11 July 2003, A3.

CHAPTER 5

The Globalization of Production, Economic Integration, and Regional Security in the Developing World

THE SECURITY rapprochement between France and Germany that followed in the wake of West European regional economic integration efforts is an alluring model for many policymakers in the developing world. It is possible that simply initiating a regional trade agreement (RTA) may improve intraregional security relations to some degree.[1] All the theory we have, however, indicates that only the *consolidation* of an RTA contributes to a significant overall shift in security relations. Forming a group does not of itself lead to the key dynamics scholars identify by which integration promotes an improved security climate: an enhanced network of transactions between citizens; deeper links of communication between policymakers; the creation of strong economic ties; spillover from dense economic cooperation to security cooperation; or a shift toward a more collective sense of interests.[2] It is the experience of deep economic regional integration that leads to these and other processes, not simply the signing of an agreement.

Unfortunately for developing countries, although forming RTAs over the past several decades has been easy, the consolidation of these groups has proven elusive. The literature on regional integration has not paid enough attention to factors that influence the consolidation of RTAs in the developing world; most studies are narrowly focused on the initial decision to pursue integration.[3] The key question this chapter will evaluate is whether the globalization of production can influence security relations in the developing world by acting as a force for the consolidation of regional economic integration.

---

[1] Mansfield and Pevehouse 2000.

[2] See, for example, the discussions in Deutsch et al. 1957; Nye 1971; Wendt 1994; and Haas 1964.

[3] The literature on regional integration is hardly unique in this respect: the consolidation, or implementation, on international agreements suffers from relative neglect in the international cooperation literature more generally. As Martin notes, "International cooperation requires states to engage in two stages of interaction: bargaining and implementation. . . . Most studies of international cooperation have in fact concentrated on the bargaining stage, asking the conditions under which states are able to reach mutually beneficial agreements." She further maintains that this relative focus is surprising, since "unless agreements are not only ratified but implemented, no real cooperation . . . has taken place" (2000, 41).

The theoretical analysis in chapter 3 indicates that competition for FDI may create enough pressure in the direction of consolidating regional integration that deep economic cooperation can emerge even among states with a long-standing history of security rivalry. However, it was shown that only under certain conditions does competition for FDI create strong incentives for the consolidation of integration: (1) the RTA is economically large but has few member states, and (2) the group's members have difficulty attracting FDI on their own. The key question is: what recent regional integration agreements in the developing world meet these two conditions?

With respect to market size, two recent developing integration agreements stand out. The first is Mercosur (the Southern Cone Common Market), which was formed in 1991. Mercosur is by far the largest developing country RTA, with a GDP of U.S.$861 billion in 1994. The second largest in economic size is the ASEAN Free Trade Agreement (AFTA), which was initiated in 1992. AFTA has a combined GDP of U.S.$539 billion in 1994.[4] It is not just the aggregate size of the group that is important; how this size is constituted is also key. In this respect, AFTA and Mercosur differ significantly. AFTA contains nine full members,[5] four of which are significant members that act as veto players: Thailand, Indonesia, Malaysia, and the Philippines. In contrast, Mercosur contains four full members,[6] only two of which are key members that act as veto players: Argentina and Brazil.

At the start of the 1990s, AFTA and Mercosur also differed greatly regarding the second condition—the ability of their respective members to obtain FDI on their own.[7] For a variety of reasons, the ASEAN region became a magnet for FDI beginning in the early 1980s, and, as a result, the group's key members were able to attract extremely high levels of FDI without having to undertake deep regional integration.[8] During the 1980s, the stock of inward FDI as a percentage of GDP

[4] See the systematic ranking of RTAs on the basis of size in Frankel, Stein, and Wei 1997, 247–48. GDP data from 1994 is presented here because this is what Frankel, Stein, and Wei employ in their analysis. Although a large number of developing country RTAs have been initiated since 1994 (see World Trade Organization 2000), they are all now smaller than Mercosur and AFTA were in 1994. The largest developing country RTA formed since 1994 is the Commonwealth of Independent States (CIS), whose 10 members collectively had a GDP of U.S.$475 billion in 1999 (data from World Bank 2001). This is less half the current size of Mercosur, whose full members in 1999 collectively had a GDP of U.S.$1,063 billion (World Bank 2001).

[5] Until 1995, ASEAN had six full members.

[6] Chile and Bolivia were added as associate members of Mercosur in 1996 (see note 4).

[7] There is no standard method for establishing a developing country's potential for attracting FDI. The method employed in this analysis is to focus on a country's inward FDI stock relative to its GDP, which is then compared to a country's own inward FDI stock in earlier years and to the average level among developing countries. For a discussion of why this method is useful, see UNCTAD 2000b, 100.

[8] ASEAN did pursue regional economic cooperation during the 1980s, but only to a very limited extent: the ASEAN Preferential Trading Agreement initiated in 1977 ultimately reduced tariffs on just 5 percent of ASEAN's intraregional trade (*Asian Wall Street Journal*, 24 January 1992, A1).

increased within the key members of ASEAN, more than tripling in Thailand (from 3 percent in 1980 to 9.3 percent in 1990), more than doubling in Indonesia (from 14.2 percent in 1980 to 36.6 percent in 1990), increasing from 24.8 percent in 1980 to 33.0 percent in 1990 in Malaysia, and rising from 3.8 percent in 1980 to 4.7 percent in 1990 in the Philippines.[9] By 1990, Thailand, Malaysia, and Indonesia all had stocks of inward FDI as a percentage of GDP that stood well above the developing country average; only the Philippines fell below this level.[10] In combination, these four ASEAN members attracted 19 percent of the total inward FDI going to developing countries in 1990.[11]

In marked contrast, the key members of Mercosur, Argentina and Brazil, were both having great difficulty attracting FDI on their own as they entered the 1990s. During the 1980s, the stock of inward FDI as a percentage of GDP was stagnant in Brazil (increasing from 7.4 percent in 1980 to 8.0 percent in 1990) and actually dropped in Argentina (decreasing from 6.9 percent in 1980 to 6.4 percent in 1990).[12] And though Brazil's inward FDI stock edged slightly upwards during the 1980s, this period marked a dramatic shift in the country's relative fortunes in terms of attracting FDI: during the second half of the 1970s, Brazil alone accounted for over a quarter of inward FDI flows to developing countries.[13] In 1990, Argentina and Brazil together accounted for only 8.4 percent of the inward FDI going to developing countries,[14] and both countries had stocks of inward FDI as a percentage of GDP that fell below the developing country average.[15]

At the beginning of the 1990s, Mercosur was thus the developing country RTA that best met the conditions specified here. Mercosur is an intriguing case to examine not just for this reason, but also because of the nature of the security relationship between Argentina and Brazil. Dating back to the 1820s, there had been a "historic pattern of rivalry and geopolitical competition between Brazil and Argentina"[16] in which the two countries "for centuries . . . had competed for regional domination and had often clashed over boundaries and water rights."[17] The historical parameters of Argentina-Brazil security relations will be described in further detail in a subsequent section. For now, the important point is that Mercosur provides an ideal laboratory for examining whether competition for FDI can induce economic cooperation even among states with a long history of security tensions.

The examination that follows consequently focuses on the experience of Mercosur. The first section shows that Mercosur made great strides toward

[9] UNCTAD 1996, 270–71.
[10] UNCTAD 1996, 262.
[11] Calculated using data from UNCTAD 1996, 230.
[12] UNCTAD 2000a, 323.
[13] UNCTAD 2000b, 99.
[14] Calculated using data from UNCTAD 1996, 228.
[15] UNCTAD 1996, 262.
[16] Hurrell 1998b, 534.
[17] Pion-Berlin 2000, 45.

consolidating integration in the years following its formation. It analyzes a series of explanations for the group's progress drawn from the main general approaches to regional integration and finds that none of them provide much leverage. The second section analyzes whether competition for FDI influenced Mercosur, and finds that it is, in fact, an important reason why the group made more progress toward consolidating integration in less time than any other developing country RTA. The final section shows that the consolidation of Mercosur helped make it possible for Argentina and Brazil to decisively move beyond their 150-year-long history of rivalry and consolidate a stable and peaceful relationship.

THE CONSOLIDATION OF MERCOSUR

Most integration efforts in the developing world have had either limited aims or a slow timetable for implementation, or both. From the outset, Mercosur was comparatively ambitious. Formed in March 1991, Mercosur aimed to eliminate tariffs on intraregional trade and create a common external tariff by 1 January 1995. The *Economist* emphasized in 1996 that the goal of creating a customs union in less than four years made Mercosur "the world's most ambitious scheme of regional integration since the birth of the European Economic Community in 1957."[18] Indeed, at its inception, Mercosur was perceived as being too ambitious. Many analysts dismissed the agreement as another example of the "ideological escalation" typical of postwar Latin American policymaking.[19] And numerous policymakers within Mercosur initially presumed that their governments would have to scale back the agreement. In Argentina, for example, Carlos Escude (an advisor to the Argentine Foreign Ministry) noted in November 1992, "I cannot see a scenario under which Mercosur becomes functional in a way that enhances free trade,"[20] while Domingo Cavallo (then economy minister of Argentina) stated flatly in May 1992 that he doubted Mercosur would be able to meet its tariff reduction targets.[21]

Against these pessimistic expectations, Mercosur made significant progress immediately after it was created. Less than four years after the group was formed, tariffs were eliminated on 95 percent of intraregional trade, and a common external tariff was established covering 85 percent of all extra-Mercosur imports.[22] Compared to the poor record of regional integration efforts in the developing world prior to the 1990s, the consolidation of integration achieved by Mercosur during its early years is impressive.

[18] *Economist*, 12 October 1996, S4.

[19] See, for example, Bouzas 1991, 5. On ideological escalation in Latin America, see Hirschmann 1979.

[20] *Washington Post*, 15 November 1992, H1.

[21] *Latin American Weekly Report*, 28 May 1992.

[22] Carranza 2000, 77.

Contrasting Mercosur with other contemporary RTAs is not as easy: because all integration efforts have vastly disparate goals, they are difficult to directly compare. The only existing effort that makes such a comparison ranks Mercosur as the most successful contemporary RTA in the developing world, yet the basis for this assessment is not indicated.[23] When we compare the consolidation of integration of different groups, we must consider not just whether the particular goals of the agreement were fulfilled but also the scope of the agreement (it is hardest, and most consequential, to fulfill the objectives of an economic union, followed, in order, by a customs union, a free trade agreement, and a preferential trade agreement) as well as the speed of the implementation period (it is hardest, and most consequential, to quickly implement the terms of the agreement). One way of comparing the degree of consolidation of integration agreements is therefore to ask three questions: (1) how expansive are the group's goals: a preferential trade agreement, a free trade agreement, a customs union, or an economic union? (2) how much progress did the group make toward the priorities it set for itself? and (3) how much time did it take for the group to reach this level of implementation?

If we use these criteria, Mercosur's early performance ranks far ahead of all contemporary RTAs in the Middle East,[24] Africa,[25] Asia,[26] and the rest of Latin America.[27] Indeed, by these criteria, Mercosur's initial record arguably compares favorably against all other regional integration efforts, including in Western Europe. Carranza asserts that "It took eight years for the European Community (EC) to become a customs union in 1968; Mercosur achieved the same goal in less than four years."[28]

This discussion should not lead one to conclude that Mercosur was an unqualified success during the early and middle 1990s. Although Mercosur came very far very quickly, it fell short of some goals during this period and only attained the status of an imperfect customs union.[29] But Mercosur achieved more

---

[23] See Mattli 1999a, 66; 1999b, 17.

[24] On the shallow nature and poor records of Middle Eastern integration efforts, see, for example, El-Agraa 1997, 7; Frankel, Stein, and Wei 1997, 276–79; and IMF Survey, 6 July 1998, 207, www.imf.org/external/pubs/ft/survey/surveyx.htm.

[25] On the poor progress by regional economic integration efforts in Africa, see, for example, Horvath and Grabowski 1997, 2; Frankel, Stein, and Wei 1997, 269–76; and Mbaku 1995.

[26] The ASEAN Free Trade Agreement (AFTA) is the key regional integration agreement in Asia among developing countries. On AFTA's lackluster progress toward consolidating integration in the 1990s, see, for example, Santiago 1995; Frankel, Stein, and Wei 1997, 267–68; Ravenhill 1995, 850; and Denoon and Colbert 1998–99, 507.

[27] On Mercosur's more significant progress during the 1990s compared to other Latin American regional integration efforts, see, for example, Kaltenthaler and Mora 2002, 92; and Markwald and Machado 1999, who conclude (63) that "Mercosur stands out as the first Latin American integration project to achieve a reasonable degree of success, after more than three decades of frustrated efforts."

[28] Carronza 2000, 100.

[29] Pereira 1999, 10–16.

in less time than any other contemporary RTA in the developing world before or since.

General Explanations for the Consolidation of Mercosur

Why did Mercosur make so much progress during the early and middle 1990s? The analysis below briefly reviews five general approaches to the study of regional integration that can be applied to the Mercosur case.[30] None offers a strong explanation for the degree of consolidation achieved by Mercosur during this period.

The approach to regional integration with the longest pedigree is neofunctionalism, which centers on the role of spillover.[31] The most common form of the argument highlights the role of a strong, expansive supranational institution as a force behind integration.[32] This perspective is not compelling for the simple reason that, as one recent analysis puts it, "Mercosur suffers from a juridical and institutional deficit."[33] It is unclear why Mercosur's institutional structure is so weak. However, Mercosur's policymakers appear to have been guided by the notion, contra neofunctionalism, that strong supranational structures actually constrain further integration: "Southern Cone policymakers . . . frequently attribute the institutional weaknesses of Mercosur to the history, and subsequent failure, of earlier ambitious undertakings in a similar vein like the Andean Pact for example, where excessive bureaucratization hampered effectiveness in carrying out their mission of resolving problems. . . . To avoid repetition of past mistakes, then, policymakers opted for a pragmatic, less bureaucratic approach."[34] Whatever the reason, the members of Mercosur created only one unsubstantial institution at the outset—an extremely small Secretariat, essentially a clearinghouse for documents.[35] Because Mercosur's institutional structure is so weak, the conditions necessary for a second prominent spillover argument— which centers on the role of large numbers of bureaucrats affiliated with regional institutions that push for enhanced integration[36]—also does not obtain in this case.

---

[30] The various problems with explanations drawn from realism and liberalism that can be applied to Mercosur will not be reviewed here since they have already been detailed elsewhere (see the discussions in Hurrell 1994, 170–73, 178; Hurrell 1995, 258; Hollist and Nielson 1998, 269–71, 274–76; Solingen 1998, 119; Grieco 1997, 175–78; and Carranza 2000, 17–19).

[31] See, for example, Haas 1958; Haas 1964; Scheinman 1966; and Lindberg and Scheingold 1970.

[32] See the discussion in Cameron 1992, 25.

[33] IADB 2001, 5; see also Gonzalez 1999; Kaltenthaler and Mora 2002, 76; and Phillips 2001, 575.

[34] Manzetti 1993, 119.

[35] *Economist*, 12 October 1996, S9.

[36] See, for example, Scheinman 1966; and Lindberg and Scheingold 1970, chap. 4.

A second general approach to regional integration that can be applied to Mercosur is customs union theory, which owes its genesis to Jacob Viner's analysis.[37] Although economists almost always use Viner's trade creation/trade diversion framework simply to determine the welfare effects of these agreements, a simple prediction that can be derived from the theory is that regional integration is more likely to be consolidated when the potential for trade creation is high. At the inception of Mercosur, evidence was mixed concerning the agreement's potential for trade creation. On one hand, the members of Mercosur traded with each other more than we would expect on the basis of gravity models of trade (at least as of 1990), thereby indicating some potential for trade creation.[38] On the other hand, the region's comparatively low intraregional trade share in 1990 (6.1 percent) suggested that Argentina and Brazil did not have especially complementary economies and that the potential for trade creation was not high (comparable figures in 1990 for the EC were 47.1 percent; for NAFTA, 24.6 percent; and for East Asia, 29.3 percent).[39] Moreover, the share of intraregional trade as a percentage of total trade undertaken by members of Mercosur was at the same level in 1990 as it was in 1965.[40] As it turns out, Mercosur has not resulted in significant trade creation. Instead, Alexander Yeats demonstrates that Mercosur resulted in much more trade diversion than trade creation.[41] Although customs union theory is certainly not irrelevant, it does not provide a particularly strong explanation for Mercosur's consolidation during the early and middle 1990s.[42]

A third potential explanation for Mercosur drawn from constructivism highlights the ideational shift in these countries in the late 1980s, away from import-substitution industrialization (ISI) policies toward international economic openness.[43] It is true that the decision to pursue regional integration does roughly correlate with the timing of this ideational shift among the members of Mercosur. However, this explanation does not tell us why regional integration was preferable to unilateral liberalization. More importantly, focusing on this

[37] Viner 1950.

[38] See Frankel, Stein, and Wei 1997, 69–72. In their analysis, the estimates for the Mercosur dummy variable are positive as of 1970, but this variable is statistically significant only in 1990.

[39] Frankel, Stein, and Wei 1997, 63.

[40] Over the entire 1965–90 period, the intraregional trade share of trade undertaken by the members of Mercosur are as follows: 1965 (6.1 percent); 1970 (5.0 percent); 1975 (4.0 percent); 1980 (5.6 percent); 1985 (4.3 percent); and 1990 (6.1 percent); see Frankel, Stein, and Wei 1995, 63.

[41] Yeats 1998.

[42] The standard Vinerian framework would at the very least predict that Mercosur would experience less trade diversion as compared to the bulk of other integration agreements in the developing world that are comprised of states whose economies are even less complementary than Mercosur. In turn, while it is true that trade complementarity among the members of Mercosur was not anything near the levels in North America, East Asia, or Western Europe in 1990, trade complementarity among the members of Mercosur was nevertheless higher than was the case among these same four countries in the 1960s (see Braga, Safadi, and Yeats 1994, 5).

[43] For a brief discussion along these lines, see Hurrell 1998a, 247–48.

ideational shift makes it very hard to explain why Mercosur outperformed other RTAs in the developing world, unless one is willing to claim that the group's members repudiated ISI more forcefully than other countries at this time—a notion that cannot be sustained with respect to Brazil.[44]

In his recent book, Walter Mattli develops a fourth general approach to regional integration that can be applied to Mercosur.[45] Mattli emphasizes that regional economic integration can have negative effects upon the economic growth of nonmembers and that states may try to join the existing RTA in response. But since this choice is often unavailable to states, the only option left is to form a rival group.[46] Significant evidence exists in support of Mattli's basic claim that the creation of Mercosur was driven partly by fears of NAFTA and the EU at the beginning of the 1990s.[47] That being said, it is very hard to explain why Mercosur achieved a greater degree of consolidation than other developing country RTAs during the early and middle 1990s by pointing to fears of NAFTA and the EU. Highlighting such a general force in the international environment makes it impossible to explain such variation. Moreover, the EU and NAFTA did not become "fortress" protectionist blocs, and hence many of the initial fears of these two groupings within Mercosur very quickly evaporated.[48]

A fifth and final general approach to integration that can be applied to Mercosur emphasizes the influence of domestic interest groups as prime shapers of regional economic integration. In the current literature, the most common version of this perspective focuses on the role played by domestic firms as key supporters and catalysts for regional integration.[49] In this view, successful regional integration is more likely to eventuate when domestic firms strongly lobby for regional integration. This perspective has very little empirical support with respect to Mercosur, however. As one analyst summarizes, "in contrast to the Canada-U.S. Free Trade Agreement and Europe's Maastricht treaty, both strongly supported and even initiated by business interests, Mercosur is largely a state-led project."[50] After Mercosur was formed, the immediate

[44] On this point, see, for example, Hufbauer and Schott 1994, 59.

[45] Mattli 1999a.

[46] Two other important recent studies of regional integration that emphasize a similar dynamic are Gruber 2000; and Lazer 1999. I focus only on Mattli's analysis here because he is the most direct in applying his framework to Mercosur.

[47] This empirical evidence is reviewed in Brooks 1994.

[48] It should be noted that a second potential explanation advanced in Mattli's book is also not compelling for Mercosur. Mattli argues that "successful integration *requires* the presence of an undisputed leader" within the group that is willing to act as a regional paymaster, help coordinate disputes, and so on (Mattli 1999a, 56). However, this key supply condition is simply not present with respect to Mercosur, as Mattli freely admits: "Brazil has been reluctant to use its economic and political position to assume active political leadership. Whenever short-term national interests have been at stake, Brazil has relegated Mercosur to second place" (160).

[49] See, for example, Milner 1997; Frieden 1996; and Chase 1998.

[50] Jenkins 1999, 42–43. For similar assessments, see Hurrell 1995, 258; Manzetti 1993, 117; Page 2000, 55; Kaltenthaler and Mora 2002, 84; and Cason 2000, 2.

reaction among domestic firms was largely lukewarm or hostile.[51] Influential business sectors, companies, and industrial associations in both Brazil and Argentina actively lobbied for delays and restrictions in the agreement.[52] Early on, the level and scope of lobbying by firms against Mercosur was significant enough to prompt many policymakers to complain that the integration project was in danger of failing due to lack of enthusiasm from business leaders.[53]

There is also little evidence in this case that supports Helen Milner's more specific argument that domestic firms characterized by increasing returns to scale (IRS) will play an important role in shaping regional integration.[54] Milner's aim is to explain why some sectors in RTAs are more liberalized than others, but her basic perspective can easily be expanded to provide an explanation for the extent of consolidation of RTAs.[55] In this view, domestic firms characterized by IRS are likely to have strong incentives to lobby their respective governments in favor of regional integration since these firms will be able to set up regional production strategies if integration is consolidated. Milner's general perspective is very compelling with respect to NAFTA and the EU, where there are scores of domestic firms characterized by IRS.[56] In Mercosur, however, there were relatively few such domestic firms before 1991, in large part because of these countries' long-standing import-substitution policies. For the most part, the companies characterized by IRS that could regionalize production if integration proceeded were not domestic companies, but rather firms based outside of Mercosur.[57] It is thus no surprise that we find, for example, little

[51] One poll taken in the summer of 1991 revealed that businessmen in all four countries were doubtful that companies from their respective countries were capable of effectively competing within the bloc: On a scale of 1 to 10, Brazilians rated their companies readiness for integration at 6.14, Argentines at 5.53, Paraguayans at 4.78, and Uruguayans at 4.82 (see Foreign Broadcast Information Service–Latin America, 23 September 1991, 1).

[52] See, for example, Jenkins 1999, 42–43; Fischer 1999, 204; *Latin American Weekly Report*, 10 September 1992, 4; August 1992, 7; 19 November 1992, 1; Foreign Broadcast Information Service—Latin America, 30 December 1992, 1; and *Washington Post*, June 19, 1991, B4. The Argentine business interests that worked most forcefully against Mercosur included steel companies, textile producers, petrochemical firms, and various agricultural interests. Important bases of business opposition to Mercosur in Brazil included the textile industry and the Federaçao das Indústrias do Estado de São Paulo.

[53] See, for example, *Latin American Weekly Report*, 28 May 1992, 1. Not all business groups lobbied against Mercosur. However, the most significant pro-Mercosur lobby, Grupo Brasil, was not formed until early 1995—that is, after the most significant steps to consolidate Mercosur had already been taken (see *New York Times*, 4 July 1995, A29).

[54] Milner 1997.

[55] In an earlier version of her analysis (1995), Milner did, in fact, extend her argument in this manner.

[56] See Milner 1997, 95–102.

[57] Not surprisingly, in a poll of businesses taken just after Mercosur's formation, MNCs were the most optimistic respondents about the agreement (see Foreign Broadcast Information Service—Latin America, 22 November 1991). See also Fischer 1999, 206.

increase in intraregional investment by domestic firms following the initiation of Mercosur.[58] Instead, MNCs based outside Mercosur have been dominant in this regard.

COMPETITION FOR FDI AND THE CONSOLIDATION
OF MERCOSUR

Mercosur achieved an impressive level of consolidation during the early and middle 1990s, and existing general approaches to integration provide relatively little leverage in explaining this outcome. The question at issue is whether, as the theoretical analysis posits, Mercosur came as far as it did during the early and middle 1990s in part due to competition for FDI. If this is the case, then we would expect to find evidence that (1) policymakers regarded Mercosur as useful for attracting increased FDI; (2) Mercosur produced substantial FDI dividends that were, in turn, recognized by policymakers; (3) Mercosur's institutional design was structured to reassure MNCs; and (4) the drive to attract increased FDI helped make it possible to overcome key early disputes in Mercosur. These four observable implications are successively reviewed below.

Policymakers View Investing in Mercosur as Useful for
Attracting Increased FDI

We would first expect to find evidence that policymakers early on saw investing in Mercosur as useful for attracting increased FDI. Decision makers in Brazil and Argentina are of central importance in this respect, since the other full members of Mercosur, Paraguay and Uruguay, have very little influence.[59] In turn, it is policymakers in the executive branch of Argentina and Brazil that are of key concern, since "Mercosur has been marked by a top-down development strategy heavily dependent upon presidential initiatives."[60]

[58] According to one estimate, Brazil's FDI in Mercosur grew only from U.S.$180 million in 1991 to U.S.$350 million in 1995 (Roett 1999, 31). According to another estimate, through mid-1997, Brazilian firms had investments or joint ventures in Argentina worth a total of U.S.$425 million, whereas Argentine firms had invested around U.S.$450 million in Brazil (IADB 1997, 15). In comparison, Brazil received more than U.S.$31 billion in FDI from MNCs based outside of Mercosur in 1999 (UNCTAD 2000a, 284).

[59] In 1999, Paraguay had a GDP of U.S.$7.7 billion, while Uruguay had a GDP of U.S.$20.8 billion. In comparison, Brazil had a GDP of U.S.$751.5 billion, while Argentina had a GDP of U.S.$283.2 billion (data from World Bank 2001).

[60] Manzetti 1993, 117. Manzetti further notes that the early stages of the integration process were characterized "by a reluctance of political parties and interest groups to commit themselves to MERCOSUR" and that "although the respective national parliaments approved the Treaty overwhelmingly, they have played a largely passive role in its progress" (117). There is widespread

Key Brazilian policymakers noted early on that attracting increased FDI was a central benefit of Mercosur. When asked in 1993 what importance Brazil attached to Mercosur, then finance minister Fernando Henrique Cardoso responded: "Mercosur will generate interest abroad because it will become a plum area for foreign investments."[61] Significant policymakers from Argentina echoed this sentiment. Domingo Cavallo, then foreign minister, noted just before Mercosur was formed that the "ultimate objective of Latin American integration is to obtain investments for Latin American countries. . . . Investments will rapidly flow through the integration process."[62] In a speech near the end of his term in office, President Carlos Menem underscored that one of the advantages of Mercosur was that it made Argentina and Brazil "more attractive for direct investment, an essential element in guaranteeing sustained long-term growth."[63]

By the end of the 1980s, attracting FDI had become a key priority for Argentina.[64] Beginning in 1989, the Argentine government undertook a number of policy changes that greatly enhanced the investment climate for MNCs in the early 1990s, including (1) the initiation of significant macroeconomic reforms in 1990; (2) a liberalization of the country's FDI regulations;[65] and (3) the signing 25 bilateral investment treaties between 1990 and 1994.[66] While these economic reforms helped make Argentina more attractive to MNCs at this time, Argentine policymakers believed that the country would continue to be handicapped in attracting FDI by the country's relatively small economic size. For that reason, Felix Pena, then undersecretary for Mercosur and inter-American relations in the Argentine Ministry of Foreign Relations, noted in 1992 that it was necessary "to change the magnitude of production in order to attract capital here. . . . Once Mercosur is in place, a manufacturer knows he has a market of almost 200 million people with an economy of $500 billion a year."[67]

---

agreement among scholars on this point; see, for example, Hurrell 1995, 258; and Jenkins 1999, 42–43. Exactly why the legislatures in the Mercosur countries delegated initiative to the respective presidents to this extent is an interesting question that requires further study (for a discussion of the reasons why legislatures sometimes choose to allow the executive to take the initiative in negotiations with other states, see Martin 2000, esp. 31–36).

[61] Foreign Broadcast Information Service—Latin America, 6 July 1993, 42.

[62] Foreign Broadcast Information Service—Latin America, 4 September 1990.

[63] "Argentina's Menem in Brazil, Stresses Improved Ties and Regional Alliance," BBC Worldwide Monitoring, 19 October 1999.

[64] See Solingen 1998.

[65] In particular, the need for prior authorization was eliminated in a host of industries (Agosin 1995, 12).

[66] Argentina signed bilateral investment treaties, which provide for various forms of protection for MNCs, with all but four members of the OECD (OECD 1997, 36). By the end of 1995, all of these bilateral investment treaties had been ratified and put in force (OECD 1997, 36).

[67] *New York Times*, 5 July 1992, C8.

As in Argentina, there was a clearly a newfound desire in Brazil to attract increased FDI by the start of the 1990s.[68] However, Brazil was in a much different situation than Argentina. The world's tenth largest economy, Brazil was large enough to be a significant draw for FDI on its own. In comparison to Argentina, however, Brazil lagged behind during the first half of the 1990s in enacting economic reforms to improve the investment climate for MNCs.[69] It was only in July 1994 that the Brazilian government began taking effective steps to restore stability in the economy with the introduction of the Real Plan. In turn, it was not until 1995 that the new Cardoso government was able to implement a significant liberalization of FDI regulations, most notably an amendment to the constitution that eliminated the distinction between "national companies" and "national companies of Brazilian capital."[70] Finally, Brazil lagged behind Argentina in initiating and implementing bilateral investment treaties in the early 1990s.[71]

Given this record, a significant benefit of Mercosur for Brazil during the early and middle 1990s was that regional integration could be used to signal MNCs.[72] Because consolidating regional integration is costly, demonstrating a firm commitment to integration could send a strong signal that Brazil was, in fact, a liberal state striving to provide a favorable long-term investment climate for MNCs. In this respect, Brazilian officials argued that it was crucial for the members of Mercosur to successfully meet the established timetable for integration in order to reassure MNCs. In August 1992, for example, Celso Lafer (foreign minister of Brazil) and Rubens Barbosa (an undersecretary in the Foreign Ministry) respectively stressed that "Mercosur is already included by multinational corporations in their strategies" and that "The first challenge is fulfilling the treaty. Failure to meet deadlines and fulfill agreements would be a blow to the credibility of the four countries."[73] Similarly, Brazilian ambassador Marcos Castrioto de Azambuja noted in 1994 that, as a result of Mercosur's extensive consolidation, "Brazil and Argentina have reinforced in all senses their credibility," and underscored that "the great international companies . . . are today investing in the two countries and are planning future investments. . . . It is important that nothing dissipate the intense focus on the construction of Mercosur. . . . The lack of success in

---

[68] See, for example, Grosse 1990.

[69] See, for example, Solingen 1998, 147; and Hufbauer and Schott 1994, 59.

[70] OECD 1997, 23.

[71] OECD 1998, 47. While Argentina had already ratified 25 treaties by the end of 1995, Brazil had signed treaties with only 12 countries by then and had not yet ratified any.

[72] The relative lateness of Brazil's economic reforms means that a common explanation for why Mexico undertook NAFTA, namely, to "lock in" a shift to market-liberal economic policies, does not apply to Mercosur (on the lock-in argument, see, for example, Ikenberry 2001, 240–41). By the time Brazil introduced the Real Plan in July 1994, the scheduled tariff reductions within Mercosur had already been almost fully implemented.

[73] "Latin America: NAFTA Brings Home Need to Speed Up Integration," Inter Press Service, 22 August 1992.

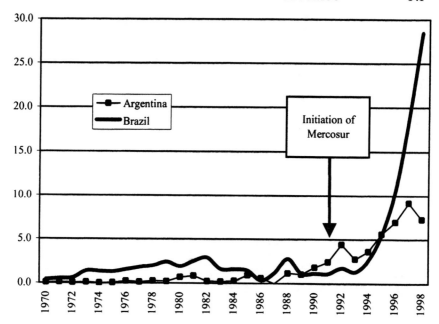

Figure 5.1 FDI Inflows to Argentina and Brazil, 1970–1998 (U.S.$billions)
Source: UNCTAD FDI/TNC database.

this common associative enterprise . . . [would] detract from the external credibility of the two countries."[74]

We also find that policymakers from Argentina and Brazil explicitly pointed to the consolidation of Mercosur during the early and middle 1990s while lobbying MNCs to invest more in the region. This was perhaps most significant at Mercosur's June 1995 summit, which 250 international businessmen were invited to attend. At that meeting, the leaders of Mercosur argued that the success of Mercosur made the region a more attractive place to invest and called on MNCs to enhance their presence in the region.[75]

Mercosur Pays Substantial FDI Dividends That Policymakers Recognize

A second piece of evidence we would expect to find is that Mercosur's significant consolidation in the early and middle 1990s would pay substantial FDI dividends that were, in turn, recognized by policymakers. As figure 5.1 shows,

[74] Castrioto de Azambuja 1994, 69 (author's translation).
[75] "Mercosur Leaders Call for Investment," United Press International, 19 June 1995.

■ Brazil & Argentina (combined)

☐ All other developing countries (combined)

1990

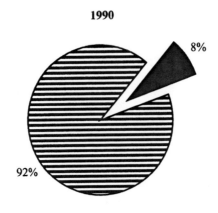

8%

92%

1998

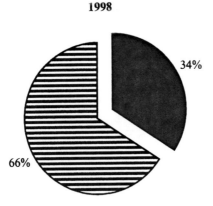

34%

66%

Figure 5.2 Share of FDI Inflows to Developing Countries Going to Argentina and Brazil, 1990 and 1998
Source: UNCTAD FDI/TNC database.

FDI inflows into Argentina and Brazil did, in fact, increase dramatically after
Mercosur was initiated in 1991, rising more than tenfold from 1990 to 1998.[76]
As a result, the stock of inward FDI as a percentage of GDP more than doubled
during this period in both Brazil (rising from 8.0 percent in 1990 to 17.1 percent

[76] Mercosur also appears to have prompted a significant rise in the quality of FDI in many sectors, particularly automobiles (e.g. IADB and IRELA 1996, 69; Tigre et al. 1999, 123; and Agosin
1995, 92).

in 1998) and Argentina (increasing from 6.4 percent in 1990 to 13.9 percent in 1998). As figure 5.2 indicates, this marked rise in FDI during the early and middle 1990s was not simply a product of growing world FDI flows: Argentina and Brazil were much more effective at competing for FDI after Mercosur was initiated.

Mercosur is clearly not the only cause of this surge of FDI into Argentina and Brazil, but analysts agree that regional integration played an important contributing role, especially during the early and middle 1990s.[77] In addition, there is much direct evidence demonstrating that MNCs took Mercosur into account when making investment decisions. First, the importance of Mercosur as a motivation for FDI appears in various surveys of MNCs. One Pricewaterhouse survey of executives representing over two hundred of the largest MNCs with operations in Latin America and the Caribbean revealed that regional integration was an important factor in their decision to invest in Mercosur.[78] Another survey of MNCs that invested in Argentina found that Mercosur was a critical factor motivating the decision, especially for manufacturing firms.[79] Finally, a recent UNCTAD survey of MNCs found that Mercosur had increased investor's confidence in Brazil as an investment site: "Among the investors already in Brazil, the Mercosur has reinforced the favorable perceptions of the optimists and has gone some way in reducing the negative impressions of the pessimists."[80] Moreover, this UNCTAD survey found that more than 80 percent of MNCs investing in Brazil viewed Mercosur as important to their regional strategies.[81]

Beyond these general surveys, it is clear Mercosur also influenced specific investment decisions by MNCs. In interviews, executives from GM,[82] Motorola,[83] Kodak,[84] Electrolux,[85] Renault,[86] and Bayer AG[87] explicitly cite Mercosur as a

---

[77] As one analysis summarizes, "In the Mercosur . . . most direct investment inflows have taken place *after* the Treaty of Asuncion. . . . These points remain valid even after allowing for the major role in FDI inflows played by privatization and debt-conversion schemes that are seen as having little to do with regional integration" (IADB and IRELA 1996, 62). Other assessments that Mercosur played an important role in stimulating inward FDI include Devlin and Davis 1999, 277; OECD 1998, 12; OECD 1997, 11; World Bank 2000, 37; UNCTAD 1998, xxiv, 17, 246, 251; UNCTAD 1999, 62; UNCTAD 2000b, 21–23; Weintraub 2000, 14, 65; Agosin 1995, 34; Lemos and Moro 1999, 19–20; and IADB and IRELA 1998, 15, 20, 87.

[78] See *Latin Finance*, June 1999, 12.

[79] Chudnovsky, Lopez, and Porta 1996, 66–67.

[80] UNCTAD 2000b, 113.

[81] UNCTAD 2000b, 112.

[82] *New York Times*, 13 September 1993, D1.

[83] *Gazeta Mercantil News*, 28 October 1996.

[84] *Business Week*, 4 May 1992, 50.

[85] O'Keefe 1997, chap. 8, 18.

[86] "Renault to Invest One Billion Dollars over Four Years," BBC Summary of World Broadcasts, 9 March 1999; and *Economist*, 12 October 1996, 10.

[87] "Mercosur Chemicals Led by Argentine Growth," *Chemical Market Reporter Outlook*, 20 December 1999.

key reason for their company's decision to undertake new FDI in the region or to upgrade existing facilities. One executive from Bayer, for example, outlined the rationale for an increased presence in Mercosur by noting: "The establishment of Mercosur has created an important trading zone which is attractive for investment and has given the region a stronger position in the world market. Its 206 million inhabitants and gross domestic product of $1.15 trillion makes Mercosur the world's third largest trading bloc, after the European Union and NAFTA (North American Free Trade Agreement) region. This makes Mercosur an important market for Bayer."[88]

We also find numerous examples of MNCs that tailored their production strategies to take advantage of Mercosur. As one European MNC executive notes: "Mercosur allows us to think about the region in terms of optimizing our production arrangements."[89] Many MNCs, including Siemens, Solvay, and Nestle, have sought to produce some inputs in one Mercosur country and other inputs in another country as part of regional or global production strategy.[90] Numerous other MNCs—including BASF,[91] FMC Corporation,[92] General Motors,[93] Hewlett-Packard,[94] Dow Chemical,[95] Xerox,[96] and Bayer[97]—have either established new plants to serve the entire Mercosur market or have consolidated into a single, upgraded plant.

Policymakers clearly recognized that Mercosur produced significant FDI dividends. In 1998, Finance Minister Malan maintained that being a member of Mercosur had made it easier for MNCs to have confidence in Brazil as an investment site, and that Mercosur thereby gave Brazil an advantage over Southeast Asia, Eastern Europe, and Russia in the competition to attract FDI.[98] In one speech in 1998, President Menem noted, "Inflows of capital continue to pour into our region, Mercosur. FDI attained an all-time record of 26 billion dollars last year. Mercosur has thus become one of the regions attracting the largest amount of investments in the world and a fundamental tool of integration for member states."[99]

---

[88] "Mercosur Chemicals" 1999.

[89] UNCTAD 2000b, 113.

[90] See Hasenclever, Lopez, and Clemente de Oliveira 1999, 183–184; *Economist*, 12 October 1996, S10; and Tigre et al. 1999.

[91] *Wall Street Journal*, 24 September 1992, R6.

[92] O'Keefe 1997, chap. 8, p. 20.

[93] *New York Times*, 25 April 1997, D4.

[94] "HP to Manufacture Laser Printers in Brazil," *Gazeta Mercantil Online*, 2 March 2000.

[95] *Business Week*, 15 June 1992.

[96] O'Keefe 1997, chap. 8, p. 20.

[97] "Brazilian Stabilization Boosts Chemical Growth," *Chemical Market Reporter Outlook*, 20 December 1999.

[98] "Malan: Brazilian Economic Situation Unlike Russian Crisis," Foreign Broadcast Information Service—Latin America, 26 August 1998. See also "Malan in Uruguay Denies New Fiscal Measures after Election," Foreign Broadcast Information Service—Latin America, 19 August 1998.

[99] "Argentine President Tells Mercosur of Need to Boost Integration Efforts," BBC Summary of World Broadcasts, 4 August 1998.

And in another speech in 1999, Menem declared that "MERCOSUR Common Market of the South is undoubtedly a successful endeavor" in part because it had helped attract increased FDI in the region.[100]

Mercosur's Institutional Design Is Structured to Reassure MNCs

In order to attract increased FDI, a state must reassure MNCs that it will not expropriate the firm's assets or engage in other forms of opportunism. International institutions are very useful in this regard, as they help make state commitments more credible: if states embed assurances against unfair treatment of MNCs within an international institution, this raises the costs of acting in a predatory manner toward MNCs and hence reduces the likelihood that governments will do so. A third piece of evidence we would consequently expect to find is that Mercosur's members would seek to shape the terms of the integration agreement to reassure MNCs that they will enjoy favorable investment conditions. This is indeed the case. In 1994, the four countries signed the Extra-Zone Foreign Investment Protocol expressly in order to reassure MNCs in this manner.[101] Some of the provisions of this protocol are briefly described below.

First, it contains assurances against unfair or discriminatory treatment of foreign investments by third parties. As one analysis summarizes: "Each member party [of the protocol] undertakes to assure that just and equitable treatment will be accorded to investment of third parties and will in no way hamper their management, their continuance, their utilization, their privileges or their realization, by any unjustified or discriminatory measures."[102] Toward this end, the protocol "provides that foreign investments coming from third parties will enjoy national treatment in Mercosur countries. The protocol also contains a most-favored nation clause that requires each Mercosur country to give investments originated in non-Mercosur countries treatment no less favorable than the treatment granted to investments of any other national origin."[103]

Second, the protocol also restricts expropriations of MNC assets: "Under the Extra-Zone Protocol, expropriation by Mercosur members of investment by third country investors may take place only as required for reasons pertaining to public utility or social interest, on a non-discriminatory basis and after due legal process. Compensation will be fair, adequate and timely. Amounts of compensation will be determined on the basis of real value."[104] The protocol

---

[100] "Argentina's Menem in Brazil, Stresses Improved Ties and Regional Alliance," BBC Worldwide Monitoring, 19 October 1999.

[101] See Naon 1996, 1105.

[102] OECD 1998, 26.

[103] Naon 1996, 1105.

[104] Argentine Ministry of Economy 1996, 45.

also establishes that compensation will be paid to investors in the event of damages caused by war, national emergencies, or insurrections.

Third, and perhaps most important, the protocol provides for binding international arbitration of disputes concerning foreign investments. States are allowed to bring disputes and, significantly, so too are MNCs themselves, which are "granted direct *ius standi* before international arbitral tribunals for claims against state parties."[105] MNCs are able to "directly submit, without prior exhaustion of local remedies, foreign investment claims against Mercosur host countries to international arbitral bodies that will make their decisions primarily on the basis of widely accepted international standards for the protection of foreign investments and investors. . . . [These panels] are detached from the national legal systems. If the parties do resort to such a panel, its decision is binding on the member countries involved in the dispute and prior exhaustion of local remedies is not required."[106]

As one legal analyst concludes, "the greatest actual delegation of sovereign powers is found in the Mercosur treaty provisions on dispute settlement. . . . In this respect, Mercosur attains an almost unparalleled level of supranationality."[107] Not only is the delegation of sovereign powers to arbitral panels substantial, but the level of delegation is also dramatic in a relative sense, since Mercosur actually gives more power to MNCs to bring claims than it does its *own* companies.[108] The delegation of sovereign powers to international arbitral panels is also noteworthy since the group's strongest member, Brazil, has sought to keep loss of sovereignty to Mercosur supranational institutions to an absolute minimum.[109] The protocol represents a marked departure from Brazil's past practices: "historically Brazil has been reluctant to accept binding arbitration between foreign economic agents and state entities on the grounds that this would affect the sovereign rights of the State."[110]

Drive to Attract FDI Helps Make It Possible to Overcome Early Disputes in Mercosur

We would also expect to find that successful resolution of early crises within Mercosur would be partly due to concerns among policymakers about how MNCs would react if disputes were not settled satisfactorily. This dynamic was

[105] Naon 1996, 1107.
[106] Naon 1996, 1107, 1108.
[107] Naon 1996, 1107, 1108.
[108] See the discussion in Naon 1996, 1105–8.
[109] See, for example, Pion-Berlin 2000, 52; and *Economist*, 12 October 1996, S9.
[110] OECD 1998, 48.

present in perhaps the two most serious crises during the initial phases of Mercosur, which occurred respectively in 1995 and 1997.

In 1995, Brazil threatened to unilaterally set quotas on imports of automobiles. Had this proposal gone through, it would have greatly damaged Argentina's automobile industry, which had attracted significant shares of FDI during the 1990–95 period—much of which was predicated on access to the Brazilian market. This prompted a huge dispute within Mercosur that threatened the agreement. Among other things, Argentina accused Brazil of unilaterally changing the rules of the agreement and thereby potentially scaring off MNCs. Guido di Tella, foreign minister of Argentina, publicly complained that Brazil's unilateral actions "do not encourage foreign investments in the region."[111] Argentina threatened to boycott a presidential summit of Mercosur countries in June 1995 unless Brazil changed its policies. The crisis was resolved by an agreement in February 1996 in which companies in either Brazil or Argentina were allowed to import parts and cars from either country duty-free, provided that the company match such imports with exports. Policymakers within Mercosur made it clear that this move was made in part with an eye toward reassuring and attracting MNCs. For example, Dorothea Werneck (Brazil's trade and industry minister) asserted, "The decisions of investors, both in the auto manufacturing and parts sectors, can now be made with a clear horizon."[112]

A second early crisis emerged in 1997 when Brazil threatened to force importers to pay for purchases in cash instead of allowing purchases to be made on credit, an action that would have greatly harmed the other members of Mercosur. Representatives from the other members of Mercosur criticized this Brazilian action, arguing, among other things, that it damaged the group's external credibility and would thereby make it harder to attract FDI. For example, Alberto Alvarez Gaiani, vice president of the Argentine Industrial Union, complained, "Although no blood is running in the streets, the most worrying aspect of this Brazilian behavior is that it demonstrates a lack of seriousness and legal insecurity to the Mercosur's foreign investors. . . . Many investors come to [Argentina] attracted by the Mercosur, aiming to direct their trade towards Brazil."[113] Brazil eventually backed down on this issue in response to complaints from the other Mercosur members.

Of course, fear among Mercosur policymakers about how MNCs would react if these crises were not satisfactorily resolved was not the sole factor that made it possible to overcome these disputes. However, the need to reassure MNCs was an important motivating force behind the reconciliation efforts in each of these two early crises.

[111] "Di Tella on Problems in Mercosur," BBC Summary of World Broadcasts, 30 June 1995.
[112] *Financial Post*, 14 February 1996, 49.
[113] "Mercosur Credibility Bruised by Brazilian Initiative," Inter-Press Service, 2 April 1997.

THE CONSOLIDATION OF MERCOSUR
AND REGIONAL SECURITY

The preceding analysis demonstrates that competition for FDI helped propel Mercosur policymakers to take great strides toward the consolidation of regional integration during the group's early years. Given the history of rivalry between Argentina and Brazil, a key question concerns the influence of Mercosur's consolidation on their security relations. This section reviews the Argentina-Brazil security relationship, focusing upon how it has changed in recent years. As will be seen below, the consolidation of Mercosur helped make it possible for Argentina and Brazil to decisively move beyond their long-standing security rivalry.

Argentine-Brazilian Security Relations prior to 1990

Conflicts between Argentina and Brazil emerged very soon after the independence of the two countries (actual hostilities over territory first broke out in 1825).[114] Thereafter the two countries became locked in a deep rivalry that lasted more than 150 years. "By the mid–nineteenth century, the language of power balancing had become well established as the dominant frame of reference for understanding the relationship. . . . High levels of mutual threat perception continued through the twentieth century and . . . the possibility of war and the importance of military preparedness were constant themes in strategic and diplomatic discussion."[115] The military establishments in Argentina and Brazil "exacerbated regional competition over resources and power, borrowing from Prussian and Nazi lebensraum theories to emphasize 'vital spaces.' Their military academies imbued generations of officers and civilians with a geopolitical perspective that stressed security dilemmas, state sovereignty, territorial disputes, and zero-sum trends in oil resources, population growth, and technological capabilities."[116]

Within Brazil, it had long been feared that Argentina was seeking to increase ties with other Spanish-speaking countries in the region in order isolate and encircle Brazil.[117] As one analyst noted in 1985: "The enduring image of Argentina as an aggressive, expansionist state lies at the core of the sense of threat that has pervaded Brazilian strategic circles for generations."[118] Brazil's force structure long reflected fears of Argentina, with the vast portion of its military capability focused on the southern part of the country. In turn, much of the design

---

[114] For a useful overview of the first century of the Argentina-Brazil rivalry, see Burr 1955.

[115] Hurrell 1998, 230.

[116] Solingen 1998, 156.

[117] See Vidigal 1989.

[118] Hilton 1985, 28.

and expansion of Brazil's transportation network of highways and railroad system in the 1950s was a direct function of the threat from Argentina.[119]

For Argentina's part, there were great concerns about the threat from Brazil, particularly as the balance of capabilities began to shift decisively in Brazil's favor after World War II. Moreover, Brazil's strengthening links in the 1960s and 1970s with Uruguay, Bolivia, and Paraguay due to augmented flows of settlers, investment, and trade—as well as the Paraguay-Brazil agreement on the Itaipu dam—caused Argentina to increasingly feel *it* was the country that was being encircled. In addition to building up its military forces to counter the Brazilian threat, Argentina followed a strategic policy "of 'empty provinces' under which, until the 1980s, no valued economic activities, and few bridges or transport systems were developed in the northern provinces as part of a geopolitical doctrine of strategic denial in the face of the Brazilian threat."[120]

Of notable concern in the region and elsewhere was that Argentina and Brazil took a dangerous turn toward a nuclear arms race in the 1970s.[121] Because it was falling behind in the conventional balance, Argentina invested heavily in developing the capability to produce nuclear weapons. Argentina's actions in this regard, particularly those in the early 1970s, prompted great concern in Brazil. In response, Brazil strongly pursued its own nuclear weapons program, particularly after 1974.[122]

Partly in response to fears of a nuclear arms race that seemed in the 1970s like it might run out of control, the leaders of Argentina and Brazil sought to dampen the security rivalry between the two countries. In 1980, Brazilian president Joao Figueiredo visited Argentina in an attempt to improve the security relationship. This visit and various subsequent agreements led to an improved climate in the 1980s.[123] While it was an improvement over the 1970s, the Argentine-Brazilian security relationship in the 1980s was hardly a cooperative one. During "the 1980s Brazil and Argentina were uneasy neighbors, each believing that it was locked in a zero-sum game to determine which country would be the dominant player in the region."[124] And although both sides were obviously concerned about the severity of the nuclear rivalry in the 1970s, even

[119] Hilton 1985, 33.

[120] Hurrell 1998a, 250.

[121] Hilton 1987, 332.

[122] As Hilton describes, Argentina developed "a nuclear program based on natural uranium reactors, whose military potential is considerably greater than that of reactors using enriched uranium—a fact carefully noted by Brazilian military observers. After inauguration of the Arucha I reactor in 1974, Argentine scientists announced that producing a nuclear weapon depended solely on a political decision, and when Argentina and India signed an atomic energy accord in May, there was immediate speculation in Brazil that the La Plata adversary in fact would be able to manufacture nuclear arms. . . . Subsequent reaffirmations of Argentina's capacity to develop a nuclear arsenal reinforced Brazil's determination to accelerate its own nuclear project" (Hilton 1985, 35).

[123] See Selcher 1985; Hilton 1985; and Pion-Berlin 2000.

[124] Roett 1999, 1.

after the demise of the military governments in both countries, in 1983 and 1985 respectively, there was "no real breakthrough in nuclear cooperation" during the 1980s.[125]

Throughout the 1980s, Brazil continued to have significant security concerns about Argentina. Early on in the decade, the Falklands/Malvinas War of 1982 was viewed by Brazil as a "worrying sign that the extreme 'territorial nationalism' in Argentina had not disappeared . . . and that armed conflict might be possible in the region."[126] After President Raul Alfonsin took over from the military government in 1983, Argentine defense policy was marked by a significant degree of continuity. With respect to conventional weapons, Argentina's rearmament program after the Falklands War was viewed with concern within Brazil.[127] Of particular significance is that "Argentina initiated the development of a very costly, sophisticated, and threatening weapon of mass destruction (the Condor II) as an integral part of the foreign policy of the first post-authoritarian government."[128] In the nuclear arena, "the surprise announcement by Argentina, in November 1983, that they had developed uranium enrichment technology through a secret program, and were proceeding to build a production plant, shocked Brazilians, [and] introduced a greater element of suspicion and distrust into the relationship."[129] During the 1980s, President Alfonsin also "maintained Argentina's opposition to the NPT (Nuclear Non-Proliferation Treaty) and refused to ratify Tlatelolco, and maintained its right to peaceful nuclear explosions."[130] More generally, security concerns within Brazil were heightened by Argentina's political instability: "Military uprisings in Argentina during the 1986–1990 period underscored the uncertainty of civilian rule and the endurance of belligerent nationalist sentiment in Brazil's most powerful neighbor."[131]

Foreign policy changes in Brazil during the 1980s were not especially dramatic, and, as a result, Argentina continued to feel anxiety about its northern neighbor. Of particular importance is that the democratic revolution in the 1980s in Brazil did not extend to the armed forces: the military continued to maintain a great deal of autonomy regarding defense policy. In particular, "the renewal of democracy in the 1980s did little to undermine Brazil's nuclear programs. . . . Sections of Brazil's military continued their 'parallel program' with weapons applications even after attempts to place all nuclear activities under democratic control."[132] Argentina also had significant concerns due to the

---

[125] Solingen 1998, 141, 152. Cf. Barletta 1999.
[126] Barletta 1999, 21. See also Hurrell 1995, 252.
[127] See Barletta 1999, 21; and Hilton 1987, 333.
[128] Griffith 1998, 172.
[129] Selcher 1985, 46; see also Hilton 1987, 333.
[130] See Solingen 1998, 141.
[131] Barletta 1999, 21.
[132] Solingen 1998, 157, 141.

enhanced scope of the Brazilian conventional weapons industry during the 1980s, which was augmented to the point that Brazil became one of the top 10 exporters of arms in the mid-1980s.[133]

Mercosur and the Transformation of the Argentine-Brazilian Security Relationship in the 1990s

While the Argentine-Brazil security climate improved in the 1980s, it was only in the 1990s that a stable, peaceful security relationship was firmly consolidated. Within the specialist literature, there is widespread agreement that an important contributing factor to this development is Mercosur.[134] This is the assessment not just of analysts, but of Argentine and Brazilian policymakers as well. For example, former president Cardoso of Brazil emphasizes: "The international order that has emerged in recent years—maturing and consolidating at an accelerated pace with the implementation of Mercosur—reduce the probability that conventional external regional conflicts involving our country will manifest."[135] Similarly, the Argentine secretary for state intelligence, Hugo Anzorreguy, stressed in 1999 that after "decades of confrontation and conflict scenarios between the countries that are now members of Mercosur . . . we now have a new scenario of cooperation."[136]

Mercosur's role in fostering improved security ties was not as a catalyst for rapprochement; Argentina and Brazil were already taking steps toward an improved security relationship in the period immediately prior to the group's creation.[137] Instead, Mercosur's key contribution was to help make it possible for the incipient security rapprochement to be consolidated in a manner that makes backtracking unlikely, and even deeper forms of security cooperation possible. It is in this respect that Roett concludes that "Mercosur is a bold and imaginative initiative that has laid to rest the traditional and spasmodic conflicts that afflicted the region."[138] Absent Mercosur, the Argentina-Brazil security rapprochement would have been more tentative and more likely to be reversed. In short, the fundamental transformation of the security relationship between Argentina and Brazil came after Mercosur and occurred partly in response to the process of integration.

[133] Hirst 1998, 105.

[134] See Roett 1999, 4; Hirst 1996, 176–77; Hirst 1998, 113; Hirst 1999, 44; Manzetti 1993, 110; Fujita 1998, 579, 581; Escudé and Fontana 1998; Guedes da Costa 1995, 9 and 1998, 229; Hurrell 1998a; Donadio and Tibiletti 1998, 111; Tulchin and Espach 1998, 175; and Weintraub 2000, 18–20, 77.

[135] Cardoso as cited in Guedes da Costa 1998, 230.

[136] BBC Worldwide Monitoring, 22 July 1999.

[137] On this point, see, for example, Hurrell 1998a.

[138] Roett 1999, 4.

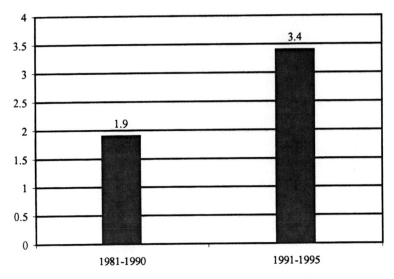

Figure 5.3 Average Number of Argentina-Brazil Presidential Meetings per Year
Source: South American Cooperation and Conflict Database, compiled by Randall Parish.

Integration theorists and others have long emphasized that regional economic integration has beneficial effects on security by improving the overall tenor of relations through the development of stronger communication links between policymakers.[139] Until recently, actual meetings between the key decision-makers in Argentina and Brazil had been rare: the presidents of Argentina and Brazil reportedly did not have a single one-on-one meeting between 1935 and 1980.[140] During the 1980s, meetings between the presidents of the two countries became more frequent. As figure 5.3 shows, Mercosur caused the scope of consultations at this level to jump to an even higher level. This sharp increase in the rate of presidential meetings during the 1991–95 period as compared to the previous decade is entirely due to Mercosur: half of the meetings during 1991–95 period (8 out of the 17) focused specifically on the integration process.[141]

Increased communication and personal contact of any sort between policymakers is likely to be beneficial: regular meetings mean less chance for diplomatic slights to be blown out of proportion, for misperceptions to develop, and so on. Mercosur has done much more than simply increase the *quantity* of interactions; it has also played a key role in shifting the *qualitative* nature of these

[139] See, for example, Deutsch et al. 1957; and Wendt 1994.

[140] Schmitter 1991, 109.

[141] All of this information is from the "South American Cooperation and Conflict (SACC)" database compiled by Randall Parish. I thank him for sharing this data.

interactions and the overall Argentine-Brazilian relationship in a more cooperative direction. As President Menem underscores, during the 1990s "Argentina and Brazil moved from being uncompromising neighbours to being indispensable partners."[142] Mercosur helped shift the locus of discussion away from "defensive" discussions of how to manage the security rivalry between the two states (as was largely the case during the 1980s) toward "positive" discussions of how to cooperate for mutual gain in a variety of areas. Hirst concludes that "economic factors have converted themselves into the most important source of the identification of common interests in the Southern Cone."[143] This has occurred not only with respect to the effort to reduce tariffs and other formal barriers to economic interactions as part of the regional integration process, but also ancillary issues such as improving transportation links in order to facilitate intraregional trade flows. As Brazilian ambassador Marcos Castrioto de Azambuja stressed in 1994, Mercosur contributed to Argentina and Brazil "confiding in each other" and thereby produced a situation in which there was "dissipating animosity for each other."[144]

As figure 5.4 indicates, the consolidation of Mercosur contributed to a dramatic expansion of trade flows in the region during the early and mid-1990s, helping to create strong vested interests in the populace for the continuation of a stable and peaceful security relationship. Virgilio Beltrán emphasizes that this "mesh of economic relations" contributed to "stable associations that . . . reduce levels of tension" and promoted "complementarities in the field of security."[145] Similarly, General Martín Balza, Argentine army chief of staff, stresses that "the development of economic interaction" contributes to "the necessary reasonableness and foresight to make the possibility of resorting to force in the solution of conflicts remote."[146]

These intensified economic interactions also put "pressure on the inadequate transportation and communications infrastructure that links the economies in the subregion [and] various physical integration projects have been undertaken to respond," including new bridges, more extensive road networks, better navigation networks on waterways, enhanced telecommunication links, and improvements in air and cargo transportation.[147] These deeper infrastructural links facilitated a higher level of interactions between Argentine and Brazilian businessmen and citizens, which likely fostered improved understanding between the two countries.[148] One indicator of these increased ties is that the 1.3 million

---

[142] BBC Monitoring Latin America, 19 October 1999.

[143] Hirst 1996, 182 (author's translation).

[144] Castrioto de Azambuja 1994, 71 (author's translation).

[145] Beltrán 2001, 59, 61 (author's translation).

[146] As quoted in Pion-Berlin 1998, 93.

[147] IADB 1996, 44; see the discussion in 44–48.

[148] On the general importance of these kinds of linkages for fostering better relations between countries, see Russett 1963; and Deutsch et al. 1957.

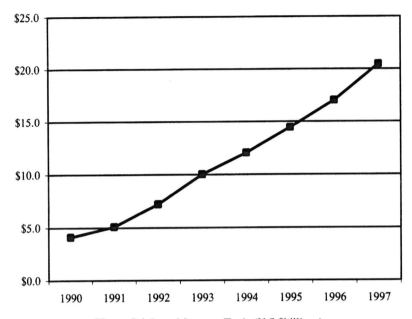

Figure 5.4 Intra-Mercosur Trade (U.S.$billions)
Source: Associación Latinoamericana de Integración Secretariat.

people traveling on airplanes between São Paulo and Buenos Aires in 1994 was double the level in 1990.[149]

A critical function of international institutions is the reduction of transaction costs.[150] Once an institution has been established—especially one that involves regular meetings and consultations of key decision-makers—the "marginal cost of dealing with each additional issue will be lower," thereby allowing "governments to take advantage of potential economies of scale."[151] Although Mercosur was not intended to be a security organization, it has increased transparency by establishing stronger communication links concerning security issues. Consultations regarding security among political leaders have become routine at Mercosur summits. Mercosur has also led to other forms of consultation over security.[152] These consultations, especially those between the Argentine and Brazilian

[149] *New York Times*, 4 July 1995, 47.
[150] See, for example, Keohane 1984.
[151] Keohane 1984, 90.
[152] As Grandi and Biezzózero note, through 1997 "ten strategic studies symposia have taken place, which began with the Argentine-Brazilian integration process and the participation of both countries' armed forces. Uruguay then became involved as a result of Mercosur negotiations, followed by Paraguay and recently Chile, which moved from being an observer to participate as a member" (1997, 45).

militaries, play a very useful role: "As the armies of the region come to know more about each other, their mutual anxieties and uncertainties are diminished."[153]

While security discussions within Mercosur have often focused upon confidence-building measures and other traditional security concerns, "nontraditional" security threats such as drugs, terrorism, and smuggling have become common areas for joint discussion.[154] In September 1998, for example, the justice ministers of Mercosur met to establish better coordination of counterterrorism actions.[155] And in April 1998, the "Mercosur Ministers of the Interior and of Justice established the Security Plan for the Triple Border, Argentina-Brazil-Paraguay. The objective of the plan is to facilitate the planning and execution of concerted efforts involving the governments of the three countries in the areas of fighting drug trafficking, automobile theft, contraband, and the trafficking of minors."[156]

Increased consultations over security are one thing; increased security *cooperation* is something much more significant. Early in the integration process, General Gleuber Vieira of Argentina noted, "The association [Mercosur], whose birth has been brought on by economic motives . . . will present to us the opportunity of cooperation in the fields of military and security."[157] This is indeed what happened: "Regional security cooperation has become a spill-around effect of the expansion of economic ties among Southern Cone countries. Hence, intraregional integration agreements have given place to a new chapter in regional security politics. . . . recent cooperative programs that sprang from the regional integration process have increased confidence and transparency among the militaries of Mercosur countries."[158] Of particular importance is that Mercosur contributed to the initiation of joint exercises between the Argentine and Brazilian militaries.[159] As General Balza of Argentina concludes: "There is no doubt that the launch of Mercosur guided the Armed Forces to think about everything related to integration from the military point of view."[160] As another Argentine military official put it: "After Mercosur, we realized we could do a lot of things together."[161] These joint military exercises

[153] Pion-Berlin 1998, 93.

[154] For example, Manzetti notes, "Mercosur has provided its member states with a forum for discussion of sensitive policy issues such as those in relation to transport and communications, nuclear proliferation (Argentina and Brazil signed a non-proliferation treaty in 1991), environmental protection, military cooperation, illegal immigration, and the drug traffic" (1993, 110).

[155] See Foreign Broadcast Information Service—Latin America, 25 September 1998.

[156] IADB 1998, 30.

[157] Vieira 1994, 12 (author's translation).

[158] The first two sentences in the quotation are from Hirst 1998, 113. The last sentence is from Hirst 1999, 44.

[159] See, for example, Rial 1995, 15. Cf. Pion-Berlin 2000.

[160] Balza 1995, 26 (author's translation).

[161] "South America Steady Route to Unity," *Jane's Defence Weekly*, 6 August 1997, 19.

have involved the armies of Argentina and Brazil, as well as the two countries' naval forces.[162]

A final, more indirect way that Mercosur has contributed to an improved security climate is by acting as a force for democratic stability. The presence of authoritarian regimes has long exacerbated security rivalries in the region, and hence the movement away from authoritarian rule has acted as a powerful force for stable security relationships.[163] The members of Mercosur have added a "democracy clause" to the agreement, that is, making democratic rule a prerequisite for membership in the agreement. The decision to institute the democracy clause followed the experience in 1996 in which Argentina, Uruguay, and Brazil used threats of expulsion from Mercosur as a strategy for promoting democracy in Paraguay.[164]

Is Mercosur an Incipient Security Community?

By the end of the 1990s, it was clear there had been a "phenomenal transformation in bilateral relations. . . . Once the region's primary competitors for geopolitical domination, Brazil and Argentina now, in Cardoso's words, share a 'common strategic vision.' "[165] Mercosur is certainly not the only cause of the marked shift in the region's security environment, but it did help to consolidate a stable, peaceful relationship between Argentina and Brazil.[166] Overall, the most visible manifestation of this new security relationship is the extensive military cooperation noted previously. On the Brazilian side, another key indicator is the changed orientation of the country's military forces. Historically, Brazil's military capability was directed southward, but "with no hypothesis of

---

[162] In September 1996, the armies of Argentina and Brazil undertook their first joint exercise (Operation Southern Cross) in Argentina, which was designed to simulate the execution of a UN peacekeeping mission. The following year, the exercise was expanded (involving 2,300 troops over 10 days) and was held in Brazilian territory. As a spokesman reported after one of these exercises, it was aimed at "improving cooperation, trust and friendship between the participants, and developing the capacity to plan and execute combined operations" (BBC Summary of World Broadcasts, 9 October 1997). For a discussion of Argentina-Brazil joint naval exercises, see Escudé and Fontana 1998, 61.

[163] See Schmitter 1991.

[164] In April 1996, Paraguay's president, Juan Carlos Wasmosy, tried to fire army general Lino Oviedo. Oviedo responded by gathering loyal troops and demanding that Wasmosy step down instead. In response, the other members of Mercosur threatened to expel Paraguay from Mercosur if Oviedo succeeded in replacing Wasmosy. As Richard Feinberg recounts, "This credible threat heartened Paraguay's democrats, sent shivers through the country's commercial classes, and helped convince General Oviedo's fellow officers that he could not prevail. . . . Within a matter of hours, General Oviedo capitulated and civilian authority was restored" (*International Herald Tribune*, 2 May 1996).

[165] Pion-Berlin 2000, 52.

[166] For useful reviews of the full range of factors contributing to this overall shift, see Hurrell 1998a; and Hirst 1998.

conflict contemplated with Argentina . . . Brazil has not only relaxed its guard at the southern frontier but has shifted military troops and installations to the northern perimeter of the Amazon."[167] As for Argentina, a significant indicator of this security reorientation in the region is its "decision to give up its policy of 'empty provinces,' . . . not only has such thinking disappeared, but increased infrastructural integration and ever-denser transborder ties have become a central part of the Mercosur project."[168]

A logical question to ask is whether the Mercosur countries are heading toward the development of a security community.[169] Karl Deutsch and his colleagues argued that security communities are more likely to develop in regions that share certain characteristics. These conditions within the region include (1) a wide range of mutual transactions and strong links of social communication; (2) a high expectation of joint economic gains; (3) a significant degree of mobility of persons; and (4) a high level of communication and transactions on more than one or two topics.[170] Before the establishment of Mercosur, these conditions were not present. In significant part due to Mercosur, these four conditions now increasingly characterize the region. As a result, there is a reasonable expectation that the establishment of Mercosur may contribute to the development of a security community in the Southern Cone.

There is, in fact, evidence of movement toward a security community. In May 1998, the member states of Mercosur announced that they would make the region defined by the common market one that was free of nuclear, chemical, and bacterial weapons, as well as conventional weapons capable of mass destruction.[171] On 24 July 1998 the members of Mercosur declared the region a "peace zone." In so doing, the signatory states agreed "to strengthen mechanisms of consultation and cooperation on existing issues of security and defense involving members and to promote their progressive coordination; and to increase cooperation in terms of measures aimed at developing trust and security, and to promote the implementation of such measures."[172] And in October 1999, Argentina and Brazil signed a declaration that designated the relations between the two countries as having reached the status of a "strategic alliance."[173]

In addition, Argentina has consistently pressed to develop an expansive and direct regional security system within the context of Mercosur. "The idea of creating a security system for the Southern Cone has been defended in Argentine academic, military and diplomatic circles. According to certain proposals

[167] Pion-Berlin 2000, 52.

[168] Hurrell 1998a, 533.

[169] This question is also explored in Hurrell 1998a; and Hirst 1998, 116–18.

[170] See Deutsch et al. 1957, 50–59.

[171] Xinhua New Agency, 9 May 1998.

[172] "Mercosur Presidents Declare Region a 'Zone of Peace,' " BBC Summary of World Broadcasts, 27 July 1998.

[173] BBC Monitoring Latin America, 19 October 1999.

this system would include the formation of a center responsible for avoiding subregional conflicts, a strategic data center, military technical exchange, and cooperation for civil protection."[174] Other proposals for security cooperation within Mercosur have been even more significant in scope. In November 1996, "the Argentine vice foreign minister, Andrés Cisneros, asserted that in the near future joint Argentine-Brazilian forces might have a single command, in the framework of subregional military integration. This statement was soon seconded by the chief of the Casa Militar of the Brazilian presidency, who said that it is very possible that agreements might soon be reached for formal military integration."[175]

Although these changes and proposals may lead to large-scale cooperation on security in the future, it is too soon to view Mercosur as a security community.[176] While Argentina and Brazil have put their long-term rivalry behind them, the two countries do not have completely overlapping interests in the security realm. In particular, Argentina frequently sought to move closer to the United States in the security realm during the 1990s, which led to frictions with Brazil. Another point of disagreement occurred in August 1997, when Argentina's president Menem announced opposition to Brazil's proposal of becoming a permanent member of the UN Security Council. Menem declared that giving Brazil the seat would "break the balance we currently have in the region" and asserted that it would be preferable if the seat were rotated among Argentina, Brazil, and Mexico.[177] In the end, the region has not yet reached the status of a security community.

CONCLUSION

There are many reasons why the consolidation of regional economic integration can enhance the prospects for peace. In the developing world, consolidating regional integration has unfortunately been difficult to achieve over the past several decades. The analysis here reveals that the globalization of production has the potential to influence security relations in the developing world by acting as a force that propels the consolidation of integration. This examination demonstrates that competition for FDI is an important reason why Mercosur made as much progress as it did during the early and middle 1990s. In turn, it was shown that the consolidation of Mercosur during this period helped make it possible for Argentina and Brazil to move beyond their long history of security rivalry and establish a stable and peaceful relationship.

While Mercosur initially made great strides, a number of serious problems have plagued the agreement during the past several years. Even before the

[174] Hirst 1998, 114.
[175] Escudé and Fontana 1998, 61.
[176] For similar assessments, see Hirst 1998; and Hurrell 1998a.
[177] NotiSur—Latin American Political Affairs, 29 August 1997.

recent free fall of the Argentine economy, there was pessimism about Mercosur's prospects.[178] Does this analysis have anything to tell us about Mercosur's recent difficulties and, more particularly, whether pessimistic projections about its future have any validity? Recall that the theoretical analysis posits that developing countries are more likely to consolidate regional integration when two conditions are met: (1) the economic size of the pact they join is large and the group is able to achieve significant economic size with relatively few members; and (2) the ability of the group's members to meet their potential for attracting FDI without pursuing regional integration is low. The first condition continues to apply to Mercosur. And, as stressed previously, the key members of Mercosur strongly met the second condition in the early and middle 1990s: for different, though complementary, reasons, Brazil and Argentina both stood to reap FDI dividends from investing in regional integration during those years. By the end of the 1990s, however, this situation changed.

In terms of attracting FDI, the prime advantage of Mercosur for Argentina—greater market size—remained essentially constant throughout the decade. Economy Minister Jose Luis Machinea stressed in 2000 that Mercosur was beneficial for Argentina "first and foremost, because we have an enlarged market and this is conducive . . . to attracting more investments."[179] In contrast, Mercosur's main FDI advantage for Brazil—using regional integration to signal MNCs—greatly declined by the late 1990s following the successful implementation of economic reforms initiated during the middle of the decade. By 1999, the U.S.$31.4 billion of FDI that flowed into Brazil placed the country second out of all developing countries, behind only China.[180] While Mercosur played an important role in improving Brazil's FDI fortunes during the early and middle 1990s, by end of the decade much of the country's success in attracting FDI had relatively little to do with regional integration per se: a 2000 survey of MNC executives found that more than 80 percent said they would consider investing in Brazil even in the absence of regional integration, whereas only one-third said they would do so in Argentina.[181] Partly due to Brazil's greatly improved ability to attract FDI on its own, its need to engage in compromises in order to promote the consolidation of Mercosur was much lower at the end of the 1990s than it was earlier in the decade.

Absent some dramatic, unexpected event that causes Brazil to once again have an overlapping need with Argentina to invest in Mercosur to compete for FDI, it is very unlikely this dynamic will continue to act as a supporting force for integration. In the end, therefore, this analysis does not provide any reason to question the current pessimistic projections about Mercosur. From the standpoint of security, however, it is important to recognize that Mercosur's work is

---

[178] See, for example, *New York Times*, 24 March 2001, B2.
[179] BBC Monitoring Latin America, 21 March 2000.
[180] UNCTAD 2000a, 50, 60.
[181] UNCTAD 2000b, 115.

already done. The long-standing rivalry that existed between Argentina and Brazil was rooted in a cycle of mistrust, misperceptions, and miscommunication. Rivalries of this kind, unfortunately, are not easy to end; they often develop a self-reinforcing dynamic and, in the extreme, can lead the respective parties to define themselves partly on the basis of their mutual opposition.[182] To move beyond a rivalry of this kind, the cycle that feeds it must be interrupted and a new basis of communication must be established; ideally, this will occur as part of a more general effort to cooperate for mutual gain. Mercosur is hardly the only factor that led to a decisive interruption of the vicious cycle of mistrust, misperceptions, and miscommunication that existed for over a century between Argentina and Brazil, but it did play an important role. Now that this cycle has been decisively interrupted, it is very difficult to envision a scenario in which it could ever start up again. In this respect, Argentine foreign minister Guido di Tella recently stressed that the "alliance between Argentina and Brazil is as solid as a rock and nothing will be able to touch it."[183] In the end, the future of Mercosur is unclear, but its positive contribution to the long-term security relationship between Argentina and Brazil is not.

[182] The discussion here draws from the work of Robert Jervis (e.g. 1976, 1978) and Alexander Wendt (e.g. 1992, 1999).

[183] BBC Summary of World Broadcasts, 22 August 1997.

CHAPTER 6

The Globalization of Production and the Economic Benefits of Conquest

THIS CHAPTER will evaluate whether the globalization of production has led to shifts in the structures of the most advanced states that would prevent a conqueror from effectively extracting economic gains from vanquished territory. It is important to recognize that many factors influence the overall profitability of military conquest, including: (1) military costs, of defeating the vanquished state, of conflicts with other states that result from conquest, and of defending the conquered territory from counterattacks, (2) the costs of economic sanctions imposed by other states in response to conquest, and (3) the benefits of capturing strategic territory. In addition to these factors, it is important to consider the cost/benefit ratio of occupying a vanquished country—that is, how many economic resources can be extracted from a society relative to the costs of policing that society. This chapter will focus specifically on how the globalization of production influences this cost/benefit ratio for occupation, which in the literature is typically referred to as the "economic benefits of conquest."[1] I will follow this terminological convention, but it should be noted that the question at issue in this chapter is not whether conquest pays in a general sense but whether the globalization of production influences a conqueror's ability to extract economic gains from the occupation of another society. This question is of critical importance, since the prospects for peace are reduced when an extractive conqueror can effectively exploit a vanquished society and use these economic gains to protect or acquire other resources.[2]

The theoretical analysis in chapter 3 specified three hypotheses concerning the expected influence of the globalization of production on the economic benefits of conquest: (1) a vanquished advanced country is unlikely to attract significant FDI, and its firms are unlikely to be able to form or sustain extensive international interfirm alliances; (2) in the most advanced states, the ability of a conqueror to extract economic resources is likely to be much lower than in previous eras because production and technological development are no longer as geographically concentrated; and (3) conquerors will be likely to pursue economic centralization, especially in a vanquished knowledge-based economy. If these hypotheses are valid, then military conquest will greatly reduce

---

[1] For the standard usage, see, in particular, Liberman 1996.

[2] For useful discussions of the various reasons why this is the case, see Van Evera 1999, chap. 5; Stam and Smith 2001; and Rosecrance 1999.

the economic dynamism of a vanquished advanced state, and, moreover, the conqueror will be in a much weaker position to immediately use the resources of a vanquished advanced society to protect or acquire other resources.

The only recent example of military conquest of any economically advanced societies in which resource extraction was attempted is the Soviet empire in Eastern Europe. Concerning the first hypothesis, it might initially appear futile to use this case to evaluate it. The reason why is that the Eastern European bloc was, for the most part, isolated from the geographic dispersion of MNC production by choice before 1990. As a result, it is impossible to ascertain whether Eastern Europe in general could have attracted FDI and sustained international interfirm alliances had it not been part of the Soviet empire. However, there is one notable exception in Eastern Europe, Hungary, that we can use to evaluate this hypothesis. Examining Hungary is useful because of the country's economic policies; because the Hungarian government strove to attract FDI after 1972; and, finally, because this positive inclination toward FDI was reinforced by policies and reforms designed to make Hungary an attractive location for MNCs. Moreover, we have data that tracks FDI inflows into Hungary, as well as joint ventures between Hungarian and international companies, from the early 1970s onward.

Because Eastern Europe was conquered by the Soviets several decades before the globalization of production gathered force, we cannot use this case to directly evaluate the second hypothesis in its entirety. The Hungarian case does, however, provide a means of evaluating an important element of it. This is because the logic of the first and second hypotheses overlaps in one important respect. Specifically, the conqueror's credibility of commitment, which is central to the first hypothesis, also bears on the second hypothesis. As stressed in chapter 3, the conqueror's credibility of commitment is a key factor influencing whether MNCs will be prone to rely on affiliates, interfirm alliances, and outsourcing partners in the vanquished country—which, in turn, greatly affects how much leverage the conqueror has over MNCs. For this reason, if MNCs shy away from FDI in the vanquished country because of the conqueror's low credibility of commitment, this result would provide a degree of support for the second hypothesis.

One seeming limitation in using this case to evaluate the third hypothesis is that within Eastern Europe, only East Germany had shifted in the direction of having a knowledge-based economy by the time the Cold War ended. This by itself is not a problem, however, for evaluating the notion that a conqueror will view it as advantageous to undertake economic centralization following the conquest of a knowledge-based economy. The theoretical analysis in chapter 3 posited that the incentives for a conqueror to pursue economic centralization in the vanquished country will be relatively higher for a knowledge-based society than for an industrial or an agricultural economy. This means that in an important respect the Soviet empire in Eastern Europe is actually a hard test of the third hypothesis.

The empirical analysis below is divided into three main sections. The first and second sections use the Soviet empire in Eastern Europe to evaluate, respectively, the two long-term hypotheses advanced here. Two overall findings emerge. First, MNCs shy away from a vanquished advanced country following conquest. Second, a conqueror is prone in advanced societies to use mechanisms of imperial control that greatly hinder innovation. In order to advance cumulative knowledge on this case, the third section integrates these specific findings concerning Eastern Europe into a systematic examination of the Soviet imperial balance sheet. The current benchmark study of the economic benefits of conquest concludes that the Soviets were able to extract significant economic gains from their empire.[3] I show that this conclusion is unjustified for the last several decades of the Soviet empire.

ECONOMIC DECLINE IN EASTERN EUROPE

Before we turn to the empirical analysis, it is useful to provide a brief overview of some basic features of East European economic performance during the last two decades of the Soviet empire. This will make it easier to understand the analysis that follows.

There is general agreement that Eastern Europe's level of innovation and overall technological capacity, and hence the region's economic value to the Soviet Union, declined markedly after the early 1970s. This trend shows up clearly in analyses focusing on overall macroeconomic indicators. In her survey, Carol Clark concludes that during the 1970s and 1980s "three notable trends emerged in the East European region: declining output growth, increasing technological backwardness vis-à-vis the advanced market economies, and deteriorating relative performance of the manufacturing sector on world markets."[4] More specifically, she finds that Eastern European "finished manufactured goods—whose marketability is closely tied to design quality and sophistication—had suffered disproportionately" and that beginning in the mid-1970s there was "a continued decline in the capacity to design finished manufactured goods of sufficient quality and technical sophistication to be marketable in the West."[5]

Studies of particular East European economies also reveal this general trend. Most relevant is the experience of East Germany, since it was the technological "crown jewel" of the Soviet empire. By 1989, it was apparent that East Germany was merely "the brightest star . . . in an otherwise dim socialist universe."[6] Telling on this score is that 17 percent of all employees in East German

---

[3] See Liberman 1996, chap. 7.

[4] See Clark 1993, 169. For similar assessments, see, for example, Van Brabant 1987; Bogomolv 1987; and Schroeder 1989.

[5] Clark 1993, 171, 167–68.

[6] Kopstein 1997, 3.

manufacturing in 1989 were required "just to keep industry's dilapidated machinery and equipment in a state of minimally acceptable repair."[7] Numerous indicators reveal that technological capacity in East Germany declined greatly after the early 1970s. One key statistic is that the share of machine tools in East Germany's exports to the OECD fell by almost half between the early 1970s and the early 1980s.[8] By 1985, even the East German State Planning Commission was willing to concede that the "export of tool and processing machines . . . has become ineffective."[9] Another key indicator of technological decline during this period is East Germany's productivity relative to West Germany: "to produce comparable value-added in the machine-building industry required 1.8 times the input in East as in West Germany in 1970; but by 1980 it required 3.9 times the input."[10] It is estimated that by 1990 the relative labor productivity in the East German manufacturing sector was only around 25 percent of the West German level.[11] These comparative 1990 productivity figures are particularly dramatic when we consider that "the area which was to become the GDR, excluding Berlin, had, by 1939, a higher net industrial production per head than the Western areas of Germany."[12]

A final important point to recognize is that it is not for lack of resources that the East European countries fell behind technologically during the 1970s and 1980s. For example, Hungary and Czechoslovakia both spent more on R&D as a percentage of GDP than the United States did in the late 1970s.[13] The same is true for manpower: the share of nonagricultural employment comprising R&D personnel was 2.2 percent in East Germany in 1979, while the corresponding figure for the United States was 0.8 percent.[14] East Germany's computer program is a prominent example of devoting immense resources to further technological innovation, with few rewards. During the 1980s, the East German government tried to produce internationally competitive computer chips and devoted between 12 and 14 billion marks to the effort. The result was a total failure: "The GDR aspired to produce 500,000 256-kilobyte memories (already outmoded abroad) and had turned out only 90,000 even after importing Western equipment . . . [Moreover,] the 256K memory cost GDR consumers 534 marks instead of 4–5 valuta [convertible] marks" that the chips cost on world markets.[15]

[7] Bryson 1995, 59–60.

[8] See Rogowski 1993, 17.

[9] Kopstein 1997, 99.

[10] See Rogowski 1993, 17.

[11] Keller 1997, 1.

[12] Childs 1988, 140.

[13] In 1978, Hungary devoted 2.5 percent of its GDP to R&D and Czechoslovakia 2.9 percent, while in 1979 the United States devoted 2.4 percent; figures are from Winiecki 1988, 188.

[14] Winiecki 1986, 545.

[15] Maier 1997, 76–77.

EVALUATING HYPOTHESIS 1: THE SOVIET EMPIRE, CREDIBILITY OF COMMITMENT, AND FDI IN EASTERN EUROPE

Beyond inefficiencies resulting from economic centralization, the growing costs of isolation from the global economy is the other principal factor scholars have identified to explain Eastern Europe's decline in technological innovation and economic competitiveness after 1970.[16] Analysts specifically highlight the dearth of FDI as a prominent problem.[17] While Eastern Europe's economic and technological efficiency was limited due to its general lack of international economic exposure—and lack of access to FDI in particular—this provides confirmatory evidence for only a portion of the theoretical analysis outlined in chapter 3. This analysis first specified why an extractive conqueror's low credibility of commitment restricts the ability of the conquered advanced country to gain access to MNCs following conquest and, second, outlined why this would lower the economic gains to the conqueror, especially over the long term. The overall Eastern European experience is certainly consistent with the notion that the long-term benefits of conquering an advanced state will be greatly reduced if the vanquished country is isolated from MNCs following conquest. But does the Soviet empire in Eastern Europe tell us whether a vanquished advanced state will have trouble gaining access to global firms following conquest?

As stressed previously, because most of the Eastern bloc was isolated from MNCs essentially by choice before 1990, we cannot examine these countries to evaluate this hypothesis. The only exception in Eastern Europe is Hungary, which strove to attract FDI beginning in the early 1970s. Hungary first permitted the establishment of joint ventures in 1970 and formally announced a decree to that effect in 1972.[18] Initially, joint ventures in Hungary were limited in a variety of ways.[19] Between 1972 and 1988, however, the Hungarian government initiated a series of liberalizations of FDI regulations as a strategy to attract MNCs.[20] In 1977, regulations on joint ventures were liberalized in several key respects, including a significant reduction in tax rates on foreign firms. In 1978, another series of reforms was initiated to smooth the establishment of joint ventures, including new sources of capital from Hungary for joint ventures and further tax concessions. In 1982, another key reform permitted some foreign firms to be considered foreign enclaves and to thereby become "exempt from

---

[16] See, for example, Clark 1993, 178; Gomulka and Nove 1984; Rogowski 1993; and Winiecki 1986, 326.

[17] See, for example, Rogowski 1993; and Clark 1993, 178.

[18] Marer 1986, 129–30. Much of the discussion in the remainder of this paragraph summarizes material in Marer.

[19] Much of the discussion here summarizes material in Marer 1986, 130–31.

[20] Simai 1988, 168.

the administrative regulations pertaining to Hungarian reforms, such as those concerning earnings . . . wages, and price determination."[21] And in 1988, Hungary passed the Act on Foreign Investments. This law "allowed foreign investors to establish a business in Hungary without any special permission (except for some sectors, such as banking and financial services). Joint ventures with at least 30 percent foreign ownership and meeting a couple of other requirements were entitled to significant tax privileges (in some cases an absolute-tax exemption for five years and further allowances afterwards, again for five years)."[22]

In short, Hungary was far ahead of the rest of Eastern Europe in providing a favorable investment climate for FDI. Indeed, Hungary was at the forefront concerning FDI policies not simply within Eastern Europe, but among *all* countries with high levels of economic centralization, including China.[23] The analysis that follows consequently focuses on the Hungarian experience to evaluate whether a state is likely to be hampered in its ability to attract FDI after it is vanquished by an extractive conqueror.

Credibility of Commitment and FDI in Hungary

Enacting policies, as Hungary did, to provide a favorable climate for FDI is one thing; making a credible commitment to them is something altogether different. In the absence of a credible commitment, even the "correct" economic policies are unlikely to influence investors.[24] As it turns out, Hungary's credibility of commitment in the eyes of MNCs was assured of remaining low so long as the Soviet empire continued to exist. Exactly why is discussed below.

Credibility of commitment will be low when the ultimate governing authority has unchecked power. As the discussion in the next section of this chapter demonstrates, the Soviet leadership had great leverage to structure the economies of Eastern Europe as it saw fit. Credibility of commitment will be reduced yet further if there are reasons to believe a government with unchecked power will not refrain from using its authority to further its own short-term interests at the expense of investors. For reasons stressed in chapter 3, conquerors rank low in this regard because of the challenges they face in governing conquered territory. In Eastern Europe, the Soviets made evident after 1968 that maintenance of stability was the key priority, and that they would pursue this goal even at the expense of economic viability within the region. Concerning Hungary in particular, the Soviets actively monitored Hungary's economy and,

---

[21] Marer 1986, 131.

[22] Antal-Mokos 1998, 45.

[23] On this point, see Kaminski and Riboud 2000, 7; and Marer 1986, 134.

[24] See the discussion in Weingast 1993.

more significantly, intervened to narrow the scope of Hungarian economic reforms, especially in the 1970s.

A related point is the primary leadership criterion used by the Soviets: the East European leader must "be capable of changing his outlook if opinion changes in the Kremlin."[25] The Soviets made it clear that they would engineer the removal of leaders who did not closely follow the directives of Moscow on economic policy. What this meant, of course, is that MNCs never had reason to place long-term faith in Hungary's economic policies: there was every reason to suspect that Janos Kadar, the leader of Hungary, would immediately reverse course on economic policy if the Soviets demanded that he do so. Kadar's loyalty to the Kremlin assured his ability to maintain power, but it was a simultaneously a fundamental limitation on Hungary's credibility of commitment. The larger point is that whether an East European leader was loyal to Moscow mattered little: in either case the regime's credibility of commitment in the eyes of foreign investors would be low so long as the country remained under Soviet control. One way or another, a shift in Moscow's mood could lead to the curtailment of economic policies that an MNC was banking on, or an even greater infringement on their revenue.

In the end, there was no reason for MNCs to place faith in Hungary's economic policies so long as the country remained within the Soviet orbit. Significant here is that Soviet constraints on Hungarian economic policies were not limited to the 1970s. Although there was some relaxation of Soviet monitoring and direction of Hungary's economic policies in the late 1970s, by the early 1980s the Soviets once again began to exert pressure. After Gorbachev assumed power, Hungary was given another green light for reforms and initiated significant economic liberalization beginning in 1986. From the standpoint of credibility of commitment, it is precisely this instability in policy that is of great concern to MNCs.

The Level and Structure of Foreign Direct Investment in Hungary before 1990

Two key conclusions emerge from the previous discussion. First, Hungary was an outlier within Eastern Europe in its policies to attract FDI after 1972. Second, MNCs had little reason to place faith in Hungarian efforts to attract FDI so long as the Soviets retained the authority to reshape the country's economic policies.

In light of this discussion, what observable implications would we expect to find concerning FDI inflows into Hungary before 1990? First of all, we would

---

[25] Dawisha 1988, 78.

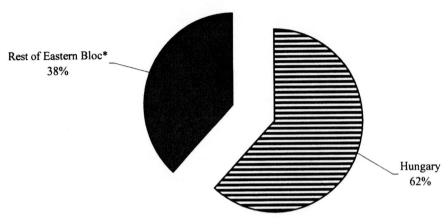

Rest of Eastern Bloc*
38%

Hungary
62%

* Includes: Soviet Union, Czechoslovakia, Bulgaria, East Germany, Poland, and Romania

Figure 6.1 Joint Ventures in the Eastern Bloc through 1987
Source: Dunning 1993b, 221.

expect that Hungary would do better at attracting FDI than any other country in the Eastern bloc before 1990. As figure 6.1 shows, it did so. This skewed distribution of joint ventures is remarkable considering that Hungary's population of 10.6 million accounted for less than 3 percent of the total of the Eastern bloc.[26]

Second, we would expect these FDI inflows to Hungary before 1990 to take on three specific characteristics. The first expectation is that large MNCs would shy away from investing in Hungary before 1990 and that most FDI during this period would instead be by individuals or small and medium-sized enterprises (SMEs) based in Europe. Large MNCs typically have great latitude in terms of where they invest: they have the financial, managerial, and logistical resources to establish facilities in countries that are geographically distant from their headquarters. As a result, large MNCs normally invest in those countries that offer the most favorable advantages. Individuals and SMEs, in contrast, do not have this degree of geographic flexibility: if they invest, they often must do so close to home because it is difficult for them to effectively monitor and manage far away holdings.

Consistent with these expectations, almost all FDI in Hungary before 1990 was undertaken by small investors, not by large MNCs.[27] In fact, a significant proportion, perhaps a majority, of the joint ventures before 1990 were undertaken

[26] Dunning 1993b, 221.
[27] Marton 1993, 117–18.

by firms with only a small number of people.[28] In turn, the majority of FDI in Hungary before 1990 came from firms based in neighboring European countries: as of 1990, German and Austrian firms alone accounted for almost half of all foreign affiliates that existed in Hungary.[29] These small, geographically proximate firms engaged in FDI in Hungary before 1990 for a simple reason: they considered "the Hungarian market as extensions of their home operations."[30]

Given the substantial risk of policy shifts in Hungary, we would also expect to find investments before 1990 to be small in terms of the financial outlay by the foreign investor. Indeed, the vast bulk of FDI into Hungary consisted of very small investments by international standards: 61.5 percent of FDI in Hungary as of 1 January 1990 consisted of investment projects that were less than U.S. \$20 million in value.[31] Significantly, those MNCs that did invest in Hungary before 1990 sought to reduce their exposure, and hence their risk, by seeking out local partners and by limiting the total value of their investment.[32] As a result, MNCs accounted for only 2 "of the 20 largest foreign investments in Hungary, up to 1 April 1990."[33]

As a side point, the small size of investments in Hungary before 1990 meant that their influence on the Hungarian economy would be limited.[34] Relative to small firms, large MNCs are desirable because they have more technology, can better assist in training, have larger pools of capital, and so on. This is not to say that FDI by small firms is not useful; however, it is investment by large MNCs that can have the greatest positive influence on a host country's economy; not surprisingly, Hungary was most keen about attracting investment by such firms.

Finally, we would expect to find that very little FDI in Hungary before 1990 consisted of manufacturing or other activities that required installation of technology that is expensive and hard to remove; the reason is that the profitability of such investments is especially dependent upon a government's long-term credibility of commitment. Instead, we would expect that most inflows into Hungary before 1990 would consist of market-seeking FDI in low-technology areas such as retail or after-sales service of products imported from abroad but sold in Hungary. This is indeed the pattern we find.[35] The net result is that there were few technology transfers to Hungary from foreign investors before 1990.[36]

---

[28] Marer 1986, 178 reports the joint ventures in Hungary "that have become operational through 1983 have been exceedingly small, in most cases involving only a small number of persons."

[29] Marton 1993, 118.

[30] Marton 1993, 118, 126.

[31] Hamilton and Adjubei 1990, 78.

[32] Marton 1993, 117.

[33] Hamilton and Adjubei 1990, 85.

[34] See the discussion in Marer 1986, 178.

[35] See Hamilton and Adjubei 1990, 90.

[36] Marer 1986, 126.

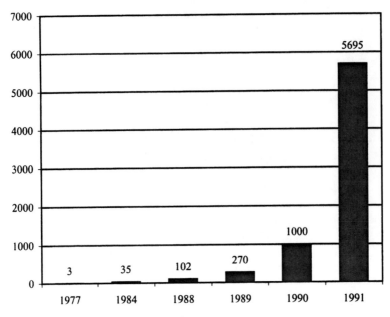

Figure 6.2 Cumulative Number of Joint Ventures in Hungary, 1977–1991
(available years)
Sources: Dunning 1993b, 221; Burant 1990, 151.

The Level and Structure of Foreign Direct Investment
in Hungary after 1990

The evidence we have just discussed concerns FDI inflows to Hungary before the collapse of the Soviet empire. If the argument presented here is valid, we would expect to find a sharp jump in FDI immediately after the collapse of the Soviet empire in the fall of 1989. This is indeed what happened. As figure 6.2 shows, the number of joint ventures in Hungary exploded at this time.[37]

According to one analysis, during the entire 1972–89 period, Hungary attracted only U.S.$595 million of FDI; in comparison, the FDI inflow amounted to U.S.$900 million in 1990 and then climbed further, averaging U.S.$1.7 billion per year in 1991 and 1992.[38] To put this into perspective, FDI inflows during the 1990–92 period were more than seven times greater than FDI during the previous 17 years. The result, as figure 6.3 shows, is that

[37] Dunning 1993b, 221; and Burant 1990, 151.

[38] MTI 1995, 126. This is the only data source of which I am aware that provides an estimate for FDI inflows into Hungary for the 1972–89 period.

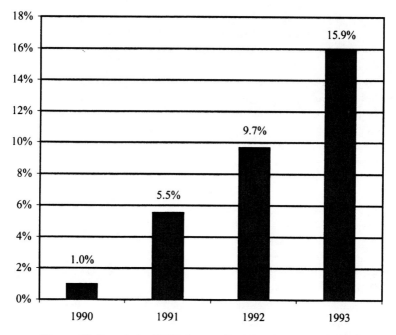

Figure 6.3 Cumulative FDI Inflows to Hungary as a Share of GDP
Source: Kaminski and Riboud 2000, 5.

cumulative FDI inflows as a share of Hungary's GDP jumped dramatically after 1989.[39]

Beyond the dramatic increase in the quantitative level of FDI immediately after 1990, we would also expect to find that the qualitative nature of FDI would stand in contrast with Hungary's pre-1990 experience. This is the case: much of the new FDI was undertaken by large MNCs and comprised investments that were significant in size and involved substantial technological investments. As one analysis summarizes: "There is abundant evidence suggesting a rapidly progressing incorporation of manufacturing capacities located in Hungary into global production networks, usually of large MNCs. The list of 100 top Hungarian companies in 1997 includes many easily recognizable subsidiaries of MNCs. Among the 20 largest firms in terms of sales there are at least six companies that are part of large MNCs."[40] Empirical analyses also indicate that MNCs engaged in significant technological investments in their Hungarian facilities during the 1990s.[41]

[39] Kaminski and Riboud 2000, 5.
[40] Kaminski and Riboud 2000, 20.
[41] See Kaminski and Riboud 2000, 12, 14.

Why Did Hungary Become So Attractive to
MNCs after 1990?

Although Hungary tried very hard to attract FDI after the early 1970s, it fell far short of its potential for doing so before 1990. What changed after 1990 that dramatically improved Hungary as a site for FDI by MNCs? The most obvious change is the shift away from the political monopoly of the Communist Party. This change, which actually occurred in 1989, greatly improved Hungary as an investment site. That being said, exclusive rule by a Communist Party and high levels of FDI are hardly incompatible, as the Chinese experience of the past 15 years aptly demonstrates. Moreover, when it came to the economic policies influencing FDI, at least by the mid-1980s, Hungary could hardly be considered a die-hard Communist regime. Hungary had long been the East European country most tied into the global economy: by the early 1980s, one-third of Hungary's trade was with the West. In 1982, Hungary joined the International Monetary Fund and the World Bank and, in 1978, was granted most favored nation status by the United States. With respect to the regulatory environment for FDI, Hungary's policies were certainly the most liberal among all Communist countries before 1990. And concerning general economic policies, Hungary took the opportunity to pursue significant liberalization reforms in 1986 after Gorbachev assumed power in the Soviet Union. Of key importance is that these reforms made Hungary's "price system . . . more flexible. . . . In a large segment of the economy, price formation became 'free,' reflecting supply and demand movements. Foreign exchange legislation became simpler and a realistic 'managed float' system was introduced."[42]

In the end, it is clear that the dramatic FDI inflows that began in 1990 were influenced by the end of the political monopoly of the Communist Party in Hungary in 1989. However, the change in the magnitude of FDI inflows after 1990 is simply far too great to be explained by this factor alone, particularly in light of the fact that Hungary had already proceeded far down the road toward economic reform before this time, both generally and with respect to FDI in particular. In Hungary, at least as of 1986, many of the key "structural" constraints on the inflow of FDI often associated with Communist regimes did not exist, or were greatly attenuated. As Fred Bancroft, president of an international business consulting firm, noted in 1990: "Well before the revolution swept over Eastern Europe a year ago, Hungary had moved away from central planning and allowed a measure of free trade and foreign investment."[43] Similarly, Warren Marcus, the vice president of Porta Systems (a U.S. telecommunications firm) emphasized at the end of 1989 that the end of political dominance by the Communist Party "won't change the [investment environment] that radically in Hungary, since that country was already well down the road to reform."[44]

[42] Simai 1988, 166.
[43] *New York Times*, 16 December 1990, sec. 6, p. 42.
[44] *Newsday*, 28 November 1989, 33.

If the end of political dominance by the Communist Party does not provide a fully satisfactory explanation for the dramatic surge of FDI into Hungary after 1990, then what else contributed to this shift? In answer to this question, many analysts highlight the Hungarian government's enhanced credibility of commitment after 1990 to maintain a favorable investment climate for FDI. Kaminski and Riboud, for example, maintain that a key reason Hungary attracted so much FDI after 1990 was the "strong political commitment to attract foreign capital."[45] Simai similarly emphasizes that before 1990, "the risk factors (including political risk) were still considered too high by Western partners."[46] After 1990, in contrast, Hungary became attractive to MNCs because "policy reversals regarding the role of the private sector seemed unlikely."[47] Hungarian policymakers also clearly recognized the significance of this credibility of commitment dynamic. For example, Karoly Grosz, then the Communist leader of Hungary, stressed in 1989 that a key "element of creating confidence is political reliability and stability. . . . Nobody would invest in a place where they had to have . . . on their minds a fear that 'those communists' will change their minds in five years and nationalize it." He went on to stress the critical importance of shaping "the political superstructure in such a way that its operation would give guarantees for preventing events [such as nationalization]" in order to attract foreign investment.[48]

Current analyses fall short by treating Hungary's enhanced credibility of commitment to maintain a favorable investment climate after 1989 as exogenously given. In other words, they do not examine why Hungary was able to credibly commit to maintain policies favorable for FDI after 1989 but not previously. The analysis here reveals why the end of the Soviet empire was of vital import on this score. Until Hungary was removed from the Soviet orbit, there was no means by which the Hungarian government could credibly commit to economic policies over the long term.

Before we can have confidence that this credibility-of-commitment dynamic helps to explain Hungary's dramatic rise in FDI after 1989, we must first consider remaining potential explanations. It is useful to consider the other main factors analysts identify as having contributed to Hungary's low level of FDI before 1990: (1) with a population of only 10.6 million people, Hungary did not have a large domestic market; (2) it was not a rich country with a high percentage of wealthy consumers; (3) its macroeconomic performance in the 1970s and 1980s was poor; and (4) the bulk of the Hungarian economy was not privatized. How did these factors change after 1989?

We cannot point to changes in any of the first three factors to explain the massive surge in FDI that began in 1990. Hungary's population did not increase by any meaningful degree. Hungary's economic wealth also did not

[45] Kaminski and Riboud 2000, 1.
[46] Simai 1988, 169.
[47] UNCTAD 1996, 66.
[48] *New York Times*, 15 May 1989, A4.

improve—in fact, its economy was characterized by negative economic growth from 1990 to 1993. Finally, changes in Hungary's economic performance in the early 1990s cannot explain the timing of FDI inflow, since great macroeconomic instability prevailed during this period. Inflation rates in Hungary were as follows: 17 percent (1989); 28.9 percent (1990); 35 percent (1991); 23 percent (1992); and 22.5 percent (1993). In turn, growth in GDP was as follows: 0.7 percent (1989); −3.5 percent (1990); −11.9 percent (1991); −4.3 percent (1992); and −2.3 percent (1993).[49] In sum, to the extent there were changes in these first three factors that analysts identify as contributors to Hungary's low FDI before 1990, they augured a *reduction* in FDI in the early 1990s, not a dramatic increase.

It is also hard to point to changes in the fourth factor, privatization, to explain the overall pattern of inflows of FDI—in particular, the early surge in FDI in 1990, 1991, and 1992. While Hungary initiated privatization reforms in 1990, the initial policies "were generally perceived as failures, and in many cases, indeed, did not bring the expected results for various reasons. . . . Foreign investors were rather unwilling to enter competition by submitting tenders."[50] In fall 1991, the *Economist* reported that "Lajos Csepi, the managing director of State Property Agency, admits to being disappointed with progress so far. His agency has the task of privatizing 2,180 companies. . . . It has approved 360 transactions worth a total of 300 billion forints ($400 million). This sounds impressive, but only two companies have been completely sold; about 90 are still wholly owned by the government and have merely been corporatised. . . . Especially discouraging has been the agency's plans to sell 20 of the country's biggest and most successful companies."[51] In response to criticism that the initial privatization program was ineffective, Hungarian policymakers initiated a new approach in 1992.[52] As a result, privatization-related FDI was very substantial in 1993.[53] It is clear that privatization in Hungary did lead to increased FDI during the 1990s, but only in 1993 do these reforms become a significant factor.

Conclusion

The collapse of the Soviet empire removed a key constraint on the inward flow of FDI to Hungary. MNCs do not like unpredictability. Until 1990, the Soviets had great leverage to shape the economic policies of Hungary. Moreover, as the next section of this chapter reveals, the Soviets demonstrated that they would

[49] Inflation and GDP figures as reported in Johnson 1997, 42.
[50] Antal-Mokos 1998, 52.
[51] *Economist*, 21 September 1991, 14.
[52] Antal-Mokos 1998, 53.
[53] See UNCTAD 1996, 67.

use this capability in an arbitrary manner in Eastern Europe. Until Hungary was free of Soviet influence, the Hungarian government could not credibly commit to any economic policies, including those that influenced the investment decisions of MNCs.

Does this mean that Hungary was only able to attract higher levels of FDI after 1990 because of the end of the Soviet imperial order? According to the logic of the formal theoretical literature on credible commitments, the answer is yes. Even with the "correct" set of reforms, the Hungarian government could not have secured significant investment by MNCs in the absence of credible protection against major changes in the economic policies that MNCs care about.[54] And so long as Hungary was part of the Soviet imperial order, credible protection against major shifts in economic policy was simply unattainable.

Although all the theory we have indicates that the huge inflow of FDI that began in 1990 would not been possible so long as Hungary remained part of the Soviet empire, the nature of this case does not allow us to draw such a strong conclusion from the empirical analysis. This is simply because two key changes that influenced the decision calculus of MNCs regarding investments in Hungary—the end of Communism and the enhanced credibility of commitment resulting from the end of the Soviet empire—occurred simultaneously. Which change was more important in facilitating the dramatic influx of FDI that began in 1990? On the basis of this case, it is impossible to say. All we can conclude is that the end of Communism does not provide a sufficient explanation for the magnitude of the FDI inflow to Hungary at the time and that the dynamic of the enhanced credibility of commitment highlighted here is necessary to understand this shift. In a counterfactual world where Hungary had decisively moved away from Communism but remained part of the Soviet empire, we would have been able to better see how important credibility of commitment was on its own. My theoretical expectation is that in such a counterfactual world, Hungarian efforts to secure enhanced FDI would have achieved insignificant results.

In sum, my conclusion is that Soviet hegemony created an underlying, structural constraint on the inflow of MNCs to Eastern Europe. This is noteworthy, since it is apparent that the dearth of access to MNCs contributed significantly to the decline of the East European economies after 1970 and thereby reduced the economic benefits the Soviet Union received from its empire during this period.[55] Of course, Hungary was the sole country in the region that strove to attract MNCs before 1990; for most of Eastern Europe, the lack of access to MNCs before 1990 was not directly constrained by

---

[54] Particularly relevant here is the discussion in Weingast 1993, 288.

[55] Hungary, for example, benefited tremendously from the inflow of capital from MNCs in the 1990s. One analysis found that "foreign firms now account for almost two-thirds of total investment" in the Hungarian economy and that the value added per employee in manufacturing of firms with 100 percent foreign ownership increased by almost 70 percent between 1992 and 1997 (Kaminski and Riboud 2000, 1, 14).

the credibility-of-commitment dynamic emphasized here. The larger point, however, is that even if there had been a broader attempt by all the East European countries to attract MNCs before 1990, the effort would have failed so long as they were part of the Soviet imperial order. So long as the Soviets retained the ability to structure the economies of Eastern Europe as they saw fit, Eastern Europe's ability to attract MNCs would be constrained because these governments could not credibly commit to economic policies that investors care about.

EVALUATING HYPOTHESIS 3: THE CENTRALIZATION
OF ECONOMIC AUTHORITY IN EASTERN EUROPE

The most prominent factor analysts have identified to explain Eastern Europe's rapid decline in the 1970s and 1980s is the growing costs associated with the centralization of economic authority.[56] A key question is whether economic centralization within the region was partly endogenous to Soviet efforts to quell resistance to their imperial control.[57] This central issue has received very little direct discussion in the literature.[58] A notable exception is a short passage in Peter Liberman's recent book: "Perhaps tyrannical rule over modern industrial societies can function only with centralized economic control. If so, then the kind of stagnation observed throughout the Soviet bloc would be an inherent liability of industrial empires. Such a conclusion might seem supported by Gorbachev's decision to introduce glasnost and perestroika before attempting to decentralize the Soviet economy. But Gorbachev's timing may have been a miscalculation; certainly the Chinese leaders inching towards market authoritarianism would think so."[59]

Two key points need to made about Liberman's remarks. First, we cannot meaningfully compare the Chinese experience with the Soviet empire in Eastern Europe for one basic reason: while the Soviets were an extractive military conqueror from a different, despised nationality, the Chinese government is not (except in Tibet). Second, Liberman cites only one author, Judy Batt, in support of his claim that economic centralization in Eastern Europe was unnecessary for promoting stability.[60] But Batt merely notes in passing that "marketisation is

---

[56] The best sources here are Winiecki 1986, 1988; and Kornai 1992. See also Clark 1993, 177; Schroeder 1989, 36; and Maier 1997, 93.

[57] I thank Jeff Kopstein, Mark Kramer, and Bill Wohlforth for helpful conversations concerning the issues examined in this section and for directing me to a number of these sources.

[58] As will become clear in the analysis below, the massive specialist literature that examines Soviet relations with Eastern Europe provides a great deal of evidence that bears on this issue, but this specific question is not a direct focus of this literature.

[59] Liberman 1996, 143.

[60] Liberman cites Batt 1988, 45, on this point.

possible without the collapse of one-party rule and democratic revolution."[61] Anything is theoretically possible in the abstract. The central issue is not what was possible, but rather the specific dynamics of imperial control in Eastern Europe and what actions the Soviets undertook to maintain stability within their empire.

A logical question arises at the outset: did the Soviets actually have extensive control over the East European economies? If not, then the East European regimes, not the Soviets, would have ultimately been responsible for the structure of their economies, and hence it would little matter whether the Soviet leadership saw economic centralization in Eastern Europe as promoting stability.

The Soviets clearly did not make all decisions within Eastern Europe. That being said, "compared to most other highly unequal inter-state relationships, the Soviet relationship was marked by a far greater number of intrusive political controls."[62] While there was frequent consultation between the Eastern European regimes and the Soviet leadership, "it was not a genuine conciliar system: consultation there was, but it was not joint consultation. The inequality of the partners was accepted, and both discussion and decision proceeded on that basis."[63] "The degree of Soviet control over [Eastern Europe] was extremely high" due to a variety of factors.[64] A key reason is that the Soviet leadership had "immense opportunities for gaining information and exerting influence down to the lowest societal level of each East European party."[65] Also crucial is that the Soviets had a strong willingness and ability to threaten or use military force to remove or install leaders. Significantly, one-third of the East European general secretaries after World War II attained or were removed from power via this mechanism.[66] It is important to realize that only when the Soviet goal of cohesion within the empire was threatened that the degree of Soviet influence over Eastern Europe became clear.[67] As Melvin Croan emphasized in the mid-1970s with respect to Soviet–East German relations, "Moscow is eminently capable of enforcing East German compliance by virtue of the Soviet Union's overwhelming preponderance over the GDR. But it need not do so unless Soviet and East German interests are in serious disalignment."[68]

Looked at one way, therefore, the Soviets clearly had centralized economic control in their empire: Moscow, the imperial center, had great leverage to shape the structure of the East European economies. The question at issue concerns what the Soviets did with this leverage. As chapter 3 emphasized, for a

---

[61] Batt 1988, 45.

[62] Kramer 1996, 109; see also the discussion in Parrott 1997, esp. 11; and Lake 1996 and 1997.

[63] Brown 1988, 49

[64] Parrott 1997, 11.

[65] Dawisha 1988, 75; for a general discussion, see Dawisha 1988, 75–80.

[66] Dawisha 1988, 103.

[67] Jones 1981, 23.

[68] Croan 1976, 15.

number of reasons a conqueror is likely to regard economic centralization as advantageous within a vanquished advanced country. The analysis that follows examines whether this proposition corresponds with the Soviet experience in Eastern Europe.

General Features of the Case

How useful is the Soviet experience in Eastern Europe for evaluating whether a conqueror will regard economic centralization as beneficial for imperial control? As noted previously, this is in one respect a hard test case for evaluating the underlying hypothesis: East Germany is the only country in Eastern Europe that had begun moving toward having a knowledge-based economy by the end of the Cold War and it is specifically in knowledge-based economies that we would expect the strongest incentives to pursue economic centralization. That being said, this case suffers from an obvious limitation: the Soviet Union had a Communist ideology. Ideology greatly influenced Soviet decisions on how to organize the economic structures of Eastern Europe, particularly regarding the initial decision to create command-style economies immediately after World War II. The Soviets' ideology disposed them toward a centralized economic structure in Eastern Europe more than we would expect a non-Communist conqueror to be; as a result, the high level of economic centralization in the region during the Cold War does not provide direct support for the hypothesis advanced here. To evaluate this hypothesis, it is necessary to look at more fine-grained evidence.

The aim of this section, therefore, is not to explain the overall nature of Soviet policies concerning the economic structure of Eastern Europe, but rather to see whether the pertinent features of this case are consistent with the hypothesis advanced here concerning military conquest and economic centralization. If the underlying hypothesis is valid, what specific kinds of observable implications would we expect to find in the historical record? We should find evidence that (1) the Soviet Union sought to exploit the leverage associated with economic centralization to shape production in Eastern Europe so as to reduce the region's freedom of action and resources for rebellion; (2) the Soviets sought to modulate the level of centralization within Eastern Europe to manage the trade-off between higher income, on the one hand, and a greater ability to challenge Soviet imperial authority, on the other; (3) leaders in the most advanced Eastern European countries were the first to recognize the costs of economic centralization and to undertake decentralization; (4) any moves undertaken toward economic decentralization within Eastern Europe made it harder for the Soviets to maintain imperial control; and (5) the Soviets actively restricted the scope of decentralization reforms in Eastern Europe to a much greater extent within the most economically advanced countries in the region, particularly East Germany. These five observable implications are successively reviewed below.

The Soviets Deliberately Structure East European Economies to Reduce Freedom of Action and Resources for Rebellion

Pursuing economic centralization in a vanquished country gives the conqueror the ability to precisely shape what is produced and what supplies are used in ways that make stability easier to maintain. One specific advantage of centralization is that it allows the conqueror to restructure production in the vanquished societies so that they depend on the conqueror, reducing the freedom to rebel. This dynamic shows up clearly in Soviet relations with Eastern Europe.

Production in Eastern Europe was plainly structured in such a way that these societies were dependent upon the Soviet Union, and it is also evident that taking this dependence was helpful to imperial authority.[69] During noncrisis periods, "the dependence of Eastern Europe on the Soviet Union for weapons and spare parts enabled Soviet commanders to wield a good deal of formal and informal control over the non-Soviet Warsaw Pact members."[70] The Soviets also structured trading relations with Eastern Europe in order to reinforce economic dependence and thereby "foster political control" in the region.[71] Of particular importance is that "the energy supplies and other raw materials purchased by the East European countries from the Soviet Union, especially those imported by East Germany, Hungary, Poland, and Bulgaria, were so vital to their economic development that cutting off these supplies would have resulted in economic chaos almost immediately."[72]

Economic centralization in the vanquished country also puts the conqueror in a strong position to monitor output carefully and, most importantly, to ensure that what is being manufactured is not supporting resistance and that the conquered country never develops the capability to defeat the conqueror. Did the Soviets pursue policies along these lines? The evidence indicates that they, in fact, did strive to ensure that Eastern European countries would not possess the capacity to defend their national territory using national means (in other words, that these countries would be unable to resist large-scale Soviet military force).[73]

An essential method for attaining this objective was to constrain the ability of Eastern Europe to manufacture arms indigenously. Before the Soviet conquest of the region, various countries in Eastern Europe, particularly

---

[69] See the discussion in Lake 1996, esp. 25.

[70] Kramer 1996, 107–8.

[71] Crane 1988, 10.

[72] Kramer 1996, 113.

[73] For a thorough analysis of this point, see Jones 1981.

Czechoslovakia and East Germany, had advanced arms industries. This changed under Soviet rule. As one contemporary analyst observed: "East European WTO members . . . are not allowed to engage in indigenous arms production of most major weapons systems—for example, tanks, combat aircraft, etc.— unless explicitly licensed to do so using Soviet designs. . . . Moscow's willingness to allow East Europeans to produce the most advanced Soviet designs has been, it is important to note, significantly more constrained than with other of the USSR's friends."[74] With respect to tanks, only Poland and Czechoslovakia were significant producers within Eastern Europe, yet by the end of the 1980s even they were still producing "older models such as the T-55" and had only just begun "full-scale production of the T-72, which is not the most modern Soviet tank."[75] With respect to fighter jets, as of the early 1980s "none of the East European states [were] allowed to assemble anything more advanced than the 30-year old Mig-21."[76]

The decision by the Soviets to undercut the East European arms industries during the Cold War and, more specifically, to prevent the East European governments from producing the most advanced Soviet weaponry had significant costs. It restricted the ability of the East European militaries to match NATO forces, as will be discussed later. It also meant that East European defense firms were constrained in their ability to be useful cooperative partners in the production of weaponry. Both of these costs were particularly apparent in East Germany, with its key strategic location and vaunted technological status within the Eastern bloc.[77]

At the same time, this strategy of denial also had key strategic benefits for the Soviets. On the one hand, it was desirable for the Soviets that the East European militaries be somewhat capable, since these forces were useful for suppressing resistance among the domestic populations. On the other hand, if the East European militaries were too capable, they would be in a position to challenge Soviet forces, and hence Soviet control. Instead, the Soviet Union ensured that if a conflict with an East European country occurred, the Soviets would possess superior weaponry: "East European armies generally use equipment one or two generations behind that of Soviet forces in the region."[78] Moreover, the weapons the East Europeans possessed could not operate independently of Soviet spare parts and other supplies. Constraining the ability of any East European country to resist Soviet military forces was thus another reason why "East European stocks of spare parts and reserve war material [were] kept deliberately low."[79] The ability on the part of the Soviets to monitor

---

[74] Nelson 1989, 329.
[75] Crane 1988, 15.
[76] Nelson 1989, 329.
[77] Crane 1988, 15.
[78] Crane 1988, 2.
[79] Dawisha 1988, 86, 82–85. See also the discussions in Eyal 1992, 63.

and control what the East European countries produced and what supplies they had to this degree was possible only because of the high level of economic centralization in these countries.

The Soviets Modulate the Level of Centralization within Eastern Europe to Manage the Income/Stability Trade-Off

Maintaining stability is not the only priority of a conqueror. As noted in chapter 3, a conqueror acutely faces a specific governance trade-off: between enhancing income, on the one hand, and lowering security threats by minimizing the resources and freedom for rebellion, on the other.[80] The level of economic centralization is a key aspect of this larger trade-off: greater economic centralization may promote stability, but at the price of reduced economic efficiency, particularly in more advanced societies.

This is not to say that economic centralization only carries economic costs for the conqueror. An advantage of centralization within the conquered territory is that it puts the conqueror in a position to ensure that what is being produced is useful. Numerous analysts stress that the Soviets did, in fact, undertake a fine-grained manipulation of production to ensure "that a significant proportion of industrial production [in Eastern Europe] was geared to Soviet demands."[81] East European policymakers also emphasize this point. Top East German economic policymaker Günter Mittag, for example, notes in his memoir: "Our industrial structure was completely tailored to the needs of the USSR: shipbuilding, railroad cars, cranes. Some firms sent 80 percent of their production to the USSR, with pressure for more every year."[82] Significantly, the East Europeans often directly complained about the costs of supplying the specific goods that the Soviets demanded.[83]

Although economic centralization in Eastern Europe initially carried no significant downside for the Soviets, circumstances changed over time. For reasons stressed in chapter 3, economic centralization in advanced vanquished societies will ultimately have a negative influence on the ability of a conqueror to reap economic gains from a vanquished society because it will lead to a reduction in innovation and hence long-term economic dynamism. At first, none of the East European economies were advanced enough to feel these costs of centralization to a significant degree. As time wore on, however, these costs rose in the most economically advanced countries in the Eastern bloc, Czechoslovakia and East

[80] North 1993, 14.

[81] Smith 1992, 81; see also Fulbrook 2000, 39, 54; Adomiet 1998, 108; Bryson and Melzer 1991, 62; Crane 1989, 98; Crane and Yeh 1991, 78.

[82] As quoted in Peterson 2002, 6.

[83] See, for example, the complaints of Honecker to the Soviet leadership reported in Kramer 1999, 149, 154–55.

Germany.[84] In these two countries, analysts and policymakers early on perceived the constraints of centralization on economic performance and technological innovation and recognized the consequent need to proceed with significant decentralization.[85]

We would expect to find that as the costs of economic centralization increased, the Soviets would be tempted to modulate the level of centralization within Eastern Europe so as to better manage the trade-off between income and stability. This is indeed the case. Whereas during the 1950s the East European regimes were not permitted by Moscow to decentralize their economies, by the early 1960s the Soviet leadership decided to give a green light to—or, at least, to not block—economic decentralization in the Eastern bloc.[86] This new Soviet stance was motivated in part by the notion that improving economic efficiency would make the regimes in Eastern Europe "more viable, more legitimate, more attractive to [their] own citizens," improving the imperial balance sheet by reducing the high costs of maintaining stability in Eastern Europe.[87]

This is most apparent in East Germany, the country in the bloc that came closest to being a knowledge-based economy.[88] The archival evidence released since 1990 "elucidates in vivid detail Soviet awareness of the costs of empire" in East Germany.[89] More specifically, this new primary evidence shows that "the Soviet leaders were perfectly aware of the main problems of imperial control in Germany. The GDR lacked legitimacy . . . the regime was unstable. It could be kept in power only by the presence of Soviet forces."[90] This new evidence also shows that by 1960 the leadership in Moscow had an "an aversion to subsidize the GDR but at the same time perceived the necessity of having to do so in the interest of safeguarding the Soviet strategic position in the center of Europe and to improve the competitive position of East Germany."[91]

The Soviet leadership's recognition at this time that economic reform in Eastern Europe would improve its imperial balance sheet shows up clearly, for

[84] See Janos 1994, 4; and Kopstein 1997, 198.

[85] With respect to East Germany, see, for example, Grieder 1999, 160–61; and McCauley 1983, 85–86. With respect to Czechoslovakia, see, for example, Myant 1989, 76–78; Golan 1973, 6–7; and Stevens 1985, 159.

[86] See, for example, Grieder 1998, 10–11.

[87] Brown 1988, 43.

[88] For statistics that indicate East Germany's advanced economic status within the Eastern bloc, see Janos 1994, 4; Kopstein 1997, 3, 198; and Fulbrook 2000, 55. One telling indicator is that only 4 percent of East Germany's economy was devoted to agriculture and forestry in 1970; the comparable figure for Czechoslovakia, which had the second most advanced economy in the Eastern bloc, is 19 percent (see ILO 1974, 284, 286).

[89] Adomeit 1998, 107.

[90] Adomeit 1998, 99.

[91] Adomeit 1998, 107. The Soviet leadership had an aversion to subsidies not just to East Germany but to Eastern Europe generally (particularly revealing on this point are the series of recently released documents concerning Soviet deliberations about the level of subsidies given to Poland and Eastern Europe in the early 1980s; see Kramer 1999, 17–18, 57, 90–91, and 154–55).

example, in a recently released transcript of a private conversation in 1960 between Khrushchev and Walter Ulbricht, the leader of East Germany.[92] In this conversation, Khrushchev first underscored the need for enhanced economic growth in East Germany ("The GDR must develop and maintain the increase [*sic*] in the standard of living of its population"). He then went on to complain bitterly about Ulbricht's demand for resources from the Soviet Union to prop up the GDR's sagging economy: "You ask us for 68 tons of gold. This is inconceivable. We can't have a situation where you buy goods and we must pay for them. We don't have much gold, and we must keep it for an emergency. . . . You will not encroach on our gold. . . . Free us from this and don't thrust your hands into our pockets. . . . You should [learn] to walk on your own two feet instead of leaning on us all the time."[93]

Although the initial move to permit economic decentralization in Eastern Europe was undertaken under Khrushchev, there is no indication that this policy shift that was favored by him alone. Significantly, even after Khrushchev was ousted in October 1964, the more conservative Soviet leadership that replaced him did not restrict the freedom of Eastern European governments to engage in economic decentralization. Indeed, this more conservative Soviet leadership actually permitted an acceleration in decentralization, as will be discussed below.

Most Advanced East European Countries Are the First to Take Advantage of the Opportunity to Decentralize

As noted previously, analysts and policymakers in both Czechoslovakia and East Germany early on perceived the constraints of centralization on economic performance and technological innovation. Awareness of this constraint is one thing; taking costly actions in pursuit of economic decentralization is much more significant. If the opportunity cost of centralization does, in fact, increase as an economy becomes more dependent on knowledge, then we would expect to find that East Germany was the first country in the region to take advantage of the aforementioned Soviet policy shift and initiate significant economic decentralization. This is indeed the case: East Germany's New Economic System (NES) was initiated in mid-1963—several years before other significant economic decentralization packages in Eastern Europe were initiated.

What of the origins of these reforms? As East Germany recovered from World War II and moved toward greater emphasis on knowledge-based industries, we would expect that Walter Ulbricht, the leader of East Germany from 1945 to 71, would have a heightened recognition that centralization was holding

[92] See the citation in Adomeit 1998, 106 n. 165.
[93] Khrushchev as quoted in Adomeit 1998, 107–8.

East Germany back in the development of advanced technologies. Scholarship on Ulbricht prior to 1990 tells a different story: he is portrayed as anything but a champion of the need to decentralize in order to promote innovation. However, a recent study by Peter Grieder based on an exhaustive review of the latest primary evidence released since 1990 shows that this conventional wisdom was wrong: "Ulbricht has traditionally been presented as a dogmatic Stalinist. . . . This view is now in need of revision. From the early 1960s, Ulbricht underwent a metamorphisis from incorrigible Stalinist to fanatical technocrat. He was the driving force behind Eastern Europe's first economic reform programme."[94]

The latest evidence also indicates that, as of the early 1960s, Ulbricht "recognized the importance of the 'scientific-technological' revolution" and, in turn, that it was his desire to promote what he referred to as "the 'locomotives' of scientific-technological development (computing, electronics, petrochemistry)" that led him to introduce in 1963 his "pioneering programme of economic reform [which] attempted to combine plan and market by circumscribing the central planning bureaucracy and granting factory managers a degree of autonomy."[95] As one recent study concludes: "Ulbricht's advocacy of reform was the result of a hard-headed appraisal of the need for change . . . if the GDR were to have a long-term future as a developed industrial state."[96]

There is little evidence that Ulbricht feared the political consequences of granting greater autonomy to managers. It is important to remember that the degree of economic centralization in a society pertains not just to the structure of economic decision making; one of the other crucial factors is the level of centralized monitoring of economic activities. Significantly, East Germany had the highest overall level of monitoring of its citizens, including their economic activities, within the Eastern bloc.[97] Members of the East German intelligence agency "were in every firm."[98]

Finally, it is also telling that the second most advanced country in Eastern Europe, Czechoslovakia, was next in line after East Germany to initiate significant economic decentralization reforms. Beginning in 1967, the Czechoslovak government initiated the "most far-reaching" economic decentralization reforms in the region.[99] The underlying goal of these reforms, in the words of its proponents, was to create "an economic system of management able to enforce a turn towards intensive growth" and promote the "scientific-technical

---

[94] Grieder 1999, 160.

[95] Grieder 1999, 161, 165, 213.

[96] Dennis 2000, 106.

[97] See, for example, Kopstein 1997, 3; Grider 1999, 5–6; Dennis 2000, 214; and Fulbrook 2000, 40.

[98] Peterson 2002, 25.

[99] Kyn 1970, 300.

revolution."[100] The reforms consisted of several basic policies: the state reduced its role as a source of investment credits; foreign trade restrictions were scaled back; central plans were abolished in favor of "so-called 'economic guidelines' containing parameters for economic policy and information about desirable output"; and firms were given much greater autonomy.[101] Although Czechoslovakia's initial economic decentralization package was quite modest, the Action Plan of April 1968 was more dramatic: it called for "the democratization of the economy," most notably "the independence of enterprises and enterprise groupings."[102]

Economic Decentralization within Eastern Europe Makes It Harder to Maintain Soviet Imperial Control

The decision in the early 1960s to permit economic decentralization was part of the Soviet effort to achieve a balance between what J. F. Brown calls "cohesion and viability" in Eastern Europe.[103] By viability, Brown means a scenario in which the East European regimes are economically efficient and legitimate in the eyes of their citizens. By cohesion, he means a situation in which there is little or no threat of challenges emerging to Soviet imperial authority from the population or elsewhere. Brown emphasizes that the "Soviet aim of balancing cohesion and viability has lain at the root of the Soviet dilemma in Eastern Europe. . . . the two aims, rather than being interacting and complementary, have in practice often been contradictory and elusive."[104] The trade-off between cohesion and viability is a central theme in the literature that examines Soviet relations with Eastern Europe.[105]

In 1968, Eastern Europe dramatically shifted away from the pursuit of economic decentralization. As the previous discussion makes clear, this was not due to the policy preferences of the leaders who were championing decentralization. Instead, it was the Soviet leadership that radically reversed course, not only clamping down on decentralization in Eastern Europe, but actually demanding recentralization. Examining the source of this Soviet policy shift concerning economic decentralization is very helpful for gaining leverage on the

---

[100] "Action Programme of the Communist Party of Czechoslovakia," adopted 5 April 1968, as quoted in Stevens 1985, 159.

[101] Kyn 1970, 302–4; the quote is at 302. See also Golan 1973, 57–84.

[102] "Action Programme of the Communist Party of Czechoslovakia," adopted 5 April 1968, quoted in Stevens 1985, 158.

[103] See Brown 1975, 2; 1988, 42.

[104] Brown 1975, 3.

[105] See Stone 1996, 39–40; Kramer 1998, 111, 164; Gati 1986, 206–7, and 1984, 6–8; Dawisha 1988, 102–18; Marer 1984a, 235; Chafetz 1993, 14, 31–32; Campbell 1984, 2; Crane 1989, 75; Neumann 1994, 217; Croan 1976, 39; and Bunce 1985, 9, 11.

specific hypothesis under examination here. If this hypothesis is valid, we would expect to find that the Soviet leadership suddenly decided to clamp down on economic centralization because they perceived it was necessary to do so in order to reduce challenges to their imperial authority.

Why then did the Soviets move to strongly emphasize cohesion within the bloc after 1968, despite reduced viability? The watershed event in this regard was the Prague Spring in Czechoslovakia in 1968. From an economic standpoint, "there were not many reasons to believe that Soviet leaders strongly opposed any basis aspect of the economic reform" program in Czechoslovakia.[106] With respect to imperial control, however, this economic reform package was of great concern because it helped to create a climate in which Soviet authority was threatened.[107] Because "a dispersal of decision-making power would have . . . given the enterprise a certain degree of separateness. . . . [it] was, therefore, a risky legitimation strategy."[108]

In the end, the Prague Spring revealed a basic conundrum for the Soviets: "In the pursuit of viability, the goal of cohesion was made less attainable."[109] For our purposes, what is important to understand is not the specifics of Soviet concerns about Czechoslovakia—which were clearly not limited to the nature of its economic reforms—nor the particulars surrounding the decision to invade Czechoslovakia in August 1968, but rather the general stance concerning economic decentralization in Eastern Europe that succeeded it.[110] To the Soviets, Czechoslovakia provided clear evidence that economic decentralization made challenges to their imperial authority easier. For this reason, the Soviet stance toward economic policy in Eastern Europe shifted decisively after 1968. As Brown summarizes: "The Soviet-led invasion of Czechoslovakia in 1968 . . . [marked] the beginning of a new period in which the relationship between cohesion and viability strongly tilted back in favor of cohesion. The trauma of Czechoslovakia . . . convinced the Soviet leaders that the spirit of innovation and experimentation . . . had to be substantially curbed. . . . After the invasion of Czechoslovakia this reform model was excoriated. . . . Any other model with even the vaguest similarities to it was bound to be subject to most critical scrutiny."[111]

Of course, one might contest Brown's conclusion by arguing that Soviet policymakers were not opposed to economic decentralization in Czechoslovakia per se, but rather that it was impossible for them to find leaders in

---

[106] Kyn 1970, 304; see also Dawisha 1981, 17.

[107] See, for example, Neumann 1994, 217; Höhmann 1982, 4–5; and Brown 1988, 46–47, 119.

[108] Neumann 1994, 217.

[109] Brown 1988, 45.

[110] For useful general treatments of the events leading up to Soviet invasion of Czechoslovakia, see, for example, Skilling 1976; Kramer 1998; and Williams 1997. See also the collection of documents in Navratil 1998.

[111] Brown 1988, 46–47, 119.

Czechoslovakia predisposed toward economic reform who would not challenge the Soviets on foreign policy. However, the actions and statements of Alexander Dubček and other Czechoslovak policymakers such as Prime Minister Oldřich Černík during this period are inconsistent with this line of argument. At one point, for example, Černík told Brezhnev: "I want to assure you that the leadership of our party and the majority of members of the party, each individual membership of the leadership of our party, is willing to sacrifice his life for Czechoslovak-Soviet friendship."[112] Recently released documents make it clear that Dubček and other economic reformers in Czechoslovakia were guided by a "lesson" they learned from the Soviet invasion of Hungary in 1956: internal reforms would be tolerated so long as Soviet foreign policy interests were completely respected and followed.[113] Because of the influence of this lesson, Czechoslovak policymakers made "frequent references to the 'unbreakable' friendship and alliance between the Soviet Union and Czechoslovakia . . . Dubček was particularly careful to issue repeated expressions of solidarity with Moscow and to pledge that Soviet interests would be safeguarded under all circumstances. He also emphasized that Czechoslovakia would uphold all its 'external' obligations to the Warsaw Pact, including its role as a leading military supporter to key Third World countries such as Vietnam."[114]

Brown's general conclusion that the Soviets learned to fear economic decentralization reforms after 1968 is echoed repeatedly in the contemporary literature on Eastern Europe.[115] This conclusion has become stronger over time following the outpouring of new evidence during the 1990s from recently declassified materials, memoirs, and interviews with newly accessible Eastern bloc officials. Detailed empirical examinations of Eastern Europe conducted after 1990 by scholars such as Stone, Maier, Kopstein, Kramer, and Grieder reveal that that the Soviet leadership not only refused to give its blessing to economic decentralization after 1968, but that policymakers in Eastern Europe were often placed under great pressure to undertake recentralization.[116] As Charles Maier summarizes, the evidence indicates that economic decentralization reforms in Eastern Europe ultimately "fell victim to the logic of imperial control. . . . In 1968 the emancipatory currents in Prague impelled Brezhnev to

[112] Williams 1997, 167.

[113] See Kramer 1998, 136.

[114] Kramer 1998, 136. See also Williams 1997, 166–67; and Valenta 1984a, who notes (137) that "the Soviets did not fear a dramatic change in Czechoslovak foreign policy, for it was clear . . . that the Dubcek government would not deviate from the basic Soviet foreign policy line."

[115] See, for example, Valenta 1984b, 106; Childs 1988, 161; Bornstein 1977, 129–30; and Fulbrook 1991, 205.

[116] See Maier 1997, 89; Stone 1996, 39–40; Kopstein 1997, 79; Grieder 1998, 16, and 1999, 167–68; and Kramer 1998, 111, 264. See also the discussions in Bryson 1995, 247; Fulbrook 2000, 39, 52; Krejčí and Machonin 1996, 89–90, 196; Williams 1997, 59, 183; Berger 1992, 34; and Chafetz 1993, 31.

insist on centralized control and forced all the reformers throughout Eastern Europe on the defensive. . . . Looking back from the 1990s it is easy to minimize the implications of the reform programs of the 1960s. . . . For all their limits, however, the reforms were potentially explosive: the logic of decentralization . . . was inherently expansive."[117]

Moreover, analyses based on the latest primary evidence show that the Soviet leadership did not simply set up general guidelines toward economic recentralization, but often actively managed this process when necessary. In Czechoslovakia, Mark Kramer concludes, the leadership initially resisted the process of "normalization" in the economic sphere following the Soviet invasion in 1968, but eventually crumbled in response to "enormous pressure" from Brezhnev, Kosygin, and other top Soviet officials.[118] Jeff Kopstein finds that in East Germany, the Soviets saw semiprivate ownership as "a danger to the system." The impetus in 1972 to eliminate "semiprivate ownership in East Germany . . . came from Moscow" and not from the East German leadership, and Brezhnev was studiously informed by Honecker about the completion of this task.[119]

It is important to recognize that ideology does poorly as an explanation of the timing of this shift on the part of the Soviets to favor recentralization in Eastern Europe after 1968. All the evidence indicates that the Soviet attitude toward economic decentralization in Eastern Europe changed specifically in 1968 in response to events in Czechoslovakia and not due to any significant ideological change in the Soviet leadership. Moreover, maintaining imperial control, not ensuring ideological consistency, remained the overriding Soviet objective vis-à-vis Eastern Europe.[120] Telling on this score are the discussions between the Soviet and Czechoslovak leadership in Cernia just prior to the Soviet invasion, in which Dubček's pledges of ideological fealty to socialism prompted Brezhnev to snap: "Don't talk to me about 'socialism.' What we have, we hold."[121]

A Varying Soviet Approach toward Decentralization Reforms after 1968

Although we cannot point to ideology to explain the timing of the shift in Soviet preferences toward recentralization in Eastern Europe, this response was undoubtedly guided by ideology to a significant degree. Put simply, recentralization

---

[117] Maier 1997, 88–89.

[118] Kramer 1998, 170–71; see also Williams 1997, 59.

[119] Kopstein 1997, 79. See also Bryson 1995, who notes (247), "The Soviets . . . simply ordered the East Germans to reorganize (nationalize) their half-private enterprises."

[120] See, for example, Campbell 1984, 21; Croan 1976, 21; and Bornstein 1977, 130.

[121] Quoted in Tucker 1981–82, 429.

was more likely to be seen as a default option for dealing with unrest because of the prevailing Communist ideology in the Soviet Union. However, elements of this case do indicate that ideology was not the only guiding force behind Soviet decisions concerning the economic structure of Eastern Europe after 1968. More general strategic issues—the logic of imperial control, as Maier puts it—also played a role in how and where the Soviets tightened the economic reins. This shows up most clearly in the contrasting approaches that the Soviets adopted toward economic decentralization in Hungary and East Germany after 1968.

THE SOVIET APPROACH TO ECONOMIC
DECENTRALIZATION REFORMS IN HUNGARY

East Germany and Czechoslovakia were not the only countries in Eastern Europe to undertake significant economic decentralization reforms during the 1960s; Hungary did so as well. Of these three East European countries, Hungary was clearly the least advanced economically and East Germany the most.[122] Even by 1970, 26 percent of the economy of Hungary continued to be based on agriculture and forestry; the comparable figure for East Germany was only 4 percent.[123] In light of the theory presented in chapter 3, the expectation that emerges is that the pressure on the Soviets to pursue centralization in order to maintain imperial control would be much lower in Hungary than in East Germany. One consideration is that Hungary clearly had less capacity for an advanced arms industry than East Germany; for this reason, the Soviets had less need to control the kinds of goods produced in Hungary as a means of constraining the potential for rebellion.

This is not the only significant strategic feature of Hungary that bears on the Soviet stance toward centralization. As stressed previously, centralization is attractive to a conqueror because it reduces freedom for rebellion. The degree of centralization is, of course, not the only factor that influences how easy it is to retain imperial control. Another standout factor in this regard is the nature of the leadership that the conqueror can draw upon in the vanquished country. In this respect, the Soviets had a unique asset in Hungary: Janos Kadar.[124] Kadar, the leader of Hungary from 1956 to 1989, was "a masterful practitioner of the art of politics" who was able to easily control his society and dampen internal unrest.[125] Kadar not only was able to retain tight control over Hungary, he did so while remaining "a relatively popular figure . . . a remarkable achievement for any East European politician."[126] Kadar was more than just an incredibly

[122] See Janos 1994, 4; and Kopstein 1997, 198.
[123] ILO 1974, 286–87.
[124] See Valenta 1984a, 143; Gati 1986, 169; and Baylis 1989, 48. An excellent analysis that outlines Kadar's unique qualities is Gati 1974.
[125] Gati 1986, 169; and Molnór 2001, 328.
[126] Valenta 1984a, 143.

skilled politician; he was also extremely loyal and deferential to the Soviets. Kadar was always careful to consult with the Soviets concerning economic policy and was unwavering in his support of all foreign policy issues that they cared deeply about.[127]

If conquerors could always rely upon leaders like Kadar in the vanquished territory, then the dilemma conquerors inevitably face between cohesion and viability would be less acute. But leaders like Kadar simply do not grow on trees: potential leaders with his great political gifts are few; individuals with such political abilities who are also willing to remain loyal to an imperial controlling power are fewer still. As a result, conquerors normally are forced to rely upon much less able and loyal figures to carry out their wishes. This was certainly the case for the Soviets in the rest of Eastern Europe[128]—especially in East Germany in the late 1960s, when Ulbricht deviated from Soviet foreign policy preferences regarding relations with West Germany and other matters.[129]

Given the nature of Hungary's economy and leadership, we would expect the Soviets' need to centralize economic control in order maintain imperial authority would be lower in Hungary than in Czechoslovakia and especially East Germany. If the logic of imperial control was an important factor guiding Soviet decision making, then we would expect to find that Hungary's economic decentralization programs would be treated more leniently by the Soviets after 1968. This is indeed the case. The Hungarian decentralization reforms were not even initiated until 1968. The fact that the Soviets allowed the Hungarians to proceed with these reforms at this time indicates that the Soviets did not insist on recentralization in East Germany and Czechoslovakia after 1968 purely for ideological reasons. If that were the case, then we would not expect any outliers to the recentralization trend after 1968.

Although Hungary was given relatively more latitude to pursue economic decentralization, this is not to say that the Soviets gave free rein to these reforms. After 1968, the Soviets actively monitored Hungarian economic decentralization reforms and, at various points, compelled Kadar to constrain them in various ways.[130] Significantly, the area of the Hungarian economy that was most decentralized between 1968 and 1986 was agriculture, where there was a fair degree of self-management. As underscored in chapter 3, decentralization of economic authority to workers in agriculture is less threatening to conquerors than reforms that give greater autonomy to urban workers; the key reason is that urban workers are more geographically concentrated and hence can more easily overcome problems of collective action and organize for rebellion. The

---

[127] See Baylis 1989, 48; and Hoensch 1988, 229.

[128] On this point, see Adomeit 1998, 122; and Brown 1988, 204.

[129] See Grieder 1999, 160–83.

[130] As Stone 1996, 40, reports, "On several occasions, Yuri Andropov was dispatched to Budapest to deliver stern warnings that the Soviet Politburo was becoming concerned about the extent of Kadar's reforms. Finally, in 1974, Brezhnev intervened personally."

fact that the Soviets permitted the greatest level of Hungarian decentralization to occur in agriculture is thus very telling. Even in this sector, however, the majority of output was still under centralized control as late as 1984: state-owned farms and cooperatives together accounted for two-thirds of Hungary's agricultural output at this time, a figure only slightly lower than in the mid-1960s.[131]

THE SOVIET APPROACH TO ECONOMIC DECENTRALIZATION REFORMS IN EAST GERMANY

It is in East Germany, the country in the region that came relatively closest to being a knowledge-based economy, where we would expect the greatest incentives for the Soviets to move against decentralization after 1968. We do indeed find that following the Prague Spring, Soviet tolerance for decentralization was much lower in East Germany than in Hungary.

After the invasion of Czechoslovakia, the Soviets shifted sharply against Ulbricht's economic reforms.[132] In a private conversation with Honecker in early 1970, for example, Brezhnev made clear that the GDR needed to shift to a more centralized economic structure, "for otherwise we will get into difficulties."[133] The evidence indicates that even before 1968, East German conservatives such as Honecker and Willi Stoph were concerned that Ulbricht's decentralization reforms carried significant political and economic risks.[134] After 1968, however, they stepped up their attacks on Ulbricht's leadership generally, and his economic policies in particular. Kopstein underscores this increased opposition was due, in part, to a "desire to please their Soviet masters," and notes that "Honecker and company received a steady stream of advice and encouragement from Brezhnev. . . . With the Soviets dissatisfied. . . . Ulbricht's rivals in the Politburo felt secure in preparing his ouster."[135] In a private conversation in 1970, Brezhnev pointedly reassured Honecker that it would "not be possible for him [Ulbricht] to rule without us. . . . After all, we have troops in your country."[136]

Of course, there is more to economic centralization than just the structure of decision making. It might be argued that if the Soviets were interested in reducing the chances of unrest by increasing centralization, a better route would have been to leave the decentralization of economic decision-making in place in East Germany after 1968 and simply monitor economic activity more

---

[131] Kornai 1986, 1701.

[132] See Grieder 1999, 168, and 1998, 16; Maier 1997, 89; and Fulbrook 1991, 205, and 2000, 39, 52.

[133] Grieder 1999, 168.

[134] Dennis 2000, 107, 136; Kopstein 1997, 71; and Roesler 1991, 55.

[135] Kopstein 1997, 70–71.

[136] As quoted in Grieder 1999, 180.

carefully. The problem is that, as mentioned previously, East Germany already had the highest overall level of monitoring of its citizens' economic activities within the Eastern bloc, in part due to Soviet preferences.[137] In the years prior to 1970, the number of full-time employees of the East German intelligence agency—for which the gathering of economic information was a core activity[138]—grew dramatically: 1,100 in 1950, 19,130 in 1961, and 43,311 in 1970.[139] It is clear the Soviets recognized the value of centralized economic monitoring in East Germany for maintaining control, but by 1970 there was little room to augment it.

Even after the Soviets expressed their strong disapproval of decentralization, Ulbricht did not abandon it after 1968. It is unclear why he refused to scrap these reforms after the Soviets expressed disapproval. Perhaps it is because East German economic performance seemed to improve somewhat afterward, both overall (between 1965 and 1970, national income grew by 29 percent and the index of gross production in industry grew by 36 percent) and also in key technological sectors Ulbricht had identified as "locomotives" of development (between 1965 and 1970, the chemical industry grew by 45 percent, metallurgy by 50 percent, and electrical engineering, electronics, and instrument building by more than 100 percent).[140] Regardless of why Ulbricht resisted recentralization, his resistance was a contributing factor in Brezhnev's decision to abandon him in favor of Honecker in April 1971.[141] In the end, Ulbricht's decentralization reform package was far from an unqualified economic success, but it was "never given sufficient time for a real trial: in the aftermath of the Czech 'Prague Spring' it was terminated for largely political rather than economic reasons."[142]

Given East Germany's relatively high level of economic development, recentralization had a high opportunity cost—more so than for any other East

---

[137] See, for example, Kopstein 1997, 25.

[138] See Kopstein 1997, 133. Peterson 2002, 25, notes, "On the local level in the country organizations, the economy was either first or second priority."

[139] Dennis 2000, 213. See also Childs and Popplewell 1996, 82.

[140] Calculated from data in Dennis 2000, 120. See also Roesler 1991, 54, who notes that the NES promoted "the consolidation of the GDR economy, which had been in a state of crisis at the beginning of the 1960s. . . . Productivity and the effective use of machinery and plant in industry had increased. . . . The long long-term decline in productivity growth-rates was halted. Further successes were achieved in the modernization of the economy."

[141] See Grieder 1999, 160, 214–15, and 1998, 8. The other main reason for Brezhnev's dissatisfaction with Ulbricht was the latter's policies toward West Germany (Grieder 1999, 178–81), which led Brezhnev to consider installing Honecker in his place in July 1970, but Brezhnev eventually decided against this course (184). But just a few months later, "Ulbricht's refusal to support the abandonment of his economic policy in September 1970 brought the leadership question back to the fore" (184). After a series of internal maneuvers by Ulbricht's conservative opponents, Brezhnev received Honecker and Ulbricht together in Moscow in mid-April 1971, and the latter was told to resign as first secretary (185–86).

[142] Fulbrook 2000, 52.

European country. We would therefore expect to find that the cohesion gains accrued as a result of recentralization in East Germany could only come at the cost of reduced viability. This is indeed the case: "By the time Honecker displaced Ulbricht in 1971, political stability could only be bought at the price of economic decay."[143] The Soviets' imperial trade-off between cohesion and viability was most apparent with respect to semiprivate enterprises in East Germany. In 1971, they accounted for 11.3 percent of production and, more importantly, "to the extent that East German industry remained internationally competitive at all, it was due in large measure to the goods produced in this sector."[144] To the Soviets, however, these semiprivate enterprises were a danger to political stability, and, for this reason, they compelled a reluctant Honecker to eliminate them in 1971.[145]

In light of the fact that the Soviets were "well aware that economic grievances have generally sparked political crises" in Eastern Europe, we would expect that they would be willing to bear significant costs to improve economic conditions in East Germany after the shift to recentralization.[146] More specifically, we would expect Soviet economic subsidies to East Germany to increase sharply after Honecker assumed power and, moreover, that East Germany would receive the highest per capita subsidies in the Eastern bloc during the 1970s.[147] As figures 6.4 and 6.5 demonstrate, this is the case.[148]

Another telling statistic is that East Germany received 34.8 percent of the total subsidies going to Eastern Europe during the 1970–78 period, even though its population comprised only 16.2 percent of the Eastern bloc as of

[143] Kopstein 1997, 2.

[144] Kopstein 1997, 77.

[145] Kopstein 1997, 79; see also Bryson 1995, 247.

[146] Crane 1989, 89. Telling in this respect is Brezhnev's comment to Honecker in a private conversation: "For us the important thing is the strengthening of the position of the GDR, its further positive economic development, and a corresponding increase in the conditions of life of the population" (quoted in Adomeit 1998, 122). This expectation is broadly consistent with David Lake's argument that side payments from the dominant state will need to be higher when a hierarchical relationship exists; see Lake 1997, esp. 42.

[147] See Bunce 1985, for a discussion of how Soviet economic subsidies provided to Eastern Europe were motivated in part by a desire of the Soviet leadership to reduce the chances of unrest in the Eastern bloc by promoting enhanced economic performance. See also the recently released documents from the Soviet deliberations during the Polish crisis in the early 1980s, which make abundantly clear the significance of this "enhancing stability" motivation for the economic subsidies sent to East Europe; see Kramer 1999, 17–18, 57, 90–91, 134–35, and 154–55.

[148] The source for this data on Soviet subsidies is Marresse and Vanous 1983. Many scholars accept the validity of the methodology that produced these estimates (see, for example, Stone 1996, 74; and Brada 1985). At the same time, Crane (1989), Marer (1984a), and Van Brabant (1987) all believe that Marresse and Vanous significantly overestimate the overall magnitude of the Soviet economic subsidy provided to Eastern Europe. However, Crane, Marer, and Van Brabant do not provide year-by-year data for the level of the Soviet subsidy to East Germany or any other East European country. For our purposes here, what is most important is the trend over time and not the magnitude of the subsidy.

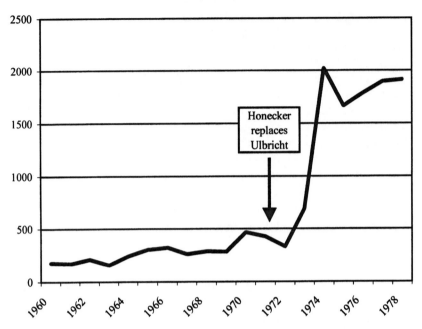

Figure 6.4 Soviet Trade Subsidies to East Germany in Current Dollars (millions)
Source: Marresse and Vanous 1983, 43.

1970.[149] Significantly, the most recent primary evidence indicates that these significant Soviet subsidies were regarded by the East German leadership as playing an important role in stabilizing the country's economy.[150]

Conclusion

This examination of the Soviet empire in Eastern Europe is consistent with the underlying hypothesis that conquerors face strong pressures to pursue economic centralization in a vanquished advanced society. This is evinced in particular by the fact that the Soviets used the leverage associated with economic centralization to reduce the region's freedom of action and resources for rebellion and also that the Soviets found that economic decentralization reforms in the region made imperial control more difficult. Although the general logic of imperial control did influence Soviet decisions concerning the economic

---

[149] Calculated using data from Marresse and Vanous 1983, 50.

[150] This is evident in various notes sent by Honecker to Brezhnev and other Soviet leaders concerning the level of subsidies that were slated to be sent to East Germany in the early 1980s; see Kramer 1999, 149.

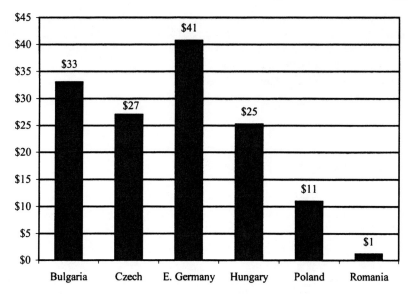

Figure 6.5 Per Capita Average Annual Implicit Soviet Trade Subsidies, 1970–1978, in 1970 Dollars (Constant)
Source: Marresse and Vanous 1983, 50.

structure of Eastern Europe, it is important to bear in mind the significance of ideology in this case. The economic structure that the Soviets put in place in Eastern Europe was clearly shaped by ideology to a significant extent. As a result, we need to be careful about the conclusions we draw from this case. What this analysis does reveal is specific patterns of evidence in favor of the notion that conquerors will face strong incentives to pursue economic centralization, especially in advanced societies. There is no reason to think, however, that the form of centralization is likely to follow the particular outlines that we observe in this case. Put another way, it is reasonable to conclude from this case that conquerors are likely to pursue economic centralization in order to enhance stability, but there is no basis for concluding that conquerors are likely to institute central planning. As the discussion in chapter 3 of the Nazi experience showed, conquerors have several options for engaging in economic centralization in the vanquished territory that vary in the extent of economic management exercised by the central authority.

Aspects of this case also provide support for the specific notion that the benefits of conquest are likely to be particularly constrained as a state shifts toward an economy reliant upon knowledge. The experience of East Germany is especially significant on this score. The costs of economic centralization were relatively most acute in East Germany, and these costs became more salient as the country became more advanced. It is also clear that East Germany was the country with the highest level of economic centralization in the region after 1970 and, in turn, that the Soviets played an important role in producing this outcome as part of an effort to enhance stability, forcing recentralization in key areas on a reluctant East German leadership.

REEVALUATING THE PROFITABILITY OF THE SOVIET EMPIRE: BRINGING IN THE REMAINING FACTORS ON THE IMPERIAL BALANCE SHEET

The aim of this section is to use the previous analysis as a springboard for an overall evaluation of whether the Soviets' gained significant economic benefits from their East European empire during the last several decades of the Cold War. This evaluation is important not just because of the intrinsic significance of the case, but also because it is the most recent example of military conquest of any economically advanced society in which extraction was attempted.

The current benchmark study of the economic benefits of conquest, Peter Liberman's *Does Conquest Pay?* argues that the Soviets were able to extract significant gains from their empire.[151] In order to facilitate cumulative knowledge, I will follow his specific method for evaluating the economic benefits of conquest in this case. This necessitates an examination of three remaining factors on the Soviet imperial balance sheet, namely (1) Soviet economic subsidies to Eastern Europe, (2) Soviet military occupation costs in Eastern Europe, and (3) the potential strategic contribution of the Eastern European militaries. As will be seen below, incorporating these additional factors strengthens the general conclusion that the Soviets did not reap significant economic gains from their empire during the last several decades of the Cold War. The Soviet imperial balance sheet was harmed not just by the region's lack of economic dynamism and declining technological competitiveness during this period; additionally, the Soviets bore substantial economic costs as part of their effort to maintain imperial control in Eastern Europe.

The Growing Burden of Soviet Economic Subsidies

The reduction in innovation owing to the centralization of economic authority in Eastern Europe and the growing opportunity cost of isolation from MNCs highlighted in the previous sections were costly in direct terms. Both of these factors reduced economic efficiency in Eastern Europe, causing the goods and

---

[151] See Liberman 1996, chap. 7, where he concludes that "many aspects of Soviet hegemony over Eastern Europe support the argument that industrial resources are cumulative" (144).

technologies developed there to be progressively less useful to the Soviets. As already emphasized with respect to East Germany, poor Eastern European economic performance after 1970 had a second, indirect effect on the Soviet imperial balance sheet: it caused the legitimacy of Eastern European regimes to plunge and thereby enhanced the need for the Soviets to increase economic subsidies to these regimes. The Soviet government increased economic subsidies throughout Eastern Europe beginning in the early 1970s in order to "prevent the economic situation from deteriorating," "stabilize the political situation," and "forestall domestic unrest."[152] Numerous scholars argue that the inflow of Soviet economic subsidies did, in fact, promote complacency in Eastern Europe.[153]

Whether these subsidies were significant in size was a matter of some contention during the 1980s. At the high end, Michael Marresse and Jan Vanous calculated that the Soviet subsidy to Eastern Europe between 1971 and 1980 amounted to around U.S.$80 billion.[154] At the low end, Paul Marer calculated that the Soviet subsidy was around U.S.$14 billion in between 1971 and 1978.[155]

Randall Stone's analysis, the most recent and best-researched account of Soviet–Warsaw Pact economic relations, puts to rest the question of whether Soviet economic subsidies were a major economic drain. Stone's ultimate conclusion is that "Soviet subsidies to the region were becoming an intolerable burden. . . . what had been a serious problem [for the Soviets] in the early 1970s had grown into a crisis of threatening proportions by the mid-1980s."[156] Stone also finds that the size of these economic subsidies remained stubbornly high even after the Soviets strove to reduce them in the 1980s. He reveals that "the Soviet premier, Nikolai Ryzhkov, had been shocked as late as 1988 by a report which estimated the Soviet subsidy to the East European allies at $17 billion per year."[157] Recently released documents also reveal that the Soviet leadership complained bitterly during internal deliberations in 1980 and 1981 over the Polish crisis that the economic subsidies sent to Eastern Europe were, in Brezhnev's words, "burdensome."[158]

Soviet Military Occupation Costs

In his analysis, Liberman argues that the Soviets were generally able to suppress popular resistance and that East European workers did not engage in

---

[152] Crane 1989, 92, 93, 89. See also Kramer 1999, esp. 52–53, 57, 60–61.
[153] The best treatment of this issue is Bunce 1985.
[154] Marresse and Vanous 1983.
[155] Marer 1984b, 179.
[156] Stone 1996, 43.
[157] Stone 1996, 45.
[158] See Kramer 1999, 57; see also 17–18, 90–91, 154–55.

many strikes. However, the East Europeans may have been quiescent only because of the large Soviet security presence. The key question is whether the
500,000 Soviet troops in Eastern Europe were meant primarily to provide external security or, whether preserving internal order was also a core mission. If
the latter, then these forces should be counted as part of the occupation costs
borne by the Soviets. Liberman argues that Soviet troops in the region were
primarily oriented toward external security, and, as a result, he concludes that
occupation costs were "not great."[159] To back up this conclusion, his only evidence is that large-scale "Soviet military intervention in Eastern Europe was
required only three times."[160] However, one could easily look at this same evidence and reach the opposite conclusion. As Brown points out, "these crises
were not random occurrences. They should be seen as symptomatic not so
much as the failure of Soviet rule *in* Eastern Europe but more as its incompat-
ibility *with* Eastern Europe."[161]

The larger problem with Liberman's conclusion is that there is widespread
scholarly agreement that the Soviet Union deployed massive numbers of troops
in Eastern Europe largely to (1) intimidate the domestic opponents of the
regimes the Soviets had installed; and (2) retain the capacity to put down any
potential uprising.[162] Charles Gati succinctly sums up this general perspective:
"The most compelling, though certainly not the only, reason for the continued
presence of Soviet troops in Eastern Europe was to *police Eastern Europe*. . . .
Stationing Soviet troops in East Germany, Czechoslovakia, Hungary and
Poland was the most credible signal of a Soviet commitment to protect vital
Soviet interests. . . . With its allies unable to obtain popular approbation, the
Soviet Union still had to commit tremendous resources to defend them not so
much from the West but from the peoples of Eastern Europe."[163]

The need to police Eastern Europe was especially high after 1968 following
the Soviet imposed economic recentralization in the region, which undermined
any hope that the Eastern European regimes would be able to secure legitimacy
on the basis of strong economic performance. In this respect, Kramer concludes: "Because of the legacy of 1968, all East European regimes lacked
the legitimacy they would have needed to sustain themselves without Soviet
military backing. . . . If Soviet leaders had once hoped that "stability" in the
Eastern bloc could be maintained by something other than coercion, the 1968
invasion put an end to those hopes."[164]

[159] Liberman 1996, 126.
[160] Liberman 1996, 133.
[161] Brown 1988, 53.
[162] See, for example, Kramer 1996, 108, and 1998, 160; Adomeit 1998, 93, 99; Pearson 1998,
172; Dennis 2000, 228; Fulbrook 2000, 40; Stent 1984, 47–48; Gati 1990, 142; Campbell 1984,
21; and Chafetz 1993, 27.
[163] Gati 1990, 142.
[164] Kramer 1998, 111, 164.

Significantly, this is not simply the perspective of Western analysts. As Brezhnev emphasized to Honecker in a private conversation in 1970: "We do have troops [stationed] with you [in the GDR]. Erich, I tell you frankly, and never forget this: The GDR cannot exist without us, without the S[oviet] U[nion], its power and strength. Without us there is no GDR."[165] Another prominent example is Viktor Kulikov, the Warsaw Pact commander from 1977 to 1989, who argued explicitly that the Warsaw Pact's main function was an internal one.[166] Recently released documents concerning the Soviet troop presence in Czechoslovakia also make this point clear: although the enhanced Soviet military presence following the Prague Spring was publicly justified in purely military terms, "transcripts from CPSU Politburo sessions and from a secret Warsaw Pact conference in September 1968 leave no doubt that Moscow's dominant motivation . . . was to obtain greater leverage over Czechoslovakia's internal politics."[167]

Finally, most specialists maintain that Liberman's key piece of evidence, that Soviet military intervention in Eastern Europe was required "only" three times, itself is endogenous to the massive Soviet military presence. As Kramer concludes: "The presence of Soviet troops in East European territory" played a key role "in precluding violent challenges to the local Communist regimes. By the same token, when specific challenges did arise in Eastern Europe, the record of previous Soviet interventions lent greater credibility to Moscow's warnings and threats, and thus helped forestall the need for direct intervention."[168]

In the end, Liberman's claim that Soviet troops in the region were primarily oriented toward external security does not have support. Contra Liberman, the Soviets clearly did bear very large military occupation costs in Eastern Europe. As a result, the general conclusion that the Soviet empire was a draining asset is strengthened.

The Potential Strategic Contribution of the East European Militaries

In sum, not only were the East Europeans producing very poor quality goods and technologies during the last decades of the Cold War, but the Soviet effort to retain control in the region itself required substantial economic subsidies and military expenditures. Before we can definitively conclude that the Soviets were unable to draw economic benefits from their empire during this period, one final issue needs to be considered. In his analysis of the economic benefits

---

[165] Brezhnev as quoted in Adomeit 1998, 122–23.

[166] See the discussion in Chafetz 1993, 27.

[167] Kramer 1998, 160. The transcript of the September Warsaw Pact conference is included in Navratil 1998, 504–12.

[168] Kramer 1996, 108.

of the Soviets' East European empire, Liberman zeroes in on the strategic significance of the East European militaries. Specifically, he attempts to undermine the notion that the Eastern European empire was an economic drain by
pointing to the supposedly large economic gains the Soviets accrued from East
European military collaboration.[169]

Whether military expenditures by East European countries should fall under
Liberman's general conception of the economic benefits of conquest is not entirely clear: factoring the military expenditures of the conquered country into
the balance sheet shades toward being a strategic benefit, as opposed to a
purely economic one, gained from holding territory.[170] If we do, in fact, use the
same terms on this case that Liberman sets out, then assessing the potential
strategic contribution of the East European militaries is crucial: his ultimate
conclusion that the Soviet empire was a net economic benefit to the Soviets
turns out to rest or fall on this issue. Liberman's analysis is surprisingly sparse
on this crucial issue. Below, I analyze this issue in greater depth. There are two
key questions that need to be addressed. First, how reliable were the Soviets'
East European allies? Second, how did the weapons deployed in East European
militaries match up with those deployed by NATO forces?

HOW RELIABLE WERE THE SOVIETS' EAST EUROPEAN ALLIES?

By Liberman's own admission, the "reliability of these [East European] forces,
and thus their contribution to Soviet power, is hard to judge."[171] However, he
later maintains that "analysts considered the East German military most reliable; the Polish, Czechoslovak, and Hungarian militaries were considered less
so, mainly because of past actual or threatened Soviet intervention in their
countries."[172] While Liberman does cite a few studies in support of this statement, his treatment of the literature on the reliability of the East European militaries is problematic.

A particular shortcoming is that Liberman does not mention the analyses of
the two leading scholars who examine this issue: Ivan Volgyes and Dale Herspring.[173] Herspring's and Volgyes's general conclusion is that during the last
decades of the Cold War, only Bulgaria was a reliable Soviet ally; that Poland,
Romania, Czechoslovakia, and Hungary were unreliable allies; and that East

---

[169] Liberman argues more specifically that Soviet economic "subsidies did not represent a net
imperial deficit for the Soviet Union" because they were less than the money spent on military expenditures by the East European countries (1996, 132).

[170] In evaluating the economic benefits of conquest, Liberman states that he leaves aside
"noneconomic benefits" such as "the strategic advantages of eliminating neighboring countries
and the utility of captured military manpower" (1996, x).

[171] Liberman 1996, 130–31.

[172] Liberman 1996, 131.

[173] See Herspring and Volgyes 1980; Herspring 1989; and Volgyes 1982 and 1990.

Germany was, at best, a doubtful Soviet ally.[174] Most analysts of this question largely mirror Herspring's and Volgyes's assessment.[175] The potential reliability of the East German military is particularly important, because they were most likely to be actively engaged with Western forces in the event of a war and since, as noted above, they are reputed by Liberman to have been the most reliable Soviet ally. In support of this conclusion, however, Liberman cites only two sources, each of which he argues was "enthusiastic about the East German Army."[176] However, each of these sources actually provides very hedged assessments of East Germany's reliability.[177]

In light of the huge reservoir of anti-Soviet sentiment that was so rapidly tapped in 1989, the general tenor of these assessments—that beyond Bulgaria, the Soviets had few, if any, reliable allies during the Cold War—seems valid. In 1989, the East European militaries not only stood by in response to unrest but, in some cases, actually helped to topple the Soviet-imposed regimes.[178] Another key barometer of the potential reliability of the East European military forces during the Cold War is their respective responses prior to the revolutions of 1989 when faced with domestic unrest. As Herspring and Volgyes summarize in their review of this issue through 1980, "In all seven cases known to the authors the armed forces consistently refused to support the regimes when confronted with serious internal disturbance."[179] The same pattern holds true after

---

[174] See Herspring and Volgyes 1980, esp. 289–90; see also Volgyes 1982, 1.

[175] See, for example, Gati 1990, 140–47; Dibb 1986, 42; Nelson 1984; Kennedy 1987, 509; Johnson, Dean, and Alexiev 1982; and Mackintosh 1984.

[176] Liberman 1996, 203n. 46. Liberman cites Johnson, Dean, and Alexiev 1982; and MacGregor 1989.

[177] The first source Liberman cites on this score, the analysis by Johnson, Dean, and Alexiev, does note that the East German officer corps have "a substantial degree of commitment to the regime," which would suggest favorable reliability (Johnson, Dean, and Alexiev 1982, 100). But beyond this, they point to many factors that suggest low reliability on the part of East German forces. In particular, they note that East German military defections were the highest in Europe (100); that East German government was reluctant to use its military forces to put down domestic insurgencies (101); and, most importantly, that "given the continuing sense of German community in the GDR, in combat against West German forces the reliability of the NPA [National People's Army of East Germany] would be more problematic than that of other Warsaw Pact states" (102). The second source Liberman cites on this point, Donald MacGregor's analysis, is highly complimentary of the East German military only in a relative sense: he notes that the "GDR has emerged as the Soviet Union's most stable and reliable ally" (Macgregor 1989, 106). At the same time, Macgregor also makes clear that in an absolute sense, East German reliability was far from perfect. He notes, for example, that within the East German military there are "those who resent Soviet military dominance and those who acquiesce to it" (72); that there existed "morale problems associated with détente and latent German nationalism" (73); and that the East German military was been plagued by a significant desertion problem "in spite of almost insurmountable obstacles to flight" (73).

[178] This is true even in Romania, where it was the Romanian secret police—not the Romanian military—that was responsible for the onset of the only violent revolution in Eastern Europe in 1989 (the military fought on the side of the populace).

[179] Herspring and Volgyes 1980, 278.

1980.[180] The significance of this record is clear. "If the reliability of these forces cannot even be assured on the home front, how can Moscow have much confidence in their utility in a war against NATO—a conflict that some of them might well see as a means to throw off Soviet domination of their countries?"[181]

The evidence from the Soviet side is consistent with the view that they did not place great faith in the East European military forces, especially after 1968. Following his review of the most recent archival evidence, Kramer reports that "the events of 1968 made clear that in the end the Soviet Union would have to rely predominantly on its own forces in Europe. Soviet confidence in Eastern European militaries was shaken . . . by the performance of the Polish, Hungarian, Bulgarian, and East German soldiers who took part in the invasion [of Czechoslovakia]."[182] "The fact that the Soviet General Staff felt it necessary to commission a study on East European reliability reveals the depth of Soviet concern about the problem."[183] Another telling indicator was emphasized previously: the Soviets greatly curtailed the ability of the Eastern Europeans to manufacture arms indigenously, and the quality of the weapons the Soviets supplied to the East European forces lagged behind those given to Soviet forces.

None of this is especially surprising given that deep-seated animosity toward the Soviet Union prevailed in almost all of Eastern Europe before the Soviets took control over the region.[184] As Volgyes notes, "It takes only a cursory glance at the national histories of the East European states to realize how important the concept of the 'traditional enemy' is. . . . The trouble for the Soviet Union is—aside from the Bulgarians and, until 1968, the Czechs and Slovaks—the Russians have been everybody's common traditional foe."[185] Beyond this, East European animosity was enhanced by the heavy-handed Soviet approach to dealing with the region. In order to quell resistance, the Soviets imposed rigid regimes in Eastern Europe that were accompanied by a strong secret police presence under the guidance or control of the Soviet Union.[186]

[180] See Herspring 1989, esp. 142; and Volgyes 1985, 363.

[181] Herspring 1989, 146.

[182] Kramer 1998, 162.

[183] Chafetz 1993, 27.

[184] Herspring and Volgyes 1980, 280; see also the related discussion in Lake 1996, esp. 26.

[185] Volgyes 1985, 371. Similarly, Herspring concludes, "The one thing that seems to unite most of the peoples of Eastern Europe is a deeply held dislike for the USSR" (1989, 131). With reference to the Cold War competition, East European fears and hatreds in the aggregate were ultimately directed much more toward Russia than the West: within Eastern Europe, Germany was the only Western country that was a traditional foe, and this was only for Poland and Czechoslovakia. Indeed, in certain Eastern bloc countries, the lopsided nature of the loyalties was even more marked. With respect to Poland, for example, there was a longstanding tradition of friendship with key NATO countries such as France, the United Kingdom, and the United States (Herspring and Volgyes 1980, 289).

[186] See, for example, Childs and Popplewell 1996, 124–25, 144.

Soviet military forces were deployed in several circumstances (most notably, in East Germany in 1953, Hungary in 1956, and Czechoslovakia in 1968) and were threatened in others. The result of these and other actions was the "reinforcement of a separate East European identity whose major defining characteristic is the fact that most East Europeans have come to dislike the Russians more than they dislike each other or the Germans."[187] It is not surprising, therefore, that Cold War surveys of East Europeans about their likely attitudes if a war were to break out between the United States and the Soviet Union ran decidedly against the latter.[188]

HOW DID THE WEAPONS IN EAST EUROPEAN MILITARIES MATCH UP WITH NATO FORCES?

The poor reliability of the East European military forces was not their only liability. Even if they had fought, the military capacity of these East European military forces would have been low. In part, this was due to the fact that East European forces were populated to a significant extent by poorly trained conscripts.[189] Even for the fraction of East European troops who were both reliable and well trained, their military effectiveness in a hypothetical war with NATO would have been limited by their weaponry.

As noted above, the Soviets did not allow any Eastern European country to have an autonomous ability to produce military weaponry. As the Cold War wore on, the weapons the Soviets supplied to their East European allies became less and less technologically competitive with those fielded by NATO forces.[190] This trend became particularly prominent in the late 1970s and 1980s:

> Continued reliance on the T-54 tank and the Mig-21 fighter, both weapons first deployed in the late 1950s, tended to be the norm in even the most sophisticated East European military establishments. . . . In most instances, the equipment stocks of the USSR's allies had come to lag anywhere from one (GDR) to two (Romania, Bulgaria) full generations behind that of Soviet forces stationed throughout the region. . . . Polish formations would have been expected to take into battle tanks

---

[187] Dawisha 1988, 20.

[188] One such survey of 4,878 East Europeans conducted in 1979 and 1980 revealed that sympathies in such a hypothetical conflict were as follows: among Czechoslovaks, 67 percent had sympathies with the United States, 6 percent with the USSR, and 19 percent were undecided; among Hungarians, 53 percent had sympathies with the United States, 16 percent with the USSR, and 21 percent were undecided; and among Poles, 64 percent had sympathies with the United States, 10 percent with the USSR, and 22 percent were undecided; see Nelson 1984, 25.

[189] Not all East European military forces suffered from this problem; the East German military was generally regarded as well trained (see, for example, Macgregor 1989; and Herspring 1998).

[190] On this point, see, for example, Johnson, Dean, and Alexiev 1982, 56–57, 139; and Herspring 1989, 135, 139, 144.

which were at least a full generation behind those used by their Danish or Dutch counterparts, not to mention West German or American holdings. The Czechoslovak and East German air forces would have flown aircraft that were two to three generations behind the systems operated by American and FRG forces in Europe. This same relationship also tended to hold true for other weapons systems, including anti-tank missiles, personnel carriers, anti-aircraft batteries, and ground support artillery.[191]

Even the technological upgrades for the East German military, which had the most advanced weaponry in Eastern Europe, were of little significance in the final phase of the Cold War.[192] By the late 1980s, the East German military forces had only 186 of the relatively more modern T-72 tanks; the 1950s era T-55 and the World War II era T-34 comprised the remaining 1,336 tanks in the East German arsenal.[193] In other words, only 12 percent of tanks in the East German military were not hopelessly outdated. Even the T-72 tanks would have been of questionable utility against NATO forces. Just as the Soviets were moving a limited number of T-72 tanks into East Germany, the United States was simultaneously deploying the M-1 tank in West Germany. The experience of the 1991 Gulf War demonstrates that the T-72 would have been essentially useless against the M-1.[194] Another telling indicator of the relative backwardness of East German military technology vis-à-vis NATO is what the West German military did with the vast store of East German military equipment it inherited following German reunification. The bulk of this equipment (thousands of tanks, armored vehicles, and artillery pieces and hundreds of helicopters and combat aircraft) was destroyed; most of the rest was given away to Pakistani peacekeepers and relief agencies, among others.[195]

Summary Assessment

In the end, it is clear that the economic gains of East European military collaboration do not, as Liberman argues, make up for all of the other negative factors on the Soviets' imperial balance sheet during the last decades of the Cold War. Indeed, the opposite may have been true: these East European forces might actually have been a net liability in a war. In a Warsaw Pact–NATO war,

---

[191] Gitz 1992, 127; see also the analysis in Herspring 1989, 139, 144.

[192] See Herspring 1998, 38; and Gitz 1992, 127.

[193] Epstein 1990, 111.

[194] Particularly useful treatments of this issue are Press 1997; and Bonsignore 1992. For a useful summary of the overlapping technological advantages the M-1 had over the T-72 tank, see Press 2001, 37. See also the discussion of this point on page 95 in chapter 4.

[195] See Herspring 1998, 157–58.

some East European soldiers—perhaps a significant number—not only would have refused to fight *against* NATO, but might have sided *with* NATO.[196] Contemporary interviews with East European émigrés indicate that anti-Soviet sentiment was rife in the East European militaries during the Cold War. As one Polish respondent noted, "The soldiers said right away that they were going to turn the tank barrels against the Soviets."[197] It is telling that many Soviets feared as much. Col. Oleg Penkovskiy, a Soviet military intelligence officer recruited as a CIA spy who is considered a reliable source on the Soviet military, put this bluntly, noting in one report that the Soviets were apprehensive that if "it comes to war, they [the East Germans] will shoot us, start fires, and commit all kinds of sabotage."[198]

CONCLUSION

The evidence analyzed in this chapter is strongly consistent with the two hypotheses delineated here concerning the long-term economic benefits of conquest. And although the short-term hypothesis was not directly examined, this analysis did provide a degree of confirmation for a key portion of it. Three specific findings emerged from this analysis.

First, the experience of Hungary in the Soviet empire indicates that MNCs will shy away from a vanquished advanced country due to the conqueror's low credibility of commitment, thereby diminishing the economic dynamism of the vanquished country and reducing the long-term benefits of conquest. The significance of this dynamic has been enhanced as the opportunity cost of being isolated from MNCs has progressively increased over the past several decades.

Second, the rise of knowledge-based economies, a trend driven in significant part in recent years by the globalization of production, reduces the economic benefits of conquest. The maintenance of high rates of innovation is crucial to the long-term economic health of knowledge-based countries. Yet the Soviet experience in Eastern Europe indicates that the mechanisms of control that a conqueror is prone to use in advanced societies will hinder innovation.

[196] Reaching this conclusion seems legitimate when one takes into consideration factors such as high desertion rates in the East European militaries; the rapidity with which the East European military forces crumbled in the face of the great upheavals of 1989; the pro-NATO sentiments expressed in interviews concerning where loyalties would lie in a Warsaw Pact–NATO war; and the great reservoir of anti-Soviet sentiment in Eastern Europe, which had long-term historical roots and was accentuated by heavy-handed Soviet rule after World War II.

[197] Alexiev and Johnson, as cited in Herspring 1989, 148. Herspring also notes that many of those interviewed in the Rand study of East European émigrés concluded that "in the event of a war with NATO . . . the majority of soldiers would desist or desert at the first opportunity" (1989, 148).

[198] Penkovskiy, as cited in Herspring and Volgyes 1980, 289.

Finally, this examination clearly shows that the Soviet Union did not derive significant economic gains from its empire during the last several decades of the Cold War. The goods and technologies produced in Eastern Europe became more and more uncompetitive during this period, and the Soviets bore increasingly large economic costs as part of their effort to maintain imperial control in the region.

CHAPTER 7

Current Security Implications of the Globalization of Production

THE GLOBALIZATION of production is a dramatic, historically unprecedented development in the global economy. The analysis in this book shows that the geographic dispersion of MNC production has already reshaped the global security environment in three specific ways. First, no state can now effectively remain on the cutting edge in military technology if it does not pursue significant internationalization in weapons production. Second, the globalization of production has greatly reduced the economic benefits of military conquest among the most advanced countries. Third, this global production shift can, under certain conditions, increase the prospects for peace by contributing to the consolidation of deep regional economic integration among long-standing security rivals.

In this concluding section of the book, I will go beyond these three findings and specify the general implications of the geographic dispersion of MNC production for interstate relations. Does it have a positive effect on security? If so, where? To answer these questions, I will follow two basic steps. The first, undertaken in this chapter, is to specify the scope of the three mechanisms examined here and derive their current collective effect for security relations in different regions of the world. On the basis of this analysis, I conclude that the globalization of production's implications are positive for security relations among the great powers, negative for security relations among developing countries, and mixed for security relations between the great powers and developing countries. In the chapter that follows, I undertake the second step: examining whether there are any other mechanisms that might eventuate in the future that could run counter to the general assessments derived in this chapter and cause them to change in the years ahead. After examining a series of additional mechanisms, I conclude that none them is likely to alter the assessments I arrive at in this chapter.

THE GLOBALIZATION OF PRODUCTION AND SECURITY RELATIONS AMONG THE GREAT POWERS

The 1990s were a period of calm among the great powers at the end of a century marked by bloody, intense competition punctuated by the two world wars and the Cold War. Although the latter conflict never became a hot war, it was extraordinarily expensive and risky and also claimed the lives of millions in proxy wars. A number of prominent analysts argue that many of the stabilizers that existed during the 1990s are fading and that we are now heading back to a world of intense security competition among the great powers.[1] All of these analysts assert that economic globalization does not dilute their pessimistic assessments: as one of them notes, "If economic interdependence could not save Europe from war in 1914, there is no compelling reason to be confident that globalization would do any better at preserving a stable peace today."[2] Is this true? The globalization of production is a novel feature of the global economy that had no precedent in 1914. Is it a new force for stability among the great powers—that is, peacefulness?

To answer this question, we first need to determine which findings from this study have a bearing upon the great powers. The finding on weapons development from chapter 4 is clearly relevant, since it applies to all countries. In contrast, the finding from chapter 5—concerning how competition for FDI can influence the consolidation of regional economic integration among developing countries—obviously does not apply to security relations among the great powers. Determining the applicability of the benefits-of-conquest finding from chapter 6 is relatively more difficult. This finding applies only to those states in which production is now significantly globalized and knowledge-based. Although no precise means are available for delineating these countries, there are measures we can use to provide a basic portrait of this group.

Production in knowledge-based economies is, for the most part, not tied to the land but must have extensive communication links, since the sharing of information and ideas is its currency. Countries whose production is knowledge-based therefore may be identified as those that for many years have had (1) less than 10 percent of the labor force in agriculture and (2) more than four hundred telephone lines per one thousand people. As of the mid-1990s, the following group of countries met these criteria: Australia, Austria, Belgium, Canada, Denmark, Finland, France, Germany, Iceland, Israel, Italy, Japan, Netherlands, New Zealand, Norway, Singapore, Sweden, Switzerland, United Kingdom, and United States.[3]

What about those countries that now have significantly globalized production? One way of distinguishing this group is to identify those states that have a substantial number of large MNCs. There are only six states that have at least 5 of the 100 largest MNCs: United States (24), Japan (16), United Kingdom (14), France (13), Germany (10), and Netherlands (5).[4] While this criterion is

[1] See Mearsheimer 2001; Kupchan 2002; Waltz 2000; and Huntington 1993.

[2] Kupchan 2002, 103.

[3] World Bank 1997b, 146–48, 272–74. Hong Kong and Bermuda also satisfy these criteria, but neither of them is an independent state: Bermuda is a "dependent territory" of Great Britain, while Hong Kong is a "special administrative region" of China. Neither of them has, for example, embassies abroad, representation in the United Nations, or responsibility for its external security.

[4] Calculated using data from UNCTAD FDI/TNC database.

helpful, these six states are not the only ones whose production has been significantly globalized. Another method is to identify those countries that have long had high levels of inward and outward FDI. With only five exceptions (Austria, Finland, Iceland, Israel, and Japan) all of the knowledge-based countries listed in the preceding paragraph also have had an inward and outward FDI stock that is greater than 5 percent of GDP since the 1980s.[5] This high level of overlap is hardly surprising in light of the fact that the globalization of production has been an important contributing force behind the rise of knowledge-based economies in recent decades. This second coding of countries with significantly globalized production seems appropriate, with the notable exception of Japan (which had an outward FDI stock that was greater than 5 percent of GDP in 1990, but did not have not an inward FDI stock above this level). Given that Japan is a country that is generally understood to have a significantly globalized economy and, in turn, that it so strongly satisfies the first, more restrictive highly globalized criteria noted above, it seems reasonable to code it as having significantly globalized production.

The net result of these two overlapping categories is the list of countries delineated in figure 7.1. Significantly, all of the countries that are now clearly great powers are on this list.[6]

The Influence of the Reduction in the Economic Benefits of Conquest

As emphasized in chapter 1, numerous scholars emphasize the economic benefits of conquest as an influence on great power stability.[7] The legacy of history is one reason for this focus: the promise of capturing economic benefits from conquered territory has often been a significant motivating force for war.[8]

It is important to recognize that the economic benefits of conquest will influence the prospects for great power stability even if states are completely insensitive to economic motivations concerning conflict. When a state seizes substantial territory beyond its borders, it will be prone to become more vulnerable to attack for a variety of reasons: supply lines are extended; more territory must be defended; military resources are dissipated across a wider geographic area;

[5] Data from UNCTAD 2001, 325–27.

[6] On this point, see Jervis 2002, who considers the United States, Japan, and the largest, most developed states of Western Europe to clearly be great powers. Jervis notes that "Russia and China . . . lack many of the attributes of great powers: their internal regimes are shaky, they are not at the forefront of any advanced forms of technology or economic organization, they can pose challenges only regionally. . . . They are not among the most developed states and I think it would be fair to put them outside the ranks of the great powers" (2002, 1–2).

[7] Three strong recent statements are Van Evera 1999, chap. 5; Stam and Smith 2001; and Rosecrance 1999, esp. 17, 81.

[8] Some of the most significant historical examples are outlined in Van Evera 1999, chap. 5.

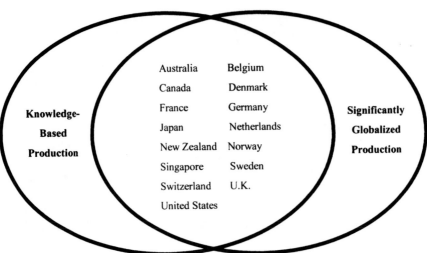

Figure 7.1 States in Which Production Is Now Significantly Globalized and Knowledge-Based

and so on. Of course, a heightened degree of vulnerability might be offset by the ability of a conqueror to extract significant economic resources from the vanquished territory. This is exactly what happened in the early phases of World War II: after Germany conquered Poland, France, Czechoslovakia, and other states, Germany's increased strategic vulnerability was largely offset because it was able to extract substantial economic resources from the territory it conquered.[9] This was a key reason why it was so difficult for the Allied coalition to beat back the German challenge to the status quo.

Ceteris paribus, the smaller the economic benefits of conquest, the more vulnerable the aggressor will be as it extends the territory under its control. For this reason, the prospects for international stability will increase if countries cannot extend their borders without increasing their vulnerability. Through its influence on the economic benefits of conquest, the globalization of production now acts as a stabilizing force among the great powers.

The Influence of the Change in the Parameters of Weapons Development

The reduction in the economic benefits of conquest is not the only reason that the geographic dispersion of MNC production enhances the prospects for great power stability. Also significant is the finding that even the great powers can no longer effectively go it alone in defense production. One consequence is that any great power that now follows an autarkic defense production strategy will

---

[9] See Liberman 1996, chap. 3.

be in a diminished position to pursue revisionist aims. The history of great power revisionism from the last 75 years reveals how consequential this is: at the time they challenged the status quo, imperial Japan, Nazi Germany, and the Soviet Union were all largely closed off from the international economy.

Significantly, all great powers, not just those pursuing autarkic defense production, will now be easier to subdue if they challenge the territorial status quo because of the changed parameters of weapons development. In the past century, revisionist great powers making challenges of this kind have (1) acted largely on their own—that is, with few or token allies; and (2) provoked a countervailing coalition that has moved to cut off supplies as part of its effort to beat back the revisionist.[10] Yet if the coalition of states does not have any particular advantage in the development of military technology over an economically isolated revisionist, then the revisionist will be more likely to be successful.

One example suffices to demonstrate the significance of this point. During World War II, a great many German weapons, especially those used by its ground forces, were technologically superior to those deployed by their Allied rivals.[11] This was despite the fact that the Allied powers undertook great efforts to impose a supply cutoff on Germany. Had Germany not been able to produce competitive weapons while subject to this supply cutoff, it would have been much easier for the Allies to prevail. Germany would not have fared nearly as well had global production been structured as is the case today: if the cost of being closed off from the global production networks had been as high as it is now, the supply cutoff imposed on Germany would have reduced its military capacity to a far greater extent and the Allied powers would have had a much easier time repelling Germany's challenge. The general implication is clear: other things being equal, revisionist great powers that act on their own will be easier to subdue if they cannot develop competitive military technologies when their access to the international economy is curtailed. For this reason, the long-term stability of the system is enhanced when the great powers no longer can be both independent and on the cutting edge in defense production, as is the case today.

Although the great powers are now less able to upset the status quo because of the changed parameters of weapons development, they are not therefore less able to successfully use force in general. Supply cutoffs will have a meaningful

---

[10] The second point is obvious: during World War I, World War II, and the Cold War, coalitions formed against those that made significant challenges to the status quo, and, in turn, supply cutoffs were initiated by the coalition. The first point is less obvious. It is clear enough that Soviet Union was essentially on its own in the Cold War, but World War I and World War II featured more than one significant country that made a challenge the status quo. In World War I, however, Germany's allies contributed very little on the battlefield. During World War II, in contrast, Germany did have a significant military ally in Japan. But Germany and Japan were so far removed from each other geographically that they were not able to pool their strength in specific military engagements, and thus each mounted essentially separate challenges to the status quo in its respective region.

[11] See, for example, the discussion in Hastings 1984, 186–95, who concludes (186) that "almost all" of the weapons used by German ground forces were superior in quality to those fielded by Allied ground forces.

effect only on those conflicts in which the battlefield effectiveness of great powers relies upon weapons or supplies that are produced or procured after fighting has begun. Although stockpiling is expensive and also locks a country into a particular technology in a fast-moving environment, great powers are likely to have a large enough inventory of weapons and supplies that supply cutoffs will not affect them in the short term. The longer the conflict, the greater the extent to which access to the global economy—or the lack thereof—will influence a great power's fortunes in war.

Even in the long term, it will be of little consequence if supplies are not cut off effectively. Significant in this regard is a key feature of economic globalization: it has greatly enlarged the pool of potential suppliers. The range of suppliers that can be easily tapped has greatly increased in response to transportation improvements and other changes. Moreover, identifying alternative suppliers, and establishing production linkages with them, is now far easier due to advances in information technology.

Judging the general potential for substitution—that is, the ability to switch from one supplier of a needed good or input to another—is not easy, but there are strong reasons to suspect that it is now very great in many sectors. For one thing, firms are aware that if a supply source temporarily becomes unavailable, they could suffer potential shutdowns and financial losses; as a result, firms typically take active steps to prevent them. One way to do so is by engaging in "multiple sourcing"—that is, relying on two or more suppliers. Although the general level of multiple sourcing is unclear, a 1999 survey of purchasing/supply management professionals in the United States revealed that 79 percent of them prefer to have multiple sources for a given item.[12] Of course, firms sometimes cannot pursue multiple sourcing or choose not to. However, even in such cases, the supply chain has been made more resilient by globalization.

Instructive on this score is what happened after the Sumitomo Chemical Company epoxy resin plant in Niihama, Japan, was destroyed by an explosion in July 1993. The case is telling because it represented an extreme example of supply concentration: this one plant produced 65 percent of the world supply of epoxy resin, which is used in the production of semiconductor chips. Moreover, there was no prior warning of a supply interruption before the Sumitomo plant was destroyed. As a result, this incident comes close to being a worst-case scenario of a supply interruption.

This case demonstrated that semiconductor firms were insulated to a significant degree from a supply shock. Alternate suppliers were able to fill the void: Sumitomo quickly arranged agreements with Nippon Kayaku, Dainippon Ink and Chemicals of Japan, and Chang Chung Chemicals of Taiwan, which, together, were capable of making up 50–60 percent of Sumitomo's original

[12] Fitzgerald 1999, 6. Beyond ensuring supply, there are three other principal advantages of multiple sourcing: it fosters price competition among suppliers, reduces the risk of being locked into a certain technological standard with a particular supplier, and helps to ensure that capacity is available to the buyer when demand for an input increases sharply.

supply of epoxy resin.[13] Dow, the U.S. chemical firm, was capable of making up the remaining epoxy resin shortage (although Sumitomo was able to reopen its plant before it was necessary to enter into any agreement with Dow).[14] The example of Dow reveals an important point that is easy to overlook when considering the degree to which producers are dependent on a certain supply source: some alternative suppliers may not be producing the good or input at the time the disruption occurs, but can do so to fill a void. The supply base, in short, is dynamic, not static. In this regard, Sumitomo also had the option of converting some of its plants in other countries to produce epoxy, but did not pursue this strategy because it was able to reopen the Niihama plant in five months.[15] Finally, this case also revealed that firms had the option of turning to alternate components produced by different suppliers (if needed, chipmakers could have switched to use higher-cost ceramic coverings, which Intel was using at the time).[16] This strategy was not utilized because of the short interruption, but it would have been available had there been a longer-term disruption. In the end, major computer and microchip producers suffered no shortage of epoxy resin despite the destruction of the Sumitomo plant.[17]

The key point is that globalization increases the ease of substitution and thereby makes evading a limited supply cutoff easier.[18] It is important to recognize that an effective supply cutoff need not be comprehensive in the number of countries it encompasses; what is crucial is that it covers a large proportion of the total number of potential suppliers in defense-related production. That being said, empirical and theoretical studies have shown that cooperation on economic sanctions is very difficult to achieve even among a small group of states.[19] When might we expect that the numerous barriers to cooperation will be superseded and an extensive supply cutoff will be established that covers a large percentage of the suppliers used in defense-related production? About the only situation in which this kind of supply cutoff is very likely to emerge is when the gravest of all international threats emerges: a fundamental challenge to the system as a whole by a revisionist great power.

The important point is that while the conditions in which an extensive supply cutoff is likely to be forthcoming are rare, the constraining effect of the

---

[13] *Wall Street Journal*, 6 August 1993, B10.

[14] *Wall Street Journal*, 6 August 1993, B10.

[15] *Chicago Sun-Times*, 22 July 1993, 53.

[16] *Chicago Sun-Times*, 22 July 1993, 53.

[17] The spot market price of memory chips doubled after the Sumitomo plant was destroyed, but the spot market accounts for only 5 percent of sales. Major computer manufacturers such as IBM and Apple, which purchase almost all memory chips, were not affected; see *Wall Street Journal*, 5 August 1993, B7.

[18] It should also be noted that because the ease of substitution is so high, disrupting an adversary's supply chain by conquering a country that your adversary depends on, or destroying its production, will be very difficult. A country pursuing such a strategy would likely need to conquer or destroy a sizable number of countries to disrupt its rival's access to supplies and inputs over the long term.

[19] See, for example, Mastanduno 1992; and Martin 1992.

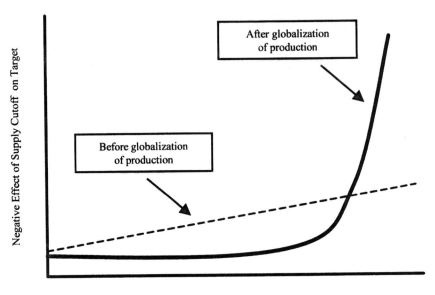

Figure 7.2 The Changing Effectiveness of Supply Cutoffs

kind of cutoff imposed on Germany in World War II would now be far stronger due to the changed ability of great powers to go it alone in defense production. In the end, recent changes concerning the role of foreign suppliers in the global economy have a cross-cutting effect on supply cutoffs: limited ones become less effective because the increase in the number of potential foreign suppliers has greatly facilitated substitution; extensive ones become harder to achieve but also far more powerful because the need for foreign suppliers in defense production is now so much greater. This dynamic is shown in the figure 7.2.

The Overall Effect on Great Power Security Relations

The changes in the economic benefits of conquest and weapons development caused by the geographic dispersion of MNC production are positive for security relations among the great powers on their own. When the economic benefits of conquest are low and great powers cannot effectively go it alone in defense production, it will be structurally harder for a great power to "run the tables"—that is, to use one instance of conquest as a springboard for the next, overturning the fundamental nature of the system through force. This basic relationship is captured in table 7.1. Put simply, the essence of a "production dispersion theory of

TABLE 7.1
Implications of Geographic Dispersion of Production
for Great Power Security Relations

	High Economic Benefits of Conquest	Low Economic Benefits of Conquest
Autarkic defense production viable	Highest danger (e.g., World War II)	Medium danger
Autarkic defense production not viable	Medium danger	Least danger (now)

conflict" is as follows: the greater the geographic dispersion of production, the better for great power stability.

In addition to the independent stabilizing effects of the change in the economic benefits of conquest and the parameters of weapons development, there is also positive interaction between them. The higher the economic benefits of conquest, the greater the ability of a great power revisionist to make itself less vulnerable to a supply cutoff. During World War II, for example, Germany was not devastated by the Allied supply cutoff in part because it was able to effectively seize so many of the economic resources it needed from the societies it conquered.[20] In today's environment, a great power revisionist will be more vulnerable to a supply cutoff not simply because the opportunity cost of being isolated from global production networks is now so much higher, but also because the only real compensating strategy available—using conquest to obtain the resources needed for defense production not available domestically—will no longer be as effective as it once was. Put another way, the size a country must be in order to effectively weather a supply cutoff has become much greater due to changes in production, which have also simultaneously reduced the ability of a great power to effectively augment its economic size through conquest.

Of course, other great power stabilizers currently exist besides the globalization of production, in particular the democratic peace, nuclear weapons,

[20] On this point, see Milward 1977, 312–13, 320–21.

international institutions, and public norms against war among advanced countries.[21] Moreover, these stabilizers existed before the globalization of production arrived on the scene. Why then can we say that the geographic dispersion of MNC production is a stabilizing force among the great powers? It is not because these other great power stabilizers are irrelevant; at present, they are very significant indeed.[22] Currently, therefore, the globalization of production is merely an additional source of stability. The key reason, however, why this global production shift is important is because it is very robust. Indeed, it may well be the most robust source of great power stability.

The democratic peace currently does constrain conflict among the great powers, but we have no assurance that all of them will always be democracies. The same is true of international institutions and public norms against war: they will not necessarily remain as constraints. Perhaps more importantly, even if these various constraints do exist, a skillful, malevolent leader could ignore or circumvent them.[23] Nuclear weapons are of course very hard for a leader to ignore or circumvent, yet not all great powers currently have them. Moreover, as Glenn Snyder's stability-instability paradox suggests, nuclear weapons do not remove the option of conventional war and, indeed, may make levels of violence short of nuclear war more likely.[24]

In raising these points, my argument is not that that these other factors are weak stabilizers, nor that they are likely to vanish in the future. The point is that even if a risk-acceptant or blundering leader of a great power does not face or overruns these constraints on war, waiting in reserve would be a constraint that no leader or country can disregard or circumvent: the globalization of production has shifted the scales against great power revisionism. By making it structurally harder for any great power revisionist to succeed, the globalization of production now serves as a powerful "reserve stabilizer."

Of course, the peace between the great powers in the decades after World War II itself created a favorable environment for the globalization of production to emerge. The key point is that now that the globalization of production exists, it presents states with a structural fact on the ground—one that independently reinforces great power stability in a positive feedback loop. Individual states can isolate themselves from the globalization of production, but they cannot summarily end it on their own. Moreover, great powers that isolate themselves still will find it just as difficult to run the tables—indeed, it will be harder because

[21] On the democratic peace, see, for example, Russett 1993. On the role of nuclear weapons, see, for example, Waltz 1993. On norms against war between advanced states, see, for example, Mueller 1989. On the stabilizing influence of international institutions, see, for example, Ikenberry 2001. For a useful general discussion, see Jervis 2002.

[22] All too frequently, scholars regard factors outside their framework as essentially irrelevant and place too much emphasis on their preferred variable; for a prominent example of an argument of this kind concerning great power stability, see Mueller 1988 and 1989.

[23] For a particularly useful and balanced discussion of this issue, see Mueller 1989, chap. 10.

[24] Snyder 1965. Also relevant is the analysis in Lieber and Press 2004.

they will be less strong militarily. Of course, the largest, most advanced states arguably have the most to gain from participation in the geographic dispersion of MNC production, and hence it is unlikely that any of them would, in fact, seek to take this self-isolation route. Pursuing independence is simply no longer an attractive option.

The globalization of production is consequential not only because it cannot be abruptly shut down or ignored by a revisionist great power. Also significant is that great power leaders do not have to understand the geographic dispersion of MNC production, or how it changes the prospects for revisionism, for it to have a stabilizing effect on great power security relations. Leaders also need not calculate costs and benefits in a rational manner, or have a particular set of preferences, for this global production shift to act as a stabilizer. As long as the globalization of production exists, it will be harder for a great power to run the tables no matter how leaders understand the global economy, how they make decisions, or what ideas they have. For the foreseeable future, nothing will change this. Ultimately, therefore, the globalization of production is a structural constraint on great power revisionism different from, say, nuclear weapons. Nuclear weapons do not necessarily operate as a stabilizer since not all great powers have them, they are subject to potential accidents, and they also may be controlled by leaders who do not make decisions using standard conceptions of rationality.[25] In addition, if nuclear deterrence fails, the negative consequences would be enormous; the globalization of production carries with it no such risks.

The bottom line is that this global production shift is very consequential. Had the globalization of production existed at the time of World War II, Germany would have been much less successful since it would not have been able to effectively seize resources from the advanced societies it conquered while also being able to produce competitive military technology under a cutoff of supplies. Given the tremendous costs and stakes associated with great power revisionism—in World War II, over 50 million were killed, and the Axis powers almost succeeded in overturning the fundamental nature of the system—having the globalization of production as a reserve stabilizer is now very beneficial indeed. Even in the absence of great power revisionism, the Cold War makes clear that the mere threat of revisionism is enough to provoke states to undertake enormous expenditures and run incredible risks to try to forestall it. Had the globalization of production been significant throughout the entire Cold War, the Soviet challenge to the system would have been significantly less acute, resulting in a less costly and less dangerous geopolitical competition. Moreover, the Cold War competition itself likely would have ended sooner, in large part because the Soviets would have more intensely felt the costs of isolation from the global economy and would have fallen behind the West in military technology much earlier on.

[25] See Sagan's discussion in Sagan 1993; and Sagan and Waltz 1995. See also Lieber and Press 2004.

Classification Issues and Policy Implications

The conclusion here is thus that the globalization of production is stabilizing among the great powers. Of course, scholars disagree concerning the classification of the great powers. One issue that needs to be considered is whether the United States should be placed in the same category as the other great powers. This conceptual issue is interesting, but need not be settled here; what it does raise is the important question of whether the preceding line of argument now applies to the United States. The answer is yes. Although the United States has a massive advantage in power over the other great powers, it is still subject to structural constraints on its ability to run the tables due to the globalization of production.

As will be delineated in a later section of this chapter, my assessment is that the geographic dispersion of MNC production promotes an even more marked U.S. military superiority. However, this is not something that undercuts the prospects for stability—at least regarding U.S. relations with the other great powers. As I have specified elsewhere, there are strong theoretical reasons indicating that an increase in U.S. military superiority will not be destabilizing among the great powers.[26] Even if one were to disagree with this perspective, it would still be necessary to come up with a compelling theoretical argument as to why the United States might use its military superiority to try to run the tables. This is not easy to do. Significantly, the fact that the globalization of production makes running the tables more difficult undercuts such a theoretical argument; particularly consequential in this regard is the reduction in the economic benefits of conquest caused by this global production shift.

In the end, the globalization of production has a cross-cutting effect on the ability of the United States to run the tables. On the one hand, the geographic dispersion of MNC production enhances U.S. military superiority—which, other things being equal, would appear to give the United States a greater ability to overturn the system through force.[27] On the other hand, the globalization of production also leads to changes that make it structurally harder for any great power, including the United States, to run the tables. The key point is that the latter effect is much stronger than the former.

A second classification issue concerns the status of Russia and China. If one regards economic and technological capacity as a core determinant of great power status, then the United Kingdom, Japan, France, Germany, and the United States are now the only countries that clearly should receive this classification. The argument on stability advanced here applies strongly to relations among these states, since they are all globalized, knowledge-based states that have significantly internationalized their defense-related production. Whether Russia and China are now best classified as great powers is ambiguous: militarily they have the attributes of great powers, yet economically and technologically they are

---

[26] Brooks and Wohlforth 2002a; see also Brooks and Wohlforth 2005.
[27] See the discussion in Hirshleifer 2001, esp. 331–32.

developing countries (Russia's GDP per capita is now slightly below that of Costa Rica's, while China's GDP per capita is just short of Namibia's).[28]

Whether or not they count as great powers, both Russia and China attract analysts' concern, especially regarding their satisfaction with the current U.S.-led international order and their possible desire to upend it. China is a particular worry, in light of its huge population and spectacular record of economic growth in recent years. Although the globalization of production does not bear on all security issues pertaining to Russia and China, it does ameliorate concerns about them in two important ways. First, the geographic dispersion of MNC production is another reason that China and Russia will not likely seek to overturn the system through force in the short term. While China and Russia are not yet globalized, knowledge-based societies, the globalization of production nevertheless restrains their ability to run the tables because it has transformed the structure of the most economically advanced states in the system in ways that reduce the economic benefits of conquest. Put another way, the systemwide opportunity for cumulative gains from conquest are now significantly reduced due to this global production shift; China and Russia are subject to this change in the system even given the current structure of their economies. Moreover, Russia and China are subject to the constraining effect of the changed parameters of weapons development, although to a relatively limited degree since it is only just now that they appear to moving toward significant globalization in defense-related production. The more internationalized they become in defense-related production, the more subject to the effect of a supply cutoff they will be.

The second, much more consequential conclusion concerns the long term. Currently, China and Russia can really only pose challenges regionally; as a result, "even the fiercest critics of Russia and China . . . do not see them as ready to launch unprovoked attacks against the United States . . . let alone as out to control the world."[29] Most of the fears about Russia and China instead concern the future: as one or both grows stronger economically, the stage may someday be set for yet another dangerous power transition of the kind so common throughout history.[30] It is true that Russia and, especially, China may eventually attain the ability to challenge the current international order through force. However, they will not be able to do so without strongly pursuing openness in defense-related production and becoming highly globalized and knowledge-based, in which case, the globalization stabilizing dynamic outlined here that now applies to relations among countries that are clearly great powers will apply equally to Russia and China. Therefore, the globalization of production

---

[28] For a helpful discussion of why China and Russia should not currently be considered great powers, see Jervis 2002, 1–2. GDP per capita figures for 2001 (from CIA 2002) are as follows: China (U.S.$4,300), Namibia (U.S.$4,500), Russia (U.S.$8,300), Costa Rica (U.S.$8,500). To put these figures in perspective, the United States' GDP per capita in 2001 was U.S.$36,300.

[29] Jervis 2002, 2–3.

[30] On power transitions, see, for example, Organski and Kugler 1980; Kugler and Lemke 1996; and Gilpin 1981.

makes long-term concerns about a dangerous power transition less acute. Russia and China may someday be very powerful, but their production then will be constituted in such a way that a power transition will be much less likely to be violent than in the past.

What implications does this analysis have for policy? As was noted in chapter 2, the globalization of production is very stable.[31] Significantly, its promotion to this point "has not required international cooperation or international institutions."[32] Instead, states have rushed in recent decades to open themselves to MNCs and to further the geographic dispersion of MNC production on an essentially voluntary, uncoordinated basis. That being said, it is certainly possible that active, collective management of the globalization of production— perhaps within the context of an international institution for FDI—may well be needed in the future. In this respect, a key question is whether active support of the geographic dispersion of MNC production can be justified on security grounds. Many countries currently assume that the answer to this question is yes. In the United States, for example, one of the few foreign policy themes common to the George W. Bush and Bill Clinton presidencies is that economic globalization will help to promote a stable security environment.[33] Yet up until now, we have had no basis for understanding whether the key driver of international commerce in today's global economy enhances international stability. With respect to security relations among the great powers, the globalization of production does, in fact, have an important positive benefit; taking any necessary actions to ensure its continued advancement during the years ahead can thus be strongly justified on security grounds.

THE GLOBALIZATION OF PRODUCTION AND SECURITY RELATIONS AMONG DEVELOPING COUNTRIES

Looking beyond the great powers, what about the security implications of the globalization of production for the so-called developing world? The exact boundaries of this region are not clear cut. For the purpose of this discussion, I will follow the designation advanced by the United Nations: the developing world includes all countries outside of North America, Western Europe, and Eastern Europe with the exception of Japan, Australia, New Zealand, South Africa, and Israel.[34] For a variety of reasons, many analysts regard the developing world as being a "zone of turmoil," both now and for the foreseeable future.[35] In light of the previous assessment concerning the influence of the globalization of production on great power relations, a logical question is whether it will

---

[31] The best treatment of this issue is Kobrin 2003.

[32] Garrett 2000, 945; see also Kobrin 1995, 24.

[33] On this point, see Rose 2003.

[34] See UNCTAD 2002b, 244.

[35] See, for example, Singer and Wildavsky 1993; and Goldgeier and McFaul 1992.

have also a positive effect on security relations in the developing world. My unfortunate answer to this question is a definitive no: the geographic dispersion of MNC production offers no reason for us to reduce our pessimism about the state of security relations among developing countries.

The Lack of Applicability of the Benefits-of-Conquest Mechanism

If the globalization of production promotes stability among the great powers, why will it not also help to make the developing world less prone to turmoil? An essential reason is that the globalization of production is not, in fact, global. As noted previously, analysts use the term *globalization of production* not because MNC production is spread worldwide, but rather because these new strategies are characterized by a geographic dispersion of MNC production across international borders. Whereas the great powers are at the vanguard of this shift, many developing countries have essentially been bypassed. Those developing countries that have participated in the globalization of production have not done so to the extent that their economies have become significantly globalized and knowledge-based.[36] As a result, while the globalization of production has transformed the economic structure of the most advanced states in ways that reduce the economic benefits of conquest, this transformation has not yet taken place in the developing world. A core reason why the geographic dispersion of MNC production is beneficial for security relations among the great powers (it reduces the economic benefits of conquest among them) thus does not apply to security relations among developing countries. Simply on this basis, we can conclude that the globalization of production will not have the same positive effect on security in the developing world that it does among the great powers.

The previous discussion showed that the globalization of production is beneficial for security relations among the great powers because (1) it has lowered the economic benefits of conquest, (2) it has changed the parameters of weapons development in ways that made it difficult for a great power revisionist to prevail, and (3) there is a positive interaction between these two changes. Since the benefits-of-conquest mechanism is not yet operative in the developing world, this latter effect does not apply. This is another reason why we should not expect the globalization of production to have a beneficial effect on developing country security relations, as it does among the great powers.

Although the benefits-of-conquest mechanism does not yet apply to the developing world, it does have implications for security in the region. Other things being equal, countries with a high GDP per capita offer the largest potential rewards to a conqueror, since they have more wealth relative to the number of people who must be controlled. The examination in this book has shown

---

[36] As figure 7.1 makes clear, Singapore is currently the notable exception in this regard.

that wealth in the most advanced states is structured in such a way that it cannot be effectively seized by a conqueror. In the developing world, in contrast, there are a number of countries with a very high GDP per capita whose wealth is not knowledge-based or significantly globalized. The standout in this regard is Kuwait, which has a land-based economy and yet has a higher GDP per capita than many advanced countries, including Canada, France, Germany, Sweden, and the United Kingdom.[37] The existence of developing countries such as Kuwait that offer high cumulative gains to a conqueror is harmful for security in the region. It is in this regard that the inapplicability of the benefits-of-conquest mechanism has repercussions for security in the developing world.

The Lack of Wide Applicability of the Regional Integration Mechanism

We need to look beyond the benefits-of-conquest mechanism to understand the security implications of the globalization of production for developing countries. Does the regional integration mechanism outlined in chapter 5 offer any reason to reduce our pessimism about security relations in this region? Policymakers in the developing world certainly envy the improved security relations in Western Europe that followed deep regional economic integration. Although developing country policymakers frequently pronounce that the consolidation of regional integration would be helpful for promoting stable security relations in their respective regions, it has been an elusive goal over the decades. For this reason, an important question is how broadly the finding in chapter 5—that competition for FDI can be beneficial for security relations by leading long-standing rivals in the developing world to consolidate deep regional economic integration—now applies throughout the developing world.

Recall that we should expect this mechanism to pertain only to those regional integration agreements that meet both of the following conditions: (1) the economic size of the pact is large and the group is able to achieve significant economic size with relatively few members; and (2) the ability of the pact's members to meet their potential for attracting FDI without regional integration is low. Chapter 5 showed that of all regional integration agreements among developing countries, Mercosur met these conditions in the early 1990s much better than any other group in the developing world. Have any groups formed since that strongly meet these conditions? The unfortunate answer is no. The largest developing country integration agreement formed since 1994 is the Commonwealth of Independent States (CIS), whose 10 members collectively have a GDP less half the size of the four members of Mercosur.[38] While possible,

---

[37] CIA 1999.
[38] Data from World Bank 2001.

it is unlikely that a new group will emerge that strongly meets these conditions or the character of an existing one will change such that it does. As the concluding section of chapter 5 showed, Mercosur itself exemplifies the elusive nature of these conditions: although it strongly satisfied them throughout most of the 1990s, by the end of the decade they no longer characterized the agreement. As a result, while competition for FDI helped propel Mercosur during its formative stages, by the end of the 1990s it no longer did.

The key constraint is the balance between size and numbers. To meet the first condition—significant economic size with relatively few members—a pact must include at least one large country. But almost all developing countries are very small economically. Argentina is instructive on this score. Argentine policymakers saw making up for the country's "small" economic size as the main FDI advantage of Mercosur, and yet Argentina was the fifth largest developing country in economic terms as of the mid-1990s. Moreover, Argentina's economy was itself significantly larger than those of three-quarters of integration agreements among developing countries: in 1994, more than half of such agreements had regional GDPs below U.S.$70 billion, and three-quarters fell below U.S.$200 billion; in comparison, Argentina's GDP was U.S.$257 billion.

The bottom line is that in most of the developing world, the lack of a large country to partner with makes unlikely an integration agreement that meets the conditions specified here. As of 2002, only three non-OECD countries has a GDP above U.S.$500 billion: China, Mexico, and India.[39] China has had great success attracting FDI on its own, and hence has little incentive to invest in consolidating economic integration with other developing countries for this purpose. As a member of NAFTA, Mexico also has little need to further regional integration with other developing countries to secure increased FDI. India is a member of the South Asian Association for Regional Cooperation Preferential Trading Arrangement (SAPTA). It seems unlikely that SAPTA will match the conditions specified here as strongly as Mercosur did in the early and middle 1990s. SAPTA was far from satisfying these conditions in the 1990s, when it was less than half the size of Mercosur even though it contained more members—seven as compared to Mercosur's four.[40] India, which by itself comprises almost 80 percent of SAPTA's GDP, also did not make attracting FDI a high priority for much of its history. Even if India continues to make attracting increased FDI a priority in the years ahead, the poor record on economic policies in the other members of SAFTA (Bangladesh, Bhutan, Maldives, Nepal, Pakistan, and Sri Lanka) means that India unlikely to reap the same FDI advantages that Brazil secured during the early and middle 1990s as a result of its partnership with Argentina.

[39] World Bank 2002.
[40] Frankel, Stein, and Wei 1997, 247.

The Influence of the Change in the Parameters of
Weapons Development

In the end, the weapons development mechanism is the only one of the three highlighted here that has wide applicability in the developing world. The previous section showed that this mechanism has a positive influence on security relations among the great powers. Unfortunately, the same is not true for developing countries.

If the great powers can no longer remain on the cutting edge in military technology while pursuing autarky in defense production, the same will be even more true of developing countries, since they are much smaller and less technologically advanced. Significant in this respect is the experience in Brazil, arguably the most technologically advanced arms producer among developing countries in the 1980s.[41] During the 1980s and for decades previously, Brazil's defense sector had been strongly reliant on domestic capabilities. By the mid-1990s, Brazil's once capable defense industry had essentially collapsed in significant part because of a continued unwillingness to relinquish the goal of "technological autonomy" in defense-related production, and a consequent failure to strongly participate in the geographic dispersion of MNC production via interfirm alliances, FDI, and international subcontracting.[42]

One should not conclude from Brazil's experience that a state's defense sector will collapse if it forgoes internationalization; what this case does show is how high the opportunity cost of closure in this sector has become for developing countries. A developing country that pursues globalization in defense production will gain access to technologies and components that otherwise would be beyond its reach or could only be produced at great cost or lower quality. It is telling that China has responded to these changed incentives. China clearly wishes to rapidly advance the technological sophistication of its weaponry and also prefers to do so while following a largely autarkic path. The analysis here shows that if China wants to catch up with the United States and Japan, it cannot pursue an autarkic strategy. Significantly, China recently began to move away from a largely autarkic strategy and has shifted toward a tentative embrace of globalization in weapons production.[43]

If the pursuit of globalization in defense-related production stabilizes relations among the great powers, why is it not also beneficial for relations among developing countries? Great powers obviously differ from developing countries in many ways; the most important systematic distinction for security affairs is that these two kinds of states have markedly different capacities for warfare. By virtue of their large, technologically advanced economies, all great

[41] See Conca 1998, 500.
[42] On this point, see Conca 1998, 509; see also 506, 509, and 511–12.
[43] See, for example, Lewis and Litai 1999; and Feigenbaum 1999.

powers have a very substantial capacity of this kind. The distinguishing feature of the developing world is economies of a certain size and character—such that they cannot match the great powers in ability to mobilize military capabilities. If we want to know whether the changed parameters of weapons development have a positive effect on developing country security relations, as among the great powers, we must factor in the significance of having, or lacking, a substantial capacity to mobilize military capabilities.

Because the great powers and developing countries differ in such capacities, conflict among the former differs from that among the latter: the stakes are different, as are the weapons produced and used. This matters greatly. Let us begin with the stakes of the conflict. Those developing countries that pursue globalization in defense-related production will become exposed to potential leverage from countries whose firms are sources of needed inputs for weaponry. Any developing country that is reliant upon global firms for key aspects of defense-related production will be more affected by a supply cutoff. And although cutting off supplies to a developing country is easier than to a great power, the incentives to cooperate on the cutoff are also much lower. Developing countries obviously have much less ability to project military force. Unlike a systemwide threat by a revisionist great power, the military actions a developing country would undertake in the region are unlikely to be sufficiently threatening to garner widespread cooperation among states for a supply cutoff. In this regard, it is important to recall that limited supply cutoffs are much less effective in today's world of many suppliers.

Developing countries who pursue globalization in weapons production are less subject to supply cutoffs not just because of the stakes of conflicts, but also because of the nature of the weapons typically employed and produced. Developing countries that are weapons producers have a manufacturing profile very different from that of the great powers. Developing countries do not generally produce large, complex weapons systems, focusing instead on less complicated, smaller systems. The significance of this difference is straightforward. The less complicated are the weapons produced, the less the need to globalize their manufacture—and hence the less effect even a comprehensive supply cutoff will have on war-fighting capacity. In turn, the less complicated the weapons that are produced, the more potential suppliers that a developing country can turn to—and hence the greater the difficulty of cutting off supplies. Finally, other things being equal, the less complex the weapons produced, the easier it is to stockpile before a conflict begins. This matters since even a comprehensive supply cutoff would not reduce the flexibility of a military action when a developing country depends only upon existing stockpiles of weapons and supplies.

In short, because of the particular stakes and weapons that predominate in developing country conflicts, the change in the parameters of weapons development does not have the same positive security effect in the region that it does among the great powers. This, unfortunately, is not all: in at least some areas of the developing world, the change is actually negative for security relations. To put it simply for now, this is because the globalization of production augments the proliferation of weapons.

Developing countries who produce advanced conventional weapons now face strong incentives to globalize their defense-related production. Those that do will produce advanced weaponry faster, cheaper, and more effectively. Although developing countries do not have many MNCs based within their territory that disperse production via affiliates and interfirm alliances, they can take advantage of globalization of production through international subcontracting—which can be very important for military technological competitiveness. Even by pursuing globalization, most developing countries cannot produce numerous advanced conventional weapons; a much larger pool of developing countries can leverage globalization and find a "niche" in which to produce a small set of such weapons.

The key point is that because of the globalization of defense-related production, developing countries can develop certain advanced weapons systems that they could not otherwise manufacture. The same basic dynamic is true for small advanced countries, some of which are now significant exporters of weapons systems to developing countries. Israel is a good example: because its companies engage in international subcontracting and other globalization strategies, Israel can produce advanced weapons systems that would otherwise be beyond its capacity, given its small economic size. Israel, in turn, exports avionics, sensors, command and control systems, guided missiles, and other advanced systems to countries such as India, potentially upsetting its arms balance with Pakistan[44].

In today's world, it would certainly be better if developing countries had fewer potential suppliers of advanced conventional weapons systems. If developing countries and small, advanced countries had not had the option to pursue globalization, the end of the Cold War could well have reduced the proliferation of weapons. By facilitating the production of advanced weapons systems and increasing the pool of potential suppliers, the globalization of production has made the proliferation problem in the developing world much worse in recent years. This undermines the developing world's security prospects for three reasons: rapid shifts in military capabilities, enhanced arms races, and a larger number of possible conflict dyads.

First, drawing on international sources of advanced technology that are far beyond their domestic capacity will make it possible for some developing countries to quickly gain an advantage over regional rivals. Although "relative military advantage is merely one component of any decision regarding war,"[45] there are reasons to believe that the emergence of windows of opportunity and

---

[44] *New York Times*, 7 September 2003, A13.

[45] Lebow 1984, 149.

vulnerability increases the likelihood of military hostilities.[46] Because it can contribute to the development of such windows, the globalization of production worsens the security situation in the developing world.

A second way in which globalization of defense production diminishes security in the developing world is through intensification of conventional arms races. As one country's military strength advances further or faster than it would without globalizing defense production itself or without purchasing weapons from another country that is doing so, other countries in the region are likely to accelerate and expand their weapons acquisition in response. Significantly, the most comprehensive statistical study of conflict to date finds that the presence of an arms race "increases the probability of all types of disputes. Importantly, the strongest associations occur in disputes that escalate to war. For these disputes, we see almost a doubling of risk associated with an arms race being present."[47]

Third and finally, by enhancing weapons proliferation the globalization of production has a negative effect on security because it increases the number dyads in which conflict can break out in the developing world. By taking advantage of the globalization of production to manufacture advanced systems they would not otherwise be able to produce, or buying from a country that is doing so, some developing countries may gain a coercive capacity against other developing countries that they previously lacked. In some cases, developing countries may seek this capacity in order to project military power in a wider geographic region. In other cases, an enhanced capacity to project force over long distances may come about more indirectly as a product of competition with a long-term security rival. For example, by globalizing its defense-related production, China could potentially produce new and powerful conventional weapons that allow it to obtain a greater coercive capacity with respect to Taiwan. Of course, Taiwan may also take advantage of the globalization of production and nullify China's advantage. Yet even if a balance were to develop, this arms buildup would in all likelihood leave China with an enhanced coercive capacity against other, more remote countries in the region (such as the Philippines) that are not trying to match China step for step. In short, the globalization of production gives some developing countries an ability to project military power over longer distances; this, in turn, increases the number of potential flashpoints, which can only be harmful for security relations.

Factoring In Weapons of Mass Destruction

The discussion up to now has focused on conventional weapons, but it also applies to weapons of mass destruction (WMD). Although this term is often used a shorthand descriptor for nuclear, biological, and chemical arms, scholars

---

[46] Van Evera 1999, chap. 4.
[47] Bennett and Stam 2003, 125.

generally agree that the latter kind of weapon should not be included in this category. As Richard Betts underscores, "chemical weapons are not really in the same class as other weapons of mass destruction, in the sense of ability to inflict a huge number of casualties in a single strike."[48] Analysts differ as to whether nuclear weapons or biological weapons now pose the greater worry. Betts points to biological weapons, arguing that they "combine maximum destructiveness and easy availability . . . [while] nuclear weapons have great killing capacity, but are hard to get. . . . An aggrieved group that decides it wants to kill huge numbers of Americans will find the mission easier to accomplish with anthrax than with a nuclear explosion."[49] Others such as Gregg Easterbrook disagree, stressing that nuclear weapons are now the greater concern because they are certain to kill massive numbers of people, whereas "historic efforts at killing large populations through biological warfare have met with mixed results."[50] This dispute is hard to resolve; what these analysts do, however, agree upon is that "chemical weapons are . . . not 'weapons of mass destruction' in any meaningful sense."[51]

Unfortunately, just as participating in the globalization of production allows developing countries to move ahead more quickly and effectively in the production of conventional weaponry, it also accelerates production of WMD. That being said, it is not the case that developing countries must participate in the globalization of production in order to produce WMD. The example of North Korea makes this point clear. Few countries are as isolated from FDI as North Korea, and yet it has an extensive, and successful, WMD program. North Korea also has no MNCs to speak of that pursue interfirm alliances or other geographic dispersion strategies. In terms of benefiting from internationalization, the key for North Korea has instead been transfers of information and technology from foreign militaries and other nonprivate groups and individuals.

It is important to recognize that although the benefits of participation in the globalization of production for developing WMD are consequential, they are smaller than for conventional weaponry. The key reason is that while much of what is needed to produce advanced conventional weaponry is dual-use—and is therefore controlled in large part by private companies—this is less true for biological and, especially, nuclear weapons.[52] At present, it is the personnel,

---

[48] Betts 1998, 30–31; see also the detailed comparative assessment of weapons lethality in Fetter 1991, who (23) ultimately concludes: "Although they are capable of causing widespread death and suffering, chemical weapons do not constitute a 'poor man's atomic bomb,' especially if used against a well-prepared adversary. Biological weapons, in contrast, could approach nuclear weapons in lethality."

[49] Betts 1998, 32.

[50] Easterbrook 2002, 24.

[51] Easterbrook 2002, 22.

[52] Companies did little work that relates to biological weapons until recently, since there was no private market in these dangerous pathogens. This is changing, however, as private companies play an ever increasing role in biodefense programs (on this point, see Hoyt and Brooks 2003–4).

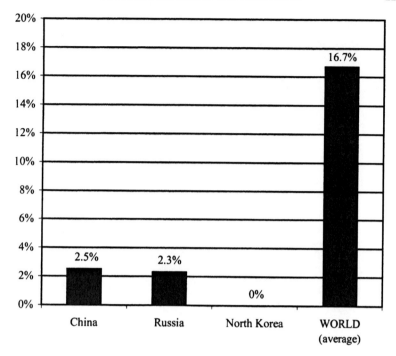

Figure 7.3 FDI Outward Stock as a Share of GDP (1999)
Source: UNCTAD 2001.

information, and materials located in universities, research institutes, and government facilities that constitute the core proliferation threat with respect to nuclear and biological weapons in the developing world. For example, the Russian interests that have made the fundamental contributions to Iran's nuclear program are a university—the Mendeleyev University of Chemical Technology—along with three different parts of the Russian government's Ministry of Atomic Energy: the Design Institute of Power Technology (NIKIET), the Experimental Machine Building Design Bureau (OKBM), and the Nuclear Energy Construction Abroad subsidiary (Zarubezhatomenergostroy).[53]

Significantly, none of the key WMD suppliers and developers are strong participants in the geographic dispersion of MNC production. The three "key supplier" countries of personnel, information, and materials that have contributed most strongly to WMD development in the developing world—Russia, North Korea, and China—all have a dearth of MNCs that are undertaking FDI abroad, as figure 7.3 demonstrates.[54] At the same time, the countries that during

[53] Monterey Institute of International Studies 2003.

[54] For the assessment that these three countries are the "key suppliers" of materials relating to WMD, see CIA 2000.

TABLE 7.2
Per Capita FDI Inflows to Countries Pursuing WMD in the 1990s

Country	Per Capita FDI Inflows in 1990s (millions of U.S.$)	Ratio of Per Capita FDI Inflows to Average World Per Capita FDI Inflows in 1990s
Syria	70	10.60%
Sudan	31.2	4.72%
North Korea	11.3	1.71%
Iran	0.52	0.08%
India	14.96	2.27%
Pakistan	31.97	4.84%
Iraq	0.43	0.02%
Libya	0	0%
World	660.4	100%

Source: UNCTAD FDI/TNC database and United Nations Population Fund.

the 1990s were most strongly pursuing the development of WMD all lagged far behind the world average of FDI inflows per capita during this period, as table 7.2 indicates.

All this being said, economic globalization certainly has contributed to WMD development by developing countries. However, the key problem in this regard has been the decisions of governments in the triad of North America, Western Europe, and Japan concerning how they regulate international exports from their respective countries rather than the geographic dispersion of MNC production. The experience of Iraq's nuclear program during the 1980s is instructive in this regard. During this time, Iraq had a dearth of production links with MNCs: of particular significance is that it received almost no FDI (a total of only U.S.$22 million) during the 1980s.[55] At the same time, Iraq greatly benefited from international trade during this period: dozens of companies from the triad exported goods from these countries to Iraq that were useful for its nuclear program during this period. Some of these exports from the triad to Iraq were illegal and only occurred because of lax enforcement of export laws by Germany and other countries, while much of the remaining trade occurred because of decisions by governments to allow it (often for political reasons, since Iraq at this time was perceived as being an ally of the United States and other key Western powers).[56] In short, Iraq's nuclear program during the 1980s was a substantial beneficiary of economic globalization, but this was due to insufficient regulation by Western governments of exports sent from their countries.

Shutting down exports of goods that can be used for developing WMD is not a straightforward task; it is, however, significantly easier to do than remotely

[55] UNCTAD FDI/TNC database.
[56] "Iraq Used Many Suppliers for Nuke Program," Associated Press, 17 December 2002.

monitoring and sanctioning the foreign production activities of MNCs. Although there has so far not been much FDI by MNCs in countries that are trying to develop WMD, this situation could, of course, change; if so, then the globalization of production could potentially contribute to WMD development to a very significant degree in the future. It is important to recognize that from an efficiency standpoint, there is no need for MNCs from advanced countries to establish foreign affiliates in any of those developing countries that are believed to now be strongly pursuing WMD development: Syria, North Korea, Sudan, and Iran.[57] None has a large number of highly trained workers, an extensive technological infrastructure, a group of universities that is well regarded in technological fields, or any other factor—including a significant domestic market—that would cause them to become attractive sites for FDI anytime soon by MNCs that produce the kind of technologies useful for WMD development. Moreover, none of these countries has the institutional and policy climate for investment that MNCs highly prize. Even if these states were to develop such a climate, none is a democracy, and so their credibility of commitment to maintain it would be low; for the same reason, MNCs could not be reassured that these governments would refrain from confiscating their assets or extracting excessive rents from them. At the same time, the firms based in these WMD-seeking states have little to offer in terms of developing new technologies, so few interfirm alliances and other deep production linkages between MNCs and companies located in these countries are likely to develop in the years ahead.

Conclusions and Policy Implications

At present, the benefits-of-conquest mechanism and the regional integration mechanism have essentially no applicability to the developing world. This is unfortunate, since each would be positive for security relations were they to apply. The lack of applicability of the regional integration mechanism is both unexpected and particularly regrettable given that so many policymakers in the developing world regard regional integration as a useful means for improving security relations. The experience of Mercosur shows that the geographic dispersion of MNC production has the potential to promote the consolidation of regional integration among security rivals in the developing world. Yet while globalization may increase the demand for institutions to reap some gain—such as attracting FDI—this does not mean that institutions will necessarily be supplied. In the end, it would certainly be favorable if Mercosur's experience during the early and middle 1990s were duplicated elsewhere in the developing world, but this is unlikely to occur.

[57] See CIA 2003. At the time that this CIA report was written, Iraq and Libya were also included on this list.

Of course, if production were to become as globalized in the developing world as it is today among the most advanced countries, then the benefits-of-conquest mechanism would apply. However, it is important not to underestimate the difficulty, and therefore overestimate the likelihood, of the economies of developing countries being transformed to look like those of the most advanced countries. No matter how significant the globalization of production, all states will never have similarly structured economies. Path dependency reduces the likelihood of dramatic economic transformations in the developing world. In addition, the need for specialization in the global economy means that not all countries can be economically structured in the same way; significantly, globalization may well increase the degree of specialization, not reduce it. For these and other reasons, most states in the developing world face tremendous constraints on their ability to shift toward economies that are geographically dispersed and knowledge-based. Irrespective of the globalization of production, a country like Kuwait is not going to look like Denmark anytime soon. That being said, it is certainly possible that some countries in the developing world will someday have economies quite similar in structure to the most advanced countries. A task of future research will be to identify what particular countries in the developing world are most likely to undergo such a significant transition.

Yet, even if the economic benefits of conquest mechanism were to apply in certain parts of the developing world in the future, the influence that the weapons development mechanism has on security relations in these areas would remain unaffected. No matter what kinds of economic changes occur in some parts of the developing world in the years ahead, the recent change in the parameters of weapons development will not have the same stabilizing influence in this region that it has on the great powers; this specific effect simply cannot be generalized to disputes among lesser states that have a much smaller capacity to mobilize for warfare. At the same time, the globalization of defense-related production makes the weapons proliferation problem even worse in the developing world with respect to both conventional weapons and WMD, and thereby worsens security relations in the region.

With respect to great power relations, promotion of the globalization of production can be strongly justified on security grounds. The same is not true with respect to developing countries. The key conclusion from this analysis is that the geographic dispersion of MNC production offers no basis to reduce our pessimism about this region's security prospects; in fact, there is reason for increased pessimism. Does this mean that any individual government that wishes to foster improved security relations in the developing world should generally restrict the globalization of production? In practical terms, individual states do not have this option and, at any rate, the positive externality for great power security relations is reason enough not to generally back away from promoting the globalization of production on security grounds. Moreover, greater exposure to MNCs in the developing world can be justified for numerous non-security-related reasons.

It is also important to bear in mind that the strongest conclusion concerns what the globalization of production is *not* doing: there is nothing to support the claim that the geographic dispersion of MNC production will make the developing world more peaceful. What is much less clear is the degree to which this global production shift actually makes security in the developing world even worse. There are reasons to doubt that the security downsides for the region will be especially dramatic during the foreseeable future. By exacerbating weapons proliferation, the globalization of production certainly does have negative implications for those developing country dyads in which at least one of the states can effectively project military force and weapons upgrades are being pursued; the rivalries between China and Taiwan and between India and Pakistan are prominent examples. However, relatively few developing countries can, in fact, effectively use military force beyond their borders; many armed forces in the region can do little more than serve internal policing functions. In large part for this reason, it is not the case that all, or even many, developing country dyads will be adversely affected by this global production shift. Put another way, although the sign on the globalization of production variable is negative for security relations among developing countries, the magnitude of its effect is likely small for the region as a whole.

In the end, therefore, the most important conclusion for policymakers is that they should not base their future foreign policy decisions on the notion advanced by Thomas Friedman and others that the globalization of production is a strong, positive security force in the developing world.[58] The globalization of production does not in any way reduce the need to take active steps to lower the likelihood of conflict in the region; instead, the opposite is true. For the foreseeable future, it would be reasonable for the United States and other countries to implement policies to reduce the repercussions that the geographic dispersion of MNC production now has in parts of the developing world. In this regard, the course with the greatest potential positive influence would be to put in place coordinated restrictions on FDI into those developing countries that are now understood to be strongly pursuing WMD development. These FDI restrictions need not be general, but can be limited to specific sectors that have the potential to significantly contribute to the development of WMD.

Putting in place such FDI restrictions on these WMD-developing states should be feasible. Although coordinated FDI restrictions among a wide range of countries would be preferable, this is not necessary in order to achieve a significant effect, for the simple reason that most FDI originates from a very small number of countries. The United States, the United Kingdom, and France collectively accounted for half of all FDI outflows in 2000; the total amount of

---

[58] See Friedman 1999, esp. 257.

outward FDI coverage increases to 85 percent if we add just eight additional states: Canada, Germany, Belgium, Luxembourg, Netherlands, Spain, Sweden, and Japan.[59] We should also expect that if coordinated FDI restrictions among some or all of these countries are put in place, they will be politically stable. As was previously noted, there is no efficiency rationale for MNCs in dual-use sectors to establish foreign affiliates in these WMD-developing countries or set up production linkages with domestic firms located within them; as a result, any restrictions that are put in place on the ability of MNCs to pursue production linkages with these countries will be essentially painless for firms. In contrast, if MNCs were required to isolate themselves from, say, Germany and its firms, then a great many MNCs would greatly suffer, and they would likely strongly protest and resist such restrictions.

THE GLOBALIZATION OF PRODUCTION AND SECURITY RELATIONS BETWEEN THE GREAT POWERS AND DEVELOPING COUNTRIES

A final question to ask is how the globalization of production influences security relations between the great powers and developing countries. The finding concerning the economic benefits of conquest does not pertain, since developing countries do not satisfy the conditions for this mechanism to apply; and while all of the current great powers satisfy these conditions, no developing country has the capacity to conquer them. The regional integration mechanism also has essentially no applicability for security relations between developing countries and the great powers. The weapons development mechanism does, however, apply strongly. As will be shown below, this mechanism ultimately has a mixed effect on security relations between the great powers and developing countries.

The Influence of the Change in the Parameters of Weapons Development

Some analysts and policymakers argue that if developing countries pursue globalization in conventional weapons production, this will "lead to the progressive erosion of the military technological advantages of the West, and particularly the United States."[60] The standard reason cited in support of this "leveling" argument is that "globalization has made the technology and resources necessary to develop sophisticated weapons more widely available."[61] As discussed in the previous section, it is certainly true that pursuing globalization

[59] UNCTAD 2001, 296.
[60] Bitzinger 1994, 191.
[61] Albright 2003; see also, for example, Libicki 1999–2000, 30.

in weapons-related production makes it easier for developing countries to produce advanced conventional weapons. But will this dynamic allow developing countries to reduce the existing gap in conventional military technology with the great powers? In addressing this question, I will focus on the United States, the great power most likely to be involved in military engagements with developing countries. As I show, for two key reasons, the geographic dispersion of production is very unlikely to reduce the American edge in military technology over developing countries in the years ahead; instead, we should expect it to enhance U.S. dominance.

The first reason concerns the greatly increased complexity of modern weapons, which in recent years has been partly driven by the globalization of defense-related production. Because modern weapons systems are so complex, developing countries may be unable to produce them even if they gained access to all needed components and technologies. It is one thing to have the tools necessary for production; it is quite another thing to possess the necessary production experience, knowledge of systems integration, and design skills to be able to use these tools effectively. While the former can be secured on the open market with relative ease, the latter cannot: firms and governments jealously guard this intellectual capital. Moreover, much of it cannot be purchased since it is largely a product of a costly and time-consuming process of trial and error. Although this is true in all advanced technological sectors, it is particularly the case in defense.[62] Developing countries have a dearth of scientists, engineers, and technicians with the relevant knowledge and experience to perform the myriad complex design and production tasks that are needed to create advanced weapons systems.[63]

It is crucial to remember that both defense production experience and knowledge are necessary to take advantage of access to parts and components. The Soviet Union shows that production experience alone does not suffice. By the final phase of the Cold War, the Soviets had acquired immense experience in weapons production—far greater than any developing country will likely have for decades. But the Soviets still had inadequate knowledge of how to use many of the parts and components used in U.S. weapons they stole or imported; for this reason, as emphasized in chapter 4, the Soviets were largely unable to translate access to weapons inputs into enhanced capability during the Cold War's last years.

Japan is another powerful example that demonstrates the inadequacy of access to parts and components alone, and the difficulty of gaining the necessary production knowledge and experience needed to produce modern weapons. Although Japan has worked with the United States in defense production over many decades, this collaboration generally has been shallow—limited largely

---

[62] Particularly helpful on this point is the discussion in Samuels 1994, chaps. 6 and 7.

[63] On this point, see, for example, Brzoska 1999, 152.

to licensing and coproduction, which is "the equivalent to following a script."[64] Japan has never developed enough "trial and error" production experience in the military sector; its production knowledge is largely limited to "know why" but not "know how."[65] Despite immense domestic technological capabilities and an intense, decades-long effort to acquire an indigenous defense production capacity, Japan still is not nearly as effective as the United States in the production of weaponry. A good example is Japan's F-2 fighter aircraft, conceived as a slightly modified version of the General Dynamics F-16C. The F-2 is a white elephant: no better than the F-16C, it is at least twice as expensive to produce.[66] The most significant technological system the Japanese brought to the table—co-cured composite technology—has led to major cost overruns and delays and has not performed well.[67] This experience has confirmed early worries that Japan would be better off using existing technologies that use more conventional materials.[68] In explaining the F-2's deficiencies, Keinichi Nagamatsu (secretary-general of the defense committee of the Federation of Japanese Industries) emphasizes the lack of skill and experience in the production process: "Although we are skilled copycats, we are not yet so good at the creativity and originality that design and system integration require."[69]

When it comes to defense production, no developing country will match Japan's capacity for many years to come. Japan's technological capacity is greater than any developing country is likely to have for decades. Japan is an important American ally, and has therefore been able to gain significant access to U.S. military prime contractors and to their store of knowledge in the production of weaponry. Finally, China is the only developing country that may approach Japan's level of defense spending in the near future.[70] Given Japan's advantages over developing countries, the fact that it is still far from matching the U.S. ability to produce cutting-edge weaponry leads one to doubt that any developing country can close the military technology gap with the United States simply because it has enhanced access to parts and components through globalization. In this respect, the *Economist* recently concluded: "Considering that Japan, which has dominated world markets for consumer electronics and cars, is not capable of building a fighter plane without America's help, [it]

---

[64] Samuels 1994, 244.

[65] See Samuels 1994, esp. chaps. 6 and 7.

[66] According to Jane's, the per unit cost of an F-16C in 1999 was U.S.$24 million, while the per unit cost of an F-2 in 2000 was 11.8 billion yen, which translates to U.S.$109.5 million per F-2 using the average market exchange rate for 2000 (Jackson 2003, 311, 668). According to a different estimate, each F-2 cost U.S.$80 million to produce in 1997 (*Economist*, 14 June 1997, S14).

[67] For a discussion of the series of problems with the co-cured composite technology, see Sekigawa 1999; and Proctor 2000.

[68] For a discussion of these early worries, see *Economist*, 24 August 1991, 58.

[69] *Economist*, 14 June 1997, S14.

[70] In 2002, Japanese defense spending was U.S.$46.7 billion at market exchange rates; in comparison, China—the highest-spending developing country by far—spent U.S.$31.1 billion (SIPRI 2003).

seems a little far-fetched [to argue] that since defense relies more and more on civilian technology, and since this is widely available, all nations will have access to the same technical resources for warfare."[71]

The experience of Japan brings up the second key reason why the globalization of production is unlikely to reduce the U.S. edge in military technology over developing countries in the years ahead: the importance of economic size. Japan has less knowledge and experience in defense production than the United States in part because the Japanese defense budget is much smaller (in 2000, around 13 percent of the U.S. total). Of course, this disparity is partly due to the fact that Japan spends a smaller proportion of its economy (about 1 percent) on defense than does the United States (about 3.5 percent). But the fact that Japan's economy is approximately half the size of the U.S. economy is obviously also crucial. The best production knowledge comes from a costly and time-consuming process of trial and error; Japan's relatively smaller defense budget means that it cannot take this route in weapons production to nearly the same extent that the United States does.[72]

A greater store of knowledge and experience is not the only advantage that economic size confers on the United States. Even with the rise of dual-use technologies, a considerable portion of weapons production is still "military specific"; there is no commercial application for stealth technology, for example. With respect to the military-specific portion of defense production, the United States continues to have two significant advantages over Japan due to its greater economic size: (1) U.S. contractors that do military specific work can more easily achieve economies of scale; and (2) the United States has a larger pool of economic resources to finance military R&D. Significantly, scale economies and military R&D have become much more important in recent years, in significant part due to the enhanced complexity of weapons.[73]

It is clear that the economic size of the United States gives it a leg up over Japan in military production. Japan's defense budget, in turn, is more than 50 percent larger than China's, the largest defense budget of all developing countries.[74] If we grant that economically larger countries now have a relatively greater advantage over smaller ones in defense production, a key question emerges: how does this enhanced significance of economic size in defense production relate to the globalization of production? The central point is that there is a positive interaction effect between economic size and the pursuit of globalization in weapons production. Put another way, globalization in weapons-related production offers relatively greater advantages for economically large states. There are several reasons for this.

For one thing, the gains to be accrued from globalization in defense production are a function of how high a state aims in the development of military

[71] *Economist*, 20 July 2002, Survey, 15–16.
[72] See the discussion in Samuels 1994.
[73] See, for example, Brzoska 1999, 150–51, 154.
[74] Source: Stockholm International Peace Research Institute (SIPRI).

technology: the higher it aims, the larger the rewards of an openness strategy. Very simply, the greater the complexity of the weapons systems that a state produces, the more expansive the number of parts, components, and technologies that are needed, and hence the greater the need to have access to a wide range of suppliers and partners. And how high a state aims in military technology, in turn, is largely a function of economic size because of the high costs of modern weapons systems, the need for significant levels of military R&D, and so on.

While a state may need economic size to aim high in military technology across the board, small states can benefit from the globalization of production by developing and producing a limited number of advanced conventional weapons. As was stressed in the previous section, this niche production strategy by developing countries exacerbates the problem of weapons proliferation. Whether taking this route will make it possible for developing countries to better match up with the United States is another question altogether. It is possible that these niche production strategies will not enable developing countries to overcome the wide range of complementary new systems that the United States is pursuing simultaneously. There are, in fact, many reasons to think that a developing country silver bullet strategy will be effectively countered by an American across-the-board upgrade strategy. For example, new antiship missiles that can better target U.S. aircraft carriers may well be countered by improved American sensors, satellites, missiles, and stealthy ships that, in combination, enhance the ability of aircraft battle groups to defend themselves from missiles as well as to attack land targets from a greater distance.

The larger point is that in terms of reducing the gap with the United States, it will matter little if a developing country takes advantage of the globalization of production to develop certain advanced conventional weapons systems but cannot use them effectively in battle against the United States. And with respect to using advanced weapons, the significance of a country's economic size has become vastly more important in recent years. Specifically, many current weapons systems depend upon state-of-the-art battlefield management—that is, having real-time, detailed information about your forces and those of the enemy, being able to quickly and effectively process this information, having seamless command and control, and so on. And effective battlefield management is, in turn, now dependent upon having information that is collected, processed, and distributed through what is sometimes called an "information architecture" that consists of computers coupled with advanced intelligence, surveillance, reconnaissance, and communications technologies (C4ISR—command, control, communications, computers, intelligence, surveillance and reconnaissance—is the U.S. military's term for this capability).[75]

---

[75] Many of the specific technological systems are specified in Owens 2000, 148. See also, for example, the discussion in Cohen 1996, 45, 50–51, 53; Betts 1998, 28–29; and Nye and Owens 1996, 23–24, 28.

Whatever this capability is termed, it is incredibly expensive and difficult to develop. The United States is currently the only state that has a fully developed information architecture for battlefield management. The European Union (EU) is currently taking some steps in this direction, most notably with the recent effort to create its own independent global positioning system. But just this one step—which will require over two dozen satellites and several ground control centers—is scheduled to take around five years, is estimated to cost almost U.S.$4 billion dollars, and will require several hundred million dollars in annual operating costs.[76] Even if Europe deploys this system, numerous other deficiencies will remain unless the Europeans rationalize their defense production and greatly increase their military spending: a recent EU report noted over forty technological shortfalls that currently constrain the ability of Europe to develop a 60,000-man rapid reaction force that can engage in military missions without U.S. assistance.[77] Not until 2012 at the earliest will the EU likely be able to field this relatively small force using its own capabilities.[78] The difficulties the EU is facing make it clear that the requisite battlefield management capability to effectively use the most advanced weapons against the United States is currently well beyond the economic and technological reach of all developing countries.

Developing countries face further hurdles in narrowing the gap in military technology with the United States. "Even if hostile countries somehow catch up in an arms race, their military organizations and cultures are unlikely to catch up in the competence race for management, technology assimilation, and combat command skills."[79] Of particular importance is that the complexity of modern warfare and the initiative required to coordinate advanced technologies require a flatter hierarchy within the military, giving greater initiative to the lower ranks to gain the value added in battlefield performance from advanced systems.[80] To achieve such flatter hierarchies, the military bureaucracy in developing countries would need to radically change doctrine and organization; moreover, the countries themselves likely will need to be democratic.[81] For political reasons, the most threatening developing countries, in general, and their military forces, in particular, are unlikely to implement the necessary organizational and bureaucratic changes to create a flatter hierarchy within their defense establishments.

In the end, it is unlikely that the globalization of weapons production will contribute to a "leveling effect" in conventional military technology, shrinking the gap between the capabilities of developing countries and those of the United

---

[76] Agence France Presse, 26 May 2003.

[77] *Financial Times*, 8 February 2002, 4. See also the discussion in Kapstein 2002, 149–50.

[78] *Sunday Telegraph*, 13 January 2002, 17.

[79] Betts 1998, 29.

[80] On this point, see, for example, Owens 2000, 23, 203–27.

[81] See Reiter and Stam 2002, esp. 64–65, 67–69, 72–73, and 75–83.

States. Indeed the reverse is likely for the foreseeable future. Yet, as noted previously, the pressure to pursue globalization in weapons production is not confined to conventional weapons; it extends to WMD as well. A key remaining question is whether the globalization of production will lead to changes regarding WMD that will significantly alter the military balance between the great powers and developing countries and thereby alter their security relations.

Taking advantage of the globalization of production does make it easier for developing countries to develop WMD—although, as the previous section emphasized, this effect is not as pronounced as is sometimes thought to be the case. When considering the implications for security relations, we need to factor in not just how the geographic dispersion of MNC production changes the ability of developing countries to develop WMD, but also how it influences the ability of great powers to counteract these weapons. Up to now, discussions by both academic analysts and policymakers of how economic globalization and WMD interact have been one-sided: only the potential downsides for the great powers have been emphasized; overlooked is that many of the tools for countering the WMD threat are partly the products of globalization.[82] With respect to WMD, the globalization of production is a double-edged sword for the great powers: it simultaneously enhances and reduces the WMD threat they face from developing countries. That capabilities for counteracting the WMD threat are partly the result of the geographic dispersion of MNC production is made apparent by efforts to counter biological weapons, for which the development of vaccines is paramount.[83]

For a variety of reasons, the cost and complexity of developing vaccines greatly increased in recent years. As recently as the early 1980s, vaccine developers in the pharmaceutical industry often had sufficient capabilities inhouse; nowadays, in contrast, the expertise required to develop vaccines has become increasingly specialized and much more widely distributed. And as the need for collaboration in order to maintain high rates of innovation in vaccines has grown rapidly in recent years, the ability to work with international partners has increased because of advances in communications and other recent technological shifts. These changing incentives have influenced not just firms that participate in vaccine development, but the entire biotechnology sector. As figure 7.4 shows, the number of interfirm alliances in biotechnology exploded beginning in the early 1980s. In turn, figure 7.5 shows that the collaboration by U.S. firms with Japanese and West European firms is almost equal in significance to that between U.S.-based firms.

Although we do not have comprehensive data on the level of international collaboration on vaccines, it is clear that international biotechnology companies have played a key role in U.S. biodefense vaccine research over the past

[82] See, for example, Bitzinger 1994, 191; and Albright 2003.
[83] For an elaboration of this point, see Hoyt and Brooks 2003–4. The material in the next two paragraphs is drawn from this article.

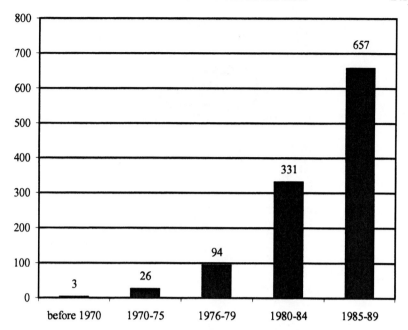

Figure 7.4 Number of Interfirm Alliances Formed in Biotechnology from the Early
1950s to 1989
Source: Hagedoorn and Schakenraad 1990, 176.

several years. Of the top six Class A biological threat agents (smallpox, anthrax, plague, tularemia, Botulinum toxin, and viral hemorrhagic fevers such
as Ebola), vaccine development efforts for all but one (Botulinum toxin) are
being pursued in collaboration with international biotechnology companies.
Acambis, a British company, and Baxter, a U.S. company, are in the late stages
of developing a new vaccine against smallpox; the actual production of the
vaccine will occur at one of Baxter's overseas affiliates in Austria. In addition
to this project, VaxGen, a California company, has begun working with Kaket-
suken, a Japanese company, to begin clinical trials on a vaccine that they jointly
developed. And Bavarian Nordic, a German Danish Company based in Copen-
hagen, is also developing a promising smallpox vaccine. As for anthrax, the U.S.
National Institute of Allergy and Infectious Diseases (NIAID) issued contracts in
October 2002 to VaxGen and Avecia of Manchester, England, to develop a civilian vaccine based on an experimental vaccine developed by U.S. Army research
scientists. Biotechnology companies from two different countries—Vical, a California company, and Crucell, located in the Netherlands—are working on a
NIAID contract to develop a vaccine for Ebola. The effort to develop defenses to
plague has an international element as well. DynPort Vaccine Company—which

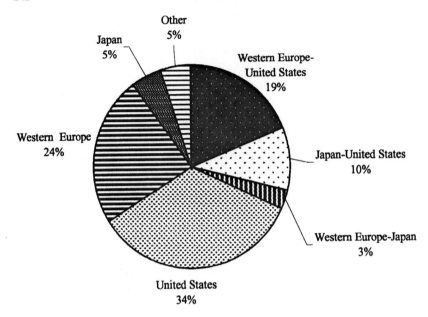

Figure 7.5 Geographic Nature of Interfirm Alliances in Biotechnology from the Early
1950s to 1989
Source: Hagedoorn and Schakenraad 1990, 177.

is a joint venture between DynCorp, based in Reston, Virginia, and Porton International, a subsidiary of French pharmaceutical company Beaufour-Ipsen—is currently in the process of developing a plague vaccine. DynPort is also working to develop a tularemia vaccine for the DoD.

Although the role of internationalization in the development of biodefense vaccines is especially apparent and consequential, it is not the only area in which the geographic dispersion of MNC production contributes to the ability of the great powers to counteract WMD. For example, the U.S. military now has the ability to destroy targets from the air with extraordinary precision, which gives the United States a greater ability to target WMD facilities. Significantly, the weapons systems that give the United States this capability are all heavily reliant on computers and other dual-use technologies—the precise areas in which the geographic dispersion of MNC production is most advanced. Because we cannot track which specific companies contribute to weapons programs at the lower tiers of production—which, it is important to recall, is where globalization is likely to occur to the greatest extent—it is impossible to know the overall contribution of the globalization of production to these new U.S. systems. At the higher tiers of production—where there are fewer barriers to identifying which companies participate in weapons systems—it is clear that numerous international companies have contributed to U.S. fighter jets. In the F-16 C/D Fighting Falcon, for example, international companies have contributed many vital technologies, including the wide-angle holographic head-up display (produced by Marconi, a British company), the secure voice system (Philips Magnavox, a Dutch company), the management flight computer (Elbit Systems, an Israeli company), the advanced radar warning system (BAE Systems, a British company), and the Terprom digital terrain navigation system (also BAE). Similarly, international companies have contributed many core technologies in the F/A-18E Super Hornet, including the mission control computers (by DY4 Systems, a Canadian company), the digital data recorder and the environmental control cockpit system (Normalair-Garrett, a British company that is now a subsidiary of Honeywell), the hydraulics system (Vickers, a British company), the landing gear (Messier-Dowty, a French company), and the defensive electronic countermeasures suite, the laser designator, the towed radar decoy, and the horizontal situation display (BAE Systems).[84]

Conclusions and Policy Implications

Only the weapons development mechanism has implications for security relations between the great powers and developing countries. The globalization of production simply reinforces the status quo in conventional weaponry. More specifically, the geographic dispersion of MNC production is not having a leveling effect, at least with respect to the United States: I find no reason to expect that in the foreseeable future, participation in the globalization of production will allow developing countries to catch up to the United States. The globalization of production thus does not appear to be altering the capacity for developing countries to use conventional weapons to deter the United States. Regarding conventional weapons, this global production shift therefore has an essentially neutral effect on security relations between the great powers and developing countries.

With respect to WMD, the production of such weapons dramatically enhances the ability of developing countries to deter the United States from using its military capacity for coercion. However, it is not the globalization of production that has put this capacity within the reach of developing countries. Consider, for example, North Korea: it has long had a significant WMD capacity despite being one of the states that is most isolated from the geographic dispersion of MNC production.

The effect of the globalization of production is to make it somewhat easier for developing countries to develop WMD. Exactly how much easier is unclear;

---

[84] Jackson 2001, 2003; and Aerospace America 2002.

however, it is evident that the geographic dispersion of MNC production is not currently the core threat with respect to the proliferation of nuclear and biological weapons. Put another way, the threat of proliferation of WMD would likely be little diminished even if the geographic dispersion of MNC production were to cease.

In short, while the development of WMD does shift the capacity of developing states to deter the United States, the globalization of production has not decisively contributed to this development. At the same time, the technologies developed through global production activities of MNCs can also enhance the ability of great powers to counteract WMD. Ultimately, it is hard to determine, with respect to WMD, how the upsides of the geographic dispersion of MNC production for the great powers compare with the downsides. Given the great significance of WMD, the only conclusion we can reach is that the globalization of production now has a mixed effect on security relations between the great powers and developing countries.

Out of all great powers, this analysis has greatest repercussions for the United States, since it will have the most extensive security interactions with developing countries in the years ahead. Significantly, economic globalization is one of the few forces, according to some analysts, with the potential to undermine the massive U.S. advantage in conventional weaponry over developing countries. Revealing that this line of argument is incorrect, this examination increases our confidence that the United States' current unipolar military status will not be diminished anytime soon.

The more general point is that when it comes to maintaining American military superiority, it would make little sense for the United States to move toward more autarkic defense production, as called for by some in Congress who recently sought to strengthen Buy American restrictions in defense procurement.[85] This analysis shows that Secretary of Defense Donald Rumsfeld was prudent to respond at this time by threatening a presidential veto of the entire 2004 defense authorization bill if it included Buy American restrictions. If Congress wants U.S. weapons systems to be as capable as possible, it should refrain from challenging the DoD's preference for globalization in defense-related production.

In terms of reducing vulnerability to WMD, U.S. policymakers would be wise to recognize that the globalization of production has a vital role to play. To date, their strategies have not recognized the significance of the geographic dispersion of MNC production. A notable example concerns the regulatory framework put in place after September 2001 to keep sensitive materials and knowledge out of the hands of adversaries trying to produce biological weapons. Although this framework is designed to bolster security, it is likely to have an

---

[85] See the conclusion of chapter 4 for a more detailed discussion of the issues raised in this paragraph.

unintended negative influence, since it creates incentives for U.S. firms developing biodefense capabilities to shift away from international collaboration. If U.S. policymakers want biodefense capabilities to advance as effectively as possible, they should remove these constraints on globalization in biodefense research and production.[86] The more general point is that U.S. policymakers who are interested in reducing the WMD threat need to avoid direct or indirect restrictions on the ability of U.S. firms to pursue globalization as part of this effort.

CONCLUSION

Over the centuries, John Stuart Mill, Immanuel Kant, Montesquieu, and numerous others have argued that enhanced international commerce will serve as a force for peace wherever it occurs. In the present day, Thomas Friedman is a prominent champion of this universalist line of argument. While the globalization of production has important security repercussions for states throughout the globe, the conclusion of this book is that it does not currently have a uniformly positive effect. Among the great powers, the geographic dispersion of MNC production is, in fact, a beneficial development: great power revisionism is now structurally harder because of this shift in the global economy. This, however, is the limit of its positive repercussions for security: my ultimate conclusion is that the globalization of production is currently a net negative for security relations among developing countries and is mixed for relations between great powers and developing countries.

Of course, the globalization of production is an ongoing process, not an end point. This raises a key question: how is it likely to influence security in the years ahead? What might arise that could alter the general assessments in this chapter? This issue is the subject of the analysis in the next chapter.

[86] For a detailed discussion of the issues raised in this paragraph, see Hoyt and Brooks 2003–4.

CHAPTER 8

Looking toward the Future

THE CONCLUSIONS in the previous chapter—that the globalization of production is positive for the great powers, negative for developing countries, and mixed for great power/developing country relations—were based upon an analysis of the three mechanisms that have been the focus of this study. In this chapter, I will analyze a series of additional mechanisms. As was noted in chapter 1, there are a total of five other mechanisms by which the geographic dispersion of MNC production can influence security. Two of these additional mechanisms were already discussed in chapter 3: (1) outward FDI from the leading state can lead to a power transition and (2) MNCs can become the key drivers of security policy. It was shown that neither of these mechanisms is likely to obtain for decades.

In the analysis that follows, I will examine in detail the remaining three mechanisms, all of which have the potential to become important but do not appear to have played a role in recent decades: (1) threats to FDI holdings in the developing world could lead to enhanced military interventions in the region by the great powers; (2) developing countries may generally be directed away from conflict with each other because the cost of being isolated from FDI has become so high; and (3) the rise of "production interdependence" could influence security relations among the great powers. Examining these mechanisms is crucial, since they could counter the assessments derived in the previous chapter concerning, respectively, great power/developing country relations, developing country relations, and great power relations. The analysis is therefore necessary for understanding whether the conclusions in the previous chapter are valid only at present or for many years to come. I conclude that, for the foreseeable future, these additional mechanisms are very unlikely to alter the general assessments derived in the previous chapter.

The final portion of the chapter then argues that future research needs to concentrate on the effect that this global production shift has on nonstate actors, especially international terrorists. I discuss the four main mechanisms by which the globalization of production can influence the severity of the international terrorist threat.

THREATS TO FDI AND FUTURE SECURITY RELATIONS
BETWEEN GREAT POWERS AND DEVELOPING COUNTRIES

Investment friction was once an "important, if not major, cause of war."[1] In his 1935 book *War and the Private Investor*, Eugene Staley recounts numerous instances in which threats to MNC holdings, and the consequent lobbying by firms for protection, contributed to the use of military force by powerful states against developing countries in the nineteenth and early twentieth centuries.[2] In light of this history, some might argue that as the amount of FDI in the world increases, the likelihood of military intervention by great powers in developing countries increases. If this argument is valid, it would tilt toward the negative the mixed assessment derived in the previous chapter concerning security relations between great powers and developing countries. However, there is little reason to think that increasing FDI will have this effect.

In the first place, since at least 1970 there do not appear to have been any cases of great powers intervening militarily in response to lobbying by MNCs whose foreign holdings were threatened. In their comprehensive survey of 412 international crises from 1918 to 1995, Michael Brecher and Jonathan Wilkenfeld code for numerous triggers, including whether an "economic threat" was perceived by the actor.[3] In no international crisis between 1965 and 1995 in which an economic threat was present do they identify lobbying by MNCs, or threats to their holdings more generally, as triggering the use of military force.[4] Some might argue that U.S. behavior toward Chile in 1973 is an exception. However, American efforts to overthrow the Chilean government headed by Salvador Allende did not involve the direct use of military force by the United States, but rather took the form of covert actions. Moreover, as Krasner shows, the decision by the United States to undertake these covert actions "cannot be explained by corporate pressure. . . . The answer lies rather in the direction of the broader political concerns at stake . . . the fear that a communist regime would come to power."[5] Some might also point to American military actions in the Persian Gulf in 1991 and 2003 as exceptions to the generalization on triggers of crises. However, neither represents a case of a powerful state intervening in order to protect MNC assets: in 1990 there was only U.S.$ 1 million of U.S. FDI in Kuwait, and there was no U.S. FDI in Iraq as of 2001, the last year for which we have data.[6]

---

[1] Wright 1935, vii.

[2] Staley 1935.

[3] Brecher and Wilkenfeld 1997, 49.

[4] On this point, see also the discussion in Lipson 1985, esp. 133–35 and 147–53; and Bilder 1980, 391–92.

[5] Krasner 1978, 311–12.

[6] UNCTAD 1993b, 495; and UNCTAD FDI/TNC database. Of course, many have argued that U.S. MNCs will benefit from contracts that are awarded to rebuild Iraq after the U.S.-led invasion

Looking forward, six overlapping changes have occurred since the time Staley was writing that, in combination, make it very unlikely that great powers will intervene in developing countries to protect FDI. In his analysis, Staley highlighted the significance of political actions in the developing world that threatened MNC holdings as an important contributing factor to interventions by great powers prior to the 1930s.[7] However, the geographic location of most FDI has changed drastically since then. In the period prior to Staley's study, most FDI was located in the developing world: in 1938, 76 percent of FDI was based outside Western Europe and North America. In recent decades, in contrast, the vast majority of FDI has been located in the most developed countries: by 1993, 70 percent of FDI was based in Western Europe and North America.[8] This is significant because countries in Western Europe and North America have long provided a safe and stable investment climate for MNCs. Staley's study found that "international investment friction has occurred almost exclusively in connection with investments in non-industrialized areas."[9] Investment in the industrialized parts of the world was not dangerous, he found, in large part because these countries provided a favorable legal and political climate that ensured that property rights of foreign investors were protected.[10]

Beyond the fact that most FDI is now located in highly developed countries that have long had a good investment climate, a second point to consider is that even in the developing world, almost all countries are striving to create a positive legal and political environment for MNCs. Developing countries that have significant levels of FDI are very unlikely to initiate policies that will threaten MNCs, since that would make it difficult to attract future FDI. One noteworthy development to recall is that the threat of expropriation has disappeared: although a significant problem in the 1960s and 1970s, it dried up beginning in the early 1980s.[11]

Third, the purpose of most FDI has changed. At the time that Staley was writing, the bulk of FDI was based around the exploitation of natural resources: in 1914, "at least three-quarters of world FDI was concerned with the exploitation of natural resources." As of the early 1990s, in contrast, only around 10 percent of FDI was devoted to natural resource extraction.[12] This shift is

---

in 2003. This is true, but it is a dynamic separate from the one at interest here. Moreover, there is little indication that U.S. firms played a key role in lobbying the Bush administration to undertake war against Iraq.

[7] See Staley 1935, esp. 164–73.

[8] Jones 1996, 43, 53. Jones does not provide data after 1993. In this section, I use figures from his study since it provides a set of recent FDI levels that can be directly compared against levels that existed earlier in the twentieth century.

[9] Staley 1935, 374.

[10] Staley 1935, esp. 380.

[11] Minor 1994, 180. See the discussion on pages 41–42 in chapter 2.

[12] Jones 1996, 32, 55.

very significant, since natural resource investments are a much more tempting target than are service-based FDI and manufacturing-based FDI.[13] Throughout history, raw materials FDI has, in fact, been much more likely to be seized than other forms of FDI.[14] This is in large part because raw materials FDI by definition has site-specific rents: "For example, the income stream created by a copper mine is specific to the place where it is located. The mine, and the resource rents associated with it, can be seized by a host country with relative ease. On the other hand, the income stream accruing to a branch plant of a manufacturing multinational corporation typically is specific to its participation in a global enterprise—it relies on managerial, marketing or technological inputs available only within the firm. While the host government can seize the factory, it cannot appropriate the rents. . . . Host governments have little incentive to take assets whose value disappears with the takeover."[15] Because MNCs that undertake raw materials investments also frequently bear high costs at the outset that can only be recouped over many years of operation, they also have much stronger incentives to lobby their home governments for protection than firms that engage in other forms of FDI.[16]

A fourth key distinction in today's environment concerns the geographic diversification of FDI. MNCs have always faced strong incentives to geographically diversify their holdings in order to guard against various forms of risk.[17] However, in the first part of this century, there were built-in constraints on geographic diversification that have been greatly reduced in recent decades. Dramatic recent advances in communications technology now make it possible for managers to easily monitor and coordinate far-flung holdings. Improvements in transportation have facilitated the shipment of goods and materials across distances that would have been uneconomical in the first part of this century. In response to these and other changes, the geographic dispersion of many MNCs' FDI holdings has increased markedly in recent years.[18] This geographic dispersion has occurred in all sectors, including raw materials. This is significant because geographic diversification significantly reduces the incentives of MNCs to lobby for military protection in response to instability that threatens their holdings in a particular country or region. So long as holdings were centered in a particular country or geographic region, instability there posed a substantial threat, and MNCs had strong incentives to lobby for intervention, while states had a strong incentive to respond. But, with more geographically

---

[13] See Frieden 1994; and Kahler 1981, 390–401.

[14] For various forms of evidence that shows this the case, see Frieden 1994, esp. 585.

[15] Frieden 1994, 567–68.

[16] Not surprisingly, the historical record indicates that "rarely have manufacturing multinational corporations attempted to bring their home governments into conflict with host countries" (Frieden 1994, 585).

[17] See, for example, the discussion in Rugman 1979 and 1980; Lessard 1982; and Dicken 1998, 218.

[18] See, for example, Vernon 1992, 14.

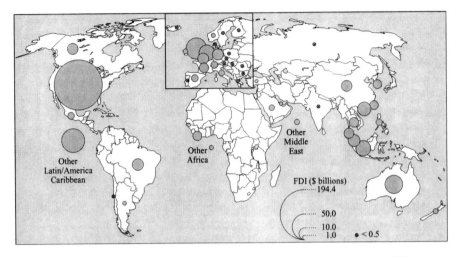

Figure 8.1 Geographic Dispersion of Japanese Foreign Direct Investment (1996)
Source: Dicken, 1998, 56.

dispersed holdings, instability in one or more countries is much less threatening both to MNCs and to the governments of countries where they are based; the reason is that another country or region where the MNC has investments can likely make up the difference.

The easiest way to grasp the significance of this point is by looking at the example of pre–World War II Japan. In the 1930s, 82 percent of Japan's FDI was based in China, and nearly-two thirds specifically in Manchuria.[19] As a result, the rise of internal unrest in Manchuria from the mid-1920s onwards was very threatening to many Japanese firms with investments there, and also the Japanese government. It is not surprising, therefore, that the growing threat to FDI holdings in Manchuria led to demands by many Japanese MNCs for protection and contributed to the Japanese military intervention in China in 1931.[20] In contrast, as figure 8.1 shows, Japan's FDI holdings are now widely dispersed throughout the world. If a challenge were now to emerge to Japanese FDI holdings in any one country or region, it would generally be much less threatening— and hence would be much less likely to lead to lobbying for intervention and a government response.

From the standpoint of powerful states, threats to raw materials investments will arguably be of greatest concern. That being said, it is also true that no one source of the resource is likely to be preferred over another since most resources are commodities. Moreover, states whose economic capacity is highly

[19] Thorne 1973, 32.

[20] See, for example, the discussion in Duus 1991, xxiv–xxvii; Junji 1991, 314, 323, 326, 328; and Jordan 1991, 2–4, 10, 14–15.

dependent upon raw materials investments undertaken by its MNCs can offer firms extra incentives to geographically diversify that go beyond the typical risk-reduction incentives that they naturally face. Japan, which receives many of the raw materials it needs via investments made by its MNCs, is noteworthy in this regard: the Japanese government has long been successful in using financial inducements to encourage an enhanced level of geographic diversification by its MNCs that are involved in natural resource extraction.[21]

The larger point is that great powers will not necessarily have any incentive to resort to military force in response to a threat to MNC holdings, even if MNCs lobby strenuously for protection. This is because powerful states have many tools other than military force to protect MNCs. One such tool is diplomatic pressure, which might take the form of linking treatment of MNCs with other issues in a bilateral relationship.[22] A more costly tool is economic sanctions.[23] Significantly, the potential leverage of sanctions has been enhanced as the opportunity cost of being closed off from the global economy has increased in recent decades. At the more extreme end of the spectrum, powerful states can undertake covert actions against states that threaten MNC holdings. These covert actions can have either minimal goals (to effect a reverse in policy that has a negative effect on MNCs) or be more comprehensive (to seek to change the character of a government itself). The existence of these other tools does not mean that they are just or consistently effective. The point is simply that these other tools can sometimes be very effective in advancing the interests of powerful states when their MNCs are threatened. Not only that, powerful governments now have a greater incentive to rely upon these other tools, in the face of the substantial constraints, both domestic and international, on the use of military force by powerful states to protect MNCs.[24] This is a fifth key change from the era when Staley's book was published that makes military intervention by powerful states to protect MNC assets unlikely in the years ahead.

Of course, not just governments in developing countries are in a position to take actions that threaten the investments of MNCs; nonstate actors can do so as well. Certain factors that lower the likelihood that threats to MNC holdings will engender lobbying for intervention—in particular, the increased geographic dispersion of FDI holdings and the reduced significance of raw materials FDI—also make any harmful actions toward FDI taken by nonstate actors less alarming to MNCs and their home governments. In addition, the high opportunity cost of being isolated from FDI means that host governments in the developing world will likely be willing to act to reduce any threats to MNCs

[21] See the discussion in Vernon 1983, chap. 5.

[22] The United States frequently used diplomatic pressure in response to threats to the holdings of its MNCs: see Krasner 1978, 151.

[23] For a discussion of various cases in which economic sanctions were used by powerful states to protect MNCs, see Lipson 1985, 153–66.

[24] See the discussion in Lipson 1985, 133–34.

that emerge from nonstate actors. Although MNCs involved in natural resource extraction are particularly vulnerable to attacks by nonstate actors, "resource companies are often large and protected by elaborate security arrangements—particularly in poor or unstable countries—in collaboration with the host government."[25] A telling example is what happened after a series of attacks by Muslim separatist rebels on Exxon's facilities in the Aceh province of Indonesia. After Exxon decided to scale back production in the region in early 2001 due to security concerns, the Indonesian "government responded by sending in more troops and ordering a military offensive in the area around the gas fields" as part of an effort to "to persuade Exxon to return."[26] In response to these efforts, Exxon resumed its operations in Aceh in July 2001.[27] The key point is that in the era when Staley was writing, it was typically home countries—that is, those powerful states where MNCs were based—that had the strongest incentive and ability to intervene when threats to MNCs emerged. A sixth and final change from this period is that presently it is host countries for FDI that are normally most likely and able to intervene on behalf of MNCs.

Ultimately, this analysis indicates that threats to FDI prompting a great power intervention in the developing world is an unlikely scenario in the years ahead. If anything, the reverse seems likely to be true: because engaging in FDI throughout the developing world is now so easy, great powers now have fewer incentives to use military force in this region. It has long been recognized that trade can substitute for conquest.[28] The same is also true of FDI. To the extent that firms from country A can selectively purchase or gain control of the most valuable portions of country B, its incentives to conquer country B lessen. In general, as a state is increasingly able to rely on MNCs to secure needed external resources and supplies, the overall willingness of that state to engage in conquest is likely to decrease. Significantly, the states with the greatest material potential to engage in conquest throughout the developing world (by virtue of the size, nature, and mobility of their military forces) are, in order, the United States, the United Kingdom, and France. These three countries are, respectively, the first, second, and third largest sources of FDI in the world, and consequently are all well positioned to have their MNCs serve as a substitute for conquest (in combination, these three countries are the source of 44 percent of the world's outward stock of FDI).[29]

In sum, a series of overlapping changes have occurred in recent decades, with the collective effect of making it very unlikely that the dynamic of the past—in which threats to FDI increased the likelihood of intervention by great powers in developing countries—will eventuate in the future. In the end, therefore, this

[25] Ross 2002, 7.

[26] *New York Times*, 24 March 2001, C2; and 19 June 2001, W1.

[27] *New York Times*, 20 July 2001, W1.

[28] See, for example, Rosecrance 1986; and Hirshleifer 2001.

[29] UNCTAD 2001, 307.

mechanism does not alter the general assessment derived previously that the globalization of production has a mixed effect on security relations between the great powers and developing countries.

ISOLATION FROM FDI AND FUTURE SECURITY RELATIONS BETWEEN DEVELOPING COUNTRIES

As stressed in chapter 2, the opportunity cost of isolation from FDI has greatly increased in recent years, especially for developing countries. This is best reflected in the fact that so many developing countries have sought to liberalize their regulations on FDI in recent years. What, if any, are the implications of the increased importance of FDI to developing countries for security relations between them? According to Thomas Friedman, this is one reason why engaging in conflict is now more costly for developing countries, and therefore less likely:

> The only place a country can go to get big checks is the Electronic Herd [MNCs and international financial investors]. Where Intel, Cisco, or Microsoft builds its next factory, or where the Fidelity global mutual fund invests its cash, is what determines who gets funded and who does not. . . . Not only will the herd not fund a country's regional war . . . the herd will actually punish a country for fighting a war with its neighbors, by withdrawing the only significant source of growth capital in the world today. As such, countries have no choice but to behave in a way that is attractive to the herd or ignore the herd and pay the price of living without it.[30]

If it were true that developing countries will generally be directed away from conflict because the costs of isolation from FDI have risen, my conclusion in the previous chapter, that the globalization of production is negative for security relations among these states, would be diluted. It is unclear whether Friedman's FDI dynamic has acted as a stabilizing influence in the developing world; at least since 1990, there do not appear to be any cases where it has so acted. There are several reasons why it appears unlikely that this mechanism will act as much of a constraint on conflict in the years ahead.

First, recent history runs contrary to Friedman's argument that states lose FDI after hostilities erupt. This is made clear through an examination of all six interstate conflicts that occurred from 1990 to 2001 (the last year for which FDI data is available).[31] In two of the six cases, the opposite actually occurred.[32] After they invaded Congo in 1998, Burundi, Rwanda, and Uganda all

[30] Friedman 1999, 257.

[31] With one exception, I follow the delineation of armed interstate conflicts during this period that is outlined in Wallensteen and Sollenberg 2000 (they do not code the 1998 invasion of Congo as an interstate conflict).

[32] FDI data in the following paragraphs is drawn from the UNCTAD FDI/TNC database.

received greater FDI inflows in 1999 (FDI inflows into Uganda increased by 14 percent, while FDI inflows into Burundi and Rwanda both increased by more than 100 percent), while Congo itself received 14 percent more FDI. In turn, following a border conflict between Peru and Ecuador in 1995, both countries received more FDI inflows the following year (FDI inflows increased by 11 percent in Ecuador and by 58 percent in Peru).

In the third case—the Iraq-Kuwait war—neither country received any inward FDI inflows in 1990, and so there was no FDI for either of them to lose the year following conflict. In the three remaining cases, one country involved in the conflict lost FDI afterwards, while the other attracted more FDI. Following the conflict between Cameroon and Nigeria in 1996, the former secured 29 percent more FDI the following year, while the latter saw its inward flow of FDI fall by 3 percent. After war broke out between Eritrea and Ethiopia in 1998, FDI inflows to Ethiopia fell by 73 percent the following year, while FDI inflows to Eritrea rose 12 percent. Finally, after the nuclear tests by India and Pakistan in 1998 and a concomitant escalation of the dispute over Kashmir, FDI inflows to Pakistan increased the following year by 5 percent, while FDI inflows to India declined by 18 percent.

In sum, of the 14 developing countries involved in conflict during the 1990 to 2001 period, 9 countries actually received more FDI in the year following hostilities and only 2—Ethiopia and India—suffered a decrease in FDI of more than 10 percent. Economic sanctions imposed by governments also explain why FDI inflows into Iraq and India were bound to fall (or, in the case of Iraq, to remain at zero) in the year following conflict, thereby leaving only 3 cases out of 14 in which a loss of FDI was perhaps driven by MNC decisions. Moreover, the experience of India also reveals that even for those states that do pay an immediate FDI price for hostile foreign policies, it may only be slight and short-lived: by 2000, FDI inflows into India were nearly 90 percent of the level before the nuclear test in 1998, and by 2001, FDI inflows were actually 57 percent higher. Although it is still too early to know for sure, the recent historical record thus indicates that Friedman is incorrect to argue that developing countries will necessarily be punished by MNCs for engaging in conflict.

Even if it does turn out to be the case that MNCs are prone to avoid investing in states that use force, there are three scope conditions that will limit the degree to which this effect constrains conflict in the developing world. The most obvious scope condition is that this argument applies only so long as states pursue—and, more importantly, are able to attract—FDI. As it turns out, the fear of losing FDI will not be a constraint on those countries in the developing world that are normally thought to be the most dangerous, since they have long had a dearth of FDI for other reasons. Table 8.1, showing the so-called states of concern from the 1990s, makes this point clear. In total, these eight states attracted just 0.0006 percent of the total world FDI inflows during the 1990s, and they all lagged far behind the world average of FDI inflows per

TABLE 8.1

Per Capita FDI Inflows to the "States of Concern" in the 1990s

Country	Ratio of per Capita FDI Inflows to Average World per Capita FDI Inflows in 1990s
Syria	10.60%
Sudan	4.72%
North Korea	1.71%
Iran	0.08%
Afghanistan	0.04%
Iraq	0.02%
Libya	0%
World	100%

Source: UNCTAD FDI/TNC database.

capita. Regardless of whether the dearth of FDI was largely by choice (e.g., North Korea), or they were prevented from attracting FDI by embargos and sanctions (e.g., Iraq), or were trying to attract MNCs but were unable to secure much FDI because of a poor investment climate (e.g., Sudan), the bottom line is that Friedman's dynamic did not apply to this group of key states since they were isolated from FDI to begin with.

The second scope condition that limits the applicability of this FDI mechanism is that some states have special traits that make them especially attractive to MNCs; these traits will, in turn, make it very unlikely that they will lose FDI if they engage in conflict. Friedman is correct that, other things being equal, MNCs prefer to avoid investing in countries that engage in conflict. However, MNCs may be willing to invest in dangerous regions if the potential gains are large. Two principal factors may cause MNCs to make such a risky investment in a state that recently engaged in conflict.

First of all, some states have a very large internal market. In the developing world, China and India clearly meet this criteria: they are the two largest countries in the region in both population and economic size. A great many MNCs will invest in these two countries even if they engage in conflict, partly to continue serving these large markets and partly to prevent competitors from establishing a stronger foothold. That the fear of losing FDI mechanism does not strongly apply to these two countries is significant, given that the Taiwan-China and Pakistan-India disputes are two of the major flashpoints in the developing world.

Another factor that may cause MNCs to make a risky investment in a country that recently engaged in conflict is that some states possess unique, highly valuable natural resources—that is, resources of which the reserves are scarce and geographically concentrated; the value added by industrial processing is not significantly higher than the market price of the natural resource; and few substitutes are available at competitive prices.[33] The principal natural resource that meets these criteria is petroleum.[34] Those few states that possess petroleum or other unique, highly valuable natural resources will be much less likely to suffer a loss of FDI if they engage in conflict. The experience of Iraq during the 1990s is a good example. It is clear that Iraq could have attracted plenty of investment by MNCs even after the invasion of Kuwait: companies from more than a dozen nations, including France, Russia, China, and Italy, reached agreements with the Iraqi government to develop the country's oil resources after 1991. These deals were constrained during the 1990s by U.N. sanctions that were imposed on Iraq during this period.[35] Absent these international sanctions, Iraq would have received substantial FDI inflows during the 1990s. In the end, in countries or regions where FDI focuses on the extraction of unique, highly valuable natural resources such as petroleum, Friedman's mechanism is very unlikely to apply. In this regard, it is significant that the developing world's most volatile region—the Middle East—is also the region with the largest reserves of petroleum.

In countries that are able to attract significant FDI and that do not have unique features that make them especially attractive to MNCs, a third scope condition limits the effect of the fear of losing FDI mechanism: countries must care enough about a potential loss of FDI to factor it into their calculations when making decisions about conflict. There do not appear to be many developing countries where the first two scope conditions delineated here are met and, in turn, where concern about the loss of FDI is sufficient to significantly influence decisions about security.[36]

In sum, there are several overlapping reasons why Friedman's FDI mechanism has limited applicability in the developing world. It should be recognized that this section has evaluated only the FDI portion of Friedman's more general argument that international investors will constrain developing countries; other kinds of investors—notably, currency traders and international portfolio investors—may better accord with his perspective.[37] Regardless, the key conclusion is that

[33] These criteria are outlined in Ullman 1991, 24.

[34] Ullman 1991, 24–25.

[35] *Washington Post*, 15 September 2002, A1.

[36] South Korea is the only possible case I am aware of in this regard. Jin Nyum, South Korea's finance minister, voiced concerns in early 2002 that an escalation of tensions on the Korean peninsula "would be a big blow to the Korean economy and Korean capital markets" and noted that "from the beginning of Korea's development to 1997, we attracted U.S.$24 billion of foreign direct investment. During the past four years of the sunshine policy, we have introduced more than U.S.$50 billion of FDI" (*Financial Times*, 6 February 2002, 10). It is possible that concerns in the South Korean government about FDI have led it to a more accommodating stance toward North Korea in 2002 and 2003 than would otherwise be the case. There are, of course, many other explanations for South Korea's accommodations during this period—most notably, the fact that its population would suffer greatly if war broke out.

[37] In the six weeks following the Indian nuclear test, for example, the Bombay stock exchange fell from 4,300 to near 3,000, while the Indian rupee lost 10 percent of its value against the U.S. dollar; *New York Times*, 23 June 1998, A19.

the dynamic Friedman points to does not challenge the conclusion in the previous chapter that the globalization of production is negative for security relations among developing countries.

THE RISE OF PRODUCTION INTERDEPENDENCE AND FUTURE SECURITY RELATIONS BETWEEN THE GREAT POWERS

The nature of economic interdependence among advanced states is now qualitatively different from previous eras. Trade among the most advanced states was high before 1914, but few linkages were formed through FDI and other production activities of MNCs. Now that FDI is largely based in advanced countries—and as MNCs have come to rely on interfirm alliances, international subcontracting, intrafirm specialization, and other strategies of geographic diversification—many firms in advanced countries now rely much more on other firms and foreign affiliates in the region for production and R&D.[38] Among the advanced economies, we now have "an interdependence of production that is far stronger than an interdependence of trade."[39]

What consequences follow from the rise of the interdependence of production among the most advanced countries? When a firm from country A is exporting finished goods to country B, the cost of interrupted linkages is reduced sales to that market; the firm from country A retains the ability to sell goods elsewhere. In contrast, interruption of production interdependence is potentially much more damaging: if a firm from country A loses access to parts, supplies, technologies, and information that it needs from its affiliates or another firm located in country B, then it is likely to suffer a reduced ability to produce for the whole world. Losing access to a particular market is one thing; losing the ability to produce generally is altogether different.

Could the recent rise of production interdependence among advanced countries undermine the conclusion in the previous chapter that the globalization of production promotes stability among the great powers? A prominent argument in the literature is that conflict becomes more likely as vulnerability—that is, the potential for a state's economy to be cut off from suppliers it depends upon—goes up. In this view, "economic interdependence . . . tends to foster security competition among states. . . . States will struggle to escape the vulnerability that interdependence creates in order to bolster their national security. States that depend on others for critical economic supplies will fear cutoff or blackmail in time of crisis or war; they may try to extend political control over the source of supply, giving rise to conflict with the source or with its

---

[38] Although international subcontracting has a wide geographic base, the vast majority of intrafirm trade flows and interfirm alliances are located within the most economically advanced countries.

[39] Rosecrance 1999, 209.

other customers."[40] According to this perspective, therefore, the rise of production interdependence will degrade stability among the great powers, an assessment contrary to the one derived in the previous chapter concerning the effect of the geographic dispersion of MNC production.

With respect to the great powers, there is as yet no evidence in favor of the argument that production interdependence leads to conflict. What about the years ahead? For a series of reasons, we should strongly doubt that the rise of production interdependence will ever have a negative influence on great power security relations. If anything, the opposite is likely.

When trade flows are used to measure the degree of interdependence between states, most studies find that interdependence reduces the likelihood of conflict among advanced states.[41] Proponents of the vulnerability-leading-to-conflict perspective could argue that the production interdependence that has emerged recently is not well captured by studies focusing only on trade flows. This is true. The existing literature on the influence of trade flows on conflict does not examine international behavior after 1992, and hence does not capture the effect of the most recent economic linkages. Nor are international trade flows a good proxy variable for the globalization of production. Trade and production do overlap in some respects—most notably, intrafirm trade—but not enough that a focus on trade gives an accurate picture of how global production linkages affect security; many aspects of the globalization of production, such as interfirm alliances, are not captured by trade data. Moreover, dyadic data on intrafirm trade is very poor and does not allow us to separate out the effects of this kind of trade from those of arm's-length trade.

We thus cannot rely on the literature on trade flows to understand how production interdependence is likely to influence security behavior in the years ahead. That being said, there are powerful theoretical reasons for discounting the argument that these new forms of production linkages will destabilize great power security relations. For one thing, even if the desire to avoid vulnerability has not dissipated among the great powers, the costs of pursuing independence have greatly escalated, as the Soviets discovered during the final phase of the Cold War.

Moreover, there are strong reasons to believe that production interdependence will not make a state feel especially vulnerable. It is true that a state could lose wealth, and hence aggregate power, if many of its MNCs lost access to external sources for production inputs. Yet while the potential for being cut off from external suppliers does exist, all indications are that this threat is not a very significant one—at least for the economy as a whole. Although advanced country firms' reliance on external sources for aspects of production has increased—which increases vulnerability to cutoffs—there has been a

---

[40] Mearsheimer 1992, 222–23. See also Waltz 1979, esp. 138; as well as the discussion and citations listed in McMillan 1997, 40–41; and Barbieri 2002, 35–37.

[41] Mansfield and Pollins 2001, 837. See the discussion in note 13 in chapter 1.

concomitant increase in the geographic spread of foreign affiliates as well as the number of partners on which firms rely via international outsourcing and interfirm alliances. This dispersal reduces vulnerability to cutoffs by making easier the substitution of a supplier or research partner located in one country for one somewhere else. As was stressed in chapter 7, there is every indication that the ease of substitution is now generally very high.

In the end, because economic globalization has facilitated substitution across suppliers in different countries, there is little reason for fears of vulnerability at the national level. This undercuts the main argument suggesting that production interdependence can increase great power tensions. If anything, we would expect the reverse. One reason is that production interdependence fosters stronger social bonds between individuals from the advanced countries. Scholars in international relations have long argued that greater contact between individuals contributes to a "we feeling" among states, and consequently improves security relations between them.[42] Compared to trade interdependence, production linkages result in more extensive personal interactions: production interdependence not only requires a greater familiarity with, and dealings with, governments abroad, but those working for MNCs are more likely to travel to another country, to live in another country, and to have extensive personal and professional dealings with its inhabitants. Indeed, some analysts argue that the managers, consultants, and others in the top echelons of international business now interact so much with their foreign peers that they form a kind of epistemic community whose members have more in common with each other than with most of their compatriots.[43]

Lobbying by MNCs is another reason that production interdependence will, if anything, promote great power stability. Firms with global business interests have not always lobbied against conflict. For example, there is no evidence of lobbying against conflict by MNCs in either Germany or Britain before or after World War I.[44] Yet, as noted previously, interruption of the kind of trade interdependence that existed before World War I—loss of a particular market—is not nearly as threatening to firms as the prospect of losing access to inputs that are needed for production throughout the world. In this regard, the key point is that not all MNCs will be equally able to find substitutes for suppliers

[42] See, for example, Deutsch et al. 1957; and Russett 1963.

[43] See the discussion in Reich 1991; and Micklethwait and Wooldridge 2000, esp. chap. 12. For a discussion of epistemic communities, see Haas 1996.

[44] The most detailed examination of the behavior of international economic actors before World War I is Papayoanou 1996. Papayoanou does find significant evidence that actors with international economic interests in both Germany and Great Britain lobbied their respective governments to refrain from war in the years prior to World War I. However, in the numerous studies that he cites, the only direct evidence is the activities of international financiers such as Albert Ballin and Ernest Cassel who worked to prevent war (see, for example, Fischer 1975, 121). No evidence is presented of any lobbying before the conflict by nonfinancial firms or by any businessmen whose firms had substantial trading interests or direct investment abroad.

or affiliates or research partners located in other countries. It is useful to think about the substitution effect in terms of three levels: (1) firm, (2) industry or sector, and (3) nation. At the industry or sector and national levels all that matters is whether firms in general are able to adjust through substitution. At these levels, there is every indication that substitution has a powerful effect. Yet even if substitution is such that loss of suppliers or partners has only minor repercussions at the levels of industry and nation, firms that cannot substitute easily will take no solace from this calm at higher levels.

Relevant here is the standard lobbying dynamic that we observe regarding protectionism: those who stand to lose from free trade have (1) a stronger incentive to lobby for protectionism because losses are more salient than gains and (2) a relatively greater ability to organize effectively because of their small size relative to the country as a whole that benefits from a lowering of trade barriers. In the same manner, any firm that will have trouble substituting if conflict emerges will have a powerful incentive to lobby against policies hostile toward other countries with which the firm has dense production links. Moreover, since the group of firms that will have trouble substituting is likely to be small, they should be able to organize themselves effectively (certainly relative to the much larger group of firms that can easily substitute).

In sum, even if the substitution effect is strong at the national and industry level, lobbying by those firms with production linkages that have trouble substituting will act as a force pushing against conflict. To return to the historical example of World War I: had the nature of interdependence been as it is today among advanced countries, it is likely that large MNCs in both Germany and the United Kingdom would have lobbied against conflict. On its own, this lobbying would not likely have prevented World War I, but it would have been a factor pointing away from conflict. This lobbying dynamic, present in our time, is beneficial for security relations, other things being equal. Moreover, the rational expectation that lobbying will occur will likely also lead leaders of advanced countries to seek to avoid conflict with other countries with which domestic firms have dense production linkages.

Ultimately, the notion that production interdependence creates vulnerabilities that will increase security tensions among the great powers is simply not compelling. Instead, production interdependence is likely to be a stabilizing influence.[45] This means that the rise of production interdependence will, if

---

[45] Although the analyses in Gartzke, Li, and Boehmer 2001 as well as Rosecrance and Thompson 2003 are greatly constrained by data limitations (see the discussion of this point in note 20 in chapter 1), their findings do provide suggestive evidence in favor of the notion that production interdependence reduces the likelihood of conflict. Also suggestive in this regard is Havard Hegre's recent study, which shows that trade among the most economically advanced states (which are the states most likely to have strong production linkages between them) has a stronger inhibitory effect on conflict than trade among either pairs of developing countries or between advanced countries and developing countries (see Hegre 2000).

anything, reinforce the assessment in the previous chapter that the globalization of production is positive for security relations among the great powers.

LOOKING BEYOND INTERSTATE RELATIONS

This book shows that the geographic dispersion of MNC production now has a varying effect on security relations: positive among the great powers; negative among developing countries; and mixed between the great powers and developing countries. The analysis in this chapter indicates that this pattern is likely to remain for many years to come.

Looking forward, a key research task will be to look beyond interstate relations. Concerning civil wars, the globalization of production might reduce the likelihood of conflict within developing countries through its effect on economic growth.[46] On the other hand, in developing economies strongly dependent on extraction of natural resources, civil wars could be exacerbated by the actions of MNCs. In some recent cases, for example, rebels have financed insurgencies through sales to MNCs of future rights to extract a natural resource.[47]

Even more pressing is the need for future research on the potential links between the geographic dispersion of MNC production and international terrorists. Since the terrorist attacks in New York and Washington, D.C., on September 11, 2001, many have argued that economic globalization increases vulnerability to terrorism. Summing up this perspective, Audrey Kurth Cronin maintains that "The current wave of international terrorism, characterized by unpredictable and unprecedented threats from non-state actors, not only is a reaction to globalization but is facilitated by it. . . . It would be naïve to assume that what is good for international commerce and communication is not also good for international terrorists."[48]

It is true that the acceleration of economic globalization has coincided with the growing threat of international terrorism. Although the two phenomena have coevolved, they are not necessarily strongly related. Significant in this regard is that many of the technological changes that have facilitated economic globalization—such as the ease of global communication—have also made it feasible for terrorists to develop worldwide networks.

To the extent that economic globalization and terrorism are linked, some aspects of the global economy may be more significant than others. There is every indication that the globalization of international financial markets does, in fact, increase vulnerability to terror. As Joseph Stiglitz and Leif Pagrotsky note, "Terrorism has highlighted the shortcomings of the global financial system in a brutal way. . . . The global financial system makes it too easy to hide

---

[46] See the discussion in Hegre and Gleditsch 2002.

[47] See the discussion in Ross 2002, esp. 8.

[48] Cronin 2002–3, 30, 45; see also Hoffman 2002, 112; Lafeber 2002, 17; and Campbell 2002, 10.

money. [The] terrorists are obviously clever and well organized, which means that they will find and exploit the many possibilities available to make anonymous transactions."[49] Does the globalization of production facilitate international terrorism to the same degree? As I show below, there are strong reasons to believe that the geographic dispersion of MNC production does not appreciably enhance the international terrorist threat, certainly to nowhere near the same extent the global financial system does.

There are four main ways in which the geographic dispersion of MNC production could intensify the international terrorist threat. First, it could make weapons more accessible, in particular biological and nuclear arms.[50] In this regard, a point advanced earlier—that the globalization of production is a double-edged sword with respect to the WMD threat that the great powers face from developing countries—is relevant to terrorists as well. The globalization of production makes it easier for terrorists to gain access to WMD; at the same time, many of the tools for dealing with the WMD threat from terrorists result from it, with vaccines being a prominent example. The more general point is that responders to terrorism may well draw upon capabilities developed through the geographic dispersion of MNC production as effectively as, or more effectively than, terrorists.

Second, the geographic dispersion of MNC production elevates the volume of imported goods, heightening the problem of monitoring incoming shipments for WMD or other weapons that terrorists can use. There are two key points to consider here. First, although a substantial portion of trade is now driven by the globalization of production, even in a counterfactual world without foreign affiliates or international subcontracting, a huge amount of goods would still cross borders. In this counterfactual world, there would be a different mix of imported goods and the overall volume would be significantly lower, but the border-monitoring problem would remain.

The second important point is that the lack of proper safeguards concerning goods that cross borders—a very significant problem—is due to a failure of government action rather than being an inherent problem with economic globalization itself. The leading analyst of U.S. border inspection issues concludes: "It is possible to keep global commerce flowing while still putting in place systems that reduce risk."[51] This is because there are numerous procedures and technologies that would be helpful for reducing the severity of the border monitoring problem—for example, requiring that shipping containers be loaded in secure facilities and, after loading, be fitted with theft-resistant mechanical seals and alarms to ensure that they remained unopened while in transit.[52] The problem is that there has been a lack of willingness to devote the necessary

---

[49] *Financial Times*, 7 December 2001, 23.
[50] See the discussion in Cronin 2002–3, 48.
[51] Flynn 2002, 62; see also Flynn 2000.
[52] Flynn 2002, 71.

financial resources to various necessary border protection measures. As of fall 2001, only 300 U.S. border control agents were assigned to monitor and intercept illegal border crossings across the 4,000 mile land and water border with Canada.[53] Surprisingly, there has been very little effort undertaken to reduce the porous nature of U.S. borders in the aftermath of 9/11: the U.S. government only made available around U.S.$200 million in grants for port security in the eighteen months following the terrorists attacks on New York and Washington, even though the overwhelming majority of goods arrive in the United States by sea.[54] And in its fiscal 2005 budget proposal, President George W. Bush's administration requested only $46 million for port security, despite the fact that the Coast Guard has estimated that more than $7 billion is needed over the next decade just to implement new port-security requirements.[55]

The third way in which the globalization of production could intensify the threat of terror is by increasing the number of targets available. For example, terrorists targeted Western MNC facilities and their personnel in Saudi Arabia several times during 2004. If Western energy firms had not invested in Saudi Arabia, these attacks could not have taken place. It is probably, true, therefore, that the globalization of production facilitates terrorism by providing extra targets. However, creating a psychological response, not destroying material or productive resources for the specific benefit of doing so, is what motivates the choice of targets. In any case, there are innumerable attractive targets for terror that have nothing to do with the internationalization of production. Certainly, a terrorist that wishes to create a lasting psychological effect will be more likely to attack one of the many infrastructural vulnerabilities in major population centers like London or New York. In the end, foreign operations of Western MNCs will continue to be targeted, perhaps in part because of their symbolic value. However, it does not seem plausible that the mere presence of these targets significantly increases the threat of terrorism beyond that which would exist in a counterfactual world where MNCs had no international production operations for terrorists to strike. Unfortunately, we live in a world where terrorists have all too many targets available.

Fourth and finally, the globalization of production may create grievances. MNC production may enrage certain groups or individuals sufficiently to motivate terror.[56] However, there is not much evidence that international terrorists are motivated by economic concerns per se;[57] instead, their grievances are political.[58] Telling in this regard is that 15 of the 19 terrorists directly involved in the attacks of September 11 were from Saudi Arabia, a rich country with a

---

[53] Flynn 2002, 60.

[54] *Baltimore Sun*, 14 March 2003, 17A.

[55] Global Security Newswire, 30 June 2004.

[56] See the discussion in Hoffman 2002, 112.

[57] See Krueger and Maleckova 2002.

[58] See, for example, the discussion in Bergen 2002, 226.

TABLE 8.2

Per Capita FDI Inflows to States Understood to Be
Significant Sources of Terrorist Activity in the 1990s

Country	Ratio of per Capita FDI Inflows to Average World per Capita FDI Inflows in 1990s
Saudi Arabia	50.55%
Egypt	20.56%
Syria	10.60%
Pakistan	4.84%
Sudan	4.72%
North Korea	1.71%
Cuba	1.04%
Iran	0.08%
Afghanistan	0.04%
Iraq	0.02%
Libya	0%
World	100%

Source: UNCTAD FDI/TNC database and United Nations Population Fund.

GDP per capita of U.S.$9,000; moreover, many of the hijackers were educated
and relatively well off.

But couldn't FDI by MNCs lead to economic and other dislocations in a
country, providing fuel for terrorist recruiting indirectly? The weakness of this
argument is revealed in table 8.2: while a few states understood to be significant sources of terrorist activity have relatively high levels of FDI, most such
states are instead characterized by a dearth of FDI.[59]

Perhaps it is FDI by MNCs in cultural industries that increases support for
terrorism against the United States and other Western countries.[60] Although it
is impossible to know how much FDI of this kind recently occurred in the
states listed in figure 8.2, it was undoubtedly very limited in light of the fact
that 8 of these 11 countries had FDI inflows per capita during the 1990s that
were less than 5 percent of the world average. Of course, it could also be
posited that support for terrorism could be generated without actual FDI by
MNCs in cultural industries. Rather, terror could result from television programs, movies, and books created by MNCs that are imported into the country
in question. Yet international trade in cultural products has always existed,
which makes it hard to explain why it now increases support for terrorism.

---

[59] This chart consists of the seven countries designated as of 2000 by the U.S. State Department as state sponsors of international terrorism. In addition, figures for Saudi Arabia, Egypt, and
Pakistan are included since by all estimations they constitute important sources of international
terrorist recruiting.

[60] See the related discussion in Barber 2001.

Moreover, it should be recognized that under current international trade rules, countries are granted a "cultural exception" that allows any country to "favor its movie, television, and radio industries with subsidies and minimize foreign competition through quotas."[61] Ultimately, it would appear that debates within countries such as "Saudi Arabia, Egypt, Algeria, Pakistan, and Iran center only in the most trivial way on Western 'contamination,' such as by pop music and video games, of their cultures."[62] Perhaps the most telling indicator in this regard is a Pew survey of opinion leaders undertaken in December 2001; 90 percent of respondents from Islamic countries said that the spread of American culture, through movies, television and pop music was either not much of a reason or only a minor reason that people in their countries disliked the United States.[63]

This same Pew survey provides additional evidence directly relevant to the possible link between MNCs and terrorism. Eighty-three percent of respondents from Islamic countries said that the growing power of U.S. MNCs was either not much of a reason or only a minor reason for resentment against the United States. In turn, 79 percent of those surveyed from Islamic countries said that globalization was either not much of a cause or only a minor cause of terrorism. The Pew survey clearly indicates that other factors now drive resentment of the United States, in particular: its support for Israel; resentment of U.S. power; and U.S. policies that may have contributed to the growing gap between rich and poor.

The Pew survey is the best snapshot we have of perceptions in the Islamic world on the link between economic globalization and terrorism. It suggests that it is not economic globalization in general or MNCs in particular that lead to deep resentment against the United States. To the extent that globalization is a factor, what appears significant is the policy environment in which it is embedded, such as U.S. protectionism of agriculture—a key export sector for developing countries.

It is worth recalling that there is no dispute among economists as to whether FDI promotes economic growth; only the magnitude of FDI's positive effect is debated. Increased FDI may reduce support for terrorism by leading to greater economic growth in the developing world. This is not because poverty per se is a root cause of terrorism; it is unclear that it is. Rather, it is because reductions in poverty may promote changes both among civilian populations and government authorities that "drain the swamp," that is, produce a less favorable climate for terrorist groups in the countries in which they operate.

This discussion of the potential links between the globalization of production and international terrorism is only a starting point. In the years ahead, much more detailed research on this topic will be needed.

[61] *New York Times*, 5 February 2003, E3.

[62] Campbell 2002, 8.

[63] Pew Global Attitudes Project, "America Admired, Yet Its New Vulnerability Seen as Good Thing," 19 December 2001.

FINAL THOUGHTS

International commerce is not what it was during the age of Plutarch, or Adam Smith, or Immanuel Kant, or any of the other philosophers who have argued over the millennia that it influences security relations. In the past several decades, we have moved away from a world in which trade was of paramount importance; nowadays, international production by MNCs is the key driver of international commerce. This is a dramatic change—one that makes it incumbent upon us to take a fresh look at how the global economy influences international security. Until now, however, research on the repercussions of international trade flows has crowded out detailed examination of the influence of the globalization of production on security. In asking how international commerce affects security, analysts have so far neglected the majority of what international commerce now consists of. The analysis in this book thus complements the work of the large community of scholars who have examined the security repercussions of trade flows over the past decade.

This examination stands in contrast to the work of those analysts who maintain that trade enhances the prospects for peace under all circumstances, since I conclude that now and for the foreseeable future the geographic dispersion of MNC production has negative repercussions for security relations among developing countries and is mixed for relations between great powers and developing countries. At the same time, this analysis greatly undercuts those who doubt that international commerce now acts as a force for peace among the great powers. A number of prominent analysts have argued that many of the factors that have long worked for peace among the great powers are fading away and that economic globalization provides no grounds for optimism.[64] With respect to the most dangerous states in the system—revisionist great powers—these skeptics highlight World War I as evidence that high levels of international commerce do not restrain efforts to overturn the system through force.[65] In other words, it is just when the stabilizing influence of international commerce is most needed that such constraints evaporate. However, the analysis in this book shows that this argument has no merit with respect to the globalization of production. The counterexample of World War I has no bearing, since the geographic dispersion of MNC production is a novel feature of the world economy in the past few decades. The globalization of production also makes success structurally more difficult for a great power revisionist, no matter what goals it has. There is every reason to believe that these peaceful effects will remain in force for many years to come.

[64] See Mearsheimer 2001; Kupchan 2002; Waltz 2000; and Huntington 1993.
[65] See Mearsheimer 2001, esp. 372; Kupchan 2002, esp. 103; and Waltz 2000.

Bibliography

Adomeit, Hannes. 1998. *Imperial Overstretch: Germany in Soviet Policy from Stalin to Gorbachev*. Baden Baden: Nomos Verlagsgesellschaft.

Aerospace America. 2002. *Aircraft Supplier Guide: An Aerospace America Special Report (April 2002)*. Reston, Va.: Aerospace America.

Aerospace Industries Association. 2003. AIA White Paper on the Industrial Base Provisions (Title VIII, Subtitle B) in the House of Representatives Version of the FY 2004 National Defense Authorization Act. Arlington, Va.: Aerospace Industries Association.

Agosin, Manuel. 1995. *Foreign Direct Investment in Latin America*. Washington: IADB.

Aitken, Brian, Gordon Hanson, and Ann Harrison. 1997. Spillovers, Foreign Investment, and Export Behavior. *Journal of International Economics* 43.

Ajami, R., and D. Ricks. 1981. Motives of Non-American Firms Investing in the United States. *Journal of International Business Studies* 12 (1).

Albright, Madeleine. 2003. Squandering Capital. *Washington Post*, July 20.

Alfaro, Laura, Areendam Chanda, Sebnem Kalemli-Ozcan, and Selin Sayek. Forthcoming. FDI and Economic Growth: The Role of Local Financial Markets. *Journal of International Economics* 64.

Alic, John A., Lewis M. Branscomb, Harvey Brooks, Ashton B. Carter, and Gerald L. Epstein. 1992. *Beyond Spinoff*. Boston: Harvard Business School Press.

Angell, Norman. 1910. *The Great Illusion: A Study of the Relationship of Military Power in Nations to Their Economic and Social Advantage*. London: William Henemann.

Antal-Mokos, Zoltán. 1998. *Privatisation, Politics, and Economic Performance in Hungary*. Cambridge: Cambridge University Press.

Argentine Ministry of Economy. 1996. Mercosur Protocols for Foreign Investment Promotion and Protection. In *OECD Reviews of Foreign Direct Investment: Argentina*, edited by OECD. Paris: OECD.

Aslund, Anders. 1989. *Gorbachev's Struggle for Economic Reform*. Ithaca, N.Y.: Cornell University Press.

Bairoch, Paul, and Richard Kozul-Wright. 1996. Globalization Myths: Some Historical Reflections on Integration, Industrialization, and Growth in the World Economy. UNCTAD Discussion Paper No. 113.

Baldwin, David. 1993. *Neorealism and Neoliberalism: The Contemporary Debate*. New York: Columbia University Press.

———. 1985. *Economic Statecraft*. Princeton: Princeton University Press.

Balza, Martin. 1995. La seguridad entre los paises del Mercosur. *Seguridad Estrategica Regional* 8.

Barber, Benjamin. 2001. Ballots versus Bullets. *Financial Times*, 20 October.

Barbieri, Katherine. 1996. Economic Interdependence: A Path to Peace or a Source of Interstate Conflict? *Journal of Peace Research* 33.

————. 2002. *The Liberal Illusion: Does Trade Promote Peace?* Ann Arbor: University of Michigan Press.

Barbieri, Katherine, and Jack S. Levy. 1999. Sleeping with the Enemy: The Impact of War on Trade. *Journal of Peace Research* 36.

Barbieri, Katherine, and Gerald Snyder. 1999. Globalization and Peace: Assessing New Directions in the Study of Trade and Conflict. *Journal of Peace Research* 36.

Barletta, Michael. 1999. Democratic Security and Diversionary Peace: Nuclear Confidence-Building in Argentina and Brazil. *National Security Studies Quarterly* Summer 1999.

Bates, Robert. 1981. *Markets and States in Tropical Africa: The Political Basis of Agricultural Policies.* Berkeley and Los Angeles: University of California Press.

————. 1991. The Economics of Transitions to Democracy. *Political Science and Politics* 24.

Batt, Judy. 1988. *Economic Reform and Political Change in Eastern Europe: A Comparison of the Czechoslovak and Hungarian Experiences.* New York: St. Martin's Press.

Baylis, Thomas. 1989. Leadership Structures and Leadership Politics in Hungary and the GDR. In *East Germany in Comparative Perspective*, edited by D. Childs, T. Baylis, and M. Rueschemeyer. London: Routledge.

Bayoumi, Tamim, David Coe, and Elhanan Helpman. 1999. R&D Spillover and Global Growth. *Journal of International Economics* 47.

Beer, Francisca M., and Suzanne M. Cory. 1996. The Locational Determinants of U.S. Foreign Direct Investment in the European Union. *Journal of Financial and Strategic Decisions* 9 (2).

Beltrán, Virgilio L. 2001. Estrategías de seguridad y estrategías de integración en el cono sur de America. In *La OTAN y los desafíos en el MERCOSUR*, edited by R. Diamint. Buenos Aires: Grupo Editor Latinoamericano.

Bengoa, Marta, and Blanca Sanchez Robles. 2003. Foreign Direct Investment and Growth: New Evidence from Latin America. *European Journal of Political Economy* 45 (1).

Bennett, Andrew. 1999. *Condemned to Repetition? The Rise, Fall, and Reprise of Soviet-Russian Military Interventionism, 1973–1996.* Cambridge: MIT Press.

Bennett, D. Scott, and Allan Stam. 2003. *The Behavioral Origins of War.* Ann Arbor: University of Michigan Press.

Bergen, Peter. 2002. *Holy War, Inc.* New York: Simon and Schuster.

Berger, W. 1992. Zu den Hauptursachen des Unterganges der DDR. *Weißenseer Blätter* 4.

Betts, Richard. 1998. The New Threat of Mass Destruction. *Foreign Affairs* 77 (1).

Bilder, Richard. 1980. International Law and Natural Resource Policies. In *Resources and Development*, edited by P. Dorner and M. El-Shafie. Madison: University of Wisconsin Press.

Bimber, Bruce. 1994. Three Faces of Technological Determinism. In *Does Technology Drive History?* edited by M. Smith and L. Marx. Cambridge: MIT Press.

Bitzinger, Richard A. 1994. The Globalization of the Arms Industry: The Next Proliferation Challenge. *International Security* 19 (2).

Blackwell, James. 1992. The Defense Industrial Base. *Washington Quarterly* 15 (4).

Blanc, H., and C. Sierra. 1999. The Internationalisation of R & D by Multinationals:

A Trade-Off between External and Internal Proximity. *Cambridge Journal of Economics* 23 (2).

Bleaney, Michael. 1988. *Do Socialist Economies Work? The Soviet and East European Experience*. New York: Basil Blackwell.

Blomstrom, Magnus, and Ari Kokko. 1997. Regional Integration and Foreign Direct Investment. NBER Working Paper No. 6019.

Bogomolov, Oleg. 1987. The Socialist Countries at a Critical Stage in World Economic Development. *Problems of Economics* 30 (8).

Bonsignore, Eric. 1992. Gulf Experience Raises Tank Survivability Issue. *Military Technology*.

Bornschier, Volker. 2000. State Building and Political Entrepreneurship. In *State-Building in Europe: The Revitalization of Western European Integration*, edited by V. Bornschier. Cambridge: Cambridge University Press.

Bornstein, Morris. 1977. Economic Reform in Eastern Europe. In *Eastern European Economies Post-Helinski: A Compendium of Papers*, edited by John Hardt. Washington, D.C.: U.S. Government Printing Office.

Bouzas, Roberto. 1991. *A US-Mercosur Free Trade Area: A Preliminary Assessment*. Buenos Aires: Facultad Latinoamericana de Ciencias Sociales.

Brada, Josef. 1985. Soviet Subsidization of Trade with Eastern Europe: The Primacy of Economics over Politics. *Journal of Comparative Economics* 9 (1).

Braga, C. A. Primo, Raed Safadi, and Alexander Yeats. 1994. Regional Integration in the Americas: Deja Vu All Over Again? *World Economy* 17 (4).

Brecher, Michael, and Jonathan Wilkenfeld. 2000. *A Study of Crisis*. Ann Arbor: University of Michigan Press.

Brooks, H. E., and B. R. Guile. 1987. Overview. In *Technology and Global Industry: Companies and Nations in the World Economy*, edited by B. R. Guile and H. E. B. Washington, D.C.: National Academy Press.

Brooks, Stephen G. 1994. Regional Economic Integration in the Developing World: Historical Trends and Future Viability. U.S. Navy Technical Report No. NPS-NS-94-001. Monterey: Naval Postgraduate School.

———. 1999. The Globalization of Production and the Changing Benefits of Conquest. *Journal of Conflict Resolution* 43 (5).

Brooks, Stephen G., and William C. Wohlforth. 2000–2001. Power, Globalization, and the End of the Cold War: Reevaluating a Landmark Case for Ideas. *International Security* 25 (3).

———. 2002a. American Primacy in Perspective. *Foreign Affairs* 81 (4).

———. 2002b. From Old Thinking to New Thinking in Qualitative Research. *International Security* 26 (4).

———. 2005. Reactions to US Primacy: Soft Balancing, or Unipolar Politics as Usual? *International Security* 29.

Brown, J. F. 1975. *Relations between the Soviet Union and Its Eastern European Allies: A Survey*. Santa Monica: Rand.

———. 1988. *Eastern Europe and Communist Rule*. Durham, N.C.: Duke University Press.

———. Brunn, S. D., and T. R. Leinbach, eds. 1991. *Collapsing Space and Time: Geographic Aspects of Communication and Information*. New York: HarperCollins.

Bryson, Philip. 1995. *The Reluctant Retreat*. Aldershot: Dartmouth.

Bryson, Philip, and Manfred Melzer. 1991. *The End of the East German Economy*. New York: St. Martin's Press.

Brzoska, Michael. 1999. Economic Factors Shaping Arms Production in Less Industrialized Countries. *Defense and Peace Economics* 10.

Buckley, P. J., and M. Casson. 1976. *The Future of Multinational Enterprise*. London: Macmillan.

———. 1988. A Theory of Cooperation in International Business. In *Cooperative Strategies in International Business*, edited by F. Contractor and P. Lorange. Lexington, Mass.: Lexington Books.

Buckley, Peter, Jeremy Clegg, and Nicolas Forsans. Foreign Market Servicing on the NAFTA Area. *Canadian Journal of Regional Science* 21 (2).

Bunce, Valerie. 1985. The Empire Strikes Back: The Evolution of the Eastern Bloc from Soviet Asset to Liability. *International Organization* 39.

Burghart, Daniel. 1992. *Red Microchip: Technology Transfer, Export Control, and Economic Restructuring in the Soviet Union*. Aldershot: Dartmouth.

Burant, Stephen. 1990. *Hungary: A Country Study*. Washington, D.C.: Library of Congress.

Burr, Robert. 1955. The Balance of Power in Nineteenth-Century South America: An Exploratory Essay. *Hispanic American Historical Review* 35 (1).

Buzan, Barry. 1984. Economic Structure and International Security: The Limits of the Liberal Case. *International Organization* 38.

Buzan, Barry, and Eric Herring. 1998. *The Arms Dynamic in World Politics*. Boulder, Colo.: Lynne Rienner.

Buzuev, Alexander. 1985. *Transnational Corporations and Militarism*. Moscow: Progress Publishers.

Cameron, David. 1992. The 1992 Initiative: Causes and Consequences. In *Euro-Politics: Institutions and Policymaking in the "New" European Community*, edited by A. Sbragia. Washington: Brookings Institution.

Campbell, John. 1984. Soviet Foreign Policy in Eastern Europe: An Overview. In *Soviet Policy in Eastern Europe*, edited by S. Terry. New Haven: Yale University Press.

Campbell, Kurt. 2002. Globalization's First War? *Washington Quarterly* 25 (1).

Campbell, Robert. 1972. Management Spillovers from Soviet Space and Military Programmes. *Soviet Studies* 23 (4).

Cantwell, J. 1995. The Globalization of Technology: What Remains of the Product Cycle Model. *Cambridge Journal of Economics* 19 (1).

———. 1998. The Globalization of Technology: What Remains of the Product-Cycle Model? In *The Dynamic Firm: The Role of Technology, Strategy, Organization, and Regions*, edited by A. Chandler, P. Hagstrom, and O. Solvell. Oxford: Oxford University Press.

Carlucci, Frank. 1988. Report on Allied Contributions to the Common Defense: A Report to the U.S. Congress. Washington, D.C.: Department of Defense.

Carr, Edward Hallett. 1946. *The Twenty Years' Crisis, 1919–1939: An Introduction to the Study of International Relations*. 2d ed. London: Macmillan.

Carranza, Mario Esteban. 2000. *South American Free Trade Area or Free Trade of the Americas?* Aldershot: Ashgate.

Cason, Jeffrey. 2000. On the Road to Southern Cone Economic Integration. *Journal of Interamerican Studies and World Affairs* 42 (1).

Casson, Mark. 2000. *Economics of International Business*. Northampton, Mass.: Edward Elgar.

Castrioto de Azambuja, Marcos. 1994. O relacionamento Brasil-Argentina: De rivais a socios. In *Temas de Politica Externa Brasileira II*, edited by G. Fonseca Junior and S. H. Nabuco de Castro. São Paulo: Paz e Terra.

Caves, Richard E. 1971. International Corporations: The Industrial Economics of Foreign Investment. *Economica* NS. 38.

———. 1982. *Multinational Enterprise and Economic Analysis*. Cambridge: Cambridge University Press.

Center for Strategic and International Studies (CSIS). 1989. *Deterrence in Decay: The Future of the U.S. Defense Industrial Base*. Washington: CSIS.

Cha, Victor. 2000. Globalization and the Study of International Security. *Journal of Peace Research* 37 (3).

Chafetz, Mark. 1993. *Gorbachev, Eastern Europe, and the Brezhnev Doctrine: Soviet Policy towards Eastern Europe, 1985–1990*. New York: Praeger.

Chase, Kerry. 1998. Sectors, Firms, and Regional Trade Blocs in the International Economy. Ph.D. dissertation, Department of Political Science, University of California, Los Angeles.

Chen, E.K.Y. 1983. *Multinational Corporations, Technology, and Employment*. New York: Macmillan.

Cheng, J.L.C., and D. S. Bolon. 1993. The Management of Multinational Research and Development. *Journal of International Business Studies* 24 (1).

Chesnais, François. 1991. Preface. In *Strategic Partnerships—States, Firms, and International Competition*, edited by L. K. Mytelka. London: Pinter.

Childs, David. 1988. *The GDR: Moscow's German Ally*. London: Unwin Hyman.

Childs, David, and Richard Popplewell. 1996. *The Stasi: The East German Intelligence and Security Service*. New York: New York University Press.

Choe, Jong Il. 2003. Do Foreign Direct Investment and Gross Direct Investment Promote Economic Growth? *Review of Economic Development* 7 (1).

Chudnovsky, Daniel, Andres Lopez, and Fernando Porta. 1996. New Foreign Direct Investment in Argentina: Privatization, the Domestic Market, and Regional Integration. In *Foreign Direct Investment in Latin America*, edited by M. Agosin. Washington, D.C.: IADB.

CIA (Central Intelligence Agency). 1982. Soviet Economic Dependence on the West. Report No. Sov 82-10012. Washington, D.C.: CIA.

———. 1983. Soviet Military R&D: Resource Implications of Increased Weapon and Space Systems for the 1980s. Washington: CIA.

———. 1985a. Domestic Stresses on the Soviet System (NIE 11-18-85). Washington, D.C.: CIA.

———. 1985b. Soviet Acquisition of Military Significant Technology: An Update. Washington, D.C.: CIA.

———. 1987a. The USSR Confronts the Information Revolution. Report No. SOV 87-10029. Washington, D.C.: CIA.

———. 1987b. The Soviet Defense Industry: Coping with the Military-Technological Challenge. Report No. SOV 87-10035DX. Washington, D.C.: CIA.

———. 1987c. Soviet Joint Ventures with the West: Much Talk, Little Action. Report No. Sov87-10072 X. Washington, D.C.: CIA.

————. 1989a. Soviet Bloc Computers: Direct Descendants of Western Technology. Report No. 89-10023 X. Washington, D.C.: CIA.

————. 1989b. The Soviet Microelectronics Industry: Hitting a Technological Barrier. Report No. Sov89-10066 X. Washington, D.C.: CIA.

————. 1990. Soviet Core Technology Needs from the West to Support Future Military Programs. Report No. SW M 90-20024. Washington, D.C.: CIA.

————. 1991. Soviet Military R&D: Scaling Back and Taking Risks. Report No. Sov 91-10053X. Washington, D.C.: CIA.

————. 2000. Unclassified Report to Congress on the Acquisition of Technology Relating to Weapons of Mass Destruction and Advanced Conventional Munitions, 1 July through 31 December 2000. Washington, D.C.: CIA.

————. 2002. *World Factbook, 2002*. Washington, D.C.: CIA.

————. 2003. Unclassified Report to Congress on the Acquisition of Technology Relating to Weapons of Mass Destruction and Advanced Conventional Weapons, 1 January through 30 June 2003. Washington, D.C.: CIA.

Clark, Carol. 1993. Relative Backwardness in Eastern Europe: An Application of the Technological Gap Hypothesis. *Economic Systems* 17 (3).

Cohen, Eliot A. 1996. A Revolution in Warfare. *Foreign Affairs* 74 (2).

Cohn, S. 1981. Adopting Innovations in a Technology Push Industry. *Research Management* 24.

Commerce, U.S. Department of. 1992. *National Security Assessment of the Domestic and Foreign Subcontractor Base: A Study of Three U.S. Navy Weapons Systems*. Washington, D.C.: Department of Commerce.

Conca, Ken. 1998. Between Global Markets and Domestic Politics: Brazil's Military-Industrial Collapse. *Review of International Studies* 24.

Cooper, Julian. 1991. Soviet Technology and the Potential of Joint Ventures. In *International Joint Ventures: Soviet and Western Perspectives*, edited by A. Sherr et al. New York: Quorum Books.

Copeland, Dale. 1996. Economic Interdependence and War: A Theory of Trade Expectations. *International Security* 20 (4).

Crane, Keith. 1988. *Eastern Europe's Contribution to Soviet Defense*. Santa Monica: Rand.

————. 1989. Soviet Economic Policy towards Eastern Europe. In *Continuity and Change in Soviet-East European Relations: Implications for the West*, edited by M. Carnovale and W. Potter. Boulder, Colo.: Westview Press.

Crane, Keith, and K. C. Yeh. 1991. *Economic Reform and the Military in Poland, Hungary, and China*. Santa Monica: Rand.

Croan, Melvin. 1976. *East Germany: The Soviet Connection*. London: Sage.

Cronin, Audrey Kurth. 2002–3. Behind the Curve: Globalization and International Terrorism. *International Security* 27 (3).

Cutler, Robert. 1992. International Relations Theory and Soviet Conduct toward the Multilateral Global-Economic Organizations: GATT, IMF, and the World Bank. In *The USSR and the World Economy: Challenges for the Global Integration of Soviet Markets under Perestroika*, edited by D. A. Palmieri. Westport, Conn.: Praeger.

Dawisha, Karen. 1981. The 1968 Invasion of Czechoslovakia: Causes, Consequences, and Lessons for the Future. In *Soviet-East European Dilemmas: Coercion, Competition, and Consent*, edited by K. Dawisha and P. Hanson. New York: Holmes and Meier.

———. 1988. *Eastern Europe, Gorbachev, and Reform: The Great Challenge.* Cambridge: Cambridge University Press.

de la Torre, Augosto, and Margaret Kelly. 1992. *Regional Trade Agreements.* Washington, D.C.: International Monetary Fund.

Dennis, Mike. 2000. *The Rise and Fall of the German Democratic Republic, 1945–1990.* New York: Longman.

Denoon, David, and Evelyn Colbert. 1998–99. Challenges for the Association of Southeast Nations (ASEAN). *Pacific Affairs* 71 (4).

Department of Defense (DoD). 1986. Defense Use of Foreign Electronic Microchips: Report to the House Appropriations Committee by the Secretary of Defense.

———. 1988. Bolstering Defense Industrial Competitiveness: Preserving Our Heritage, Securing Our Future. Washington, D.C.: Report to the Secretary of Defense by the Undersecretary of Defense (Acquisition), July.

———. 1989. The Impact of Buy-American Restrictions Affecting Defense Procurement. Report to the United States Congress by the Secretary of Defense, July.

———. 1990. Critical Technologies Plan. Washington, D.C.: DoD.

Deudney, Daniel, and G. John Ikenberry. 1991. Soviet Reform and the End of the Cold War: Explaining Large-Scale Historical Change. *Review of International Studies* 17.

Deutsch, Karl W., et al. 1957. *Political Community and the North Atlantic Area: International Organization in the Light of Historical Experience.* Princeton: Princeton University Press.

Devlin, Robert, and Ricardo French-Davis. 1999. Towards an Evaluation of Regional Integration in Latin America in the 1900s. *World Economy* 22 (2).

Dibb, Paul. 1986. *The Soviet Union: The Incomplete Superpower.* Urbana: University of Illinois Press.

Dicken, Peter. 1992. *Global Shift: The Internationalization of Economic Activity,* 2d ed. London: Paul Chapman.

———. 1998. *Global Shift: Transforming the World Economy,* 3d ed. New York: Guilford Press.

Dicken, Peter. 2003. *Global Shift: Reshaping the Global Economic Map in the Twenty-First Century,* 4th ed. New York: Guilford Press.

Donadio, Marcela, and Luis Tibiletti. 1998. Strategic Balance and Regional Security in the Southern Cone. In *Strategic Balance and Confidence Building Measures in the Americas,* edited by J. Tulchin and F. R. Aravena. Washington, D.C.: Woodrow Wilson Center Press.

Doyle, Michael W. 1997. *Ways of War and Peace: Realism, Liberalism, and Socialism.* New York: Norton.

Dunning, John. 1977. Trade, Location of Economic Activity, and the MNE: A Search for an Eclectic Approach. In *The International Allocation of Economic Activity,* edited by B. Ohlin, P. O. Hesselborn, and P. M. Wijkman. London: Macmillan.

———. 1980. Towards an Eclectic Theory of International Production: Some Empirical Tests. *Journal of International Business Studies* 11 (1).

———. 1988. *Explaining International Production.* London: Unwin Hyman.

———. 1992. *Multinational Enterprises and the Global Economy.* Reading, Mass.: Addison-Wesley.

———. 1993a. *Explaining International Production.* London: Unwin Hyman.

————. 1993b. *The Globalization of Business: The Challenge of the 1990s*. London: Routledge.

————. 1994. Globalization, Economic Restructuring and Development. Department of Economics, University of Reading.

————. 1995. Reappraising the Eclectic Paradigm in an Age of Alliance Capitalism. *Journal of International Business Studies* 26.

————. 2000. Regions, Globalization, and the Knowledge Economy: The Issues Stated. In *Regions, Globalization, and the Knowledge Economy*, edited by J. Dunning. Oxford: Oxford University Press.

Duus, Peter. 1991. Introduction: Japan's Informal Empire in China, 1895–1937: An Overview. In *The Japanese Informal Empire in China, 1895–1937*, edited by P. Duus, R. H. Myers, and M. R. Peattie. Princeton: Princeton University Press.

Easterbrook, Gregg. 2002. Term Limits: The Meaningless of WMD. *New Republic*, 7 October.

El-Agraa, Ali M. 1997. General introduction. In *Economic Integration Worldwide*, edited by A. M. El-Agraa. New York: St. Martin's Press.

Ellman, Michael, and Vladimir Kontorovich, eds. 1992. *The Disintegration of the Soviet Economic System*. New York: Routledge.

————, eds. 1998. *The Destruction of the Soviet Economic System: An Insider's Account*. Armonk, N.Y.: M. E. Sharpe.

Epstein, Joshua. 1990. *Conventional Force Reductions: A Dynamic Assessment*. Washington, D.C.: Brookings Institution.

Escudé, Charles, and Andrés Fontana. 1998. Argentina's Security Policies: Their Rationale and Regional Context. In *International Security and Democracy: Latin America and the Caribbean in the Post–Cold War Era*, edited by J. Dominquez. Pittsburgh: University of Pittsburgh Press.

Ethier, Wilfrid. 1998a. The New Regionalism. *Economic Journal* 108.

————. 1998b. Regionalism in a Multilateral World. *Journal of Political Economy* 106 (6).

Evangelista, Matthew. 1988. *Innovation in the Arms Race: How the United States and the Soviet Union Develop New Military Technologies*. Ithaca, N.Y.: Cornell University Press.

————. 1996. Stalin's Revenge: Institutional Barriers to Institutionalization in the Soviet Union. In *Internationalization and Domestic Politics*, edited by R. O. Keohane and H. Milner. Cambridge: Cambridge University Press.

————. 1999. *Unarmed Forces: The Transnational Movement to End the Cold War*. Ithaca, N.Y.: Cornell University Press.

Eyal, Jonathan. 1992. Military Relations. In *The End of the Outer Empire*, edited by A. Pravda. New York: Sage.

Feenstra, Robert. 1999. Facts and Fallacies about Foreign Direct Investment. In *International Capital Flows*, edited by M. Feldstein. Chicago: University of Chicago Press.

Feenstra, Robert, and Gordon Hanson. 1996. Globalization, Outsourcing, and Wage Inequality. NBER Working Paper No. W5424.

Feigenbaum, Evan. 1999. Who's behind China's High-Technology "Revolution"? How Bomb Makers Remade Beijing's Priorities, Policies, and Institutions. *International Security* 24 (1).

Fernandez, Raquel, and Jonathan Portes. 1998. Returns to Regionalism: An Analysis of Nontraditional Gains from Regional Trade Agreements. *World Bank Economic Review* 12 (2).

Fetter, Steve. 1991. Ballistic Missiles and Weapons of Mass Destruction: What Is the Threat? What Should Be Done? *International Security* 16 (1).

Fioretos, Karl-Orfeo. 1997. The Anatomy of Autonomy: Interdependence, Domestic Balances of Power, and European Integration. *Review of International Studies* 23 (3).

Firth, Noel E., and James H. Noren. 1998. *Soviet Defense Spending: A History of CIA Estimates, 1950–1990*. Houston: Texas A&M Press.

Fischer, Fritz. 1975. *War of Illusions: German Politics from 1911 to 1914*. New York: Norton.

Fischer, Klaus. 1999. Business and Integration in the Americas: Competing Points of View. In *The Americas in Transition: The Contours of Regionalism*, edited by G. Mace and L. Belanger. Boulder, Colo.: Lynne Rienner.

Fitzgerald, Kevin. 1999. Profile of the Purchasing Professional. *Purchasing Magazine Online*, 15 July.

Fitzgerald, Mary C. 1987. Marshall Ogarkov and the New Revolution in Soviet Military Affairs. *Defense Analysis* 3 (1).

Florida, R. 1997. The Globalization of R&D: Results of a Survey of Foreign-Affiliated R&D Laboratories in the USA. *Research Policy* 26 (1).

Flynn, Stephen. 2000. Beyond Border Control. *Foreign Affairs* 79 (6).
———. 2002. America the Vulnerable. *Foreign Affairs* 81 (1).

Frankel, Jeffrey, Ernesto Stein, and Shang-Jin Wei. 1995. Trading Blocs and the Americas: The Natural, the Unnatural, and the Super-natural. *Journal of Development Economics* 47.
———. 1997. *Regional Trading Blocs in the World Economics System*. Washington, D.C.: Institute for International Economics.

Friedberg, Aaron. 2000a. *In the Shadow of the Garrison State: American Anti-Semitism and the Conduct of the Cold War*. Princeton: Princeton University Press.
———. 2000b. The United States and the Cold War Arms Race. In *Reviewing the Cold War*, edited by O. A. Westad, London: Cass.

Frieden, Jeffry A. 1994. International Investment and Colonial Control: A New Interpretation. *International Organization* 48.
———. 1996. The Impact of Goods and Capital Market Integration on European Monetary Politics. *Comparative Political Studies* 29 (2).

Frieden, Jeffry A., and Ronald Rogowski. 1996. The Impact of the International Economy on National Policies. In *Internationalization and Domestic Politics*, edited by R. O. Keohane and H. V. Milner. New York: Cambridge University Press.

Friedman, Thomas. 1999. *The Lexus and the Olive Tree: Understanding Globalization*. New York: Anchor Books.

Fujita, Edmundo. 1998. The Brazilian Policy of Sustainable Defense. *International Affairs* 74 (3).

Fulbrook, Mary. 1991. *History of Germany, 1918–1990*. London: Fontana Press.
———. 2000. *Interpretations of the Two Germanies*. London: Macmillan.

Furubotn, Eirik, and Rudolf Richter. 1993. The New Institutional Economics: Recent Progress; Expanding Frontiers. *Journal of Institutional and Theoretical Economics* 149 (1).

Gaddis, John. 1987. *The Long Peace: Inquiries into the History of the Cold War*. New York: Oxford University Press.

———. 1992–93. International Relations Theory and the End of the Cold War. *International Security* 17 (3).

———. 1997. History, Theory, and Common Ground. *International Security* 22 (1).

Gaddy, Clifford. 1997. *The Price of the Past*. Washington, D.C.: Brookings Institution.

Garrett, Geoffrey. 2000. The Causes of Globalization. *Comparative Political Studies* 33 (6–7).

Gartzke, Erik, Quan Li, and Charles Boehmer. 2001. Investing in the Peace: Economic Interdependence and International Conflict. *International Organization* 55.

Gati, Charles. 1974. The Kadar Mystique. *Problems of Communism* 23 (3).

———. 1984. Burdens and Benefits of the Soviet Union in Eastern Europe: Kennan Institute for Advanced Russian Studies.

———. 1986. *Hungary and the Soviet Bloc*. Durham: Duke University Press.

———. 1990. *The Bloc That Failed: Soviet-East European Relations in Transition*. Bloomington: Indiana University Press.

General Accounting Office (GAO). 1989. *Industrial Base: Adequacy of Information on the U.S. Defense Industrial Base*. Washington, D.C.: GA Office.

———. 1991. *Industrial Base: Significance of DOD's Foreign Dependence*. Washington, D.C.: GA Office.

Gerbet, Pierre. 1983. *La construction de l'Europe*. Paris: Imprimerie Nationale.

Geron, Leonard. 1990. *Soviet Foreign Economic Policy under Perestroika*. London: Pinter.

Gerschenberg, I. 1987. The Training and Spread of Managerial Know-How: A Comparative Analysis of Multinational and Other Firms in Kenya. *World Development* 15.

Gholz, Eugene, and Daryl Press. 2001. The Effects of Wars on Neutral Countries: Why It Doesn't Pay to Preserve the Peace. *Security Studies* 10 (4).

Gilpin, Robert. 1975. *U.S. Power and the Multinational Corporation: The Political Economy of Foreign Direct Investment*. New York: Basic Books.

———. 1981. *War and Change in World Politics*. Cambridge: Cambridge University Press.

———. 2000. *The Challenge of Global Capitalism*. Princeton: Princeton University Press.

———. 2001. *Global Political Economy: Understanding the International Economic Order*. Princeton: Princeton University Press.

Gitz, Bradley. 1992. *Armed Forces and Political Power in Eastern Europe: The Soviet/Communist Control System*. New York: Greenwood Press.

Glaser, Charles L. 1997. The Security Dilemma revisited. *World Politics* 50.

Glyn, Andrew. 1997–98. Egalitarianism in a Global Economy. *Boston Review*, December–January.

Golan, Galia. 1973. *Reform Rule in Czechoslovakia: The Dubcek Era, 1968–1969*. Cambridge: Cambridge University Press.

Goldgeier, James, and Michael McFaul. 1992. A Tale of Two Worlds: Core and Periphery in the Post–Cold War era. *International Organization* 46.

Gomulka, Stanislaw, and Alec Nove. 1984. *East-West Technology Transfer*. Paris: OECD.

Gonzalez, Flavio Floreal. 1999. Mercosur: The Incompatibilities between Its Institutions and the Need to Complete the Customs Union. *Integration and Trade* 3 (9).

Gorbachev, Mikhail S. 1987. *Izbrannye rechi i stat'i.* Moscow: Izdatel'stvo politicheskoi literatury.

———. 1996. *Memoirs.* New York: Doubleday.

Gourevitch, Peter. 1978. The Second Image Reversed: The International Sources of Domestic Politics. *International Organization* 32 (4).

Graham, Edward, and Paul Krugman. 1991. *Foreign Direct Investment in the United States.* Washington, D.C.: Institute for International Economics.

Grandi, Jorge, and Lincoln Biezzózero. 1997. Towards a Mercosur Civil Society: Old and New Actors in the Sub-regional Fabric. *Integration and Trade* 1 (3).

Green, Donald, Soo Yeon Kim, and David Yoon. 2001. Dirty Pool. *International Organization* 55.

Green Cowles, Maria. 1995. Setting the Agenda for a New Europe: The ERT and EC, 1992. *Journal of Common Market Studies* 33.

Grieco, Joseph. 1997. Systemic Sources of Variation in Regional Institutionalization in Western Europe, East Asia, and the Americas. In *The Political Economy of Regionalism*, edited by E. Mansfield and H. Milner. New York: Columbia University Press.

Grieco, Joseph, Robert Powell, and Duncan Snidal. 1993. The Relative-Gains Problem for International Cooperation. *American Political Science Review* 87.

Grieder, Peter. 1998. The Overthrow of Ulbricht in East Germany. *Debatte* 6 (1).

———. 1999. *The East German Leadership, 1946–1973.* Manchester: Manchester University Press.

Griffith, Ivelaw. 1998. Security Collaboration and Confidence Building in the Americas. In *International Security and Democracy: Latin America and the Caribbean in the Post–Cold War Era*, edited by J. Dominquez. Pittsburgh: University of Pittsburgh Press.

Grosse, Robert. 1990. *Multinationals in Latin America.* London: Routledge.

Gruber, Lloyd. 2000. *Ruling the World: Power Politics and the Rise of Supranational Institutions.* Princeton: Princeton University Press.

Guedes da Costa, Thomas. 1995. Condiciones para la integracion do politicas de defense. *SER 2000* 7.

———. 1998. The Role of the Armed Forces in Brazil's Democratization. In *Civil-Military Relations: Building Democracy and Regional Security in Latin America, Southern Asia, and Central Europe*, edited by D. Mares. Boulder, Colo.: Westview.

Haas, Ernst B. 1958. *The Uniting of Europe: Political, Social, and Economic Forces, 1950–1957.* Stanford: Stanford University Press.

———. 1964. *Beyond the Nation State: Functionalism and International Organization.* Stanford: Stanford University Press.

Haas, Peter M. 1996. *Knowledge, Power, and International Policy Coordination.* Columbia: University of South Carolina Press.

Hagedoorn, John. 1993. Strategic Technology Alliances and Modes of Cooperation in High Technology Industries. In *The Embedded Firm*, edited by G. Grabher. London: Routledge.

———. 2002. Inter-firm R&D Partnerships: An Overview of Major Trends and Patterns since 1960. *Research Policy* 31.

Hagedoorn, John, and Jos Schakenraad. 1990. Inter-firm Partnerships and Cooperative Strategies in Core Technologies. In *Perspectives in Industrial Organization*, edited by J. Dankbaar, J. Groenewegen, and H. Schenk. Dordrecht: Kluwer.

———. 1992. Leading Companies and Networks of Strategic Alliances in Information Technologies. *Research Policy* 21.

Haggard, Stephan. 1995. *Developing Nations and the Politics of Global Integration.* Washington, D.C.: Brookings Institution.

Haglund, David, and Marc Busch. 1990. "Techno-Nationalism" and the Contemporary Debate over the American Industrial Base. In *The Defense Industrial Base and the West*, edited by D. Haglund. London: Routledge.

Hall, John. 1996. *International Orders*. Cambridge, Mass.: Polity Press.

Hamilton, Alexander (Publius). 1961. The Federalist No. 6. In *The Federalist Papers*, edited by C. Rossiter. New York: Mentor.

Hamilton, Geoffrey, and Yuri Adjubei. 1990. Analysing the First Wave of Foreign Direct Investment to the Countries of Eastern Europe, 1987–1990: Structures, Actors, and Motives. In *New Dimensions in East-West Business Relations: Framework, Implications, Global Consequences*, edited by M. Schenk and W. Czege. Stuttgart: Gustav Fischer Verlag.

Hanson, Gordon, Raymond Mataloni, and Mathew Slaughter. 2001. Expansion Strategies of U.S. Multinational Firms. NBER Working Paper No. 8433.

Hanson, Philip. 1991. The Internationalization of the Soviet Economy. In *International Joint Ventures: Soviet and Western Perspectives*, edited by Alan B. Sherr et al. New York: Quorum Books.

Hanson, Philip, and Keith Pavitt. 1987. *The Comparative Economics of Research and Development in East and West: A Survey*. London: Hardwood Academic Publishers.

Hasenclever, Lia, Andres Lopez, and Jose Clemente de Oliveira. 1999. The Impact of Mercosur on the Development of the Petrochemical Sector. *Integration and Trade* 3 (7–8).

Hastings, Max. 1984. *Overlord and the Battle for Normandy*. New York: Simon and Schuster.

Hegre, Havard. 2000. Development and the Liberal Peace: What Does It Take to Be a Trading State? *Journal of Peace Research* 37 (1).

Hegre, Havard, and Nils Peter Gleditsch. 2002. Globalization and Internal Conflict. In *Globalization and Conflict*, edited by G. Schneider, K. Barbieri, and N. P. Gleditsch. Boulder, Colo.: Littlefield.

Heinrich, Jeff, and Denise Konan. 2000. Foreign Direct Investment and Host-Country Trading Blocs. *Journal of International Economic Integration* 15 (4).

Held, Bruce, and Edward Sunoski. 1993. Tank Gun Accuracy. *Armor* 102 (1).

Held, David, Anthony McGrew, David Goldblatt, and Jonathan Perraton. 1999. *Global Transformations*. Stanford: Stanford University Press.

Hermes, Niels, and Robert Lensink. 2003. Foreign Direct Investment, Financial Development, and Economic Growth. *Journal of Development Studies* 40 (1).

Herrera, Geoffrey L. 1995. The Mobility of Power: Technology, Diffusion, and International System Change. Ph.D. dissertation, Department of Politics, Princeton University.

Herspring, Dale R. 1989. The Soviets, the Warsaw Pact, and the Eastern European

Militaries. In *Central and Eastern Europe: The Opening Curtain?* edited by W. E. Griffith. Boulder, Colo.: Westview.

———. 1990. *The Soviet High Command, 1967–1989: Personalities and Politics.* Princeton: Princeton University Press.

———. 1998. *Requiem for an Army: The Demise of the East German Military.* Lanham, Md.: Rowman and Littlefield.

Herspring, Dale R., and Ivan Volgyes. 1980. Political Reliability of the Eastern European Warsaw Pact Armies. *Armed Forces and Society* 6 (2).

Hewett, Ed. 1988. *Reforming the Soviet Economy: Equality versus Efficiency.* Washington, D.C.: Brookings.

Hewett, Ed, and Clifford Gaddy. 1992. *Open for Business: Russia's Return to the Global Economy.* Washington, D.C.: Brookings Institution.

Heymann, Hans. 1990. Modernization and the Military-Civil Competition for Resources: Gorbachev's Dilemma. In *Soviet National Security Policy under Perestroika,* edited by G. Hudson. Boston: Unwin Hyman.

Hoensch, Jörg. 1998. *A History of Modern Hungary, 1867–1986.* London: Longman.

Hilton, Stanley. 1985. The Argentine Factor in Twentieth Century Brazilian Foreign Policy Strategy. *Political Science Quarterly* 100 (1).

———. 1987. The Brazilian Military: Changing Strategic Perceptions and the Question of Mission. *Armed Forces and Society* 13 (3).

Hirschmann, Albert. 1979. The Turn to Authoritarianism in Latin America and the Search for its Economic Determinants. In *The New Authoritarianism in Latin America,* edited by D. Collier. Princeton: Princeton University Press.

Hirshleifer, Jack. 2001. *The Dark Side of the Force: Economic Foundations of Conflict Theory.* Cambridge: Cambridge University Press.

Hirst, Monica. 1996. *Democracia, seguridad e integración: América Latina en un mundo en transición.* Buenos Aires: Grupo Editorial Norma.

———. 1998. Security Policies, Democratization, and Regional Integration in the Southern Cone. In *International Security and Democracy: Latin America and the Caribbean in the Post–Cold War Era,* edited by J. Dominquez. Pittsburgh: University of Pittsburgh Press.

———. 1999. Mercosur's Complex Political Agenda. In *Mercosur: Regional Integration, World Markets,* edited by R. Roett. Boulder, Colo.: Lynne Rienner.

Hobson, John. 1965. *Imperialism: A Study.* Ann Arbor: University of Michigan Press.

Hoffman, Stanley. 2002. The Clash of Globalizations. *Foreign Affairs* 81 (4).

Höhmann, Hans-Herman. 1982. Economic Reform in the 1970s—Policy with No Alternative. In *The East European Economies in the 1970s,* edited by A. Nove, H.-H. Höhmann, and G. Seidenstecher. London: Butterworths.

Holloway, David. 1982. Innovation in the Defense Sector. In *Industrial Innovation in the Soviet Union,* edited by R. Amann and J. Cooper. New Haven: Yale University Press.

Hollist, W. Ladd, and Daniel Nielson. 1998. Taking Stock of Inter-American Bonds: Approaches to Explaining Cooperation in the Western Hemisphere. *Mershon International Studies Review* 42 (Suppl. 2).

Holmes, John. 1986. The Organization and Locational Structure of Production Subcontracting. In *Production, Work, and Territory: The Geographical Anatomy of Industrial Capitalism,* edited by A. J. Scott and M. Storper. Boston: Allen and Unwin.

Holsti, Kolevi. 1991. *Peace and War: Armed Conflicts and International Order, 1648–1989*. Cambridge: Cambridge University Press.

Horvath, Julius, and Richard Grabowski. 1997. Prospects for African Integration in Light of Theory of Optimum Currency Areas. *Journal of Economic Integration* 12 (1).

Hough, Jerry F. 1986. *The Struggle for the Third World: Soviet Debates and American Options*. Washington, D.C.: Brookings Institution.

———. 1988a. *Opening Up the Soviet Economy*. Washington, D.C.: Brookings Institution.

———. 1988b. *Russia and the West: Gorbachev and the Politics of Reform*. New York: Simon and Schuster.

Hoyt, Kendall, and Stephen Brooks. 2003–4. Wielding a Double-Edged Sword: Globalization and Biosecurity. *International Security* 28 (3).

Hufbauer, Gary, and Jeffrey Schott. 1992. *North American Free Trade: Issues and Recommendations*. Washington, D.C.: Institute for International Economics.

———. 1994. *Western Hemisphere Economic Integration*. Washington: Institute for International Economics.

Huntington, Samuel. 1993. The Clash of Civilizations? *Foreign Affairs* 72 (3).

Hurrell, Andrew. 1994. Regionalism in the Americas. In *Latin America in a New World*, edited by A. Lowenthal and G. Treverton. Boulder, Colo.: Westview.

———. 1995. Regionalism in the Americas. In *Regionalism in World Politics: Regional Organizations and International Order*, edited by L. Fawcett and A. Hurrell. Oxford: Oxford University Press.

———. 1998a. An Emerging Security Community in South America? In *Security Communities*, edited by E. Adler and M. Barnett. Cambridge: Cambridge University Press.

Hurrell, Andrew. 1998b. Security in Latin America. *International Affairs* 74 (3).

Hymer, S. 1976. *The International Operations of National Firms: A Study of Direct Foreign Investment*. Cambridge: MIT Press.

Ikenberry, G. John. 2001. *After Victory: Institutions, Strategic Restraint, and the Rebuilding of Order after Major Wars*. Princeton: Princeton University Press.

Information Technologies Association of America. 2003. The Unintended Consequences of "Buy American": How HR 1588 Could Stall Commercial Procurement at DoD. Arlington, Va.: ITAA.

Inter-American Development Bank (IADB). 1996. *Intal Mercosur Report No. 1* Buenos Aires: IADB.

———. 1996. *Intal Mercosur Report No. 1: July–December 1996*. Buenos Aires: IADB.

———. 1997. *Intal Mercosur Report No. 3: July–December 1997*. Buenos Aires: IADB.

———. 1998. *Intal Mercosur Report No. 4: January–June 1998*. Buenos Aires: IADB.

———. 2001. *Intal Mercosur Report No. 7: 2000–2001*. Buenos Aires: IADB-INTAL.

IADB and Institute for European-Latin American Relations (IRELA). 1996. *Foreign Direct Investment in Latin America in the 1990s*. Madrid: IRELA.

———. 1998. *Foreign Direct Investment in Latin America: Perspectives of the Major Investors*. Madrid: IRELA.

International Labor Office (ILO). 1974. *Year Book of Labour Statistics*. Geneva: ILO.

Irwin, Douglas. 1996. *Against the Tide: An Intellectual History of Free Trade*. Princeton: Princeton University Press.

Ismail, M. N. 1999. Foreign Firms and National Technological Upgrading: The Electronics Industry in Malaysia. In *Industrial Technology Development in Malaysia: Industry and Firm Studies*, edited by K. S. Jomo, G. Felker, and R. Rasiah. London: Routledge.

Jackson, Paul, ed. 2001. *Jane's All the World's Aircraft: 2001–2002*. London: Jane's.

———, ed. 2003. *Jane's All the World's Aircraft: 2003–2004*. London: Jane's.

Janos, Andrew. 1994. Continuity and Change in Eastern Europe: Strategies of Post-Communist Politics. *East European Politics and Societies* 8 (1).

Jenkins, Barbara. 1999. Assessing the "New" Integration: The Mercosur Trade Agreement. In *Racing to Regionalize: Democracy, Capitalism, and Regional Political Economy*, edited by R. Thomas and M. A. Tetreault. Boulder, Colo.: Lynne Rienner.

Jensen, Nathan. 2003. Democratic Governance and Multinational Corporations: Political Regimes and Inflows of Foreign Direct Investment. *International Organization* 57.

Jervis, Robert. 1976. *Perception and Misperception in International Politics*. Princeton: Princeton University Press.

———. 1978. Cooperation under the Security Dilemma. *World Politics* 30.

———. 2002. Theories of War in an Era of Leading-Power Peace. *American Political Science Review* 96 (1).

Johnson, A. Ross, Robert Dean, and Alexander Alexiev. 1982. *East European Military Establishments: The Warsaw Pact Northern Tier*. New York: Crane, Russak.

Johnson, D. Gale. 1997. *Economies in Transition: Hungary and Poland*. Rome: United Nations.

Jones, Christopher. 1981. *Soviet Influence in Eastern Europe*. New York: Praeger.

Jones, Geoffrey. 1996. *The Evolution of International Business*. London: Routledge.

Jordan, Donald. 1991. *Chinese Boycotts versus Japanese Bombs: The Failure of "Revolutionary Diplomacy," 1931–1932*. Ann Arbor: University of Michigan Press.

Judy, Richard, and Virginia Clough. 1989. *The Information Age and Soviet Society*. Boulder, Colo.: Westview.

Junji, Banno. 1991. Japanese Industrialists and Merchants and the Anti-Japanese Boycotts in China, 1919–1928. In *The Japanese Informal Empire in China, 1895–1937*, edited by P. Duus. Princeton: Princeton University Press.

Kahler, Miles. 1981. Political Regime and Economic Actors: The Response of Firms to the End of Colonial Rule. *World Politics* 33 (3).

Kaltenthaler, Karl, and Frank Mora. 2002. Explaining Latin American Economic Integration: The Case of Mercosur. *Review of International Political Economy* 9 (1).

Kaminski, Bartlomiej, and Michelle Riboud. 2000. *Foreign Investments and Restructuring: The Evidence from Hungary*. Washington, D.C.: World Bank.

Kang, Nam-Hoon, and Kentaro Sakai. 2000. International Strategic Alliances: Their Role in Industrial Globalization. OECD Science, Technology, and Industry Working Paper No. 2000/5.

Kant, Immanuel. 1957. *Perpetual Peace*. Translated by Lewis White Beck. New York: Bobbs-Merrill.

Kapstein, Ethan B. 1991–92. International Collaboration in Armaments Production: A Second-Best Solution. *Political Science Quarterly* 106 (4).

———. 1992. *The Political Economy of National Security*. New York: McGraw Hill.

———. 2002. Allies and Armaments. *Survival* 44 (2).

Kass, Ilana, and Fred Clark Boli. 1990. The Soviet Military: Back to the Future? *Journal of Soviet Military Studies* 3 (3).

Katzenstein, Peter J., Robert O. Keohane, and Stephen D. Krasner. 1998. Preface: International Organization at Its Golden Anniversary. *International Studies Quarterly* 52 (4).

Kaysen, Carl. 1990. Is War Obsolete? *International Security* 14.

Keller, Wolfgang. 1997. From Socialist Showcase to Mezzogiorno? Lessons on the Role of Technical Change from East Germany's Post–World War II Growth Performance. Cambridge, Mass.: NBER.

Kennedy, Paul. 1987. *The Rise and Fall of Great Powers: Economic Changes and Military Conflict from 1500–2000*. New York: Random House.

———. 1993. *Preparing for the Twenty-first Century*. New York: Random House.

Kenney, M., and R. Florida. 1993. *Beyond Mass Production*. Oxford: Oxford University Press.

Keohane, Robert O. 1984. *After Hegemony: Cooperation and Discord in the World Political Economy*. Princeton: Princeton University Press.

Keohane, Robert O., and Joseph S. Nye Jr. 1998. Power and Interdependence in the Information Age. *Foreign Affairs* 77 (5).

Kiewiet, D. Roderick, and Matthew McCubbins. 1991. *The Logic of Delegation*. Chicago: University of Chicago Press.

Kim, Soo Yeon. 1998. Ties That Bind: The Role of Trade in International Conflict Processes, 1950–1992. Ph.D. dissertation, Political Science, Yale University.

Kobrin, Stephen. 1995. Regional Integration in a Globally Networked Economy. *Transnational Corporations* 4 (2).

———. 1997. The Architecture of Globalization: State Sovereignty in a Networked Global Economy. In *Governments, Globalization, and International Business*, edited by J. Dunning. Oxford: Oxford University Press.

———. 2003. Technological Determinism, Globalization, and the Multinational Firm. Wharton School, University of Pennsylvania.

Kontorovich, Vladimir. 1990. The Long-Run Decline in Soviet R&D Productivity. In *The Impoverished Superpower: Perestroika and the Soviet Military Burden*, edited by H. S. Rowen and C. J. Wolf. San Francisco: Institute for Contemporary Studies.

———. 1992. Technological Progress and Research and Development. In *The Disintegration of the Soviet Economic System*, edited by M. Ellman and V. Kontorovich. New York: Routledge.

Kopstein, Jeffrey. 1997. *The Politics of Economic Decline in East Germany, 1945–1989*. Chapel Hill: University of North Carolina Press.

Kornai, János. 1986. The Hungarian Reform Process: Visions, Hopes, and Reality. *Journal of Economic Literature* 24.

———. 1992. *The Socialist System: The Political Economy of Communism*. Princeton: Princeton University Press.

Kramer, Mark. 1996. The Soviet Union and Eastern Europe: Spheres of Influence. In *Explaining International Relations since 1945*, edited by N. Woods. Oxford: Oxford University Press.

——. 1998. The Czechoslovak Crisis and the Brezhnev Doctrine. In *1968: The World Transformed*, edited by C. Fink, P. Gassert, and D. Junker. Cambridge: Cambridge University Press.

——. 1999. Soviet Deliberations during the Polish Crisis, 1980–1981. Cold War International History Project, Special Working Paper No. 1.

Krasner, Stephen D. 1978. *Defending the National Interest: Raw Materials Investments and U.S. Foreign Policy*. Princeton: Princeton University Press.

Krejčí, Jaroslav, and Pavel Machonin. 1996. *Czechoslovakia, 1918–92: A Laboratory for Social Change*. New York: St. Martin's Press.

Krueger, Alan, and Jitka Maleckova. 2002. Does Poverty Cause Terrorism? The Economics of the Education of Suicide Bombers. *New Republic*, 24 June.

Krugman, Paul. 1995. Growing World Trade: Causes and Consequences. In *Brookings Papers on Economic Activity*.

Kugler, Jacek, and Douglas Lemke. 1996. *Parity and War: Evaluations and Extensions of the War Ledger*. Ann Arbor: University of Michigan Press.

Kupchan, Charles. 2002. *The End of the American Era: U.S. Foreign Policy and the Geopolitics of the Twenty-first Century*. New York: Knopf.

Kyn, Oldrich. 1970. The Rise and Fall of Economic Reform in Czechoslovakia. *American Economic Review* 60 (2).

LaFeber, Walter. 2002. The Post September 11 Debate over Empire, Globalization, and Fragmentation. *Political Science Quarterly* 117 (1).

Lake, David. 1996. Anarchy, Hierarchy, and the Variety of International Relations. *International Organization* 50.

——. 1997. The Rise, Fall, and Future of the Russian Empire: A Theoretical Interpretation. In *The End of Empire: The Transformation of the USSR in Comparative Perspective*, edited by Karen Dawisha and Bruce Parrott. London: M. E. Sharpe.

Lazer, David. 1999. The Free Trade Epidemic of the 1860s and Other Outbreaks of Economic Discrimination. *World Politics* 51 (4).

Lebow, Richard Ned. 1984. Windows of Opportunity: Do States Jump Through Them? *International Security* 9 (1).

Lemos, Mauro, and Sueli Morb. 1999. Inserção Interocionol do Sistema Agroalimentar do Mercosul: Desafios e Opportunidades.

Lenin, Vladimir. 1917. *Imperialism: The Highest Stage of Capitalism*. New York: International Publishers.

Lessard, D. R. 1982. Multinational Diversification and Direct Foreign Investment. In *Multinational Business Finance*, edited by D. K. Eiteman and A. Stonehill. Reading, Mass.: Addison-Wesley.

Levy, D. 1993. International Production and Sourcing: Trends and issues. *Science, Technology, Industry Review* 13.

Levy, Jack S. 1989. The Causes of War: A Review of Theories and Evidence. In *Behavior, Society, and Nuclear War*, edited by P. Tetlock et al. New York: Oxford University Press.

Lewis, John Wilson, and Xue Litai. 1999. China's Search for a Modern Air Force. *International Security* 24 (1).

Liberman, Peter. 1996. *Does Conquest Pay? The Exploitation of Occupied Industrial Societies*. Princeton: Princeton University Press.

Libicki, Martin. 1999–2000. Rethinking War: The Mouse's New Roar. *Foreign Policy* 117.

Libicki, Martin, Jack Nunn, and Bill Taylor. 1987. *US Industrial Base Dependence/Vulnerability: Phase II, Analysis*. Washington, D.C.: National Defense University.

Lieber, Kier, and Daryl Press. 2004. End of Mutual Assured Destruction? Paper presented at the meeting of the American Political Science Association, Chicago, 1 September–5 September.

Lindberg, Leon, and Stuart Scheingold. 1970. *Europe's Would-Be Polity: Patterns of Change in the European Community*. New York: Prentice-Hall.

Lipsey, Richard G. 1997. Globalization and National Government Policies: An Economist's View. In *Governments, Globalization, and International Business*, edited by John Dunning. Oxford: Oxford University Press.

Lipsey, Robert E. 1998. Internationalized Production in Developed and Developing Countries and in Industry Sectors. Cambridge, Mass.: NBER.

———. 2000. Inward FDI and Economic Growth in Developing Countries. *Transnational Corporations* 9 (1).

Lipson, Charles. 1985. *Standing Guard: Protecting Foreign Capital in the Nineteenth and Twentieth Centuries*. Berkeley and Los Angeles: University of California Press.

Lundestad, Geir. 2000. Imperial Overstretch, Mikhail Gorbachev, and the End of the Cold War. *Cold War History* 1 (1).

Lunn, J. L. 1980. Determinants of US Direct Investment in the EEC, Revisited Again. *European Economic Review* 13.

MacGregor, Douglas. 1989. *The Soviet-East German Military Alliance*. Cambridge: Cambridge University Press.

Mackintosh, Malcolm. 1984. The Warsaw Treaty Organization: A History. In *The Warsaw Pact: Alliance in Transition?* edited by D. Holloway and J. Sharp. Ithaca, N.Y.: Cornell University Press.

Maddison, Angus. 1995. *Monitoring the World Economy, 1820–1992*. Paris: Organization for Economic Cooperation and Development.

Maier, Charles. 1997. *Dissolution: The Crisis of Communism and the Collapse of East Germany*. Princeton: Princeton University Press.

Malone, T., and J. Rockhart. 1993. How Will Information Technology Reshape Organizations? Computers as Coordination Technology. In *Globalization, Technology, and Competition: The Fusion of Computers and Telecommunications in the 1990s*, edited by S. Bradley, J. Hausman, and R. Nolan. Boston: Harvard Business School Press.

Mansfield, Edward, and Jon Pevehouse. 2000. Trade Blocs, Trade Flows, and International Conflict. *International Organization* 54.

Mansfield, Edward, and Brian Pollins. 2001. The Study of Interdependence and Conflict: Recent Advances, Open Questions, and Directions for Future Research. *Journal of Conflict Resolution* 45 (6).

Manzetti, Luigi. 1993. The Political Economy of Mercosur. *Journal of Interamerican Studies and World Affairs* 35.

Marer, Paul. 1984a. Intrabloc Economic Relations and Prospects. In *The Warsaw Pact:*

Alliance in Transition? edited by D. Holloway and J. Sharp. Ithaca, N.Y.: Cornell University Press.

———. 1984b. The Political Economy of Soviet Relations with Eastern Europe. In *Soviet Policy in Eastern Europe*, edited by S. Terry. New Haven: Yale University Press.

———. 1986. *East-West Technology Transfer: A Study of Hungary, 1968–1984.* Paris: OECD.

Markwald, Ricardo, and Joao Bosco Machado. 1999. Establishing an Industrial Policy for Mercosur. In *Mercosur: Regional Integration, World Markets*, edited by R. Roett. Boulder, Colo.: Lynne Rienner.

Marrese, Paul, and Jan Vanous. 1983. *Implicit Subsidies and Non-market Benefits in Soviet Trade with Eastern Europe.* Berkeley and Los Angeles: University of California Press.

Martin, Lisa. 1992. *Coercive Cooperation.* Princeton: Princeton University Press.

———. 2000. *Democratic Commitments: Legislatures and International Cooperation.* Princeton: Princeton University Press.

Marton, Katherine. 1993. Foreign Direct Investment in Hungary. *Transnational Corporations* 2 (1).

Masson, Paul. 2001. Globalization: Facts and Figures. IMF Policy Discussion Paper PDP/01/4, October 2001.

Mastanduno, Michael. 1992. *Economic Containment: CoCom and the Politics of East-West Trade.* Ithaca, N.Y.: Cornell University Press.

Mattli, Walter. 1999a. *The Logic of Regional Integration: Europe and Beyond.* Cambridge: Cambridge University Press.

———. 1999b. Explaining Regional Integration Outcomes. *Journal of European Public Policy* 61 (1).

Mbaku, John. 1995. Emerging Global Trade Blocs and the Future of African Participation in the World Economy. *Journal of Economic Integration* 10 (2).

McCauley, Martin. 1983. *The German Democratic Republic since 1945.* New York: St. Martin's Press.

McKeown, Timothy J. 1991. A Liberal Trade Order? The Long-Run Pattern of Imports to the Advanced Capitalist States. *International Studies Quarterly* 35 (2).

McMillan, Susan M. 1997. Interdependence and Conflict. *Mershon International Studies* 41.

Mearsheimer, John J. 1992. Disorder Restored. In *Rethinking America's Security: Beyond Cold War to New World Order*, edited by G. Allison and G. F. Treverton. New York: Norton.

———. 2001 *The Tragedy of Great Power Politics.* New York: Norton.

Micklethwait, John, and Adrian Wooldridge. 2000. A Future Perfect: The Challenge and Promise of Globalization. New York: Random House.

Mill, John Stuart. 1920. *Principles of Political Economy.* London: Longman, Green.

Milner, Helen. 1988. Trading Places: Industries for Free Trade. *World Politics* 40 (3).

———. 1989. *Resisting Protectionism: Global Industries and the Politics of International Trade.* Princeton: Princeton University Press.

———. 1995. Industries, Governments, and the Creation of Regional Trade Blocs. Chicago: APSA.

————. 1997. Industries, Governments, and Regional Trade Blocs. In *The Political Economy of Regionalism*, edited by E. Mansfield and H. Milner. New York: Columbia University Press.

Milward, Alan. 1977. *War, Economy, and Society: 1939–1945*. Berkeley and Los Angeles: University of California Press.

Minor, Michael. 1994. The Demise of Expropriation as an Instrument of LDC Policy, 1980–1992. *Journal of International Business Studies* 25 (1).

Molnór, Miklár. 2001. *A Concise History of Hungary*. Cambridge: Cambridge University Press.

Monnet, Jean. 1978. *Memoirs*. Translated by Richard Mayne. London: Collins.

Monterey Institute of International Studies. 2003. Russian Nuclear and Missile Exports to Iran. Monterey, Calif.: Monterey Institute of International Studies.

Montesquieu, Charles de Secondat, baron of. 1989. *The Spirit of the Laws*. Cambridge: Translated by Anne Cohler, Basia Miller, and Harold Stone. Cambridge University Press.

Moodie, Michael, and Brenton Fischmann. 1990. Alliance Armaments Cooperation: Toward a NATO Industrial Base. In *The Defense Industrial Base and the West*, edited by D. Haglund. London: Routledge.

Moran, Theodore H. 1990. The Globalization of America's Defense Industries. *International Security* 15 (1).

Morse, Edward L. 1970. The Transformation of Foreign Policies: Modernization, Interdependence, and Externalization. *World Politics* 22.

MTI Media Data Bank. 1995. *Hungary: Essential Facts, Figures, and Pictures*. Budapest: MTI Media Data Bank.

Mueller, John. 1988. The Essential Irrelevance of Nuclear weapons: Stability in the Postwar World. *International Security* 13 (2).

————. 1989. *Retreat from Doomsday: The Obsolescence of Major War*. Rochester: University of Rochester Press.

Myant, Martin. 1989. *The Czechoslovak Economy, 1948–1988: The Battle for Economic Reform*. Cambridge: Cambridge University Press.

Mytelka, L. 1991. *Strategic Partnerships: States, Firms, and International Competition*. Rutherford, N.J.: Fairleigh Dickinson University Press.

Naon, Horacio. 1996. Sovereignty and Regionalism. *Law and Policy in International Business* 27.

Narula, Rajneesh. 2001. Multinational Firms, Regional Integration, and Globalising Markets: Implications for Developing Countries. MERIT-Infonomics Research Memorandum Series No. 2001-036.

National Security Archive. 1998. The End of the Cold War in Europe—The Reagan/Gorbachev Years: A Compendium of Declassified Documents and Chronology of Events. Critical Oral History Conference, Brown University. May 8–10.

Navratil, Jaromir. 1998. *The Prague Spring, 1968: A National Security Archive Documents Reader*. Budapest: Central European University Press.

Nelson, Daniel. 1984. The Measurement of East European WTO Reliability. In *The Warsaw Pact and the Issue of Reliability*, edited by D. Nelson. Boulder, Colo.: Westview.

————. 1989. Power at What Price? The High Cost of Security in the WTO. *Journal of Soviet Military Studies* 2 (3).

Neumann, Iver. 1994. Conclusion: Soviet Foreign Policy towards Its East European Allies. In *The Soviet Union in Eastern Europe, 1945–89*, edited by O. A. Westad, S. Holtsmark, and I. Neumann. New York: St. Martin's Press.

Nichols, Thomas M. 1993. *The Sacred Cause: Civil-Military Conflict over Soviet National Security*. Ithaca, N.Y.: Cornell University Press.

North, Douglass. 1993. Institutions and Credible Commitment. *Journal of Institutional and Theoretical Economics* 149 (1).

North, Douglass, and Barry Weingast. 1989. Constitutions and Commitment: The Evolution of Institutions concerning Public Choice in Seventeenth-Century England. *Journal of Economic History* 49.

Nye, Joseph S., Jr. 1971. *Peace in Parts: Integration and Conflict in Regional Organization*. Boston: Little, Brown.

Nye, Joseph S., Jr., and William Owens. 1996. America's Information Edge. *Foreign Affairs* 75 (2).

Obstfeld, Maurice, and Alan M. Taylor. 1998. The Great Depression as a Watershed: International Capital Mobility over the Long Run. In *The Defining Moment: The Great Depression and the American Economy in the Twentieth Century*, edited by M. D. Bordo, C. Goldin, and E. N. White. Chicago: University of Chicago Press.

Odom, William. 1985. Soviet Force Posture: Dilemmas and Directions. *Problems of Communism* 34.

———. 1990. The Soviet Military in Transition. *Problems of Communism* 39.

———. 1998. *The Collapse of the Soviet Military*. New Haven: Yale University Press.

Ohmae, Kenichi. 1995. *The End of the Nation State: The Rise of Regional Economies*. New York: Free Press.

O'Keefe, Thomas Andrew. 1997. *Latin American Trade Agreements*. Irvingston, N.Y.: Transnational Publishers.

Okolo, Julius Emeka. 1985. Integrative and Cooperative Regionalism: The Economic Community of West African States. *International Organization* 39.

Oliva, Maria Angels, and Luis Rivera-Batiz. 2002. Political Institutions, Capital Flows, and Developing Country Growth: An Empirical Investigation. *Review of Development Economics* 6 (1).

Olson, Mancur. 1993. Dictatorship, Democracy, and Development. *American Political Science Review* 87.

Oneal, John, France Oneal, Zeev Maoz, and Bruce M. Russett. 1996. The Liberal Peace: Interdependence, Democracy, and International Conflict, 1950–85. *Journal of Peace Research* 33 (1).

Oneal, John R., and Bruce M. Russett. 1997. The Classical Liberals Were Right: Democracy, Independence, and Conflict, 1950–1985. *International Studies Quarterly* 41.

———. 1999. Assessing the Liberal Peace with Alternative Specifications: Trade Still Reduces Conflict. *Journal of Peace Research* 36 (4).

Organisation for Economic Cooperation and Development (OECD). 1991. *Technology in a Changing World*. Paris: OECD.

———. 1992. *Technology and the Economy: The Key Relationship*. Paris: OECD.

———. 1997. *OECD Reviews of Foreign Direct Investment: Argentina*. Paris: OECD.

———. 1998. *OECD Reviews of Foreign Direct Investment: Brazil*. Paris: OECD.

———. 2001. Globalisation and Transformation: Illusions and Reality. OECD Development Centre Technical Paper No. 176. Paris: OECD.

———. 2002. Intra-industry and Intra-firm Trade and the Internationalisation of Production. *OECD Economic Outlook* 71.

Organski, A.F.K., and Jacek Kugler. 1980. *The War Ledger*. Chicago: University of Chicago Press.

Orme, John. 1997. The Utility of Force in a World of Scarcity. *International Security* 22 (3).

Office of Technology Assessment (OTA). 1988. *The Defense Technology Base: Introduction and Overview*. Washington, D.C.: U.S. Government Printing Office.

———. 1989. *Holding the Edge: Maintaining the Defense Technology Base*. Washington, D.C.: U.S. Government Printing Office.

———. 1990. *Arming Our Allies: Cooperation and Competition in Defense Technology*. Washington, D.C.: US Government Printing Office.

———. 1991. *Redesigning Defense: Planning the Transition to the Future U.S. Defense Industrial Base*. Washington, D.C.: U.S. Government Printing Office.

Overy, Richard. 1986. German Multinationals and the Nazi State in Occupied Europe. In *Multinational Enterprise in Historical Perspective*, edited by A. Teichova et al. Cambridge: Cambridge University Press.

Owens, Bill. 2000. *Lifting the Fog of War*. New York: Farrar, Straus and Giroux.

Oye, Kenneth. 1986. Explaining Cooperation under Anarchy: Hypotheses and Strategies. In *Cooperation under Anarchy*, edited by K. Oye. Princeton: Princeton University Press.

Page, Sheila. 2000. *Regionalism among Developing Countries*. London: Oversea Development Institute.

Pages, Erik. 1996. *Responding to Defense Dependency: Policy Ideas and the American Defense Industrial Base*. Westport, Conn.: Praeger.

Palmieri, Deborah Anne. 1992. The Origins of Gorbachev's Foreign Economic Policy. In *The U.S.S.R. and the World Economy: Challenges for the Global Integration of Soviet Markets under Perestroika*, edited by D. A. Palmieri. Westport, Conn.: Praeger.

Papayoanou, Paul. 1996. Interdependence, Institutions, and Balance of Power: Britain, Germany, and World War I. *International Security* 20 (4).

Parrott, Bruce. 1997. Analyzing the Transformation of the Soviet Union in Comparative Perspective. In *The End of Empire: The Transformation of the USSR in Comparative Perspective*, edited by Karen Dawisha and Bruce Parrott. London: M. E. Sharpe.

Patrick, Suzanne. 2003. July 9, 2003 Testimony of Suzanne Patrick (Deputy Under Secretary for Industrial Policy, Dept. of Defense) at the Hearing of the House Committee on Small Business. *Preserving U.S. Defense Industrial Base*. Available at http://wwwc.house.gov/smbz/hearings/108th/2003/030709/patrick.asp.

Pearce, Robert. 1993. *The Growth and Evolution of International Enterprise: Patterns of Geographical and Industrial Diversification*. Aldershot: Edward Elgar.

Pearson, Raymond. 1998. *The Rise and Fall of the Soviet Empire*. London: Macmillan.

Pearton, Maurice. 1982. *The Knowledgeable State: Diplomacy, War, and Technology since 1830*. London: Burnett Books Unlimited.

Pereira, Lia Valls. 1999. Toward the Common Market of the South: Mercosur's Origins, Evolution, and Challenges. In *Mercosur: Regional Integration, World Markets*, edited by R. Roett. Boulder, Colo.: Lynne Rienner.

Peterson, Edward. 2002. *The Secret Police and the Revolution: The Fall of the German Democratic Republic*. Westport, Conn.: Praeger.

Phillips, Nicola. 2001. Regional Governance in the New Political Economy of Development: "Relaunching" the Mercosur. *Third World Quarterly* 22 (4).

Pion-Berlin, David. 1998. From Confrontation to Cooperation: Democratic Governance and Argentine Foreign Relations. In *Civil-Military Relations: Building Democracy and Regional Security in Latin America, Southern Asia, and Central Europe*, edited by D. Mares. Boulder, Colo.: Westview.

———. 2000. Will Soldiers Follow? Economic Integration and Regional Security in the Southern Core. *Journal of Interamerican Studies and World Affairs* 42 (1).

Polachek, Solomon W. 1992. Conflict and Trade: An Economics Approach to Political International Interactions. In *Economics of Arms Reduction and the Peace Process: Contributions from Peace Economics and Peace Science*, edited by C. Anderton and W. Isard. Amsterdam: North Holland.

Press, Daryl. 1997. Lessons from Ground Combat in the Gulf: The Impact of Technology and Training. *International Security* 22 (2).

———. 2001. The Myth of Air Power in the Persian Gulf War and the Future of Warfare. *International Security* 26 (2).

Proctor, Paul. 2000. F is Forever? *Aviation Week and Space Technology*, 2 September.

Quinlan, Joseph, and March Chander. 2001. The U.S. Trade Deficit: A Dangerous Obsession. *Foreign Affairs* 80 (3).

Rangan, Subramanian. 2001. Explaining Tranquility in the Midst of Turbulence: U.S. Multinationals' Intrafirm Trade, 1966–1997. Washington, D.C.: U.S. Department of Labor.

Ram, Rati, and Kevin Houglin Zhang. 2002. Foreign Direct Investment and Growth: Evidence from Cross Country Data for the 1990s. *Economic Development and Cultural Change* 15 (1).

Ravenhill, John. 1995. Economic Cooperation in Southeast Asia. *Asian Survey* 35 (9).

Reich, Robert. 1991. *The Work of Nations*. New York: Alfred A. Knopf.

Reiter, Dan, and Allan C. Stam. 2002. Democracies at War. Princeton: Princeton University Press.

Rial, J. 1995. Actitud de las fuerzas armadas en el Mercosur. *SER 2000* 7.

Roesler, Jörg. 1991. The Rise and Fall of the Planned Economy in the German Democratic Republic. *German History* 9 (1).

Roett, Riordan, ed. 1999. *Mercosur: Regional Integration, World Markets*. Boulder, Colo.: Lynne Rienner.

Rogers, Everett. 1983. *Diffusion of Innovations*. New York: Free Press.

Rogowski, Ronald. 1993. Adaptation to the World Economy in the Former German Democratic Republic.

Rose, Gideon. 2003. Imperialism: The Highest Stage of Capitalism. *National Interest*, spring.

Rosecrance, Richard. 1986. *The Rise of the Trading State: Commerce and Conquest in the Modern World*. New York: Basic Books.

———. 1996. The Rise of the Virtual State. *Foreign Affairs* 75 (4).

———. 1999. *The Rise of the Virtual State: Wealth and Power in the Coming Century.* New York: Basic Books.

Rosecrance, Richard, and Peter Thompson. 2003. Trade, Foreign Investment, and Security. *Annual Review of Political Science* 6.

Ross, Michael L. 2002. Booty Futures: Africa's Civil Wars and the Futures Market for Natural Resources. Paper presented at the Meeting of the American Political Science Association, Boston, 29 August–2 September.

Rugman, A. M. 1979. *International Diversification and the Multinational Enterprise.* Lexington, Mass.: Lexington Books.

———. 1980. Internationalisation as a General Theory of Foreign Direct Investment: A Reappraisal of the Literature. *Weltwirtschaftliches Archiv* 116 (2).

Rumsfeld, Donald. 2003. Letter to Congressman Duncan Hunter, 8 July 2003. Available at www.ndia.org/advocacy/action/07auth_conf_secdef_ltr.pdf. Accessed 24 August 2003.

Russell, R., and C. Russell. 1992. An Examination of the Effects of Organizational Norms, Organizational Structure, and Environmental Uncertainty on Entrepreneurial Strategy. *Journal of Management* 18.

Russett, Bruce M. 1963. *Community and Contention: Britain and America in the Twentieth Century.* Cambridge: MIT Press.

———. 1993. *Grasping the Democratic Peace: Principles for a Post–Cold War World.* Princeton: Princeton University Press.

Russett, Bruce M., and John R. Oneal. 2000. *Triangulating Peace: Democracy, Interdependence, and International Organizations.* New York: Norton.

Sagan, Scott. 1993. *The Limits of Safety: Organizations, Accidents, and Nuclear Weapons.* Princeton: Princeton University Press.

Sagan, Scott, and Kenneth Waltz. 1995. *The Spread of Nuclear Weapons: A Debate.* New York: Norton.

Samonis, Valdas. 1995. *Foreign Investments in the East: Modeling the Experience.* Commack, N.Y.: Nova Science Publishers.

Samuels, Richard. 1994. *Rich Nation, Strong Army.* Ithaca, N.Y.: Cornell University Press.

Sandholtz, Wayne, and John Zysman. 1989. 1992: Recasting the European Bargain. *World Politics* 42.

Santiago, Joseph. 1995. A Postscript to AFTA's False Start: The Loss of Sovereignty Issue. *ASEAN Economic Bulletin* 12.

Sassen, Saskia. 1998. *Globalization and Its Discontents.* New York: Free Press.

Scheinman, Lawrence. 1966. Some Preliminary Notes on Bureaucratic Relationships in the European Economic Community. *International Organization* 20.

Schive, Chi. 1990. *The Foreign Factor: The Multinational Corporation's Contribution to the Economic Modernization of the Republic of China.* Stanford: Hoover Institution.

Schmickle, William. 1992. Soviet Foreign Trade Reforms under Gorbachev. In *The U.S.S.R. and the World Economy: Challenges for the Global Integration of Soviet Markets under Perestroika,* edited by D. A. Palmieri. Westport, Conn.: Praeger.

Schmitter, Philippe C. 1991. Change in Regime Type and Progress in International Relations. In *Progress in Postwar International Relations,* edited by E. Adler and B. Crawford. New York: Columbia University Press.

Schroeder, Gertrude E. 1989. The Implementation and Integration of Innovations in Soviet-Type Economies. *Cato Journal* 9 (1).

Sekigawa, Eiichiro. 1999. F-2 Wing Cracks Lead Ministry to Study Development Delay. *Aviation Week and Space Technology*, 16 August.

Selcher, Wayne A. 1985. Brazilian-Argentine Relations in the 1980s: From Wary Rivalry to Friendly Competition. *Journal of Interamerican Studies and World Affairs* 27 (2).

Shambaugh, George. 1996. Dominance, Dependence, and Political Power: Tethering Technology in the 1980s and Today. *International Studies Quarterly* 40.

Shepsle, Kenneth. 1991. Discretion, Institutions, and the Problem of Government Commitment. In *Social Theory for a Changing Society*, edited by P. Bourdieu and J. Coleman.

Shmelev, Nikolai, and Vladimir Popov. 1989. *The Turning Point: Revitalizing the Soviet Economy*. New York: Doubleday.

Silberner, Edmund. 1946. *The Problem of War in Nineteenth Century Economic Thought*. Princeton: Princeton University Press.

Simai, Mihaly. 1988. Hungary and the Transnational Corporations. In *Transnational Corporations and China's Open Door Policy*, edited by T. Weizao and N. T. Wang. Lexington, Mass.: Lexington Books.

Singer, Max, and Aaron Wildavsky. 1993. *The Real World Order: Zones of Peace, Zones of Turmoil*. Chatham, N.J.: Chatham House.

Skilling, H. Gordon. 1976. *The Interrupted Revolution*. Princeton: Princeton University Press.

Smith, Alan. 1992. Economic Relations. In *The End of the Outer Empire*, edited by A. Pravda. New York: Sage.

Smith, Gordon. 1983. Technology Transfer and Soviet Innovation. *Problems of Communism* 32.

Snyder, Glenn H. 1965. The Balance of Power and the Balance of Terror. In *The Balance of Power*, edited by P. Seabury. San Francisco: Chandler.

Snyder, Jack. 1991. *Myths of Empire: Domestic Politics and International Ambition*. Ithaca, N.Y.: Cornell University Press.

Snyder, Jim. 2003. Retired Lt. Gen Farrell Sees Peril for Defense Industry in Buy-U.S. Rule. *The Hill*, 8 July 2003.

Solingen, Etel. 1998. *Regional Orders at Century's Dawn: Global and Domestic Influences on Grand Strategy*. Princeton: Princeton University Press.

Sölvell, Örjan, and Julian Birkinshaw. 2000. Multinational Enterprises and the Knowledge Economy: Leveraging Global Practices. In *Regions, Globalization, and the Knowledge Economy*, edited by J. Dunning. Oxford: Oxford University Press.

Staley, Eugene. 1935. *War and the Private Investor: A Study in the Relations of International Politics and International Private Investment*. Garden City, N.Y.: Doubleday.

Stam, Allan C., and Alastair Smith. 2001. Issues, Stakes, and the Nature of War. Paper presented to the Annual Meeting of the American Political Science Association, San Francisco.

Stent, Angela. 1984. Soviet Policy toward the German Democratic Republic. In *Soviet Policy in Eastern Europe*, edited by S. Terry. New Haven: Yale University Press.

Stevens, John. 1985. *Czechoslovakia at the Crossroads: The Economic Dilemmas of Communism in Postwar Czechoslovakia*. New York: Columbia University Press.

Stockholm International Peace Research Institute (SIPRI). 2003. *SIPRI Yearbook 2003: Armaments, Disarmament, and International Security*. Oxford: Oxford University Press.

Stone, Randall. 1996. *Satellites and Commissars: Strategy and Conflict in the Politics of Soviet-Bloc Trade*. Princeton: Princeton University Press.

Strange, Susan. 1996. *The Retreat of the State*. Cambridge: Cambridge University Press.

Tejinder, Sara, and Benjamin Newhouse. 1995. Transaction Costs and Foreign Direct Investment in Developing Countries. *International Advances in Economic Research* 1 (4).

Terpstra, V., and B. Simonin. 1993. Strategic alliances in the Triad: An Exploratory Study. *Journal of International Marketing* 1.

Thorne, Christopher G. 1973. *The Limits of Foreign Policy: The West, the League, and the Far Eastern Crisis of 1931–1933*. New York: Putnam.

Tigre, Paulo Bastos, Mariano Laplante, Gustavo Lugones, and Fernando Porta. 1999. Technological Change and Modernization in the MERCOSUR Automotive Industry. *Integration and Trade* 3 (7–8).

Towell, Pat. 2003. House Squares Off with Rumsfeld over Change in "Buy America" Policy. *Congressional Weekly Quarterly*, 1401.

Tsai, Pan-Long. 1994. Determinants of Foreign Direct Investment and Its Impact on Growth. *Journal of Economic Development* 19 (1).

Tucker, Robert. 1981–82. Swollen State, Spent Society: Stalin's Legacy to Brezhnev's Russia. *Foreign Affairs* 60 (2).

Tulchin, Joseph, and Ralph Espach. 1998. Confidence Building in the Americas. In *Confidence Building Measures in the Americas*, edited by J. Tulchin and F. R. Aravena. Washington, D.C.: Woodrow Wilson Center Press.

Turner, Frederick. 1988. Technology Transfers (TT) and the Soviet Union. *Journal of Soviet Military Studies* 1 (4).

Ullman, Richard. 1991. *Securing Europe*. Princeton: Princeton University Press.

United Nations Conference on Trade and Development (UNCTAD). 1992. World Investment Report 1992: Transnational Corporations as Engines of Growth. Geneva: United Nations.

———. 1993a. World Investment Report, 1993: Transnational Corporations and Integrated International Production. Geneva: United Nations.

———. 1993b. *World Investment Directory*. Vol. 3: *Developed Countries*. New York: United Nations.

———. 1994. World Investment Report, 1994: Transnational Corporations, Employment, and the Workplace. Geneva: United Nations.

———. 1995. World Investment Report, 1995: Transnational Corporations and Integrated International Production. Geneva: United Nations.

———. 1996. World Investment Report, 1996: Investment, Trade, and International Policy Agreements. Geneva: United Nations.

———. 1998. World Investment Report, 1998: Trends and Determinants. Geneva: United Nations.

———. 1999. World Investment Report, 1999: Foreign Direct Investment and the Challenge of Development. Geneva: United Nations.

————. 2000a. World Investment Report, 2000. Geneva: United Nations.

————. 2000b. *FDI Determinants and TNC Strategies: The Case of Brazil.* Geneva: United Nations.

————. 2001. World Investment Report 2001: Promoting Linkages. Geneva: United Nations.

————. 2002a. World Investment Report 2002: Transnational Corporations and Export Competitiveness. Geneva: United Nations.

————. 2002b. *The Least Developed Country Report.* New York: United Nations.

Valenta, Jiri. 1984a. Revolutionary Change, Soviet Intervention, and "Normalization" in East-Central Europe. *Comparative Politics* 16 (2).

————. 1984b. Soviet Policy toward Hungary and Czechoslovakia. In *Soviet Policy in Eastern Europe*, edited by S. Terry. New Haven: Yale University Press.

van Brabant, Jozef. 1987. Economic Adjustment and the Future of Socialist Economic Integration. *Eastern European Politics and Societies* 1 (1).

Van Crevald, Martin. 1989. *Technology and War: From 2000 BC to the Present.* New York: Free Press.

Van Evera, Stephen. 1990–91. Primed for Peace: Europe after the Cold War. *International Security* 15.

————. 1999. *Causes of War: Structures of Power and the Roots of International Conflict.* Ithaca, N.Y.: Cornell University Press.

Vawter, Roderick. 1986. *US Industrial Base Dependence/Vulnerability, Phase I: Survey of Literature.* Washington, D.C.: National Defense University.

Vernon, Raymond. 1966. International Investment and International Trade in the Product Cycle. *Quarterly Journal of Economics* 80.

————. 1983. *Two Hungry Giants: The United and Japan in the Quest for Oil and Gas.* Cambridge: Harvard University Press.

————. 1992. Transnational Corporations: Where Are They Coming From, Where Are They Headed? *Transnational Corporations* 1.

Vernon, Raymond, and Ethan B. Kapstein. 1991. National Needs, Global Resources. *Daedalus* 120 (4).

Vidigal, Armando A. F. 1989. Uma nova concepçào estratégica para o Brasil. Um debate necessário. *Política e Estratégica* 7 (3).

Vieira, Gleuber. 1994. La variable estrategica en el proceso de constitucion del Mercosul. *SER 2000* 5.

Viner, Jacob. 1950. *The Customs Union Issue.* New York: Carnegie Endowment for International Peace.

Volgyes, Ivan. 1982. *The Political Reliability of the Warsaw Pact Armies: The Southern Tier.* Durham: Duke University Press.

————. 1985. The Reliability of the Warsaw Pact Armies. In *The Soviet Union: What Lies Ahead: Military-Political Affairs in the 1980s*, edited by Kenneth Currie and Gregory Varhall. Washington, D.C.: United States Air Force.

————. 1990. The Lesser Allies' View: Eastern Europe and the Military Relationship with the Soviet Union. In *The Soviet-East European Relationship in the Gorbachev Era: Prospects for Adaptation*, edited by A. Braun. Boulder, Colo.: Westview.

Wallensteen, Peter, and Margareta Sollenberg. 2000. Armed Conflict, 1989–1999. *Journal of Peace Research* 37 (5).

Wallerstein, Immanuel. 1996. The Inter-state Structure of the Modern World-System. In *International Theory: Positivism and Beyond*, edited by S. Smith, K. Booth, and M. Zalewski. Cambridge: Cambridge University Press.

Waltz, Kenneth N. 1979. *Theory of International Politics*. Reading, Mass.: Addison-Wesley.

———. 1993. The Emerging Structure of International Politics. *International Security* 18.

———. 2000. Globalization and American Power. *National Interest*, spring.

Way, Christopher. 1998. Manchester Revisited: A Theoretical and Empirical Evaluation of Commercial Liberalism. Ph.D. dissertation, Stanford University.

Weingast, Barry. 1993. Constitutions as Governance Structures: The Political Foundations of Secure Markets. *Journal of Institutional and Theoretical Economics* 149 (1).

Weintraub, Sidney. 2000. *Development and Democracy in the Southern Cone: Imperatives for U.S. Foreign Policy in South America*. Washington: CSIS.

Wendt, Alexander. 1992. Anarchy Is What States Make of It: The Social Construction of Power Politics. *International Organization* 46.

———. 1994. Collective Identity Formation and the International State. *American Political Science Review* 88.

———. 1999. *Social Theory of International Politics*. Cambridge: Cambridge University Press.

Williams, Kieran. 1997. *The Prague Spring and Its Aftermath: Czechoslovak Politics, 1968–1970*. Cambridge: Cambridge University Press.

Winiecki, Jan. 1986. Are Soviet-Type Economies Entering an Era of Long Term Decline? *Soviet Studies* 38 (3).

———. 1988. *The Distorted World of Soviet-Type Economies*. Pittsburgh: University of Pittsburgh Press.

Wohlforth, William Curti. 1993. *The Elusive Balance: Power and Perceptions during the Cold War*. Ithaca, N.Y.: Cornell University Press.

World Bank. 1997a. Global Economic Prospects and the Developing Countries, 1997. Washington, D.C.: World Bank.

———. 1997b. *World Development Indicators, 1997*. Washington, D.C.: World Bank.

———. 1999. *World Bank Development Report, 1999/2000*. New York: Oxford University Press.

———. 2000. *Trade Blocs*. Oxford: Oxford University Press.

———. 2001. *World Development Indicators, 2001*. Washington, D.C.: World Bank.

———. 2002. *World Development Indicators, 2002*. Washington, D.C.: World Bank.

World Trade Organization. 2000. Mapping of Regional Trade Agreements. World Trade Organization Secretariat Study No. WT/Reg/W/41.

———. 2001. Annual Report. Geneva: WTO.

Wright, Quincy. 1935. Foreword to *War and the Private Investor*, by Eugene Staley. Garden City, N.Y.: Doubleday.

Yarbrough, Beth, and Robert Yarbrough. 1992. *Cooperation and Governance in Internation Trade: The Strategic Organizational Approach*. Princeton: Princeton University Press.

Yeats, Alexander. 1998. Does Mercosur's Trade Performance Raise Concerns about the Effects of Regional Trade Agreements? *World Bank Economic Review* 12 (1).

Index of Sources

General Index

Acambis (U.K.), 241
Act on Foreign Investments (Hungary; 1988), 166
Action Plan (Czechoslovakia; 1968), 185
advanced states: conquest of, 49–50, 58, 59–60, 61, 63, 66, 70–71, 161, 163, 219; economic centralization in, 66–70, 195; extraction of economic resources from, 70; FDI in, 248; interdependence of production in, 257, 258–59; interfirm alliances in, 64, 70; knowledge-based economies in, 65, 208; MNCs in, 61, 63, 205. *See also* great powers; knowledge and knowledge-based economies; individual countries
Aerospace Industries Association, 93, 128
Africa, 133
AFTA. *See* ASEAN Free Trade Agreement
agriculture, 69, 190–91, 208, 265
Alfonsin, Raul, 150
Algeria, 265
Allende, Salvador, 247
Alvarez Gaiani, Alberto, 147
Andean Pact (1969), 134
Angell, Norman, 12n
Anzorreguy, Hugo, 151
Argentina: automobile industry in, 147; democracy and, 156; domestic business and interest groups in, 137; economic issues in, 139, 158–59, 223; FDI in, 131, 138, 139, 141–43, 147, 159; Mercosur and, 140–41, 147, 151–56, 159, 223; military issues in, 148, 149–50, 154–56, 157; MNCs in, 139, 143, 159; security issues in, 14, 131, 148–56, 157–58, 160; trade and economic issues in, 135, 147. *See also* Mercosur
Argentine Industrial Union, 147
ASEAN (Association of South East Asian Nations). *See* ASEAN Free Trade Agreement
ASEAN Free Trade Agreement (AFTA), 130–31, 133n. *See also* individual member countries
Asia and East Asia: FDI in, 144; outsourcing to, 21; RTAs in, 133; SAPTA and, 223; trade creation in, 135; and trade relations with China, 2

Aslund, Anders, 118
Association of South East Asian Nations (ASEAN). *See* ASEAN Free Trade Agreement
AT&T, 35, 36–37
Australia, 91, 208
Austria, 66, 169, 208
Avecia (U.K.), 241

BAE Systems (U.K.), 243
Balza, Martín, 153, 155
Bancroft, Fred, 172
Bangladesh, 223
Barbosa, Rubens, 140
BASF, 144
Batt, Judy, 176–77
Bavarian Nordic (Germany, Denmark), 241
Baxter, 241
Bayer AG, 143–44
Beaufour-Ipsen (France), 242
Belgium, 82, 208, 234
Beltrán, Virgilio, 153
benefits of conquest. *See* economic benefits of conquest
Bentham, Jeremy, 1
Betts, Richard, 228
Bhutan, 223
Bhutto, Benazir, 54
biological agents, 240–42
Bitzinger, Richard, 6
Boldin, Valery, 113
Bolivia, 130n, 149. *See also* Mercosur
Brazil: automobile quotas in, 147; democracy and, 156; domestic business and interest groups in, 137, 140; economic issues in, 140; FDI in, 138–39, 140, 141–43, 147, 159, 223; Mercosur and, 140–41, 146, 151–56, 159; military issues in, 148, 149–50, 154–57, 224; MNCs in, 140, 143, 159, 224; outsourcing to, 91; payment crisis in, 147; security issues in, 14, 131, 148–56, 157, 158, 160; trade and economic issues

CPSIA information can be obtained
at www.ICGtesting.com
Printed in the USA
LVOW12s0831141216
517216LV00007B/54/P